MW01015970

International Political Economy Series

General Editor: **Timothy M. Shaw**, Professor of Political Science and International Development Studies, Dalhousie University, Halifax, Nova Scotia

Titles include:

Glenn Adler and Jonny Steinberg (*editors*)
FROM COMRADES TO CITIZENS
The South African Civics Movement and the Transition to Democracy

Glenn Adler and Eddie Webster (*editors*)
TRADE UNIONS AND DEMOCRATIZATION IN SOUTH AFRICA, 1985–1997

Einar Braathen, Morten Bøås, Gutermund Sæther (*editors*)
ETHNICITY KILLS?
The Politics of War, Peace and Ethnicity in Sub-Saharan Africa

Deborah Bräutigam
CHINESE AID AND AFRICAN DEVELOPMENT
Exporting Green Revolution

Gavin Cawthra
SECURING SOUTH AFRICA'S DEMOCRACY
Defence, Development and Security in Transition

Jennifer Clapp
ADJUSTMENT AND AGRICULTURE IN AFRICA
Farmers, the State and the World Bank in Guinea

Neta C. Crawford and Audie Klotz (*editors*)
HOW SANCTIONS WORK
Lessons from South Africa

Susan Dicklitch
THE ELUSIVE PROMISE OF NGOs IN AFRICA
Lessons from Uganda

Kevin C. Dunn and Timothy M. Shaw (*editors*)
AFRICA'S CHALLENGE TO INTERNATIONAL RELATIONS THEORY

Kees Kingma
DEMOBILIZATION IN SUBSAHARAN AFRICA
The Development and Security Impacts

Clever Mumbengegwi (*editor*)
MACROECONOMIC AND STRUCTURAL ADJUSTMENT POLICIES IN ZIMBABWE

Nana Poku
REGIONALIZATION AND SECURITY IN SOUTHERN AFRICA

Howard Stein, Olu Ajakaiye and Peter Lewis (*editors*)
DEREGULATION AND THE BANKING CRISIS IN NIGERIA
A Comparative Study

Peter Vale, Larry A. Swatuk and Bertil Oden (*editors*)
THEORY, CHANGE AND SOUTHERN AFRICA'S FUTURE

International Political Economy Series
Series Standing Order ISBN 0–333–71708–2 hardcover
(*outside North America only*)

You can receive future titles in this series as they are published by placing a standing order. Please contact your bookseller or, in case of difficulty, write to us at the address below with your name and address, the title of the series and the ISBN quoted above.

Customer Services Department, Macmillan Distribution Ltd, Houndmills, Basingstoke, Hampshire RG21 6XS, England

Theory, Change and Southern Africa's Future

Edited by

Peter Vale
Visiting Professor of International Relations
Stellenbosch University
South Africa

Larry A. Swatuk
Lecturer
Department of Political and Administrative Studies
University of Botswana

and

Bertil Oden
Head of Secretariat of the Expert Group on Development Issues
Ministry for Foreign Affairs
Sweden

First published 2001 by
PALGRAVE
Houndmills, Basingstoke, Hampshire RG21 6XS and
175 Fifth Avenue, New York, N.Y. 10010
Companies and representatives throughout the world

PALGRAVE is the new global academic imprint of
St. Martin's Press LLC Scholarly and Reference Division and
Palgrave Publishers Ltd (formerly Macmillan Press Ltd).

ISBN 0–333–80276–4

This book is printed on paper suitable for recycling and
made from fully managed and sustained forest sources.

A catalogue record for this book is available
from the British Library.

Library of Congress Cataloging-in-Publication Data
Theory, change and southern Africa's future / edited by Peter Vale,
Larry A. Swatuk, Bertil Oden.
        p. cm. — (International political economy)
    Includes bibliographical references and index.
    ISBN 0–333–80276–4
    1. Africa, Southern—Politics and government—1994– 2. Africa,
    Southern—Economic conditions—1994– 3. Africa, Southern–
    –Social conditions—1994– 4. Africa, Southern—Forecasting.
    I. Vale, Peter C. J. II. Swatuk, Larry A. (Larry Anthony), 1957–
    III. Odén, Bertil, 1939– IV. International political economy series.
    DT1182 .T47 2000
    968.06'5—dc21
                                                    00–065263

10   9   8   7   6   5   4   3   2   1
10   09   08   07   06   05   04   03   02   01

Printed in Great Britain by Antony Rowe Ltd, Chippenham, Wiltshire

To the Memory of Carlos Cardoso,
Journalist, Freedom Fighter, Friend

Contents

List of Tables

List of Acronyms

ACP	Africa, Caribbean, Pacific (groups of states associated with EU)
AEC	African Economic Community
AIDS	Acquired Immune Deficiency Syndrome
ANC	African National Congress
BSAC	British South Africa Company
BLNS	Botswana, Lesotho, Namibia, Swaziland (group of states)
CAMPFIRE	Communal Areas Management Programme for Indigenous Resources
CBI	Cross-Border Initiative
CBO	Community-based organization
CBMNR	Community-Based Management of Natural Resources
CCT	Coxian critical theory
CITES	Convention on International Trade in Endangered Species
CMA	Common Monetary Area
COMESA	Common Market for Eastern and Southern Africa
CONTRALESA	Congress of Traditional Leaders of South Africa
COSATU	Congress of South African Trade Unions
CSCE	Conference on Security Cooperation in Europe
CSBM	Confidence and Security Building Measures
CT	Critical theory
DEIC	Dutch East India Company
DRC	Democratic Republic of the Congo
ECOMOG	ECOWAS Monitoring Group
ECOWAS	Economic Community of West African States
EEIC	English East India Company
EPZ	Export processing zone
ESKOM	Electricity Supply Company (South Africa)
EU	European Union
FISCU	Finance and Investment Coordinating Unit
FLS	Frontline states
G-7	Group of Seven (industrialized countries)
GATT	General Agreement on Tariffs and Trade
GDP	Gross domestic product

GEAR	Growth employment and redistribution
GNP	Gross national product
GNU	Government of National Unity
GPT	Green political theory
HIPC	Highly indebted poor countries
IDASA	Institute for a Democratic Alternative in South Africa
IFI	International financial institutions
IGADD	Inter-Governmental Authority on Drought and Desertification
IGO	Inter-governmental organization
IMF	International Monetary Fund
IPE	International political economy
IR	International relations
IRT	International relations theory
ISDSC	Inter-State Defence and Security Committee
Mercosur	Common Market of the South
MFN	Most favored nation
MNB	Multinational bank
MNC	Multinational corporation
MVA	Manufacturing value added
NAFTA	North American Free Trade Agreement
NATO	North Atlantic Treaty Organization
NEDLAC	National Economic Development and Labour Council
NEF	National Economic Forum
NGO	Non-governmental organization
NIC	Newly industrialized country
NSI	National self interest
NTB	Non-tariff barrier
OAU	Organization of African Unity
OSCE	Organization for Security Cooperation in Europe
PAC	Pan-African Congress
PPE	Population, poverty, environment (spiral associated with UNICEF)
RDP	Reconstruction and development programme
RMA	Rand Monetary Area
SAARC	South Asian Association for Regional Cooperation
SACCAR	Southern African Centre for Cooperation on Agricultural Research
SACP	South African Communist Party
SACU	Southern African Customs Union
SADC	Southern African Development Community

SADCC	Southern African Development Coordination Conference
SAHRNGON	Southern African Human Rights NGO Network
SALT I & II	Strategic Arms Limitation Talks I & II
SANCO	South African National Civics Organization
SAP	Structural adjustment programme
SAPP	Southern African Power Pool
SATCC	Southern African Transport and Communications Commission
SCU	Sector coordinating unit
SSA	Sub-Saharan Africa
TAZARA	Tanzania–Zambia Railway
TEBA	The Employment Bureau of Africa
TNC	Transnational corporation
UN	United Nations
UNCED	United Nations Conference on Environment and Development
UNCLOS	United Nations Convention on the Law of the Sea
UNDP	United Nations Development Programme
UNEP	United Nations Environment Programme
UNICEF	United Nations Childrens' Emergency Fund
UNITA	National Union for the Total Independence of Angola
UNU	United Nations University
US	United States
WIDER	World Institute for Development and Economic Research
WTO	World Trade Organization
ZCTU	Zimbabwe Congress of Trade Unions

Preface

The project which underpinned this collection of essays was conceived in West Sussex in the northern summer of 1996. In the gracious surroundings offered by Wilton Park, the weighty issues of Southern Africa were under review by another gathering of chiefly northern-based 'experts' and the glitter provided by Southern Africans especially flown in for the grand occasion. This project might not have happened had it not been for a flock of sheep grazing in a field adjacent to the conference hall. As the conference moved its way across the routine interpretations offered by mainstream Southern Africa, the sheep followed each other from one side of the field to another. In Peter Vale's mind the link between the agri-pastoralism outside in the June sunshine was closely linked to the simple muddle-headedness of those inside the Wiston House. During a tea-break he suggested to fellow participant Bertil Odén that together they do a collection which might look beyond the prosaic interpretations of the region which were the main fare of the conference.

For all the potential said to be offered by recent change, events in Southern Africa continue to be viewed through the same timeless lenses opened first by the Boer War a full century ago. These European viewings of Africa have successively shaped the value of nation, state and state-system and, on the other side of the same coin, markets, metals and the lives of both men and women. Their derivative values have been expressed in the language of war weapons and that old faithful which enjoins both, security. At very few moments in the political debates on Southern Africa have other capillaries been used to view the region; even human rights was drawn to the fore by the debate on state's rights. It has taken the last three years to put this project and its product together: far too long, to be sure. But then again, perhaps not too long when weighed against the cumulative ruminations offered by the mainstream.

This collection covers the chief strands of, and underpinnings in, recent theoretical thinking on the region's future. It is principally aimed at students in sociology, political science, international studies and international economics. But we believe that it will be able to bridge the existing gap between policymaking and recent international theory and therefore be of significant interest and use also to practitioners in the Southern Africa regions and internationally.

The Centre for Southern African Studies, CSAS, at the University of Western Cape, South Africa and the Nordic Africa Institute, Uppsala, Sweden may be far apart geographically, but have for many years shared a common interest in analysing the regionalization process in Southern Africa. Vale's idea of putting out a counter-sheep collection resulted in a joint workshop where early versions of most of these papers were presented. The staff and researchers of the CSAS, in addition to a number of other scholars, were actively involved in making the workshop a success. Great appreciation goes to them and to the Nordic Africa Institute for its funding of the workshop, as well as the editorial work.

Peter Vale and Bertil Odén want to record their special thanks to Larry Swatuk without whom the book would not have appeared. For much of 1999 and 2000, he beavered away in Gaborone, Harare and Toronto without help to deliver the final product to the publisher. Larry Swatuk would like to thank Mike Lefler at Sheridan College who helped ensure a soft landing following a laptop crash. He would also like to dedicate his work to the late Bill Graf whose scholarship continues to inspire and provide support for the long nights spent in front of word processors across the African sub-continent.

Peter Vale, Larry Swatuk and Bertil Odén
Cape Town, Gaborone and Stockholm (November 2000)

Notes on Contributors

Andre du Pisani is Dean of Social Sciences at the University of Namibia in Windhoek. He is also a photographic artist whose work has been exhibited at several venues in Southern Africa.

Björn Hettne is professor and director of Peace and Development Research Institute at Göteborg University (Padrigu), Sweden and has written a number of publications on development theory, ethnicity and nationalism, regionalism and international political economy.

Merle Holden is professor and head, Department of Economics and Management Sciences, University of Natal, Pietermaritzberg, South Africa. She has written extensively on theories of economic integration with a more recent specific interest in Southern Africa.

Anthony Leysens teaches global political economy at the Department of Political Science, University of Stellenbosch. He also assists in the coordination of the department's international studies programme. His publications have centred on the political economy of South Africa's relations with Latin America, the political economy of export-led growth, and the political economy of Southern Africa. He has also edited a volume on South Africa's relations with the IMF and World Bank. Currently, he is working on the issue of states and survival strategies in Southern Africa, focusing on the Caprivi region in Namibia.

Michael Niemann is an Associate Professor in the International Studies Program at Trinity College. He works and teaches on African political economy with an emphasis on Southern Africa, global human rights issues and political geography. He is the author of *A Spatial Approach to Regionalism in the Global Economy*.

Bertil Odén, as senior researcher at the Nordic Africa Institute in Uppsala, Sweden during 1989–98 conducted a research programme on South Africa and the regionalization process in Southern Africa. Before that he held positions at the Swedish International Development Authority (1968–73, 1980–85), the Ministry of Planning, Mozambique (1977–79), the Ministry of Finance, Tanzania (1986–87) and in the secretariat for a Swedish Parliamentary Commission on Development Cooperation

(1973–76). Since 1999 he has been head of the Secretariat of the Expert Group on Development Issues in the Swedish Ministry for Foreign Affairs. Odén has edited a number of books from the Nordic Africa Institute, among them *Southern Africa After Apartheid* (1993) and *Regional Cooperation in Southern Africa* (1989). He has also published *Regionalisation in Southern Africa* (UNU/WIDER 1996) and contributed to two of the volumes of the UNU/WIDER study *Globalism and the New Regionalism* (Macmillan, 1999; 2000).

Hussein Solomon is Research Manager at the African Centre for the Constructive Resolution of Disputes (ACCORD). Prior to moving to ACCORD, he was Senior Researcher of the Human Security Project at the Institute for Security Studies in Midrand, South Africa.

Larry A. Swatuk graduated from Dalhousie University with his PhD in 1993. In 1988 he was awarded the Joseph Howe Prize for Poetry at Dalhousie and continues to use this as a signpost when the feeling of being lost in the thickets of modernity gets a bit overwhelming.

Lisa Thompson is a senior lecturer at the School of Government, University of the Western Cape. She has held the position of postgraduate coordinator since 1997 and was recently appointed acting Director at the Centre for Southern African Studies which is located within the School. She has a PhD in international relations from UWC, an M.A and Honours degree from Rhodes University, and a BSocSc from the University of Cape Town. She lectured in the Political Science Department at Stellenbosch University for five years before joining the School of Government in 1995. Her field of research is primarily international political economy and the Southern African region, with specific attention to gender.

Balefi Tsie schooled at the Universities of Botswana, Columbia in New York, and Leeds in the UK where he received his PhD. He is presently Associate Professor in the Department of Political and Administrative Studies at the University of Botswana. His research interests focus on the intersection of political economy, security, development and international relations in Southern African. He is the author of *The Political Economy of Botswana in SADCC* (1995).

Peter Vale, at the time of the conference which anchored this collection was Professor of Southern African Studies at the University of the Western Cape. He has subsequently been Acting Vice-Rector for Academic Affairs at the same institution.

1
'IR Theory, I Presume': an Introduction

Larry A. Swatuk and Peter Vale

The modern world system is in the process of coming to its end. This is not per se good or bad; it all depends on what will be constructed in its place … [I]ts course is not predetermined … We are in effect being called upon to construct our utopias, not merely to dream about them. Something will be constructed. If we do not participate in the construction, others will determine it for us.
                                                    – Immanuel Wallerstein (1996: p. 106)

As we contemplate rewriting IR methods, feminists remember that we cannot be banished for our sins. We are, after all, already among the homeless in the field.
                                                    – Christine Sylvester (1994: p. 139)

Before I entered a doctoral program in IR, I had assumed that it was an inter-disciplinary field, and that was part of its attraction to me, having spent a lot of time in various countries … [I]t's been some disappointment for me to discover the narrowness of the discipline and its failure to be either aware of or appreciative of interdisciplinary scholarship.
                                                    – anonymous (cited in Sylvester, 1996: p. 269)

Introduction

The aim of this book is to encourage scholars in Southern Africa, particularly those working in the field of international relations, to theorize their region, the discipline and, we believe, their daily lives. As suggested by Wallerstein above, new 'utopias' are being visited on the region. This should encourage those interested in Southern Africa to think hard about preferred visions of and for the future. Depending where one stands, the region can look more varied than unified, more divisive than accepting of diversity, more stable than insecure. What is Southern Africa? Is there an objective definition we might aim for? How inclusive is that picture? What future(s) for those 'inside', and for those without?

At the same time, we hope to encourage scholars to theorize their discipline: its epistemology, ontology, methodology. For the most part, contributors to this volume are of like minds: we share a deep dissatisfaction with the 'tools' we have been given for ordering what we see. The so-called 'neo-neo synthesis', so celebrated by mainstream IR scholars, seems a rather remote and abstract dialogue, one lacking meaning for the lives of the vast majority of Southern Africans, one whose high-flying 'categories' stand far above experiences on the ground – though the 'neo-neo' impact on this region and our lives is significant as this opening chapter will demonstrate.

In terms of this book, we hoped to provide bold and fanciful visions of the future and biting critiques of the state of IR as theorized and practised in and on Southern Africa.

Perhaps another group of scholars will put such a much needed collection together. What the reader will find here is rather more 'down to earth'. 'Visions' are too often predictable; critiques mostly limited to the capacity of a particular theory to solve a certain puzzle. How to explain this? It seems to us, in at least three ways. One is to suggest that we are prisoners of ontology, in particular the unquestioning acceptance of states and markets as the primary forces of international politics, power and individual self-regard as the prime motivators.

A second suggests that scholars and policymakers in Southern Africa are central to the theory and practice of mainstream IR, and are so limited by the parameters of the dominant discourse. In some ways this seems counter-intuitive. For are we not everyday told that South(ern) Africa is of marginal concern in 'great power politics'? In global trade? And are we not told that the region's irrelevance has increased since the end of the Cold War? One might then expect to encounter a freedom of thought and action in the region. Like Sylvester's feminists, are not Southern Africa's IR scholars already among the homeless in the field? The facts seem to suggest something quite different, however.

Since 1994 the region has played host to an unending stream of disciplines and their disciplinarians: in particular, those in favour of globalism, liberalism, anti-statism, and populism (within reason, of course).

At every turn, the academic and policy making community of the region is coopted to follow this research agenda, encouraged to establish think tanks and non-governmental organizations (NGOs) in support of these many isms. All this attention (and money) has left scholars feeling rather flattered. It has also led many down the garden path toward 'lending expert knowledge' rather than toward critique. In other words, toward Enlightenment rather than enlightenment (see Paterson quoted in Swatuk, Chapter 12 below). At the same time, given decades of apartheid rule and authoritarian state structures, one can understand the desire, indeed novelty, felt by scholars, policymakers and activists in the region to speak out in support of 'democracy', a limited state, and for the 'people' whoever and wherever they may be.

A third way to explain the absence of fancy is to point to the dire problems facing the region: from AIDS to the former Zaire, Southern Africa is rife with trouble. Thus, with so many problems, it seems naïve to abandon 'problem-solving' theory. Prisoners of ontology, perhaps, but the simple fact of the matter is that Southern African realities for the most part prohibit a complete turn toward post-positivist or post-structuralist theorizing. This does not mean necessarily a ready acceptance of unreflective theories and theorizing. To the contrary, most contributors to this volume are well aware of the 'tension between the need to study "what is" and the danger of therefore reproducing "what is"' (Zalewski, 1996: pp. 341–2). Save for two or three contributors, all are keen to (re)fashion theory so that those too long at the margins are moved to the centre of inquiry.

Thus, even where there are more creative attempts at theorizing, not one of the contributors is willing to abandon an empancipatory project. While some are more or less critical and reflective in their theorizing, and others more or less supportive of what Ashley (1996) quite correctly labels 'the achievements of post-structuralism', this group of scholars retains what might be termed an 'enlightened' Enlightenment vision for Southern Africa.

How likely are those emancipatory visions to be realized, partial, disunited and contentious though they may be, especially given the limiting tendencies highlighted above – of ontology, of extant forms of power/knowledge, of distressing reality – and their impact on one's ability to theory? A flippant answer might be, not bloody likely. In the balance of this chapter, however, we will probe this question more fully.

To do so, we explore several of the main themes that emerge from the text. Borrowing from Zalewski (1996), we have organized our discussion by grouping together those chapters which (more or less) view theory either as a tool, as critique, or as everyday life. In the end, we make several suggestions regarding the future of theory and theorizing in the region. Like the anonymous quotation at the outset of this introduction, we hope at minimum to root IR in the lives of real people living real lives.

Tool making and honing

In Chapter 2, Vale expresses the desire to invent a tradition of theory in the region, one which places suffering humanity at the centre of its theoretical project. But, it may be asked, why the need to 'invent' a tradition? Are there not plenty of good theories to go around? Might it not perhaps be better to improve on existing theories than pursue radical departures?

This is, indeed, the position taken by several contributors to this volume. According to Zalewski (1996: p. 341), to think of theory as a tool, means to regard it as 'something that is used by those wishing to make sense of events in international politics'. This take on theory most closely aligns itself with traditional, positivist approaches to the study of IR. It is an approach that accepts the possibility of separating the knowing subject from the object of investigation and of explaining where 'events of interest to international scholars are ontologically prior to our theories about them' (Zalewski, 1996: p. 343). Reason and rationality are brought to bear in judging the adequacy of one's theory. Following Zalewski (ibid., p. 344), '[I]t is the debate about which is the most appropriate theory to study IP that seems to be of most concern to those who write about theory as a tool, given that they seem satisfied about the nature of theory and its relationship to the "real world"'.

In this volume, we consider the chapters by Solomon, Holden, Oden, and Du Pisani as having these characteristics. Each examines a particular theory, traces its lineage in the discipline, and seeks to apply it to the study of international relations in Southern Africa. Hussein Solomon writes on realism, and as a realist. Merle Holden writes from the perspective of a (neoclassical) development economist. Bertil Odén critically assesses theories of hegemony and Andre du Pisani examines regime theory in the context of the Southern African Development Community (SADC).

In this collection, the chapters by Tsie, Leysens and Hettne are also explicitly concerned with theory as a tool. Balefi Tsie examines realist, liberal and structural varieties of IPE, their accounting of the changing role and place of the state, and in particular what he feels to be the most appropriate tool for understanding Southern Africa – critical political economy. Björn Hettne looks at 'regionalism', in particular his take on what he calls the 'new regionalism'. Anthony Leysens applies Robert Cox's critical theoretical framework to Southern Africa in hope of unearthing better insights into the motor forces of the region, thereby leading to better strategies for positive political change.

These three authors go some way beyond using theory as a tool. They are also centrally concerned with how the world got to be the way it is. They collapse the artificial distinction between subject and object and acknowledge that theorizing is not a benign activity, but is rife with serious political and moral implications (see more generally, Zalewski, 1996: p. 345). In some cases they borrow insights from post-structuralism, in particular Foucault's notion of knowledge/power, in order to better locate the political projects inherent in theory building.

Taken together, these chapters reproduce the so-called inter-paradigm debate as applied to the region, with Solomon staking out the 'realist' high ground and Holden providing economic support for this position, Odén and Du Pisani pursuing more classically liberal institutionalist lines of argument, and Tsie, Leysens and Hettne coming down most firmly in support of a neo-Marxist approach. What is particularly interesting is the confidence with which each of these authors write in support of their positions, based as they are on imported theoretical framings.

In support of common sense

Solomon's argument, in Chapter 3, is classically realist in two senses. First, he supports unequivocally both the ontology – from anarchical states system to balance of power – and the epsite-methodology of realism – from correspondence theories of truth to a mix of inductive and deductive theory building. Second, he appeals both to logic and to common sense: as long as hate, envy, greed, and egotism motivate humanity people are going to need protection and this historically has been found within the state. And, as long as one state is stronger than another, it is wise for leaders of these states to act accordingly in protection of their 'national interests'. In support of his argument he provides a compelling and entertaining *tour d'horizon* of inter-state conflict through both space and time.

The upshot, however, is counsel for 'more of the same'. South Africa, as the strongest state will determine the course of events in the region. As a relatively weak global actor, however, South Africa must run that much faster in a competitive and globalizing world, especially if it is to avoid further economic marginalization. There may be room for strategic alliances primarily of the bilateral sort (with, for example, Botswana and Zimbabwe, perhaps also Zambia and Mozambique) but policy-makers should avoid entering into any binding agreements with potential to harm South Africa's national interests. So, agreements which benefit South Africa are to be encouraged, like those facilitating the free movement of trade and finance; those involving such things as the free movement of labour in the region are to be avoided. It is up to policy-makers in other states to pursue their own national interests. In the 'new' Southern Africa there are to be no free lunches.

Holden, in Chapter 7, marshals evidence that seems to support the 'self-regarding state' thesis. Her chapter addresses a question of fundamental interest to policy-makers in the SADC countries: 'Is a regional free trade agreement good for Southern Africa?' Holden frames her argument within the context of evolving theories of development economics. She identifies Southern Africa as a group of states comprising part of the developing world. She presents evidence suggesting that globalization itself is an uneven process and that Southern Africa risks economic marginalization if it does not move to counteract negative trends. Indeed, for 93 developing countries having data available, trade ratios over the last 20 years were seen to decrease in 44 of them. Where trade ratios had increased, only 10 countries accounted for 75 per cent of that increase. Is a regional trade accord the answer to this seeming economic 'marginalization'?

Interestingly, building on Krugman's work in the area of economic geography, she suggests that regional agglomeration effects will only be offset if regional economics are 'really open'. Partial openings, however, are likely to exacerbate 'dual economy' tendencies. So, a regional trade accord will benefit South Africa even though its wage rates are higher relative to other SADC members. At the same time, the rest of SADC stands to lose from such an agreement. World Bank evidence, she says, suggests that it is better for smaller developing countries to unilaterally liberalize than to pursue regional integration.

Strength in numbers

While predicting similar self-regarding state outcomes, both Odén in Chapter 8 and Du Pisani in Chapter 9 are less sanguine (as in the case of Solomon) or apolitical (in the case of Holden) in their assessments. Odén takes a neo-institutionalist look at hegemonic stability theory as applied to Southern Africa. Du Pisani uses regime analysis to assess the likelihood that SADC will eventually emerge as a strong regime in the tradition of the European Union. Du Pisani quite clearly states that regime analysis is 'not a theory but a conceptual framework and a research agenda'. Unlike Holden and Solomon, both Du Pisani and Odén write from outside of these theories looking in, not as 'true believers' so to speak. As such, they are better able to comment on the political project masked by neo-institutionalism's technical and intellectual approach.

Du Pisani, for example, cites Strange's critique of 'regimes' as simply concerned with 'problem solving' and thus 'value laden in favour of order over justice or autonomy'. Solomon in contrast cites Henry Kissinger in support of the status quo: 'If history teaches anything it is that there can be no peace without equilibrium and no justice without restraint'. Holden and Odén seem to be the most 'objective' in their analysis, though both are clearly concerned with bringing peace and prosperity to Southern Africa. They are diametrically opposed to each other regarding the means to realize such a goal, however. Whereas Holden counsels unilateral liberalization, Du Pisani – like Odén, Tsie and Hettne – regards a collective approach to regional development as the only option for Southern Africa. Otherwise, to paraphrase Tsie, neoliberalism will ensure that divided and marginal states remain hewers of wood and drawers of (increasingly scarce) water in the global political economy.

Following his 'qualitative analysis' of five arguments against South Africa's emergence as a 'benign' or 'benevolent' hegemon, Odén states that, in the absence of firm South African leadership and/or a strong regional institutional framework, 'it is likely that market driven, spontaneous regionalization will take place in which concern for regional balances and sustainability is limited or non-existent'. Du Pisani, in his chapter, does little to allay this fear. In a detailed examination of SADC, he highlights the tension between SADC's stated desire to forge a supranational development community and the state-centredness of its institutional structures and decision-making processes. In a region of weak and underdeveloped states, each holds jealously to its sectoral allocation(s), as these help generate revenue from the donor community. Both Odén and Du Pisani suggest that pursuing issue-specific, neofunctional cooperation (in the areas of water resource management, telecommunications, agricultural research) may be a middle way forward. However, in the absence of 'enough internal cohesion and political will to negotiate the terms of subordination', warns Du Pisani, the IMF will write the ground rules and South Africa will call the tune.

Theory and reflection

Implicitly or explicitly, each of these four contributors accepts a more or less liberal definition of the state. As such, according to Tsie in Chapter 6, Hettne in Chapter 5, and Leysens in Chapter 10, their theories can never get to the root of the problem. It is not enough to accept the state system as a given, as though it constituted an unchanging and objective universe. Rather, one must probe the structures of that universe in order to reveal underlying principles of operation. For Tsie, Hettne and Leysens this involves a more nuanced framework whereby states constitute one important social form in a complex universe. In classical structuralist style, they identify the underlying structure of the world system as one determined primarily by modes and relations of production. To accurately locate Southern Africa in this world system, Hettne falls back on 'good old dependency theory' where the world is now at a stage of higher integration and delinking is no longer an option. According to Hettne – and this would also stand for both Tsie and Leysens – 'In spite of the current wave of post-structural thinking in international relations theory, it still makes sense to conceive the world as a structural system'. Thus, Hettne, like Solomon, attempts to bring common sense to bear on theory building.

Whereas the state is accepted as given in the analysis of Solomon, Holden, Odén and Du Pisani, it becomes a focal point of critical inquiry for Tsie, Hettne and Leysens, all of whom are sympathetic to the theoretical work of Robert Cox. Within the context of globalization, state forms are changing. For Hettne, many have come to the 'unpleasant realization' that the Westphalian state guarantee of security and welfare for its citizens, 'can no longer be taken for granted'. Tsie examines four hypotheses regarding the position of the state in the late twentieth century: (i) the state remains central and dominant as it always did; (ii) the end of the state is upon us (which is tantamount to 'globalist triumphalism'); (iii) the state is in irrevocable decline; (iv) the state is adapting to changing circumstances (although some states lack the capacity for any sort of 'adaptation'). Leysens uses Cox's framework to look inside the state, to reveal what has been hidden and to give voice to those who have been long silenced.

Asking better questions

Realism and (Neo) Liberalism are judged inadequate to the task of theorizing the state in the late twentieth/early twenty-first century. Tsie acknowledges that there are insights to be gleaned from both realism and liberalism, primarily because policy-makers do act as if anarchy were real thereby making it real, and because the world is populated by multiple actors and issues outside of the state, each having differing capacities. Nevertheless, both he and Hettne feel that critical political economy provides better tools for analysing the world as it really is. Indeed, both authors are quite critical of IR, in particular the mainstream. Tsie, quotes Strange: 'IPE denotes a set of questions around the social, economic and political arrangements affecting the global system of production, exchange and distribution... Who benefits from the existing world economy, and at whose expense is the key question that IPE poses'. In addition, and quite unlike mainstream IR, critical political economy 'focuses on multiple axes of exclusion in the existing regional/world order'. In other words, in focusing primarily on interstate relations, mainstream IR asks the wrong questions. Its theories, therefore, are largely irrelevant as they do not pursue, in Tsie's words, 'an emancipatory vision for humanity as a whole'.

This is an overtly normative position, one typical of structuralist analysis. Indeed, Hettne claims, among other things, that while development theory needs to abandon its state centric focus, IPE needs to take on the dynamic and normative concerns central to development theory. Both Tsie and Hettne quite correctly question the motives driving realist and neoliberalist theorizing. Hidden behind the so-called 'objective', the 'timeless', and the 'universal' is an agenda of domination. Just as the state is a tool of a dominant class, so too are state-centred theories tools of that same privileged group.

There emerges an unresolved tension in their analyses, however. While both are critical of current state forms, and put forward rather hopeful visions of Southern Africa beyond Westphalia, each falls back on a statist discourse (including the central position of international law) in suggesting ways forward for Southern Africa. Both Tsie and Leysens, like Du Pisani, attempt to resolve this contradiction by, one, placing emphasis in the potential for subnational actors to become transnational forces, and two, arguing in support of better – read more popularly democratic – state forms. For Leysens, the continuing failure to acknowledge and empower 'marginalized and subordinate social forces' presents a major problem for future regional relations.

Hettne envisions something quite different. Unlike Holden's rather narrow, official policy-oriented framing, Hettne focuses on the multiple responses to globalization manifest at regional level. Accordingly, the 'new regionalism' includes economic, political, social and cultural aspects and goes far beyond preferential trade arrangements. Drawing on the work of Polanyi, he concludes that the new regionalism marks a concerted response against the forces of globalization in the same way that, in an earlier era, social democratic forces organized at state level in order to reign in the worst aspects of the free market. In other words, the new regionalism is part of a second 'double movement'. 'The struggle against peripheralization', he states, 'is the struggle for increasing regionness'.

Must Southern Africa's future reside with the interactions of a constellation of sovereign states? Although the consensus among those contributors considered thus far seems to be 'yes', Hettne says 'not necessarily'. Clearly, in the face of both globalist pressures and outright state failure, many individuals and groups are reverting to pre-Westphalian identities and resorting to sub-national 'security communities'. However, a transnational, regional response is also possible: 'Sooner or later, there must be some reorganization of social power and political authority', he says. An extended nationalism drawing on traditional flows of people and resources may emerge. 'The point is not that a "regional" political structure is inherently better than a "national" one, which would be nonsense since all political communities are "imagined"'. However, all contributors to this volume – save perhaps for Solomon – perceive of a region 'beyond Westphalia' as more desirable than 'more of the same'.

Are the theoretical tools presented thus far up to the positivist tasks of hypothesis formulation and verification? In other words, of theory building? If so, then why are desired outcomes so far from realization? What is the point of theory if not to better inform policy? In the context of Southern Africa, these seem to be reasonable questions, ones rarely asked by Ashley's 'itinerant condottiere' – the IR theorist who is everywhere and nowhere, who skims across the top of the world rarely stooping to see what is really happening so far down below. If the categories of state, regime and world system so rarely speak to those on the ground, should we not perhaps reconsider their value in explaining the world 'as it is'? More politically, and self-consciously, should we not inquire as to how these theories at once reflect and constitute a particular and most peculiar world?

Theorizing the discipline/theorizing the self

Tsie, Leysens and Hettne go some way in addressing these issues. At the same time, however, their ability 'to theory' is limited by the fact that they are so deeply rooted in materialism and the struggle for (state) power. Emancipation, therefore, revolves around a more equitable allocation of resources: a worthy project indeed.

While Vale, Niemann, Thompson and Swatuk share strong sympathies with the critical theorists, their chapters aim for a somewhat different sort of theorizing, one which more fully embraces or locates itself within social theory as opposed to IR or IPE. In Chapter 2, Peter Vale provides a searing indictment of the Westphalian state-building project in Southern Africa and the practice and theory of 'international relations' which flowed from it. In Chapter 4, Michael Niemann goes furthest of all contributors in reimagining the region beyond inherited boundaries, conceiving Southern Africa in terms of social space. Lisa Thompson, in Chapter 11, provides an overview of feminist theorizing and its implications for (re)conceptualizing 'security' in Southern Africa. In the final chapter, Larry Swatuk uses 'green lenses' to both locate and critique IR in the region.

Space for debate

Vale, Niemann, Thompson and Swatuk present fundamentally different readings of the construction of the region in time and space. Vale argues that Westphalian-centred discourses lead directly to 'ritualized responses which repeat the mistakes of the past'. He provides a counter-narrative to the dominant statist history of the region by highlighting another region: the 'rich underbelly' that finds itself absent from or held constant in any and all theorizing of Southern Africa.

While Vale, like all the others, is unwilling to abandon a modernist 'emancipatory' agenda, he nevertheless suggests that only a post-structuralist methodology, and a non-statist ontology can begin to free the region from the tyranny of received epistemologies. In his words, 'the interpretative choice is clear'.

Niemann, too, is highly critical of IR routines. Nowhere is the nexus of power and knowledge more visible than in IR, he states. For him, 'The power/knowledge nexus manifests precisely in the unquestioned acceptance of a "common sense" meaning while eschewing any analysis of the manner in which this "common sense" is constructed and maintained'.

In his estimation, the same may be said about theories of regionalism and regionalization. Niemann, like Vale, is interested in opening space for debate. Are there other ways of conceptualizing the 'region'? Are we limited simply to states, markets and state-bound civil societies? Judging from the chapters already discussed, the answer seems to be 'yes'. However, Vale has alluded already to the existence of a 'rich underbelly'. Niemann places this concept in more formalized terms.

IR theory, bound as it is to Newtonian physics and Euclidean geometry, spends little time thinking about space. Space in IR is conceptualized either as a neutral background or as a fixed unit, that is 'secure sovereign space'. Drawing on the work of Lefebvre, Niemann argues that social space is socially produced. 'States simply constitute one layer of this space with state boundaries conceived as ambiguous continuities rather than as clear divisions.' In explication of this in the Southern African context, Niemann uses Lefebvre's conceptual triad of 'spatial practice' (how social forces produce spatial structures), 'representation of space' (how space is conceived in society by the dominant discourse), and 'spatial representations' (how space is directly lived). In the region, the second tends to contradict the third: that is, state-centred discourses tend to stand at odds with the lived experiences of people, resources, animals, diseases, etcetera on the ground. To privilege the state and the study of inter-state relations is to barely touch the surface of lived social space in the region.

Niemann then goes on to theorize the region not in terms of geography but in terms of rights. Can one conceive of Southern Africa as a space of rights? Both Thompson and Swatuk build on this conceptualization of space. Swatuk argues that the dominant framings of the environment in IR theory have served only to divide people and deplete resources. A green critique of the IR project would focus, like Niemann, on a reconceptualization of space, one which perhaps conceives of Southern Africa as an interlocking mesh of what Leopold calls 'biotic communities'. And also like Niemann, it would rethink questions of 'ethics', not limiting them to intra-state discourses around the rights of the citizen, but around humans as part of an integrated ecosystem and its protection. Within the context of competing states in an anarchical system, nature continues to be considered solely for its 'use value', however.

Like nature, women in Southern Africa have long been considered as objects (of desire, to be protected) and for their 'use value' (reproduction of the labour force, a symbol supporting a call to arms). The state in Southern Africa is a hypermasculine construct, geared toward 'power over' and the conceptualization of security as that obtained through the threat and use of force. For realists, such as Solomon, this is simply the way the world is. For others in this volume, and in particular Thompson, this is a socially constructed world whose theoretical framings have too long been blind to their complicity in the reproduction of human insecurities.

Thompson, in reviewing varieties of feminist theorizing, argues that it is not enough to reframe traditional theories of liberalism, socialism and Marxism in the light of gender. To do so is to leave the 'essential structure of dominant metanarratives unchanged'. Like others in this collection, she is strongly supportive of postmodern techniques and insights. She identifies herself as a critical feminist whose main task is 'unpacking and challenging dominant metanarratives'. 'Critical feminism', she says, 'insists on talking about humanity as such'.

Thompson turns a keen eye to the construction of 'security' in the region. In Southern Africa, states have often used women as reasons for war: apartheid South Africa's policy of regional destabilization partly rested on defence of white women from the 'black peril'. More recently, she argues, SADC leaders have increasingly militarized security while 'feminizing' development. Gender critiques have been absorbed and neutralized by national (state-led) discourses on development, so constructing and separating development (a 'caring' activity) from security (a 'protecting' activity). In the region, 'protection' is increasingly located within the ambit of SADC's Organ on Politics, Defence and Security, chaired by Zimbabwe's President Robert Mugabe, and commonly called 'Mugabe's organ'. The phallic allusion could not be more apt. For Thompson, the 'military metanarrative' has become the regional priority among a host of others. While state-centred framings serve only to divide the region, and encourage self-regarding behaviours, 'deeply entrenched global gender inequality renders a critical feminist approach to security borderless'.

Like Niemann, Vale and Swatuk, Thompson encourages us to theorize our everyday practices, to lead questioning lives. As Zalewski (1996: p. 346) suggests, the theory that counts is not that confined to 'expert knowledge'. Neither is it true that the choice of substantive issues to study in international politics is the result of 'natural selection' or 'neutral judgement'. To the contrary, it is a reflection of specific interests (ibid., p. 351). Thus, as Vale reminds us in Chapter 2, 'to write is to choose'.

Choices, voices and futures

It is our hope that this book will begin a dialogue in and about both theory and the region. To be sure, ours is a modest start. In closing this introductory chapter, we would like to make two points about theorizing the region, the discipline and the self. The first point is about 'old debates'. Whereas the so-called 'inter-paradigm debate' may seem outdated, in Southern Africa it remains lively and important. Realism and the policies that emanate from it have been highly destructive in the region. Nevertheless, policy-makers continue to set their 'foreign' policies within realist theoretical frameworks. Both 'pluralism' (particularly its neo-institutionalist form) and 'globalism' (in particular, its neo-Marxist variant) provide important counter-narratives to the dominant discourse. Neo-Marxist analysis draws attention to the vast inequalities that inhere in the region. Neo-institutionalism seeks to articulate ways and means of cooperating beyond the state. It also seeks to provide space for other actors, forces and factors to operate in a suspect state system. In our view, the inter-paradigm debate is an important conversation within the Southern African IR community and so should be encouraged. The vitality of this debate is understandable: in a region with so many problems, it is virtually impossible – indeed, madness – to abandon 'problem-solving' theory.

This leads to our second point. There are many in the IR community who feel it to be fundamentally important to go beyond the discipline in the direction of a more self-conscious, and holistic social theory, one which extends both beyond and below the purview of mainstream IR. Clearly, the ontology of IR, in particular its conceptualizations of state, sovereignty and anarchy, are unhelpful in the extreme. Niemann's focus on space, Swatuk's on ecology and Thompson's on gender – all central aspects of Vale's 'rich underbelly' – begin the necessary task of constructing a different language whereby we can become 'partners in a political conversation oriented towards diversity and the common, towards world rather than self' (Wendy Brown quoted in Sylvester, 1996: p. 272). These chapters in particular indicate a desire to begin a conversation located far from the centres of state power, far from the intellectual dominance of mainstream discourse, in order to privilege the voices of those Sylvester calls 'insubordinate border dwellers' (1996: p. 271). In other words, 'We must locate the people of international politics in their places of actions' (ibid., p. 264).

Can international relations facilitate such a turn toward the subaltern? Can it sustain it? In other words, can it become relevant to more than those in the academy and the policy making community? In Southern Africa the answers to these questions are not clear. What is clear, however, is that a wide variety of disciplines – language and literature, architecture, philosophy, sociology, geography, history and theatre – have had more trenchant things to say about theory and lived space in the region than IR or political science ever did. We hope that the IR community will carefully consider this criticism. With Ashley

(1996: p. 249), we remain doubtful that IR can (re)gain relevance, can ever do what it purports to do (for a very different view, compare with Bobrow in the special issue of *International Studies Review* 1/2, 1999). In any event, we leave it for readers to decide for themselves.

A note on organization

Given that this introduction has focused primarily on theory, a few words are necessary regarding the layout of the text which moves from a focus on theory and the region, to the region and theory, then back again. In Chapter 2, Vale issues what might be termed the challenge to theory, where 'theory' may be read as both a noun and a verb. Highlighting what he feels to be the distressing consequences of state-based/positivist theorizing in the region, he argues for a constructivist turn. In Chapter 3, Solomon states the case in defence of both realism and the state. In supporting a mix of classical and neo-realism, he is in fact supporting what might be termed a refined theoretical 'status quo'.

Chapters 4 and 5 (Niemann and Hettne) locate Southern Africa in global and historical social space and, like Solomon and Vale, do so in grand theoretical fashion. Chapters 6 to 10 utilize specific theories in order to project regional futures and to assess the adequacy of specific theoretical framings (Tsie on IPE, Holden on development economics, Odén on hegemonic stability, Du Pisani on regimes, and Leysens on Coxian critical theory).

Finally, like a bellows first raised, then squeezed, then raised again, or a tide in flow and ebb, Chapters 11 and 12 return to grander narratives – Thompson on feminism and Swatuk on environmentalism/ ecology – and larger questions raised by Vale and Niemann and in some ways rebuffed by Solomon in the earlier chapters.

References

Ashley, Richard K. (1996), 'The achievements of post-structuralism', in Steve Smith, Ken Booth and Marysia Zalewski (eds), *International Theory: positivism and beyond* (Cambridge: Cambridge University Press).
Bobrow, Davis B. (ed.) (1999), 'Prospects for International Relations: Conjectures about the Next Millennium', *International Studies Review* 1/2 (summer).
Sylvester, Christine (1994), *Feminist Theory and International Relations in a Postmodern Era* (Cambridge: Cambridge University Press).
Sylvester, Christine (1996), 'The contributions of feminist theory to international relations', in Steve Smith, Ken Booth and Marysia Zalewski (eds), *International Theory: positivism and beyond* (Cambridge: Cambridge University Press).

Wallerstein, Immanuel (1996), 'The inter-state structure of the modern world system', in Steve Smith, Ken Booth and Marysia Zalewski (eds), *International Theory: positivism and beyond* (Cambridge: Cambridge University Press).

Zalewski, Marysia (1996), '"All these theories yet the bodies keep piling up": theories, theorists, theorising', in Steve Smith, Ken Booth and Marysia Zalewski (eds), *International Theory: positivism and beyond* (Cambridge: Cambridge University Press).

2
Dissenting Tale: Southern Africa's Search for Theory[1]

Peter Vale

> History is the only laboratory we have in which to test the consequences of thought.
>
> – Etienne Gilson (1976)

Introduction

To write is to choose. To twist the cliche confirms that words, like currencies, are weighted. To recognize this is to acknowledge that academics – whose work is words (Booth, 1994) – can never enjoy a neutral place, and to believe that intellectual progress is built more than anywhere else, on the idea of contestation. If life was a linear process, we might end here but we cannot because, as the central motif of this chapter argues, ideas produce consequences (Ashley, 1988). This also makes the interpretative choice clear because, like life, it is hard to avoid (Said, 1993: p. 313).

Like much writing in international relations, this chapter is associated with both ending and beginning:[2] the ending of apartheid and the beginning associated both with South Africa's re/emergence into the international community and the country's re/integration into Southern Africa.

On two previous occasions, Southern Africans have tried to ignite an interest in issues of international theory. In the early 1980s, a group associated with the South African Institute of International Affairs (SAIIA) tried to operate along the lines of the old British Committee on the Theory of International Politics; while there was no publication, Roger Spegele was motivated to write several important papers which preceded his highly acclaimed book (Spegele, 1985; 1996). A second meeting, held in Grahamstown, South Africa in the gruesome 1980s, saw twenty three (then younger) scholars meet and a slim collection of papers emerge (Frost, Vale and Weiner, 1988).

In comparison, there emerged during the 1970s and the 1980s a rich and still largely unmined theoretical literature focusing on Southern African political economic issues at the Centre for Southern African Studies in Maputo. This creative school was the progeny of the intellectually vibrant work done in Dar es Salaam in the late 1960s and early 1970s during that university's heyday (Temu and Swai, 1981).

This small but concentrated effort at inventing a tradition of theoretical exploration in the region suggests a consciousness of the need to bridge the gap between theory and practice. But if those who gathered in the embattled Maputo or Eastern Cape all those years ago thought they were dealing with practical issues, they were seriously mistaken. The real challenges had hardly begun. This only reinforces another academic cliche that theory follows practice; because so, this chapter draws more from new beginnings than old endings.

The following real world questions seem to mark the spot of where all theory in Southern Africa ought to begin. Are we going to see ever larger and larger political units in Southern Africa? Or are we to see the break-up of several states into smaller ones? Why are we seeing a large-scale migration of millions of peoples? Why is a new apartheid becoming a metaphor for the regional order? Why is the very texture of regional history changing before our eyes? These certainly demand real world answers but as they do, theoretical questions are also needed.

On a first reading, this chapter appears to be preoccupied with statist framings of the region. The idea that states are the cornerstones of international relationships is at the heart of conventional perspectives on the ways of Southern Africa. This state-centric discourse seems to have a long and honourable lineage. But is this so? Or has this tradition, like thinking theoretically in the region, been haphazard, incidental and most slim?

There is more than a conceptual game at play here; it has deadly serious outcomes, as any reading of the region's history suggests. The framing idea turns on the enabling concept of sovereignty – the right to exert authority within a geographical space; to put it as a lawyer might, within this space a legitimate authority exercises order. This is the point of Walker's powerful notion of 'inside/outside' (Walker, 1993). In Southern Africa's case, as we shall see, the clear demarcating lines which this implied were at all times illusory. There seldom was domestic harmony; as those in Grahamstown more than a decade ago were constantly reminded and as those in Maputo passionately conveyed, the opposite was true. Discord, in which ironically the international community played a very influential role by the imposing of sanctions, was the norm. In Hobbesian terms, as was so powerfully demonstrated in the 1980s, South Africa was never a peaceful and prosperous island in a sea of potential regional conflict (Held, 1995: pp. 42–3).

The politics which flow from these accepted understandings of sovereignty are the very stuff of the daily press in every country in the region. In South Africa this view is virulent as can be seen in the work of a new class of state-makers associated with the Institute of Security Studies and the revamped SAIIA (for example, see Chapter 3 below).

Given its role as theory in everyday political practice (George, 1994: p. 3), it has seemed perfectly natural to rechart Southern Africa after apartheid by using the same realist theodolite. But has it been helpful, hopeful or, as suggested here, harmful? In other words, is a peaceful and prosperous regional future to be located within the context of presently constituted Westphalian sovereign state forms? Or is the continuing dominance of this state form at the very heart of regional insecurity? (See Swatuk and Vale, 2000).

Southern Africa and the curse of the nation-state

To borrow from Basil Davidson is to understand the flow of our own history, not merely the history of others (Davidson, 1992). The post-apartheid recreation of Southern Africa has tended to stress that the borders which are said to separate its states are fixed, determine the points of entry to, and exit from, a regional state system. It assumes therefore that states in the region exercise a closed, and a close, control over their sovereign affairs and, as they interact with their neighbours, they maximize their respective 'national interests'.

This way of interpreting Southern Africa has found strong support in the 'new' South Africa. Not surprisingly, the process of national re/discovery – including the search for the 'national interest' – has been easy in South Africa where the tradition of public discussion, ironically, is more established than in the neighbourhood. As the press and policy pundits nudge the government in different directions in the region, ideas on what determines the national (as opposed to the regional) interest are seldom far below the surface of public discourse. Four dominant propositions have emerged, each linked to theoretical interpretations of international society.

First, it is said that the region is unsafe and, as a result, South Africa requires a modern and well-equipped force to defend itself. Second, the development of capability, through the arms industry, is linked both to the country's international competitiveness and the creation of much-needed 'jobs at home'. Third, states of the region also require their own militaries; in a highly competitive world, these are best built in parallel with South Africa's. And fourth, following the old African dictum, militaries are powerful instruments of nation building (Vale and Daniel, 1995: pp. 85–7).

It has not been as easy, however, for South Africa's neighbours to set their regional priorities. Establishing 'national interest' in a regional context is proving very difficult for weaker states and it is easy to understand why. In previous decades, the mantra 'ending apartheid' was integral to the national interest of each of South Africa's neighbours. With this goal attained how are these states now to set priorities in a region still dominated by South Africa? The search for immediate answers had been complicated by crippled economies, and by the crises in their political systems, the latter somewhat masked by the continuing thrust towards liberal democracy (see, especially, Saul, 1999; and Swatuk and Vale, 1999). Given this situation, there is no prospect for a regional 'balance of power', to use the old realist dictum – except in Vattel's view that a strong South Africa will 'lay down the law to others' (compare the views of Solomon, Holden and Odén in this volume).

In South African policy circles, this option for the region is not without its attractions or precedents. Despite – no, because of – Bosnia, regional order promised by the tested precepts of power is understandably preferable to the sheer unknown. The idea of building the region around the currency offered by a strong South Africa has a long history. The Harvard historian, Robert I. Rotberg, triumphantly sketched it recently by recalling that (Rotberg, 1995: p. 9):

> Cecil Rhodes, the British imperialist, mining entrepreneur, and successful colonial politician, forcefully gave the region its current shape. By thrusting iron tentacles relentlessly northward from Cape Town into what is now Botswana, Zimbabwe, Zambia and Zaire, he tied the region's mining centres and population magnets together and bound them to the ports of South Africa. His conquest of Zimbabwe, his attempted conquest of Zaire and Mozambique, his successful assertions of economic suzereignty over Zambia and Malawi also forged links which ... endure in the administrative, legal and linguistic, educational, cultural, political and economic structures of the region.

It is certainly true that the region's incorporation into modernity was located in its mineral wealth and, equally so, that its development was forged by the multiple probings which reached outwards not so much from Cape Town – where Cecil Rhodes' bust broods over the city's rich southern suburbs – but from the mineral rich Johannesburg where, undoubtedly, his ghost watches over Africa's strongest stock exchange.

If however, the debates over historiography teach anything, it is that selective interpretations of the past distort, rather than advance, our understandings of the future. So consider the following reading of the same history.

The coincidence of British capital, American technology and African muscle first turned a geographical backwater into a candidate of modernization in the late 1880s. Prior to this moment, a set of quasi-states – mainly Boer republics and colonial fragments – operated within a crudely defined regional system. The turning point came with the establishment of the region's first Westphalian-type state, the Union of South Africa in 1910. It took nearly 50 years for the next orthodox state in the region, Tanganyika in 1962, to emerge. By the time it did, South Africa and its interests dominated the region in every possible way. Other states when they emerged were modelled in and on the organizational core represented by 'modern' South Africa (Vale, 1996b).

So, modernization and the state-building project were two sides of the same coin in Southern Africa. The idea of state structures followed from – not predated – the thrust towards both regional economic development and integration. And states in the region, as South Africa has always shown, were required to enforce and legitimize the power of markets.[3]

In this interpretation, South Africa set the conditions for membership of the region's inter-state system; put differently, and drawing from historical sociology, the other states in the region were defined not so much by an interaction of internal forces but by their external setting towards the state called South Africa (Vale, 1996c).

Drawing upon a familiar idiom to reinforce the point: all the region's maps[4] were charted upon and around the emergent South African state and its interests. The most obvious example was the recruitment of mine labour from the region: a process which commenced not long after the discovery of gold in what is now called Gauteng. But other examples follow: the region's extensive and relatively efficient railway system, the powerful electricity grid, veterinary research and the creation of a Southern African Customs Union (SACU), to cite but four examples. In this framing, therefore, the moment of state creation in 1910 enshrined a series of power relations in the region in which, to deliberately belabour the point, South Africa was the first among unequals. This conclusion is therefore inescapable: South Africa's dominant position distorts not balances the region. So, in both my and Rotberg's readings, the ritual of state relations rests on the idea of power but the interpretation of its consequences is very different.

International relationships – even in Southern Africa – are not always marked by conflict; how are we to explain this? Here, there are many threads. Some are to be found in the work of Smith and Ricardo, the latter arguing that trade could function to the benefit of all states. The British international theorist, Martin Wight, called this kind of cooperation 'rationalist', as opposed to his other famous categories, 'realist' and 'revolutionary', and explained it by drawing on the work of Hugo Grotius.

Wight saw this as a mixed international condition, one in which conflict and cooperation existed alongside each other (Wight, 1977). If international society is to be built, various paths, including economic paths, are to be used. These lie beyond the brute force of realism and mercantilism in the idea of sharing: rules, customs, norms, ideals, institutions and values each would play a part in developing a society of states (see, in particular, Du Pisani in this volume).

In Southern Africa, a perpetual peace, to draw on Kant's central theme, might be driven by the economic benefits of trade and the values attached to mutual respect. Practically, it seems this is possible. A Southern African Customs Union (SACU) – whose membership includes Botswana, Lesotho, Namibia, Swaziland and South Africa – has existed since 1910 and, as the century ended, many still believed that it represents the only painless way to re/integrate the countries of the region (see Holden and Odén in Chapters 7 and 8 below). In a parallel way, others have urged the adoption of a Human Rights Charter for the region. This fits the idea that regimes, in this particular case a regime around rights, could both protect the region's peoples and advance the cause of regional peace (see, especially, the chapters by Niemann and Du Pisani below).

Understanding this approach offers perhaps two, admittedly statecentric, theoretical keys to the future practice of regional relations in Southern Africa. It was shared political values, especially but not exclusively the struggle to end apartheid, which gave birth to the region's other important multilateral organization, the Southern African Development Community (SADC).[5] But it was the fear of South Africa which enabled SADC's predecessor, SADCC, to grow and flourish throughout the 1980s. Here the operating mechanism was decidedly 'functional' and the participants drew, albeit unconsciously at first, on the theoretical work done in the early 1940s by the Fabian Socialist, David Mitrany (see Mitrany, 1943; Claude, 1971).

Like Mitrany, the participants in SADC were not geared, nor indeed were they prepared, to surrender their sovereignty. Rather, the SADC project sought to consolidate areas in which state loyalties might be transferred – for example, in fisheries or transportation and communications development – towards a 'working peace system'. As this happened, Mitrany argued, bureaucratic elites would be drawn closer together in a common process of building working communities across national boundaries. In any event, without the willing participation of South Africa, its success was impossible (see Niemann in Chapter 4). Moreover, in the face of active South African regional destabilization, this goal seemed all the more fanciful.

Less confidently understood, in theoretical frames, is to borrow an image and idea from the French Africanist, Jean-Francois Bayart (1993): the rich underbelly of Southern Africa, that vast interchange and exchange of people and ideas which is taking and has taken place across the region from time immemorium. These do not show up on any of the accepted maps, be they theoretical or practical. Why?

Three further examples suggest that theoretical understandings of the processes at work in Southern Africa are at best partial ones. First, analysing the notorious practice of 'black-birding' at 'Crooks' Corner' in what is now South Africa's Northern Province, Murray (1995: p. 383) writes,

> By the 1910s … competition had forced freelance poachers to push their illicit recruiting activities hundreds of miles northward … Gangs of labour thieves staked out territorial claims to recognized labour routes, took up arms to protect business operations, and assumed virtual carte blanche sovereignty over large tracts of land.

Second, writing about the 1960s, the Botswana citizen and politician Michael Dingake who served on Robben Island for 15 years for furthering the aims of the African National Congress (ANC), drew attention to a kind of regional community below both the colonial and apartheid 'states'.

> Before political independence we depended very much on our South African brothers when we earned a livelihood in their economy. We were never subjected to subtle discrimination … except by the

common enemy – the colour bar/apartheid state...[O]ur black brothers taught us how to survive, how to cheat the pass laws...we were welcome...in the ghettos, in the factories, in the schools...[Our success is the product] of the hospitality and magnanimity of our black brothers across the border

(Dingake, 1987: p. 241).

Third, Allister Sparks, the South African journalist, in a 1996 article described a small corner of the region's biggest city where a whole community of Zairois live in Johannesburg, speak only French and participate primarily in the informal sector (Sparks, 1996).

In all three cases, the 'fact' of borders and understandings of 'sovereignty' and 'community' appear palpably different. This helps explain why the region's maps seem unable to hold the organizational dimensions of time and space which they once promised.

It is not that these points about the duplicity of sovereignty framings have been entirely missed in conventional analysis. Security analysts for instance have identified 'threats to security' – like illegal migration, arms and drug smuggling – from these features within the underbelly (see Rotberg and Mills, 1997); and development economists, ever anxious to stress the informal sector as a source of employment, have lauded the efforts of women traders from Zimbabwe who use the entire region to generate economies of scale. The conceptual problem is that analytically capturing them within the set routines of realism, neoclassical economics and the Westphalian state places them at the margins. But do they belong there?

A wider point is undeniable: change of seismic proportions in the 1990s has, it seems, succeeded in widening the gap between the theory and the practices of inter-state relations in Southern Africa. Does this mean the region is disintegrating? If traditional realist maps are used, the answer may well be yes, with enduring conflicts in Angola and the Democratic Republic of Congo being cases in point.

If other framings are used, the region seems closer together and less threatened than it has ever been, as recent developments appear to be forging an identity which is both new and old (Vale, 1996a). The power of cross-border religious sects, for example, has never been stronger and the search for cross-border ethnic identity is undeniable. How and when these admittedly sketchy maps both become more clearly framed and play out in practice promises to be the most compelling feature of inter-state relations in Southern Africa in the twenty-first century. How they play out in theory will entirely change our appreciations of both politics and international relationships. This suggests that developments on the ground will lead to further theory. The question is: will the present plans to restructure the region help or hinder their emergence?

It is not surprising that political organization around states has captured the ground in Southern Africa. '[I]n ... the modern world states have managed to more or less monopolize our understanding of what political life is and where it occurs' (Walker, 1990: p. 4). To fully appreciate the genesis of state formation in Southern Africa, we must reach back across the centuries. Holiday records that 'the first Dutch settlement at the Cape of Good Hope in 1652 took place one year after Hobbes had published Leviathan' (Holiday, 1993: p. 6). Using this to locate the worldview of those who made that perilous journey, Holiday's purpose is to emphasize the difficulties of continuing conversation between colonizers and colonized.

His prescience opens a window on regional relations by helping to locate the conceptual seeds of the state that was to become South Africa – the state which has defined Southern Africa. Holiday notes that its earliest settlers brought to that place not only distinct understandings of their own superiority but a particular hostility to any world other than their own. As they re/located themselves, their own cultural practices were privileged over that of the 'brute other' (Holiday, 1993: p. 8).

This inclusion of the bearers of superior culture and ways, and exclusion of indigenous people has been a constant thread in the lived (if not written) history of South and Southern Africa (see Niemann in Chapter 4 below). It was weaved into racist ideology, and it was this same idea that enabled South Africa to take its place in the international community in 1910, and four years later to fight in a European War which, perhaps more than other issues, was about the determining power of borders.

The South African state experience brought to the ritualized practice of state-to-state relations in Southern Africa very sharp ideas about white/non-white, European/non-European, 'civilized' community/'primitive' tribe. As the self-image of the state called South Africa mutated through its regional policy, especially during the apartheid years, primordial feelings of superiority were transferred from a domestic location on to the immediate neighbourhood, in patronizing, patriarchal and often very violent ways (see chapters by Swatuk and Thompson below).

These theoretical ideas which linked identity to borders and the practice of inclusion/exclusion are not unique to Southern Africa; this pattern has occurred elsewhere (for examples, see Chapter 3 below). However, the South African case, especially during the apartheid years, enables us to isolate strains of statist theory which can be linked to particular policy outcomes.

One strain – call it liberal – theorized about regional relations within the language of the traditional empiricism of the English school of international relations. South Africa's post-1960s relations with its neighbours were, as a result, overwhelmingly framed within the limiting discourse set by a limited number of white men with closely shared social origins. By drawing, as they did, on selective historical interpretations, they entirely ignored the lived reality of the majority of the region's peoples, that is the aforementioned rich underbelly.

A second, neo-conservative, strain was more virulent and linked to the passion of the second Cold War.[6] Here, state formation ensured 'that boundaries [were] constructed, spaces demarcated, standards of legitimacy incorporated, interpretations of history privileged, and alternatives marginalized' (Campbell, 1990: p. 266). With time, international relations, in the guise of regional policy, shifted from a preoccupation with the relations between states to the creation of boundaries that 'constitute, at one and the same time, the state and the international system, the domestic and the external, and the sovereign and the anarchic. As they emphasized the power of states and the ritual of state systems, their sense of international community…was… characterized by anarchy, not community' (Ashley, 1987: p. 404).

In the legitimating context of a new Cold War, South African policy-makers embarked on a path of 'total strategy', the strategic doctrine which underpinned South Africa's regional policy. As a view of the world and an approach to policy, it was imbued with doctrinaire Christianity which reinforced the proverbial power of realism (Brewer, 1994: p. 314). Regionalism became the nexus for 'inter-state' conflict as South Africa's security problems, particularly in the 1970s and the 1980s, were defined by the 'brute other non-state' in Southern Africa. Fed by this understanding, South Africa plunged the region into a devastating war whose consequences will be felt well into the next century (Manzo, 1992: p. 55). It was an horrific moment in the history of any continent, in any epoch: one million people are thought to have been killed and it is said to have cost billions. What lessons must the academy draw from this?

The present efforts to reconstruct Southern Africa around its states run, in my view, the risk of repeating the disasters of the past. It is of course perfectly true that South Africa's domestic situation is entirely different, that, as noted, truly historic events have taken place in South Africa. But it has also been stressed here that bad theory and poor mapping prescribed the route to the horror of regional destabilization.

The ending of apartheid has not made the making of regional policy in Southern Africa any easier. The pressures on the regular policy processes have been complicated both by the pace and magnitude of the changes which have taken place, and shifts in the global economy. Moreover, the region's unthinkable event, the end of apartheid, caught many governments and, most certainly, the region's multilateral organizations unawares. John Lewis Gaddis's bemused response to the question regarding the end of the Cold War – 'this possibility had never occurred to any of us' – might well have applied to officials and leaders throughout the region. In these circumstances one can sympathize with Aziz Pahad, South Africa's Deputy Minister of Foreign Affairs who often laments about making 'foreign policy all the time!'

Those in the academy who advise policy-makers regarding the quickly changing tempo of regional affairs it seems seldom think about all this. Like the hapless Mr Pahad, they have been caught up in the sheer pace of day-to-day developments and the need to provide answers to an eager and ill-prepared public. 'Policy-oriented intellectuals have internalized the norms of the state, which when it understandably calls them to the capital, in effect becomes their patron' (Said, 1993: p. 366). As they do so, they reinforce the traditional frameworks in profound ways. In these circumstances, it is easy to see why rote and ritual rather than rigour or imagination mark thinking about the immediate cause, and future course of the region's affairs. Can this change?

A helpful beginning can be made by accepting Cox's well-known distinction between 'problem-solving' and 'critical' theory (Cox, 1981). The former accepts the world as it finds it and tries to engineer ways of making it run more smoothly; to achieve this, problem-solving sets limits to the inquiry it makes. As a rule it accepts the world as good and seeks to maintain existing structures (Vasquez, 1983: p. 16). The proponents of the other view, critical theorists,

> work on the basis of a theory of history which gives them a handle on historical processes, enabling them to assess the existing structure of reality in terms of the historical evolution of the international system. These theorists are not only interested in analyzing the world, they wish to restructure the established order … [T]heir intention is to adopt a position which makes it

possible for them to transcend the existing order and look for ways
of transforming it.

(Little, 1995: p. 66)

If the primary concern of theoreticians is the same punditry much
loved by policy-makers, then the future vision of Southern Africa seems
really no different from the tragic consequences of its Westphalian-ori-
ented and Euro-centric historical mapping. If, however, the purpose of
theory is to understand the existing conditions in Southern Africa and
to explore the possibilities for structural change, new framings may
emerge. In turn, these may help to build new regional understandings.

Contrary to realist framings, there can be no neat divorce in either
theory or practice between South Africa and its neighbours. Because
South Africa was built on a single core, there is no dividing line
between what is 'regional' and what is 'domestic', one orderly the other
anarchic. A deep moral question follows. Why is it that structures, such
as states, enjoy a greater weighting than do people (see Linklater, 1990;
1994)? Why have states meant more than the people who have built
Southern Africa? The answer lies in the way the region's maps have
been drawn around the interests of the powerful, silencing the majority
of its people (Smith, 1995: p. 2).

Orthodox theories, then, seem to have advanced Southern Africa no
further than the regional circumstances which prevailed at the moment
of 'birth' of the state we call South Africa. They have left tremendous
gaps, both theoretical and practical, in our understanding of the affairs
of the region. On the central issue of apartheid, the traditional matrix
was not able to amplify the point that South Africa's people had more
to fear from the government of their own country than from armies in
neighbouring countries (Booth and Vale, 1995). On the evolving policy
challenge of migration, they offer no explanation except to fall back on
their narrow logic and to urge tough responses. And they cannot
explain the success, in regional and world terms, of the 80-year old
Southern African Customs Union.

If the same inadequacies in understanding led, amongst other hor-
rors to regional destabilization, what futures await the region's people
in the twenty-first century? This question usefully brings this analytical focus to a close.

In slow and painful ways, international relations in Southern Africa
is recognizing its manifold weaknesses. At the global level, widening
interest in framings suggests that 'knowledge on the subject is no
longer established; it is contested' (Booth, 1995: p. 329); and that there

is deep 'theoretical tumult in international relations' (Williams, 1996: p. 1).[7] In Southern Africa this has taken some of us, among other directions, towards the conceptualization of a 'culture of caring' (van Aardt, 1993), and opened up the idea that it might be best to organize the affairs of the region in a neo-functionalist way, say for example, around water resource access and use (Swatuk and Vale, 1999).

Clearly, this chapter reveals a bias towards an approach which 'places suffering humanity at the centre of its theoretical project' (Wheeler, 1996: p. 127). But here, too, there may be more than meets the eye: without criticism, a country cannot know itself; without understanding their behaviour in the world through the lens provided by critical theory a people cannot know themselves in the world.[8] All this has profound consequences for Southern African governments, especially that in South Africa. If South Africans, in Sparks's (1996) words, 'don't want to be seen as the gringos of Africa', they will have to use different maps to think about Southern Africa and their role in it.

It does not stop here. Countries outside the region are also touched by this. If Botswana buys tanks to build its sense of security, might not the question 'who benefits' be asked alongside the question of 'which map' of the region's future is being used?

Ritualized responses will repeat the mistakes of the past; a new beginning can be made by accepting that choices generate beginnings (Ashley, 1988; George, 1993), that theories are, to use Cox's well-worn but trenchant phrase, 'always for someone, and for some purpose' (Cox, 1995: p. 31). There is no end of history in Southern Africa or anywhere else, as Fukuyama (1992) would have us believe. As politicians constantly remind us, there is much work to be done in Southern Africa, most of it practical, as the bureaucrats invariably assert, but it all begins with theory.

Notes

1. Many of the ideas in this paper are drawn from Peter Vale (1996d), *South Africa and Southern Africa – Theories and Practice, Choices and Ritual* (Inaugural Lecture, UNESCO Africa Chair, Faculteit der Letteren, Universiteit Utrecht).
2. As a cautionary tale on this now familiar theme in International Relations, Rob Walker's critique of endings and epochs in Booth and Smith (1995) is compulsory reading.
3. This follows Latham's (1996: p. 5) assertion that 'capitalist markets are perhaps the ultimate modern form in that they smash all sorts of relations before them'.
4. This image is too often used and, like much in international relations, too seldom explored (Bialas, 1997).

5. SADC was formed by treaty out of the Southern African Development Coordination Conference (SADCC). SADCC itself was initiated in 1980
   by the Frontline States. The Frontline States included Angola, Botswana,
   Mozambique, Zambia, Zimbabwe and Tanzania. SADCC's membership
   included these states plus Lesotho, Malawi and Swaziland. Namibia joined
   SADCC in 1991. SADC, created in 1992, includes the 10 SADCC member
   states plus South Africa (1994), Mauritius (1995), the Democratic Republic
   of Congo (DRC) and Seychelles (both 1997). See Du Pisani in Chapter 9 for
   details.
6. The names commonly associated with this epistemic community are Jack
   Spence, John Barratt, James Barber and Deon Geldenhuys. Each was a trained
   historian and, only with the exception of the first, each studied within
   the Oxbridge tradition. The first three were closely associated throughout
   their professional lives: Geldenhuys's PhD was supervised by Spence and
   examined by Barber; he wrote his important book on South Africa's foreign
   policy and his more controversial work on Southern Africa whilst in the
   employ of the SAIIA where John Barratt was then the Director. For a representative selection of their work, see Barber and Barratt (1990) and
   Geldenhuys (1984).
7. Nic Rengger's footnote captures a few of their strands: 'positivist' versus 'post-
   positivist'; 'modern' versus 'postmodern'; 'critical' versus 'traditional'; 'rationalist' versus 'reflectivist'; 'neo-realist' versus 'neo-liberal' (Rengger, 1996).
8. I was brought to this recognition after reading an interview with the
   Mexican writer, Octavio Pax in *The Observer Review* (London, 23 June 1996).

References

Ashley, Richard K. (1987), 'The Geopolitics of Geopolitical Space: Toward a
   Critical Social Theory of International Politics', *Alternatives* 12, 403–34.
Ashley, Richard K. (1988), 'Geopolitics, Supplementary Criticism: A Reply to
   Professors Roy and Walker', *Alternatives* 13.
Barber, James, and John Barratt (1990), *South Africa's Foreign Policy: the search for
   status and security 1945–1988* (Johannesburg: Southern Book Publishers in
   association with the South African Institute of International Affairs).
Bayart, J.-F. (1993), *The State in Africa: The Politics of the Belly* (London and New
   York: Longman).
Bialas, Zbigniew (1997), *Mapping Wild Gardens: The Symbolic Conquest of South
   Africa* (Essen: Die Blaue Eule).
Booth, Ken (1994), 'A Security Regime in Southern Africa: theoretical considera-
   tions', *Southern African Perspectives: A Working Paper Series*, no. 30 (Bellville:
   Centre for Southern African Studies).
Booth, Ken (1995), 'Dare not to Know: International Relations Theory versus
   the Future', in Ken Booth and Steve Smith (eds), *International Relations Theory
   Today* (London: Polity Press).
Booth, Ken, and Steve Smith (eds) (1995), *International Relations Theory Today*
   (London: Polity).
Booth, Ken, and Peter Vale (1995), 'Security in Southern Africa: after apartheid,
   beyond realism', *International Affairs* 19, 285–304.

Brewer, John D. (1994), *Black and Blue: Policing in South Africa* (Oxford: Clarendon Press).

Campbell, David (1990), 'Global Inscriptions: How Foreign Policy Constitutes the United States', *Alternatives* 15, 263–86.

Claude, Inis (1971), *Swords into Ploughshares: The Problems and Prospects of International Organization* (New York: Random House).

Cox, Robert W. (1981), 'Social Forces, States and World Orders: beyond international relations theory', *Millennium* 10, 126–55.

Cox, Robert W. (1995), 'Critical Political Economy', in Bjorn Hettne (ed), *International Political Economy: Understanding Global Disorder* (Halifax: Fernwood Books Ltd).

Davidson, Basil (1992), *The Black Man's Burden: Africa and the Curse of the Nation State* (London: James Currey).

Dingake, Michael (1987), *My Fight Against Apartheid* (London: Kliptown Books).

Frost, Mervyn, Peter Vale and David Weiner (eds) (1988), *International Relations: a debate on methodology* (Pretoria: HSRC Series on Methodology).

Fukuyama, Francis (1992), *The End of History and the Last Man* (London: Hamish Hamilton).

Geldenhuys, Deon (1984), *The Diplomacy of Isolation* (London: Macmillan).

George, Jim (1993), 'Of Incarceration and Closure: Neo-Realism and the New/Old World Order', *Millennium* 22/2, 197–234.

George, Jim (1994), *Discourses of Global Politics: A Critical (Re)Introduction to International Relations* (Boulder, CO: Lynne Rienner).

Gilson, Etienne (1976) 'Concerning Christian Philosophy', in R. Klibansky and H. J. Paton (eds), *Philosophy and History* (Oxford: Oxford University Press).

Held, David (1995), *Democracy and the Global Order: from the modern state to cosmopolitan governance* (Cambridge: Polity Press).

Holiday, Anthony (1993), 'Conversations in a Colony: Natural language and primitive interchange', *Pretexts* 4, 3–18.

Latham, Robert (1996), 'Modernity and Security: An Argument Sketch', paper presented at the annual meeting of the International Studies Association, San Diego, California (April).

Linklater, Andrew (1990), 'The Problem of Community in International Relations', *Alternatives* 15, 135–53.

Linklater, Andrew (1994), 'Dialogue, Dialectic and Emancipation in International Relations at the End of the Post-War Age', *Millennium* 23, 119–31.

Little, Richard D. (1995), 'International Relations and the Triumph of Capitalism', in Ken Booth and Steve Smith (eds), *International Relations Theory Today* (London: Polity).

Manzo, Kate (1992), 'Global Power and South African Politics: A Foucauldian Analysis', *Alternatives* 17, 23–66.

Mitrany, David (1943), *A Working Peace System* (London: Royal Institute of International Affairs).

Murray, Martin J. (1995), ' "Blackbirding" at "Crook's Corner": Illicit Labour Recruitment in the Northeastern Transvaal, 1910–1940', *Journal of Southern African Studies* 21, 373–97.

Rengger, Nic (1996), 'Clio's Cave: historical materialism and the claims of "substantive social theory" in world politics', *Review of International Studies* 22, 213–31.

Rotberg, Robert I. (1995), 'Centripetal Forces: Regional Convergence in Southern Africa', *Harvard International Review* XVII/8–9, 78–9.

Rotberg, Robert I., and Greg Mills (eds) (1997), *War and Peace in Southern Africa: Crime, Drugs, Armies and Trade* (Washington: Brookings Institution).

Said, Edward W. (1993), *Culture and Imperialism* (New York and London: Vintage Books).

Saul, John (1999), ' "For Fear of Being Condemned as Old Fashioned": Liberal Democracy versus Popular Democracy in Sub-Saharan Africa', in Kidane Mengisteab and Cyril Daddieh (eds), *State-Building and Democratization in Africa: Faith, Hope and Realities* (Westport, CT: Praeger).

Smith, Steve (1995), 'The Self-Images of a Discipline: A Genealogy of International Relations Theory', in Ken Booth and Steve Smith (eds), *International Relations Theory Today* (London: Polity).

Sparks, Allister (1996), 'Africa's poverty threatens SA', *The Star* (Johannesburg), 1 May 1996.

Spegele, Roger (1985), 'Theory and Process in the Recent Study of International Relations', *Jerusalem Journal of International Relations* 7/4, 1–27.

Spegele, Roger (1996), *Political Realism in International Theory* (Cambridge: Cambridge University Press).

Swatuk, Larry A., and Peter Vale (1999), 'Why Democracy is Not Enough: Southern Africa and Human Security in the Twenty-first Century', *Alternatives* 24, 361–89.

Swatuk, Larry A., and Peter Vale (2000), 'Southern Africa Beyond Sovereignty', paper presented at the annual meeting of the International Studies Association, Los Angeles (March).

Temu, A. J., and Bonaventure Swai (1981), 'The intellectual and the state in postcolonial Africa: The Tanzanian case', *Social Praxis* 8/3–4.

Vale, Peter (1996a), *Southern Africa: Exploring a Peace Dividend* (London: Catholic Institute for International Relations Briefing Series).

Vale, Peter (1996b), 'Southern Africa's Security: Six Propositions for the Twenty-First Century', *Disarmament* XIX/1, 53–72.

Vale, Peter (1996c) 'Southern African Security', *Alternatives* 21, 361–91.

Vale, Peter (1996d), 'South Africa and Southern Africa: Theories and Practices, Choices and Ritual', Inaugural Lecture: UNESCO Africa Chair Faculteit der Letteren, Universiteit Utrecht.

Vale, Peter, and John Daniel (1995), 'Regional Security in Southern Africa in the 1990s: Challenging the Terms of the Neo-Realist Debate', *Transformation* 28, 84–93.

van Aardt, Maxi (1993), 'In search of a more adequate concept of security for Southern Africa', *South African Journal of International Affairs* 1/1(Spring): 82–101.

Vasquez, John (1983), *The Power of Power Politics: A Critique* (London: Francis Pinter).

Walker, R. B. J. (1990), 'Security, Sovereignty and the Challenge of World Politics', *Alternatives* 15, 3–27.

Walker, R. B. J. (1993), *Inside/Outside: international relations as political theory* (Cambridge: Cambridge Studies in International Relations).

Walker, R. B. J. (1994), 'On pedagogical responsibility: a response to Roy Jones', *Review of International Studies* 20, 313–22.

Wheeler, Nick (1996), 'Guardian Angel or Global Gangster: a review of the ethical claims of international society', *Political Studies* 44, 123–35.

Wight, Martin (1977), *Systems of States*, edited by Hedley Bull (Leicester: Leicester University Press).

Williams, Michael (1996), 'Institutions of "Security"', paper presented at the annual meeting of the International Studies Association, San Diego, California (April).

3
Realism and its Critics[1]

Hussein Solomon

Introduction

This chapter examines the bewildering state of the latter half of the twentieth century and illustrates the need for a reliable theoretical framework through which we may interpret global change. Although ridiculed by critics wearing the broad mantle of the 'progressive left', incorporating critical theory, postmodernism, post-structuralism and the like (that is, virtually every other contribution to this book), it is argued that realism – especially the classical realism of Carr, Morgenthau and Niebuhr but also the structural or neo-realism of Waltz and Krasner – is best suited to understand the turbulent world in which we live. At all times the interface between theory and practice is exposed.

We are living in a dynamic and turbulent period of world history, fecund with seeming contradictions. In an era which has witnessed the end of some of the most intractable conflicts of the twentieth century – the Cold War and apartheid – and therefore seemingly to herald a new era of peace, the killing fields of the former Yugoslavia and Zaire are once more awash with blood, while Angola and Afghanistan continue to mock all international efforts to bring about peace. In an era where the winds of democracy have ostensibly signified the end of the one-party state, authoritarianism and human rights abuses are still the order of the day in much of Africa where the Mugabes, the Mois and the Kabilas still reign.

Moreover, in Eastern Europe, ultra-nationalists such as Vladimir Zhirinovsky are gaining ground; while the *apparatchiks* of the former communist regimes are being returned to power under the banner of the 'Reconstituted Left' like a warped rendition of the 'Star Wars

Trilogy'. In an era where one hears increasing talk of a global economy, the possibility of several trade wars occurring is a reality. In an era where there is talk of a global culture, various types of insular and virulent cultural chauvinisms are expressed. In an era where there is increasing talk of a harmonious global polity, the world is wracked by conflict generated by secessionist movements wearing mantles of ethnicity, nationalism or religious fundamentalism.

To make sense of the confusing world we inhabit we need theory. Theory, according to Kenneth Waltz, 'is an intellectual construction by which we select facts and interpret them' (George, 1994: p. 126). However, theory, especially theory in the social sciences – and as inferred from the above definition – cannot be objective (Booth, 1994: pp. 1–3). This, then, creates the basis for competing theories to develop.

What this chapter sets out to do is to briefly describe the key features of realism and to critically evaluate the theoretical challenge to it. Above all, it aims to show that realism/neo-realism does have a case and that its critics are misguided in their opposition to a paradigm which is so useful in coming to understand the turbulent world in which we live.

What is realism?

Realism as a distinct school of thought in international relations theory places its emphasis on the state as the primary actor in world politics (Walker, 1990: p. 3; George, 1994: pp. 72–4; Booth, 1991b: p. 313). Its central proposition is that since the purpose of statecraft is national survival in a hostile, anarchic environment the acquisition of power is the proper, rational and inevitable goal of foreign policy (Booth, 1991a: p. 2). International Politics can then be defined as a struggle between power-maximizing states in an anarchical environment (Morgenthau, 1960; Booth, 1991a: p. 2). Hence realism is sometimes referred to as the power politics school of thought (Evans and Newnham, 1992: p. 277).

The concept of 'anarchy' as noted above is an important pillar of the realist paradigm. Anarchy stems from the fact that states answer to no higher authority and so must look to themselves to protect their interests and ensure their survival. Thus the concepts of 'self-help' and 'sovereignty' become integral parts of the realist view of global affairs (Walker, 1990: p. 7; George, 1994: p. 200; Booth, 1991b: p. 313; Carim, 1995: p. 2). Since all states seek to maximize power in such an anarchic world, realism emphasizes the endemic nature of conflict and competition in world politics. This, in turn, necessitates the acquisition of military capabilities by states, sufficient at least to deter attack in a dangerous and uncertain world (Evans and Newnham, 1992: p. 277).

Acceptance of the persistence of conflict in the system, however, does not mean that such conflict should go unchecked since this would imply a threat to the entire state system. The favoured realist technique of conflict management is through the Balance of Power where 'stability and order are the result of skilful manipulations of flexible alliance systems: they do not stem from the authoritative force of International Law or Organization, which in any case is minimal' (Evans and Newnham, 1992: p. 277).

The truism of the above has been borne out historically time and again. However, three relatively recent incidents illustrate the point. In the 1980s, the United States mined the harbours of Sandinista Nicaragua. General Daniel Ortega took the US to the International Court of Justice (ICJ) at The Hague. The US refused to show up, however, declaring that it does not see itself as bound by the decisions of the ICJ. In the 1980s, too, New Zealand asked for the extradition of a French secret service agent to face charges of international terrorism relating to the bombing of the Greenpeace vessel, *Rainbow Warrior*. France refused to extradite the agent and used her veto in the United Nations Security Council to 'kill' the issue in that august world body. Closer to home, the apartheid South African state destabilized its neighbours both militarily and economically in defiance of international legal norms.

These cases illustrate the fact that power, or the lack of it, is the central organizing principle of international politics – not international law or organization – and that international law and world bodies like the UN are cynically used and abused by the powerful to further their own interests as it has been done for centuries. Even more prosaically, it underlines the correctness of the realist paradigm which views the structure of the international system as a hierarchy based on power capabilities; where the principle of equality between states is non-existent since states have different power capabilities; and where weak states are at the mercy of more powerful states (Evans and Newnham, 1992: p. 277).

However, it is important to distinguish the classical realism of Carr, Morgenthau, Niebuhr and Schwarzenberger from the structural or neo-realism of, among others, Waltz, Krasner, Stein and Keohane (George, 1994: pp. 14–15).

While retaining many of the basic features of classical realism, for instance power as a central analytical concept, neo-realism directs attention to the structural characteristics of an international system of states rather than to its component units. In this 'Waltzian' formulation the concept of 'structure' refers to the hierarchical ordering of a system. In the words of Evans and Newnham (1992: pp. 216–17), in the neo-realist view:

> [t]he system is still anarchical, and the units are still deemed to be autonomous, but attention to the structural level of analysis enables a more dynamic and less restrictive picture of international political behaviour to emerge. Traditional realism, by concentrating on the units and their functional attributes, is unable to account for changes in behaviour or in the distribution of power which occur independently of fluctuations within the units themselves. Neorealism, on the other hand, explains how structures affect behaviour and outcomes regardless of characteristics attributed to power and status.

In this chapter the term 'realism' will be used to refer to both the classical and structural varieties. This is possible due to the strong continuities, as noted above, running from realism to neo-realism.

The progressive left challenge

Realism, in one form or another, has dominated academic considerations of world politics and the thinking of foreign-policy makers over the past few decades. However, in this post-Cold War period realism is coming under fire from the progressive left. The progressive left flame has been carried into the realm of international relations theory by the likes of Booth (1991a; 1994), George (1994; 1993b), and Walker (1990). In Southern Africa it has been carried by the likes of Vale (1994; also Chapter 2 above), Booth and Vale (1995) and Carim (1995).

These scholars view realism as an 'anachronistic residue of the European Enlightenment and, in general, mainstream [positivist] Western philosophy, which continues the futile quest for a grand (non) theory of existence beyond specific time, space and political purpose' (George, 1994: p. 12; Walker, 1990: p. 7).

Critics assert that realism presents its knowledge of the world in terms of generalized, universalized and irreducible patterns of human behaviour, which reduces the complexity of global patterns to the incessant anarchical power struggle among states and 'rational' inter-state activity to the single utilitarian pursuit of self-interest (Carim,

1995: p. 4; George, 1994: p. 4). It is also argued that realists view reality in 'essentialist, unitary and universalist terms', thereby arriving at the 'erroneous' positivist conclusion of a 'singular, stable, knowable reality' (George, 1994: p. 29). These critics, in contrast, see reality in a state of perpetual flux – of movement, change and instability. They believe that their acceptance of heterogeneity and diversity make them uniquely positioned to address the ambiguities and paradoxes of global life (Carim, 1995: p. 3).

As a result critics argue that realism has become increasingly irrelevant to policy-makers and ordinary people; and that realist dominated international relations theory has been reduced to 'the gibbering of apes' (George, 1993: p. 197). Frequently it is cited that realism's 'failure' to predict the end of the Cold War or the demise of Soviet Russia is indicative of the irrelevance of realism to the complex world we inhabit (George, 1994: p. 4; Carim, 1995: p. 5).

Ultimately, these critics aim to facilitate a broader, more inclusive understanding of global human relations and seek to illustrate how it is possible to think and act beyond the seemingly immutable principles of international relations orthodoxy, 'where identity, state sovereignty and international anarchy are presented as unchanging, ahistorical "givens" in the global system' (Carim, 1995: pp. 2–4).

However, the progressive left is not without its critics, and this writer takes grave exception to the way they transform realism from a sophisticated, complex, and successful tradition which seeks to analyse global life into a caricatured, simplified narrative.

Will the true realists please stand up?

The progressive left generally presents realism as a static body of thought; which, because of its aversion to change, is becoming increasingly irrelevant in this post-Cold War era. Walker (1990: p. 12), for example, notes the following:

> Since the eighteenth century, Western political theory has been guided by a reading of history as a grand march from barbarism toward enlightenment and modernity. [Realist] theories of international relations, however, build on an intense suspicion of any theories of progress, indeed about the possibility of fundamental change of any kind. Progress is possible within states, but, it is said, between states there can only be the same old rituals of power politics played over and over again.

What this section aims to do, then, is to disprove the notion of realism as a single homogenous strand of thought unchanging in the face of a world characterized by change, movement and turmoil.

Historically, realism went through three phases. The first phase began in 1948 with the publication of Hans Morgenthau's *Politics Among Nations*. This saw the emergence of realism in the classic power-politics sense. The second phase began in the late 1950s and ended with the end of the Vietnam War. This saw a shift in the realist research orientation: the discipline came to be dominated by behaviouralist approaches to Cold War strategic issues (George, 1994: p. 70). The third, or neo-realist, phase formally began with the publication of Kenneth Waltz's *Theory of International Politics* in 1979. This marked the start of a more international political economy (IPE) approach to international relations (see Tsie in Chapter 6).

Notwithstanding the above, critics continue to berate the 'static' nature of realism. Carim (1995: p. 15), for instance, uses the terms 'realist' and 'neo-realist' interchangeably and George (1994: p. 70) claims to see no substantive difference between classical realism and its neo-realist heir. However, substantive differences between the two easily can be illustrated. Niebuhr, for example, one of the founding fathers of classical realism, belonged to a tradition of strong Christian pessimism. As a result, he saw a fallen human nature at the root of war and other international problems (Booth, 1991a: p. 6). Waltz (1979), however, explains war in terms of the anarchical structure of the states system. This determining structure imposes a self-help logic on states. From this perspective, wars occur because there is nothing to stop them when a state believes it must defend or further a 'vital interest' by force.

One can also demonstrate substantive difference not only between classical realism and neo-realism, but also within neo-realism. On the role of regimes in international politics, two camps may be broadly identified within the structural realist paradigm. These may be identified as conservative and liberal. The conservative approach of Waltz (1979) expresses itself in his rejection of any meaningful role accorded to regimes in international affairs. This may be contrasted with the more liberal approaches of Stephen Krasner and Robert Keohane who,

> accept the basic analytical assumptions of [conventional] structural realist approaches, which posit an international system of functionally symmetrical, power-maximizing states acting in an anarchic environment. But [it] maintains that under certain conditions involving the failure of individual action to secure Pareto-optimal

outcomes, international regimes may have a significant impact even in an anarchic world.

(George, 1994: p. 118)

Substantive differences not only exist between the classical and structural realist schools, and also within the respective schools of thought; they also exist between realists belonging to the same school on specific issue areas. Clearly the debate surrounding the hydrogen bomb (H-bomb) and Vietnam were two such issue areas (see, for example, Gaddis, 1992; Kennan, 1984).

Moreover, there are substantial differences to be found within the writings of a single realist. For instance, the last page of Carr's, *Twenty Years Crisis* (1966) spoke of a world community beyond borders; similarly, the state-centric Hans Morgenthau later in life advocated world government (Boyle, 1985: pp. 70–74).

What is clear from the above is that realism, both in theory and practice, is not as simple as critics claim it to be. This fact, however, has serious implications for the progressive left critique of realism. George (1994: p. 104) posits the notion that realism leads to war and devastation; and Vale in Chapter 2 of this volume suggests that realism drove apartheid's foreign and domestic policies, in particular the thinking behind 'Total Strategy'. However, if one accepts the complexity of realism in theory and practice, one would find such an overly simplistic causal relationship between realism and war, or realism and apartheid difficult to sustain. Such monocausal analysis might also lead us to conclude that Nietzsche's writings directly led to the rise of Naziism, Auschwitz and Dachau. No further historical analysis is needed.

Realism versus Nostradamus

As noted above, critics accuse realism of being increasingly irrelevant in this age of rapid global change, citing in particular the example of realism's inability to come to grips with the demise of the Soviet superpower and the end of the Cold War (Carim, 1995: p. 5). George (1994: p. 4) puts it this way:

> Indeed Gaddis has illustrated how the analytical emperor of International Relations is naked after all. More precisely the dominant perspective in International Relations, articulated latterly as neo-Realism, has illustrated that it cannot adequately explain that which it assured a generation it understood – the behaviour of the Soviet

Union as power politics actor in the anarchical system. This is primarily because Realism, in any of its guises, represents its knowledge of the world in terms of generalized, universalized, and irreducible patterns of human behaviour, which reduces global politics to the incessant, anarchical power struggle among states and 'rational' interstate activity to the single utilitarian pursuit of self-interest. From such a perspective there can be no 'rational' explanation for Soviet behaviour in peacefully relinquishing its power status and systemic authority other than in traditional power politics terms.

This is an interesting argument. In the first instance, George rests his attack on realism's lack of predictive power, dubious criteria indeed by which to judge the relevance or usefulness of knowledge. Clearly, the complexity inherent in human nature makes it difficult to predict the future of human relations with the same level of accuracy as the interaction between atoms. But, the question still remains: did realism fail to predict the demise of the Soviet superpower? The work of Cold War historian J. L. Gaddis (1992) provides an answer.

In Gaddis's estimation, John Foster Dulles is generally regarded as the archetypal realist and Cold Warrior yet he did foresee the end of the Soviet superpower. In 1955 Dulles met the Chinese Nationalist Foreign Minister George Yeh and had the following to say:

> Washington regarded the disintegrative process as inherent in the nature of a communist dictatorship, and as inevitable. The communist regimes were bound to crack, if for no other reason than their inability to satisfy the needs of their own people. What was required was faith that the dissolution of this evil system is gradually taking place even when there is no surface evidence … External pressures hasten the destructive process.
>
> (Gaddis, 1992: p. 76)

Dulles identified one of the fault lines of the Soviet Union as being its large and volatile ethnic mix. He likened the Soviet empire's 'multinational' problem to the problem of ethnic nationalism in the Austro-Hungarian empire before it. Like the Austro-Hungarian empire, he maintained that ethnic nationalism constitutes such a severe destabilizing factor that it could precipitate a crack in the Soviet monolith (Gaddis, 1992: p. 77).

Moreover, in the last years of Dulles' life, he came to see that changes within communist states might alter their external behaviour more rapidly than the deliberate application of pressure without

(Gaddis, 1992: p. 79). History has proven Dulles correct in asserting that economics and ethnicity, internal as opposed to external forces, would result in the demise of the Soviet superpower. What the above illustrates is the lie in George's statement that from a realist perspective there can be no 'rational explanation for Soviet behaviour in peacefully relinquishing its power status and systemic authority other than in traditional power politics terms'.

Realism and the misappropriation of historical figures

George (1994: p. 193) also takes issue with what he terms the 'problematic nature of neo-realism's textual foundations'. According to George, in attempting to appropriate Thucydides's *History of the Peloponnesian War* as a realist text neo-realism ignores Thucydides's own emphasis on the significance of human actors as the conscious initiators of events and his antipathy to structuralist principles 'that posit the foundation of an anarchical world in the (external) power distribution of actors' (George, 1994: p. 193). Similarly, George (1994: p. 195) finds the representation of Machiavelli's *Prince* as part of a realist 'doctrine' problematic. George claims that Machiavelli's primary concern in *The Prince* is *virtu* and the problem of violence in the pursuit of a good life.

George's critique notwithstanding, Thucydides's and Machiavelli's contributions to realist theory are undeniable. Evans and Newnham (1992: p. 277) note that Thucydides's *History of the Peloponnesian War* was the first sustained effort to explain the origins of international conflict in terms of the dynamics of power politics. More importantly any reading of the book itself will illustrate that Thucydides's concentration on human actors like Pericles and Alcibiaedes did not negate the importance of various structural factors like the alliance between Sparta and Persia against Athens. More importantly, it could be argued that Machiavelli's *Prince* (1513) and Hobbes's *Leviathan* (1651) provided crucial components of the realist tradition in their conceptions of interest, prudence, and expediency as prime motivators in the anarchic arena of world politics. Moreover, it could be argued that George's own comments elsewhere in the same book undermine his own argument. For instance he notes that the first Machiavellian principle of power politics is 'that virtue in International Relations dictates that aggression must be met with greater aggression if meaningful order is to be maintained' (George, 1994: p. 3).

Even more important is the fact that any academic endeavour necessarily borrows rather eclectically from that which has gone before.

For instance, Marx's materialist conception of history borrowed extensively from Hegel; Marx's critique of capitalism and the notion of surplus value were borrowed from Smith and Ricardo; and Marx's conception of the state owed a great intellectual debt to the anthropologist Henry Morgan. Similarly, postmodernism's intellectual roots are just as eclectic: *inter alia*, feminism, Marxism of the Frankfurt school, the anti-structuralism of Gramsci, post-structuralism, hermeneutics, language philosophy, and postempiricist philosophy of science. One wonders how Hegel would have felt with Marx making his dialectic 'to stand on its head'; equally, one wonders how Marx, the positivist, the modernist and the determinist, would feel about being 'misappropriated' by postmodernists.

Realism and morality

It has been argued by Walker (1990: p. 8) that realism's concentration on power-politics results in a dichotomy between power and morality. He also asserts that realism negates the usefulness, or indeed, the relevance of ethics in the international arena. Vale makes a similar point, but goes further by implying a link between realism and immoral apartheid (Vale, 1994: pp. 28–9, 11–14). Is this true? Does realism, both as theory and practice, separate power from ethics? Put simply, does realism advocate immorality in international politics?

On the theoretical side one could repudiate this challenge by simply turning to Carr's *The Twenty Years' Crisis 1919–1939* (1966), one of the chief scrolls in the realist faith. It is generally regarded that this text effectively repudiated the tenets of Wilsonian idealism and set forth the basic principles of power politics on which Morgenthau, Niebuhr, Reynolds and others built. However, a closer examination of the book itself provides a more tempered view of the role of power and an appreciation of morality in international politics. In fact, Carr (1966: p. 89) suggests a combination of power and morality, and he describes politics and law as a 'meeting place' for ethics and power (Booth, 1991a; Fox 1985).

On a theoretical level, then, we can note that realism is not as immoral as it has been made out to be. But what of the more practical level? Since critics are so fond of citing the case of the US during the Cold War, it is to that country's foreign policy that we now turn.

The Vietnam War and the Watergate scandal raised questions about the 'moral relativism' of US politics generally and US foreign policy in particular. The combined effect of all this was to bring about by the mid-1970s, a serious debate about the relationship between morality and foreign policy. Basically, the argument revolved around two competing priorities: order and justice.

The realist position on this was clear: order was the prerequisite for justice. This was not a negation of human rights in foreign policy. Niebuhr worked out the realist position as early as 1942 when he pointed out that human rights could not flourish in conditions of war, anarchy, or revolution (Gaddis, 1992: p. 59) – a viewpoint embraced by then US Secretary of State Henry Kissinger. 'The true task of citizenship', he argued in 1975, 'is to draw from the balance of power a more positive capacity to better the human condition'. Or, as he put it in his memoirs, 'If history teaches anything it is that there can be no peace without equilibrium and no justice without restraint' (quoted in Gaddis, 1992: p. 59).

But, the opposite view which regarded human rights as the primary American interest overwhelmed the realist position, on what one suspects to have been more domestic political than intellectual reasons. The most forceful proponent of such a view was Jimmy Carter, who during the 1976 presidential campaign declared, 'We've seen a loss of morality … and we're ashamed of what our government is as we deal with other nations around the world. What we seek is … a foreign policy that reflects the decency and generosity and common sense of our own people' (in Gaddis, 1992: p. 60).

The result was that, during the Carter presidency, human rights gained a much higher priority than at any other point in the history of the Cold War. Ironically, the effect of this was to intensify the Cold War rather than to make it possible to move beyond it, as Carter had hoped to do. Complaints about human rights violations in the Soviet Union undermined the atmosphere of relative goodwill that had developed between Washington and Moscow during the Nixon and Ford administrations. The most prominent casualty was progress in the Strategic Arms Limitation Talks, in particular SALT II. Carter's preoccupation with human rights, meanwhile, induced the Soviets to exploit what they saw as American weaknesses in places such as Angola, Ethiopia, Mozambique, and Afghanistan. Moreover, Carter's attempts to disassociate the US from authoritarian regimes in Iran and Nicaragua backfired when these governments gave way to outspokenly anti-American regimes, which, in addition, were not too sympathetic on the question of human rights either (Gaddis, 1992: p. 60).

What the above demonstrates are the disastrous consequences of making human rights both ends and means of foreign policy, rather than allowing human rights to flow from order as realists propose. Let us concretize this a little more and create a hypothetical future scenario.

Currently, the Mugabe regime in Zimbabwe is growing more authoritarian with the arrest and torture of journalists – Mark Chavunduka being a case in point. In addition, an independent judiciary is being undermined and the power of the military inside Zimbabwe is increasing rapidly. Opposition parliamentarians and prominent leaders of civil society organizations are being harassed and intimidated. An anti-realist position taken by South African policy-makers would immediately slam the Mugabe government for gross human rights abuses, possibly break off diplomatic relations, and provide some sort of assistance to the 'oppressed'. The repercussions of this would be disastrous, however. South Africa would lose a valuable trading partner, adversely affecting the South African economy. The possibility of regional integration would be dealt a severe blow. Other countries in the region would view South Africa with suspicion: is Pretoria's anti-Mugabe stance really motivated by a concern for human rights or does South Africa want to marginalize Harare with the intention of maintaining total control over the Southern African Development Community? More importantly, how are other countries, such as Swaziland, with poor human rights records supposed to feel about the Republic's new found role as protector of human rights?

A realist view would proceed along a different route to arrive at the same objective – the end of human rights abuses in Zimbabwe. For example, a realist-based foreign policy would ensure that the project of regional integration – which after all would be for the benefit of all the region's people – continues. The question of human rights abuses can be privately raised by way of the exercise of diplomacy with the Mugabe administration. At the same time, Harare could be offered various carrots (for example, various trade incentives) to nudge (as opposed to push) it along the human rights route. This would result in a good marriage between human rights and foreign policy, between morality and the national interest.

Realism and anarchy

George (1994: p. 204) challenges realists by asking them to account for regime cooperation in a situation of endemic anarchy. As has been noted above, however, this is precisely the question that occupied the minds of Waltz and other neorealists. It is not my intention in this section to reiterate these arguments; rather, it is to attempt to clarify the meaning and consequences of anarchy in realist thought.

Anarchy is a central pillar in realist thought. Its literal meaning is 'absence of government'; however, this should not be interpreted as disorder, confusion and chaos (as George wrongly does). Anarchy and order are not necessarily mutually exclusive in traditional international relations theory. States, realists note, do in fact form a primitive society with rules, norms and values (such as respect for the territorial sovereignty of states) (Vincent, 1986: pp. 123–5). However, these rules, norms and values are not as well developed between states as they are within states. The cases cited earlier regarding US mining of Nicaragua's harbours; French bombing of the *Rainbow Warrior*; and apartheid South Africa's regional destabilization policies in defiance of international norms all demonstrate the tentative nature of what is termed 'international law'. Nevertheless, a primitive form of society exists within this anarchy – that is, what Bull termed 'the anarchical society' (Bull, 1977).

The concept of anarchy, however, holds other implications. Lack of a common government or a universally recognized common external authority is what distinguishes the international from the domestic realms of politics and law. The notions of sovereignty and independence in this way are either a consequence of or a reason for this condition (Evans and Newnham, 1992: p. 12). However, demarcating domestic from international politics does not necessarily mean seeing one in isolation from the other; rather, 'domestic' and 'foreign' are interrelated. For example, at the Congress of Vienna in 1815, Prussia's Metternich and other conservative monarchies, fearing the spread of the ideas of the French Revolution decided to band together to stop the spread of such revolutionary ideas. Thus Metternich's 'Concert' system proposed a kind of international policing regime for he feared that revolutionary French ideas like 'equality' might become a factor in the *domestic* politics of conservative Prussia. Similarly, in an effort to bolster their own territorial integrity and sovereignty, Southern African states formed the Southern African Development Coordination Conference (SADCC) in 1980 to reduce their economic dependence on apartheid South Africa which used this economic dependence to force compliance from neighbouring states in a number of issue areas.

The example cited above is also instructive for another reason: it explains why states which are necessarily in competition with each other cooperate. States, history emphasizes, cooperate with each other when it is in their interest to do so. It is instructive to note that after the conservative monarchies of Europe weathered the storm of the populist

1848 revolutions, very little in common remained between them and the Concert system all but fell into disarray. When the Crimean war broke out in 1854 it officially sealed the death of the Concert system (Evans and Newnham, 1992: p. 50). Similarly, the demise of apartheid South Africa and the inclusion of its post-apartheid successor into the SADC fold in 1994 has resulted in increased competition between South Africa and Zimbabwe for regional leadership. I return to the concept of national self interest (NSI) in the 'anarchical society' in the next section.

Realism and the withering away of the state

Realists have been attacked by critics for according to the state the role of primary referent in international affairs (George, 1994: p. 72).

The state as an 'ahistorical given'

One aspect of this criticism relates to the fact that realists see the state as an 'ahistorical given in the global system' (Carim, 1995: p. 2). Critics contend that the state is a relatively recent historical form; that the birth of the modern state is to be found in the Treaty of Westphalia of 1648 which formally ended the Thirty Years War. Campbell, for example, argues that the state emerged out of particular circumstances and that in the present era of massive global change it shows every indication to be on the wane (Campbell, 1990: p. 271; see, also, Tsie's discussion in Chapter 6).

However, such a view is extremely problematic. Does this mean that Julius Caesar did not rule over a state? Does this mean that Shaka or Moshoeshoe I did not rule over states in nineteenth-century Southern Africa? Does this mean that Montezuma's sophisticated Aztec polity was not a state? And what of King Solomon's Israel, rulers of the mighty kingdoms of Mali and Ghana, Atahualapa's vast Inca empire, and the sophisticated Indus Valley polity which existed millennia before the birth of Christ?

These questions necessitate a more fundamental question: what exactly is a state? The classic political science definition of a state is a people occupying a specific territory, having rulers (government) who pass laws that are binding on those people (Rodee *et al.*, 1976: p. 20). By this definition, all the above historical examples are indeed states. More importantly, it illustrates a deep Eurocentric bias among those scholars who claim that the state is a relatively recent historical phenomenon that began with the Treaty of Westphalia in 1648.

Those who argue that the state is withering away lack an under-standing of human history, which shows that states are complex and ever-changing social structures. As such, the state as defined by Rodee *et al.* above will always be with us in one form or another. After all, somebody has to see to it that my garbage is picked up on Thursdays, that my post is delivered to me, that sees to the education of my daughters, that provides me with some form of a social security net if I lose my job, and that provides me with protection from the mugger in the dark alley or the army of a foreign government.

State versus non-state actors

Another aspect of the critique relates to the 'fact' of the state withering away. Proof of this is said to be the tremendous growth of social move-ments, non-governmental organizations (NGOs), transnational corpo-rations (TNCs) and the like (Carim, 1995: p. 15; George, 1994: p. 204; Vale, 1994: p. 10). Unfortunately for the critics, the situation is far more nuanced. History shows that state and non-state actors have *always coexisted*: that sometimes they have been in opposition to each other, and that in other cases they have worked together; that at times the power of the state was predominant and at other times the power of non-state actors was predominant. But, and this is an important qualification, where the power of non-state actors has been predomi-nant it did not mean a death-knell to the existence of the state.

Consider here the case of some of the earliest TNCs – the English East India Company (EEIC) and the Dutch East India Company (DEIC). The EEIC set about the conquest of India and, to use a more contemporary phrase, members of its 'board' became governors of the various con-quered Indian provinces. Similarly, the DEIC set about the conquest of Java (later to be renamed Dutch Batavia) and it was members of its board – the Council of 17 – who ordered Jan van Riebeeck to come to the Cape in 1652. Both companies had their own warships and, indeed, one could ask whether the power of these TNCs was not greater then than now. In considering the development of apartheid in South Africa, it is difficult to separate it from the demands of capital. Consider in this regard, the demands of the mining magnates and the development of native reserves (a precedent for the later development of bantustans) and the contract labour migrant system (Davenport, 1991).

It is important to note here, too, that the power of the state in each of the above instances was enhanced by the activities of private capital. Indications today are that not much has changed. Consider the case of Lonrho, the British conglomerate, which while operating in several countries cannot escape the label 'British'. More importantly, the British state benefits from Lonrho's activities as can be seen in the assistance the company's overseas activities receive from the British state. The same could be said about Anglo American and Toshiba.

Talking of things Japanese, it is interesting to note that the US trade deficit with Japan is caused by Japanese companies operating inside the United States which insist on importing Japanese goods for their plants as opposed to using American-made inputs in motor vehicle assembly. This illustrates an important point – the underlying nationalism of sup-posedly international companies and the support they get from their respective national governments. Similarly, it is the South African state which is attempting to defend its conglomerates' domestic market while attempting to acquire market access for them abroad. The completed European Union–South Africa free trade agreement is a case in point.

Regarding the power and position of social movements, history is replete with examples of strong social movements – disproving critics of realism who argue that this is a relatively recent historical phenome-non. In 1374 BC, for instance, Pharoah Amenhotep IV introduced monotheism into ancient Egypt. This revolved around worship of the Sun-God Aten. However, Amenhotep faced stiff opposition from the priests of other gods, and especially the priests of Amun. So severe was this opposition that Amenhotep's successor had to recant the tenets of monotheism and once more had to embrace polytheism, thus making place for the god Amun and his priests. A similar incident occurred in 1669 when Hindus in northern India rebelled against the rule of Aurangzeb who banned their religion and burnt their temples.

There are strong historical parallels to be drawn involving today's worker movements. In 1428, for example, Japanese transport workers went on strike against high food prices as famine struck Japan. They were joined by farmers who wrecked warehouses, temples and private homes. A similar incident occurred in 1563 when the Japanese feudal lord Ieyasu placed heavy taxes on rice. Japanese workers once more went on strike and embarked upon what Sam Shilowa would describe as 'mass action'. History also provides examples where workers' organi-zations actually took power in states – for instance the 1917 Bolshevik Revolution in Russia – and cities – for example in 1413 Paris butchers led by Simon Caboche took over the city in an effort to 'make the government more efficient'.

The question arises, what happens when social movements actually capture state power? Does the state, to paraphrase Marx and Engels, wither away? The answer to this is a definite no. In fact, quite the opposite is true: where social movements capture state power, the state is imbued with greater legitimacy. This, in turn, enhances its power *vis-à-vis* citizens and other social formations found within the territorial boundaries of the state. Such was the case when Engelbrecht Engelbrechtsen led a peasant revolt in Sweden which resulted in King Eric VII fleeing and Engelbrechtsen occupying the throne. Such was the case, too, in Gaur in India when African slaves revolted and put their own leader on the throne. Such was the case of the trade union movement Solidarity in Poland in the 1980s.

The case of the African National Congress (ANC) in South Africa can also be said to fit this pattern. It could be argued that the ANC from its inception in 1912 until just prior to coming to power on 27 April 1994 was more a social and nationalist movement than a political party. It fought for a South African nationalism blind to the colour of a person's skin and fought for the upliftment of what Frantz Fanon termed 'the wretched of the earth' (see Vale in Chapter 2).

Clearly, social movements, trade unions, and the like do not view the state as an empty husk or shell; rather; it is viewed as the repository of real power and that one has to capture it or influence it in order to affect desired social change. Thus, the anti-state Vale (1994: p. 3) unwittingly emphasizes the importance of the state to academics by stating:

> If progressive intellectuals are to promote the prospects for a better world – and, I believe they must – they will have to anticipate and help shift debates within the resulting spaces, by changing the way *policy-makers* think about the region. To repeat the overall point in a causal chain – we need to – change – the way – *bureaucrats* – think – in order – to – change – their – behaviour – in order – to secure – a different future for the region's people (my emphasis).

To return to the question of the ANC and the South African state: the anti-apartheid movement, epitomized by the ANC, has captured state power. For the first time the new government has a mandate from the South African people as a whole, as opposed to one section of it. This point is emphasized by the fact that the ANC has an alliance with both the South African Communist Party (SACP) and the Congress of South African Trade Unions (COSATU) – the tripartite alliance – and has a working relationship with the South African National Civics Organization (SANCO). Indeed, it is not unusual to find a member of the ANC also being a member of the SACP, COSATU and SANCO. This accords the new government greater popular legitimacy, and strengthens the hand of the new state considerably. President Mbeki's government, like Mandela's before, can use the police to curb worker and student unrest, use the army against striking policemen in Transkei and force SANCO and the Congress of Traditional Leaders of South Africa (CONTRALESA) to reach an agreement over local government elections as occurred in November 1995. In each of the above, the Government of National Unity embarked upon punitive measures, yet still retained popular support. The underlying point here is that states are far more resistant to historical change than critics of realism suggest.

The state and the national interest in an era of interdependence and integration

To some observers, regional integration and global interdependence undermine state sovereignty (Walker, 1990: pp. 18–22). However, one finds reality to be far more nuanced. What is often missing from progressive left accounts of interdependence are the structural disparities and exclusions that form part of the process of interdependence and integration in modern world politics. Consider here the level of interdependence between the US and Mexico within the North American Free Trade Association (NAFTA). Can one argue that the US is as dependent on Mexico as Mexico is on the US? Similarly, within the ambit of the South African Customs Union, can one argue that South Africa is as dependent on Lesotho as Lesotho is on South Africa? The answer to both these questions is obviously 'no'.

The point is that critics' accounts of interdependence invariably attempt to show it as a harmonious, horizontal and equitable process (compare Du Pisani in Chapter 9 below). Reality, however, suggests the opposite. Vertical or unequal relations guided by national self interest (NSI) have been the norm. States cooperate with each other on a specific issue because it is in the national interest to do so; however, where cooperation comes into conflict with the interest of the state or NSI such behaviour ceases rather quickly. Interdependence, in this way, has been with us for millennia and will be with us for millennia to come. Consider here the temporary alliance of Angola and Zimbabwe with Kabila's Congo. President Dos Santos aimed to cut Union for the Total Independence of Angola (UNITA) supply routes through the Democratic Republic of the Congo. Hence his military support to Kabila in order to weaken UNITA's military and diplomatic position within Angola and the region. Similarly President Mugabe's support for the Kinshasa regime reflects Zimbabwe's extensive economic interests in Kabila's Congo.

Regional interdependence and integration, or inter-state cooperation generally, should not be seen as the forerunner of some sort of global polity. It should be seen instead as the workings of NSI. Those who doubt it need only consider here the US's ambivalent position within the Pacific Community, the disintegration of the East African Community, Nigeria's behaviour within ECOWAS, or the fears of smaller SADCC states of Zimbabwean hegemony of this regional organization in the 1980s (Chan, 1987: p. 173; Manning and Stern, 1994: pp. 79–93). As SADCC evolved into SADC, these fears have now shifted to South Africa as a possible regional hegemon (see Odén in Chapter 8 of this volume).

These are not isolated occurrences. Consider the recent case of Norway's 'no' to membership of the European Union (EU). The major reason for Oslo's refusal is that membership would mean giving up farm subsidies and embracing free trade. Open markets and free competition, the Norwegians feel, would sound the death knell for its agricultural sector. However, Norway's refusal to join the EU does not mean, to paraphrase Samir Amin, 'delinkage' from the European colossus: Norway remains a member of the European Economic Area and of NATO. Norway's soldiers will still patrol Western Europe's only border with Russia, and its lobsters will still be served in Belgian restaurants (*The Economist*, 3 December 1994). What the case of Norway demonstrates is that states will choose to cooperate with certain other states if they derive benefit from it, however where such cooperation is not in the national interest, they will either refrain from or qualify the nature of that cooperation.

The utility of NSI for academics to understand the behaviour of states is underlined by the confusion critics of realism face in their quest to come to terms with state behaviour. For example, Vale (1994: p. 2) asks, 'How is one to explain the regional policy of a country [South Africa] which relied on its neighbours to deliver it from oppression but threatens to turn on an electric fence to keep them out'. The answer to this question obviously relates to the fact that it is not in South Africa's interest to have millions of illegal immigrants from neighbouring countries (irrespective of their contribution to the 'struggle') entering South Africa.

Biological research has demonstrated how self-interest on the part of states is readily explicable from a consideration of biological and cultural forces that have shaped human history from the beginnings of time (Dawkins, 1976; Mansbridge, 1990; Shaw and Wong, 1989; Wilson, 1975). For instance, Hatcher (1994: pp. 8–11) delineates the biological roots of self-interest, and reveals how self-interest at the group or national level is a logical outgrowth of biological considerations. Moreover, it is argued that many of the factors which limit selfishness at the individual level are absent at the inter-group or international level. This Hatcher asserts leads to unbridled self-interest at these levels, practically guaranteeing a world of conflict between groups and nations.

Those still unconvinced of the predominance of national self interest in global politics should simply ponder the following question: can they provide an example of one country which conducts its foreign policy without first considering the national interest? What the above demonstrates is that interdependence and integration are not some forerunner of the emergence of a global polity heralding the disappearance of the state; rather it must be viewed as simply the workings of the national interest. A concomitant of this is that there can be no talk of a 'waning state'.

The state and the new security agenda

It has been argued that threats to security in the 1990s arise increasingly from processes that are worldwide in scope – potentially massive ecological disruptions; drug-trafficking; refugees and small arms proliferation. It is asserted that these transnational security threats necessitate inter-state cooperation and the development of collective security, thereby diminishing state sovereignty (Walker, 1990: p. 3; Vale, 1994: p. 3; George, 1994: p. 209).

While it is true that insecurity is increasingly taking on a transnational character there is no evidence that this *necessarily* leads to inter-state cooperation. Consider the new ecological threats to security and their effects on state behaviour. Southern Africa is an arid region, as such water is a valuable commodity. In 1992 Zimbabwe decided to build a dam on the Saabi river. The Botswana government, realizing that this would decrease the flow of water downstream, opposed this decision. They maintained that Harare's insistence to build the dam constituted a national security threat to Botswana. So severe was this crisis that, at one stage, Gaborone placed its troops on alert. A similar incident occurred between the state of California and Mexico in the 1980s over the waters of the Rio Grande (Solomon, 1995; see also Swatuk in Chapter 12 below).

The underlying point is that scarce natural resources have not fostered a spirit of cooperation. Instead, they have fuelled the fires of inter-state rivalry. A similar point can be made regarding refugees.

As noted earlier, the appearance of the 'refugee problem' has resulted in strong nationalist feelings, bordering on xenophobia. The resultant anti-foreigner sentiments have not exactly helped the case of regional cooperation. Indeed, respect for sovereignty and the territorial integrity of member states are among the guiding principles of the Treaty establishing the Southern African Development Community. Once more one can conclude that the new security agenda does not mean the 'withering away of the state' (see also Buzan, 1987).

A viable alternative to the state?

In light of so much criticism, is there an alternative form of political community to the state? In answer to this question Booth (1994: p. 14) makes the following observation:

> Modern states are too large to satisfy some human needs, and too small to cope with the requirements of guidance for an increasingly interdependent planet. The logical conclusion of this argument is that power should be more diffuse. It is desirable to take it away from states to more local communities (to cater for cultural diversity, for example), while wider problems such as economic and environmental issues, could be more effectively dealt with by designated regional or global function organizations.

Booth's is not an argument against the state – it is an argument against a specific *type* of state (unitary) in favour of another *type* of state (federal). If Booth is talking about even greater autonomy to cater for cultural diversity, how might this be applicable to the South African scenario? Apartheid South Africa justified its bantustan policies following similar logic.

But, what of Booth's other idea that 'wider problems such as economic and environmental issues could be more effectively dealt with by regional or global function organizations'? In the first instance, economic regimes such as the Uruguay Round of the General Agreement on Trade and Tariffs (GATT) which led to the formation of the World Trade Organization (WTO) have failed to achieve its stated objective of 'tariff disarmament' as US–Japanese trade relations indicate. Neither is this an isolated incident if the 'chicken wars' between South Africa and the US are anything to go by. On the question of environmental regimes one may simply point out how global environmental concerns foundered on the rocks of national self interest at the Rio Earth Summit in 1992 (Speth, 1992).

To emphasize the point, both brutally and simply, there is no practical alternative to the state. Walker (1990: p. 5) puts it this way: 'The state is a political category in a way that the world, or the globe, or the planet, or humanity is not'. Also stressing the centrality of the state, UN Secretary-General Boutros Boutros-Ghali (1992: p. 9) observes: 'The foundation-stone of this work [that is, peace and economic development] is and must remain the State. Respect for its fundamental sovereignty and integrity are crucial to any common international progress'.

The strongest argument in support of the state comes not from its many and varied successes but rather from its failure. State collapse in Somalia, for example, has not been met with cries of jubilation from its now 'emancipated' inhabitants (compare Booth, 1991b: pp. 313–26). Rather, tragedy and misery have greeted Somalis with its collapse. This is why the state must and should remain the primary referent in domestic and international affairs. The principle of state sovereignty is the most plausible way of reconciling claims about universality and diversity. Without the apparatus of a strong state, the way becomes clear for the Mohammed Farah Aideeds of the world to appear. Without the apparatus of a strong state, the world will be plunged into Somali-style warlordism of the Dark Age variety.

Conclusion

In summary, in this chapter the progressive left challenge to realism has been tested, and shown to be wanting. Realism remains the single most reliable analytical framework through which we can understand and evaluate global change. Critics provide no practical alternatives to the realist paradigm. We know what a realist world looks like (we are living in one); what of an alternative to realism? As long as hate, envy, greed and egotism motivate humanity, realism will continue to be of invaluable worth to policy-maker and scholar alike. In this regard it is perhaps instructive to note that, from the end of the Second World War until 1992, 100 major conflicts around the world left some 20 million human beings dead (Boutros-Ghali, 1992: p. 7). Neither has the end of the Cold War shown any sign that such conflict will end. By the end of 1993, 53 wars were being waged in 37 countries across the globe (Bendana, 1994: p. 3). By 1996, Africa alone accounted for six million of the world's 13 million refugees. Until a fundamental change in human nature occurs realism will continue to dominate the discipline of international relations. The most fundamental problem with realism's critics is in assuming a more optimistic view of human nature. The killing fields of Andulo, Kisangani and Algiers all bear testimony to the folly of such a view.

Note

1. The views expressed in this chapter are my own and do not necessarily reflect those of my employer, ACCORD.

References

Aronowitz, S. (1992), 'The Tension of Critical Theory: Is Negative Dialectics All There Is?', in S. Seidman and D. G. Wagner (eds), *Postmodernism and Social Theory* (Cambridge, MA: Basil Blackwell): 289–321.
Bendana, A. (1994), 'A New Global Order', paper presented to the 'Conference on Global Change – Imperatives for the South' organized by the Southern African Non-Governmental Development Organization Network (SANDON); Centre for Southern African Studies; Centro de Estudios Internacionales, Managua, Nicaragua; and the Foundation for Contemporary Research, Protea Hotel, Brackenfell (23–25 February).
Booth, Ken (1991a), *Security in Anarchy: Utopian Realism in Theory and Practice* (Aberystwyth: University College of Wales).
Booth, Ken (1991b), 'Security and Emancipation', *Review of International Studies* 17, 313–26.
Booth, Ken (1994), 'A Security Regime in Southern Africa: Theoretical Considerations', *Southern African Perspectives: A Working Paper Series* 30 (Bellville: Centre for Southern African Studies).
Booth, Ken, and Peter Vale (1995), 'Security in Southern Africa: after apartheid, beyond realism', *International Affairs Bulletin* 71/2.
Boutros-Ghali, Boutros (1992), *An Agenda for Peace: Preventive Diplomacy, Peacemaking and Peace-keeping* (New York: United Nations).
Boyle, F. A. (1985), *World Politics and International Law* (Durham, NC: Duke University Press).
Bull, Hedley (1977), *The Anarchical Society: A Study of Order in World Politics* (London: Macmillan).
Buzan, Barry (1987), *An Introduction to Strategic Studies: Military Technology and International Relations* (London: Macmillan Press in association with the International Institute for Strategic Studies).
Campbell, David (1990), 'Global Inscription: How Foreign Policy Constitutes the United States', *Alternatives* 15, 263–86.
Carim, Xavier (1995), *Critical and Postmodern Readings of Strategic Culture in the 1990s*, paper presented to the conference on 'A Culture of Peace in Commemoration of Dr. Martin Luther King, Jnr' organized by the Department of Political and Administrative Studies, University of Zimbabwe in cooperation with the United Nations Educational, Scientific and Cultural Organization (UNESCO), Harare, Zimbabwe (13–17 February).
Carr, E. H. (1966), *The Twenty Years Crisis 1919–1939. An Introduction to the Study of International Relations*. 3rd edn (London: Macmillan).

Chan, Stephen (1987), *Issues in International Relations: A view from Africa* (London: Macmillan).

Davenport, T. R. H. (1991), *South Africa: A Modern History*, 4th edn, (London: Macmillan).

Dawkins, Richard (1976), *The Selfish Gene* (New York: Oxford University Press).

Economist (1994), 'Marital problems' (3 Dec.).

Economist (1994), 'Norway's No' (3 Dec.).

Evans, G. and J. Newnham (1992), *The Dictionary of World Politics: A reference guide to concepts, ideas and institutions* (New York: Harvester-Wheatsheaf).

Far Eastern Economic Review (1994), 'India: Pride and Prejudice' (3 Nov.).

Far Eastern Economic Review (1994), 'Zones of competition' (22 Dec.).

Far Eastern Economic Review (1994), 'Enter the Dragon' (22 Dec.).

Fox, W. T. R. (1985), 'E H Carr and Political Realism: vision and revision', *Review of International Studies* 11, 1–16.

Gaddis, John Lewis (1992), *The United States and the End of the Cold War: Implications, Reconsideration, Provocations* (Oxford: Oxford University Press).

George, Jim (1994), *Discourses of Global Politics: A Critical Reintroduction to International Relations* (Boulder, CO: Lynne Rienner).

George, Jim (1993), 'Of Incarceration and Closure: Neo-Realism and the New/Old World Order', *Millennium: Journal of International Affairs* 22/2, 197–234.

Hatcher, J.W. (1994), 'The Problem of Self-interest: from Gene to International Relations', *The Indian Ocean Review* (8–11 Dec.).

Kennan, George F. (1984), *The Nuclear Delusion: Soviet-American Relations in the Atomic Age* (London: Hamish Hamilton).

Manning, R. and P. Stern (1994), 'The Myth of the Pacific Community', *Foreign Affairs* 73/6 (Nov.–Dec.), 79–93.

Mansbridge, J. J. (ed.) (1990), *Beyond Self-Interest* (Chicago: University of Chicago Press).

Morgenthau, Hans (1960), *Politics among Nations: The Struggle for Power and Peace*, 3rd edn (New York: Alfred A. Knopf).

Rodee, C. C., T. J. Anderson and C. Q. Christol (1976), *Introduction to Political Science*, 3rd edn (New York: McGraw-Hill).

Shaw, R. P. and Y. Wong (1989), *Genetic Seeds of Warfare, Evolution, nationalism and patriotism* (Boston: Unwin and Hyman).

Solomon, Hussein (1995), 'Global Change and the Challenge to International Relations Theory', *Politeia* 14/1, 37–54.

Speth, James G. (1992), 'A post-Rio Compact', *Foreign Policy* 88.

Vale, Peter (1994), *Of Laagers, Lepers and Leanness: South Africa and Regional Security in the mid-1990s* (Bergen, Norway: Chr. Michelsen Institute).

Vincent, R. J. (1986), *Human Rights and International Relations* (Cambridge: Cambridge University Press).

Walker, R. B. J. (1990), 'Security, Sovereignty and the Challenge of World Politics', *Alternatives* 15, 3–27.

Waltz, Kenneth N. (1979), *Theory of International Politics* (Reading, MA: Addison-Wesley).

Weekly Mail (1995), 'Ecuador and Peru in Border War' (10 Feb.).

Wilson, E. O. (1975), *Sociobiology: The new synthesis* (Cambridge, MA: Harvard University Press).

4
Unstated Places – Rereading Southern Africa

Michael Niemann

Introduction

The very visible increase in regional efforts by states in many parts of the globe has again generated an academic interest in such efforts. This is, of course, not the first time in the century or so of systematic thinking about regionalism in the field of international relations (IR). The torturous developments of the European Union generated significant academic effort during the 1950s and the 1960s which sometimes even spilled over into investigations of the non-European world. The current interest, emerging as it is after almost two decades of disciplinary silence on matters of regional concern, tends to be based on the theoretical models and ideas introduced during the earlier period. This is understandable but not necessarily helpful, especially if these models are resurrected without a critical eye towards their implicit and explicit assumptions.

The nexus of power and knowledge so eloquently elaborated by Foucault is nowhere more visible than in the discipline of IR. If the social sciences in general have always been a 'state centric activity' (Taylor, 1996: p. 19), then IR theory has been the most explicit in its links to and reliance on state power. Since its formal origins after the First World War, it has been increasingly concerned with determining the language which 'is used to maintain the hegemony of [a] privileged discourse' (Dear, 1988: p. 266). This discourse consists of unquestioned assumptions about the nature of global politics, the actors which participate in it and the strategies and policies which warrant attention. Nowhere is the power of this discourse more visible than when teaching a course on IR theory to students in the US who have, on the whole, little knowledge of and exposure to issues of a global nature and yet have a fully formed imagery of the nature of global affairs. This is the crux of Foucault's argument: the power/knowledge nexus manifests precisely in the unquestioned acceptance of a 'common sense' meaning while eschewing any analysis of the manner in which this 'common sense' is constructed and maintained (Solomon in Chapter 3 being a case in point).

The same can be said for the theorizing about regionalization. It is my purpose in this chapter to challenge this discourse and, instead, call for a radically open dialogue about regionalization and the meaning of regions with a specific focus on Southern Africa. My effort in this chapter is based primarily on conceptualizations of space and how these can provide an avenue for such a dialogue. In the following section I will outline a critical review of regional theory in IR to be followed by a reintroduction of space into the debate about IR and regions. The third section will provide one perspective from which to read Southern Africa and the final section will offer suggestions for future directions of this dialogue.

IR theory and statism

As with any academic discipline, international relations has its 'lore' of foundational texts and theoretical battles fought over its core assumptions and foundations. Part of such 'lore' is the obligatory reference to the 'great debates' which have marked its development since 1919. However, one question which was not part of these 'debates' was the basic assumption that states are the primary if not the only actors in international relations. While the Liberals believed that the causes of war were related to 'bad' states negotiating in secret (Wilson, 1996), Realists maintained that the drive for power existed in all human beings and therefore, by extension, in all states like some sort of international original sin (Morgenthau, 1960). Waltz (1959; 1979) dismissed either notion and, as one of the original neo-realists, claimed that the workings of the system, specifically anarchy, was the reason behind the recurrence of war. What is common to all these positions is the basic description of states as personified entities, as 'hyper individuals'. The crudest example of such an anthropomorphism is the appropriation of the Rousseauian image of the stag hunt by Waltz (1959: p. 167 *et seq.*), but others equally embraced such individualized notions.

There is an interesting paradox here and it transcends the supposed distinctions between the parties of the 'debate'. States are ascribed the qualities of 'primitive individuals' (Sylvester, 1992: p. 157), that is, selfishness, lust for power, and so on. These 'qualities' are taken from the worst notions held of human beings outside the bounds and strictures of society. Yet, the fact that human beings in everyday life do not exhibit these tendencies, except in extreme circumstances, is explained by the 'civilizing' role of society. In other words, human beings are assumed to have overcome or controlled these tendencies in our lives only because they live in a social context which imposes hierarchical structures. The paradox, of course, lies in the assumption that the very institutions which keep our worst tendencies in check also inherit these tendencies only to display them at the international level. How can it be that eminently social constructs, that is, states, exhibit the archetypal human behavior which they are supposed to control in the first place? This Janus face of the state as protector of order on the one hand and creator of disorder on the other pervades the intellectual propositions on either side of the first 'great debate' without ever being recognized or properly theorized.

It is clear that the process of turning the state into a 'hyper individual' is problematic to say the least but even if we were to accept this transfiguration for the moment, there is still no reason to accept the assumption that these individualized states must therefore exist in an anarchic system. The latter notion achieves common sense status only as a result of the unquestioned transfer of the basic tenets of liberal philosophy of the individual to the state, particularly the state of nature images employed by Hobbes, Spinoza, Rousseau and others. In developing the liberal theory of society, Hobbes and others created fictional human beings, fictional men to be correct, who, in the words of Christine Di Stephano, appear like 'orphans who have raised themselves, whose desires are situated within and reflect nothing but independently generated movement' (1983: p. 639). These 'rugged individual' men[1] interact with each other only on combative or contractual terms and the latter type of interaction is only possible through the intervention of the Leviathan.

Once this image is employed in IR, states take the places of individuals and, just as the Hobbesian man appears out of nowhere like a mushroom, states exist without a historical dimension which is concerned with origins and trajectories. Just as the Hobbesian man is doomed to continuous warfare without the intervention of the Leviathan, states in the international system face a similarly dangerous future. There is no sense of connections between states, that one state's existence is tied to, made possible by or otherwise connected with another state's existence. They exist as autonomous, isolated entities, just like billiard balls, except that they generate their movement from within. Most importantly, the anthropomorphic conception of the state robs it of any spatial quality. Instead of a particular spatial extension, shape and place, the state is reduced to an idealized, disembodied, one-dimensional entity which exists only in the temporal dimension. This despatialized state then becomes a common sense entity, something no longer questioned and analysed.

This exclusion of space from the analysis is, in my opinion, a major reason for the inability of IR theory to come to grips with regionalization and globalization. For it is the abstraction of the state, the hyperindividualization referred to above, which turns the state into an idealized entity without any spatial dimension. By endowing this entity with the human qualities envisioned in liberalism, behaviour is automatically limited to conflictive or contractual relations, the latter being the only possible cooperative behavior. In the social contract story of liberalism, contractual (cooperative) relations are only possible if guaranteed through an institution which has monopolized access to the means of violence, the state. It is this absence of violence in society which makes contractual relations possible. In international relations, the absence of this monopolization of the means of violence is taken to be one of the basic constituent aspects of the system. In other words, the entire anarchy problematic (Ashley, 1988) which is the foundational myth of IR relies on the despatialized, individualized image of the state.

In light of the preceding arguments, it is not surprising that theoretical efforts to deal with cooperative behavior of states have, on the whole occupied marginal positions in the field and the analysis of regionalism has been one of the victims of this dominance of the anarchy problematic. This is not the place to provide an in depth review of regional integration theory (see also Holden and Odén in this volume). However, a few points will demonstrate the manner in which the despatialized statist nature of IR theory has influenced the analysis of regions.

Whereas the pioneer of theorizing on cooperative behavior, David Mitrany, still conceived of multiple overlapping spaces as the solution to the problems of modern politics, those who took his functionalist theory as a starting point to analyse regionalization in Europe quickly abandoned the non-statist perspective and reasserted the state as the central actor in regional projects. Mitrany envisioned a functional system based on the transfer of loyalty from existing social-nationalist centres to new functional entities which provided their respective services, in effect an integration of functions at whatever happened to be the most appropriate scale. Haas a major proponent of neo-functionalist theory on the other hand, saw integration as a transfer of loyalty from old centres of political power to a new centre of power, replacing multiple pre-existing centres of power with a single new centre (Haas, 1958: p. 16). Instead of the decentralized collection of functional agencies envisioned by Mitrany, Haas substituted a new 'super state' for the previously independent states.

Efforts to address regionalization in the context of the periphery of the world system tended to follow the lead of Europe centred analysis. Few efforts were undertaken to unravel the overlapping puzzles made up of the multiple layers of ethnicity, statehood and proto-nationalism which constitute current peripheral and semi-peripheral states. As Vaitsos (1978: p. 720) has pointed out, there has been a concern with the methodology of integration rather than a concern with the socio-economic circumstances in which integration occurs in the periphery of the world economy. This emphasis on the methods used, that is, free trade areas, customs unions, policy coordination, was always based on the assumption that the goal of integration was that of improved development, industrialization, and so forth (compare Du Pisani in this volume).

Embedded in the economic development debate, integration efforts were regarded as tools for development and consequently were analysed with regard to their efficacy towards reaching that goal. This is true both for the neo-liberal perspective of 'northern' economists and the *dependencia* approach of the ECLA-inspired Latin American efforts. If integration efforts failed, and that was the norm, the failure was situated at various levels, be it failure to distribute the benefits and costs equally, lack of sufficiently strong regional institutions to enforce individual state compliance (see also Holden in this volume). Rarely was the reason for failure located in the unquestioned transfer of 'northern' ideology and concepts for the solution of entirely different problems:

> To put it bluntly, the economic integration failures of the underdeveloped countries are an impressive monument to the professional arrogance of most 'conventional wisdom' economists from the industrially advanced North, the intellectual sheepishness of the flock of their unconditional followers in the underdeveloped areas both on the technical and policy-making levels, and the inability of the States and dominant political structures to work out any sort of longer-term

development policies suitable for the solution of problems which the present-day advanced societies never faced, even at the beginning of the first industrial revolution in the eighteenth century.

(Wionczeck, 1978: p. 781).

The conventional wisdom referred to above includes, in particular, the despatialized image of the state as the sole representation of a society's interest outside the boundaries which are assumed to constitute that state.

The spaces of global politics

Let me begin with the obvious question: What is a region? Although we all use the term and we all assume that it has a clear meaning, the reality is far from it. First employed in the eighteenth-century to designate a 'natural' physical division of the land, the term was conceived of in terms of 'the integration of all phenomena (natural and human) of an area into an individual unit distinct from those of neighboring areas' in the nineteenth-century (Kimble, 1996: p. 493). Generally, most proponents of the term in the field of geography agreed on the fact that regions existed while disagreeing on which factors could best be used to define the extent of such regions. Early conceptualizations of the region focused on the physical characteristics such as climate, geology or vegetation. Dissatisfaction with this mode of definition – 'Nature's "curtains" are fashioned of more malleable material than iron!' (ibid., p. 498) – led to an emphasis on social phenomena (see Swatuk in Chapter 12 below). However, all attempts to arrive at a coherent universal definition failed, leading to the admission that 'our regions are merely fragments of land whose determination involves a considerable degree of arbitrary judgement' (ibid., pp. 498–9). Kimble concludes that the standard concept of the region was in effect a continental European concept 'sired by Feudalism and raised in the cultural seclusion of a self-sufficing environment' (ibid., p. 507).

While Kimble took the indeterminacy of the term as an argument for its abolition, I would like to suggest here, that the term does have utility as long as we are willing to accept its fluidity and embeddedness in larger contexts. A region is first and foremost a spatial entity at a different scale from those usually associated with global politics – the global scale of the globe, the intermediate scale of the state and the local scale (see Taylor, 1981; 1982). It may exist both at a scale between the local and the state – most regional studies in geography are concerned with such regions – and between the scale of the state and the globe, the scale in which we are interested in this volume. While this statement does not seem dramatically different from the received wisdom of the IR 'lore' I suggest here that conceiving of regions as spaces represents the first step towards the dialogue on regionalism advocated in the introduction to this section.

Space is not something we usually think about in our daily lives, except in so far as it manifests itself as distance to be overcome. Generally, we assume space to be a container of people and things. For over two millennia, the Euclidian concept of space has dominated the Western mental representation of space. Euclidian space was homogeneous, smooth and infinitely divisible and constituted the basis for two and three-dimensional geometry. The equivalent of this mathematical conception of space in physics was that of Newtonian absolute space which viewed space as 'a neutral background against which the positions of objects can be pinpointed and their motions described' (Couclelis, 1992: p. 220). This view of space-as-container has also been embraced by international relations (IR) theory in its treatment of the state. IR theory spends little time thinking about space because its practitioners assume that the question of space has already been settled. The state is seen as a fixed unit 'of secure sovereign space' (Agnew, 1994: p. 106) and as a container of society (Taylor, 1994). The international system, in turn, has come to be regarded as an agglomeration of states and a region is simply a smaller agglomeration of states which happen to share a certain geographical proximity.

Yet within the span of the century that is now ending, the introduction of relativistic space in modern physics has ended the Newtonian space-as-container notion and laid the foundation for a conception of space in which its structure 'both influences the distribution and motion of objects and is governed by them' (Couclelis, 1992: p. 221). The classical distinction between matter on the one hand and the empty void on the other hand is untenable in this new physics; likewise Einstein's relativity theory flatly states that 'there is an infinite number of spaces which are in motion with respect to each other' and these spaces are not voids but are full and dynamic, with the power of 'partaking in physical events' (Einstein, quoted in Kern, 1983: pp. 136, 154). These dramatic changes in the conception of space and the world in the natural sciences have had few if any impact on the conception of space in other disciplines. International relations (IR) theory in particular has persisted in embracing the view of space-as-container in its treatment of the state and the global system. One is left to wonder why, despite these dramatic new visions of the universe and space, the space-as-container view persisted. Lefebvre's observation regarding this question is worth quoting here:

> To picture space as a 'frame' or container into which nothing can be put unless it is smaller than the recipient, and to imagine that this container has no other purpose than to preserve what has been put in it – this is probably the initial error. But is it error or is it ideology? The latter more likely. If so, who promotes it? Who exploits it? And why and how do they do so?
>
> (Lefebvre, 1991: p. 94)

The answers to these questions lie to some extent in the manner in which modernity has fixed space so as to 'privilege historicity and sociality at the expense of spatiality' (Soja, 1993: p. 114). With the emergence of post Enlightenment rationalism, both in its idealist and materialist forms, modern thinking fell into the trap of what Lefebvre calls the 'double illusion' of transparency and opacity (1991: p. 27). The illusion of transparency perceives of space as 'luminous' and easily apprehensible – 'innocent [and] free of traps or secret places' (ibid., p. 28) – with a clear correspondence between social space and space as mental construct; the illusion of opacity, on the other hand, conceives of an objective, 'opaque' space as a natural thing which has more reality than thought and which can be measured and described (Soja, 1996: pp. 63–5). However, it would be incorrect to regard this double illusion as a conflict of competing philosophies. Instead, each is linked to the other so that '[t]he rational is thus naturalized, while nature cloaks itself in nostalgias which supplant rationality' (Lefebvre, 1991: p. 30).

I propose here that it is more helpful to think of social space as a social product (ibid.), rather than as a pre-given normalized abstraction or a mere mental construct. Like any production process, the production of specific spaces, be they buildings, cities or states 'imposes a spatial and temporal order upon related operations' (ibid., p. 71) so that the manner in which societies use and structure space ultimately determines the physical appearance of that space, which in turn has an impact on social practices. Social space exists both as the precondition for and the outcome of social action and, as such, articulates the relationships of things and actions in their simultaneity (ibid., p. 73).

This role of guiding social action while being the product of it is a crucial aspect of social space. Since it prohibits certain social actions at any given time, those who wish to commit such action will always feel the need to resist, subvert, and overcome space that has been produced previously and by others. Whether or not this need leads to action depends on the specific constellation of social forces. Social space will be altered if the social forces which experience it as a constraint achieve sufficient weight. But the alteration itself again constitutes an obstacle to further social action in the future. In Harvey's words, '[s]pace can be overcome only through the production of space' (Harvey, 1985: p. 60). The specific space of any particular time period therefore reflects the general economic structure and mode of production of the society which produces it. Thus for example, the space produced by the Xhosa people did not lend itself easily to colonial appropriation in that the different conceptions of land tenure and usage presented themselves as obstacles to the expansion of white settlers.[2]

With the arrival of Europeans in the Americas, the entire world was in one way or another tied into what I call global social space. This global social space consists of interconnected layers (Lefebvre, 1991: p. 86) whose textures are the result of human action. Texture in this particular context refers to the appearance, that is, the landscape that can be identified at any point in this space during a given time span. States simply constitute one layer of this space with state boundaries conceived of as ambiguous continuities (ibid., p. 87), rather than as clear divisions. In short, the global system did not emerge as an additive outcome of the emergence of states, just as the global economy did not emerge out of the addition of multiple national economies (von Braunmühl, 1976: p. 276). Rather, states and national economies represent different layers of one global social space; they are the constitutive components of that space contributing to its richness and variation. These layers are historically contingent, not permanent, and subject to changes as the constellations of social forces which created them change. Layers may disappear and new layers may emerge in response to new and different dynamics. Particular layers may be more enduring than others and may appear as an obstacle to forces attempting to create new layers or consolidate existing layers. But the degree to which layers appear as obstacles depends on the relative importance of closure versus continuity, in other words, the ambiguous continuities referred to above.

Regions constitute a specific example of layers in the global system. For example, the US National Resources Planning Board described a region as the 'locus of a problem' (Mitrany, 1966: p. 53). This definition is helpful in so far as it de-emphasizes the physical aspects of geography and focuses instead on social relations. Similarly, Martin

(1986, p. 100) viewed the extent of a region as defined by the degree of interconnectedness of production processes. While these definitions based on social relations avoid the problems of geographical arbitrariness, they in turn pose their own problems in that if we accept Taylor's global scale, all production processes everywhere are by definition interconnected. However, such a claim fails to recognize the manner in which different layers of global social space are connected to each other. Regions represent spaces which are constituted through the specific social interactions which, while having a global dimension, always manifest themselves in particular local forms (Taylor, 1981: pp. 186–8). Finally, regions, like all layers, always also have temporal boundaries which articulate the cyclical developments of the world economy at various locales.

Lefebvre (1991: pp. 33, 38 *et seq.*) suggests that the analysis of social space is best approached from a 'conceptual triad' consisting of spatial practice, representations of space and spatial representations. Spatial practice refers to the manner in which social forces produce the spatial structures through which they organize their practices and which is directly apprehendable by the senses. Representations of space refer to the manner in which space is conceived in a society by those who participate in the creation of the dominant discourses. Spatial representations, finally, incorporate both of the previous legs of the triad and refer to 'space as directly *lived*, with all its intractability intact, a space that stretches across images and symbols that accompany it, the space of "inhabitants" and "users"' (Soja, 1996: p. 67). This focus on the actual, lived spaces enables us to analyze 'counterspaces, spaces of resistance to the dominant order' (ibid., p. 68). My objective for the following sections is to outline this conceptual triad as it applies to Southern Africa. The next section will focus on the spatial practices and the representations of space from a macro or state producing perspective.

Spatial practices in Southern Africa

There is little reason to speak of southern Africa as a coherent region before the middle of the nineteenth-century. As a land mass at the southern tip of the African continent it was inhabited by peoples with various modes of social reproduction ranging from the San, who were hunter/gatherers, to the Khoi, who were pastoralists, to the Bantu-speaking mixed farming communities which had established themselves in its eastern part in the aftermath of what Thompson (1995: p. 13) calls a 'migratory drift' from the north two millennia ago.

Omer-Cooper (1994: p. 4) indicates that trade between the Indian Ocean coast and the Eastern Cape area had been established 'by the earlier years of the second millennium AD'. This Indian Ocean connection represented the southwestern end of the extensive and intensive Chinese system of trade which tied Eastern Africa and Southern Africa to the Arab peninsula, India and other parts of the Indian Ocean world (Newitt, 1995: p. 4; Abu-Lughod, 1989).

Although the presence of Europeans in the subcontinent dates back to 1482 when Portuguese ships first arrived at the Congo coast, this presence was limited to coastal areas which initially became part of a vast Atlantic/Indian Ocean region which tied together control over trade routes, the Atlantic slave trade and colonial possessions in Southeast Asia. The most crucial challenge faced by the colonizers was what Braudel calls the 'tyranny of distance'. In terms of spatial production, the overcoming of this distance through the production of space was the basis for the establishment of the Cape Colony and the Portuguese occupation of the East African coast. The spaces initially occupied by Europeans were therefore extensions of other spaces, more specifically the Atlantic space which connected Brazil to the other colonial possessions of Portugal and the Dutch colonial space which linked its possessions in the East Indies to their other trading networks. Once established, however, the new spaces created new possibilities and imposed their own strictures. Bender (1978) provides a cogent analysis of the role of slave trade and the practice of sending convicts to Angola in Angola's development and Newitt (1995) analyses the Portuguese impact on the Indian Ocean trade.

During the early nineteenth century, the combined impact of ecology and European pressures both directly and indirectly led to a massive dislocation and movement of indigenous peoples, usually referred to as the *mfecane*, which had a profound impact on the size of political communities and their respective distribution. These in turn led to the creation of fewer but larger African states, far more organized and bureaucratized than the smaller chiefdoms which had coexisted with one another (see Thompson, 1995: pp. 80–7; Omer-Cooper, 1994: pp. 54–74; Newitt, 1995: pp. 290–96; and Martin, 1987: pp. 866–8) and finalized the settlement patterns of Africans in the subcontinent.

The consolidation of power, the elimination of rival sources of power within specific areas and the bureaucratization of political rule along either military or lineage lines (Martin, 1987: p. 867) facilitated control over the production of desired goods and their flows between these communities while imposing singular control over larger expanses.

These incidents of migrations and state building by indigenous peoples were accompanied by similar activities of the *voortrekkers*, the Dutch speaking descendants of the first European settlers in the Cape. These migrations were inspired by their rejection of increasing anglicization after the official takeover of the Cape Colony by the British, in particular the prohibition of slavery and the legal equalization of Khoikhoi and Europeans in the early 1800s (Manzo, 1996: pp. 77–9).

It is here that we can see the beginning of the creation of a Southern African region. The mass migrations and dispersal of indigenous peoples and *voortrekkers* set up connections from the Orange River in the south to Lake Tanganyika in the north.[3] The treks and paths formed during this process served as the guide for the next defining moment for southern Africa, the discovery of diamonds and gold which turned a secondary interest of British imperialism into a source of mineral riches of massive proportions. In their drive to exploit these and other reported mineral deposits, British imperialists, Cecil Rhodes being the foremost, followed the treks of the *mfecane* and built upon these spatial foundations the infrastructural links which still serve as the routes along which labour migration takes place.

If the migrations of the early and mid nineteenth century laid the foundations for a Southern African region, the discovery of the mineral resources and the efforts to secure their exploitation towards the end of the century constitutes the temporal beginning of that region. It is here that we find the link between state building and the construction of the region. Whereas access to and control over these and other (imaginary or real) resources constituted a crucial part of the drive to establish the various states in the subcontinent, the need to exploit the mineral resources, which, after all, was the basis of state formation, necessitated the creation of a regional space. This process was clearly not uncontested and the conflicts of the period, from the Zulu wars to the South African wars attest to the conflictive nature of the process of spatial production. Once settled, however, the connections between region and state emerged ever more clearly.

In South Africa, the need for labour and capital immediately made the spatial confines of the Union territory an obstacle to be overcome. Since African agriculture as a basis for independent reproduction had not yet been destroyed (see Bundy, 1979), securing the necessary supply of labour constituted the perennial problem which was only exacerbated by the discovery of mineral resources. Similarly, the efforts to establish state power in and demonstrate effective occupation of Mozambique led the Portuguese to grant charters to private companies in order to complete the administration and pacification of the areas north of the 22nd Parallel. These companies in turn saw their opportunity in making profits by either renting out the indigenous inhabitants as labourers to South African and Rhodesian mine owners and farmers or through the fees and revenues from the regional use of ports and other transport facilities (Newitt, 1995: pp. 361–85) and thus expand the number of labourers that already crossed the boundaries from below the 22nd Parallel.

We see therefore that from the very beginning of Southern Africa as a coherent concept, social forces were actively creating different layers of social space even though they may not have been conscious of it. Ohlson and Stedman (1994: p. 36) point out that this process of 'bordering' eliminated a viable basis for the Portuguese colonies, led to the destruction of the capacity for independent reproduction of African peoples in the region and the resulting 'crystallization of ethnicity' (ibid., p. 37) as a strategy of coping with these disruptions. Mozambique, the British South Africa Company (BSAC) territories and the Protectorates quickly became part of a regional space which was primarily but not exclusively characterized by a pattern of labour flows centred on the mines in South Africa and, to some extend, in Southern Rhodesia and Northern Rhodesia and the need for agricultural labour throughout the region. A complementary aspect of this region was the circuit of capital which combined British and German capital with some local capital and created the transportation links which were to become the physical structures of this region.

The processes of industrialization, initiated in South Africa and Rhodesia as a result of mineral production, soon began to seek the region as a market for manufactured goods, adding in the process another dimension to the regional space (see Libby, 1987: p. 49; Seidman, 1980: p. 155; and Davies, 1993: p. 73), so that by the beginning of the decolonization process, Southern Africa as a region was defined by an intricate web of relations which consisted of a flow of people (labour), commodities (increasingly manufactures) and capital (both of South African and foreign origin). These flows were facilitated through a network of transportation facilities which, in distinction to networks in other part of Africa, actually helped define the region.

The beginning of the decolonization process brought independence first to Malawi, Tanzania and Zambia and later Lesotho and Swaziland but also the inauguration of the armed struggles which eventually brought independence to the rest of the region and lasted into the 1990s. Decolonization brought to the forefront the problems facing the

majority-ruled states in a regional space which was produced to prevent the majority from ever ruling. From the very beginning of the
independence period therefore, attempts to inaugurate regional policies which were geared to oppose the remaining white-minority-ruled
states both in ideological and material terms proved to be if not impossible at least extremely costly. From the first implementation of the
embargo against Rhodesia in 1965, Zambia in particular had to cope
with the fact that the structures and textures of the region presented
an enormous obstacle to the pursuit of its policy. One answer was an
attempt at reconstructing a part of the region through the Tanzania–
Zambia Railway (TAZARA) project.

   A similar situation developed upon the independence of Mozambique
which saw itself faced by the contradictory demands of solidarity with
the armed struggle in Rhodesia and its dependence on the revenue
from the Rhodesian use of the port of Beira. The connections of southern Mozambique to the Transvaal created a similar situation where the
spatial make-up of the region was set in juxtaposition to the policy
aims of the revolutionary state. As a result, the Mozambican government found itself in a position of having to rely on revenue produced
by its connection to South Africa in the form of labour remittances and
railway and port fees for Maputo while also serving as a base and training ground for African National Congress (ANC) fighters. These contradictions ultimately were untenable as the infamous Nkomati Accords
highlighted (see Anglin, 1985).

   The inauguration of the SADCC (Southern African Development
Coordination Conference, the predecessor to SADC; see Du Pisani in
this volume) in 1980 was hailed as a milestone in the efforts of the
anti-apartheid struggle and as a precedent for a new kind of cooperation between peripheral states (see Lee, 1989). Its goals, as outlined in
the Lusaka Declaration, are best summarized by two main aspects,
reduction of dependence on South Africa and the forging of new
regional ties in order to foster equitable development. On the surface,
these objectives call for a spatial reorganization of the region, albeit a
region which at that time did not include South Africa. It is here that
the fundamental problem of SADCC was situated. Its two major goals
were in effect contradictory. It proved to be impossible to build a new
region while reducing dependence on South Africa since the entire
region, as Vale highlights in Chapter 2, had been constructed around
South Africa with the peripheral states tightly integrated into the South
African core. The region was more than simply a set of inter-state relations which could be rearranged at will.

From the spatial perspective developed here, the SADCC must there-fore not be understood as an effort to create a different regional inte-gration but as an effort to escape or circumvent the effects of the existing integration. Clearly, South African destabilization during the 1980s played a significant role in obstructing efforts to create a new regional space (see Johnson and Martin, 1988). At the same time, the record of SADCC also highlights the inability of the states involved to coordinate policies in order to advance new patterns of regional inter-action. Østergaard (1989) demonstrated such limits in his study of the tractor industry in the region. Instead, each of the member states sought a way to overcome the strictures represented by the regional space by attempting to extricate itself from the region and embracing a global economy in the form of closer relations to the European Community and the Nordic states (Niemann, 1991).[4]

Representations of Southern Africa

In Lefebvre's view, the representations of space reflect the manner in which space is conceived of in a society. It is the space of 'technocratic subdividers and social engineers – all of whom identify what is lived and what is perceived with what is conceived' (Lefebvre, 1991: p. 38). This description could not be more fitting for Southern Africa. Whereas the spatial practices in which social forces engaged during the period in question without doubt contributed to the production of the regional space we call Southern Africa, that very space was conceived of in terms of national states. Imbued with the ideology of nationalism emanating from Europe, the conception of territorial space was consid-ered the sole spatial form in which to secure a political community. The efforts of the *trekboers* to establish their own republics after 1850 demonstrate the power of this territorial conception of space. Similarly, the British efforts to block possibility of a connection between the Portuguese colonies, the *Boer* republics and the German colony of South West Africa reflected the desire to define power in terms of delimited territories.

This is not the place to recount the history of state building in Southern Africa over the past century. Suffice it to say that such efforts were not dramatically different from similar processes in Europe (see Tilly, 1990; 1985). Political forces relied on the resources extracted from economic operators in order to eliminate alternative sources of vio-lence within specific territories which in turn allowed such operators to engage in accumulation. The construction of such delimited spaces, however, was never without contradictions and these contradictions were contained in the conception of race.

The early European discursive conceptualization of their contact with the indigenous population mostly reflected religious and civilizational prejudices, that is, the characterization of Africans as 'heathens' and 'savages' served as the moral justification for the expropriation of their land, cattle and labour rather than the imputed racial differences (Frederickson, 1981: pp. 54–136). Consequently, there was not yet a clear spatial separation between Africans and Europeans. Even sexual relations reflected the relatively lax attitudes towards spatial/racial mixing (ibid., pp. 108–24).[5]

However, British attempts to impose a more *laissez faire* free labour policy (Ordinance Number 50 of 1828 and the emancipation of slaves during 1834–38) led to a hardening of racial thinking among the Boers. Consequently, once they had created their new republics, the Boers began to establish the ideological basis for the spatial segregation of Africans from Europeans. As late nineteenth-century thinking about race shifted decisively towards the notion that differences between the races were permanent and not erasable through religious conversion or 'civilizing influences' there was little opposition when, after the establishment of the Union, these antecedents were adopted as a whole for the entire Union.

The influence of this racial thinking proved to be the major contradiction in conceiving of Southern Africa in terms of territorial states. The idea of the territorial state depends on the 'inside/outside' distinction so expertly interrogated by Walker (1993). State-building in Europe reflected the transition from a Christian universalism to a rational particularism confined to a specific space which made possible the idea of separation, of spatial differentiation, of public and private and of inside and outside (Ruggie, 1993: p. 151). However, the conceptualizations of race which dominated Southern Africa made such separation and differentiation impossible. The desire to separate Africans from Europeans in spatial terms – formalized in the Land Act of 1913 (and its later amendments) which established the 'native reserves' or 'homelands' which, in turn, served as the basis for the policies of apartheid instituted after 1948 – imposed spatial structures which undermined any attempt to create a uniform 'inside'.

The desire and resulting policies to create spatial structures on the basis of the European conceptualization of race were not limited to South Africa. All over the subcontinent, policies were enacted which regulated the physical presence of indigenous people in so-called 'white' areas.[6] These discourses of space and race ultimately had their meeting point in the body. Spaces were identified by the skin colour of those who were permitted to live through them. It was possible to read off the body of an individual whether or not that individual was in the proper space and the pass laws in South Africa, the housing of labour in hostels and compounds adjacent to mines and, later, manufacturing facilities all reflected this racialization of space in Southern Africa (Bundy, 1992).

In short, although the representations of space were clearly in following with the dominant territorial view, the very racial thinking which dominated both boers and the British, led to policies which weakened the territorial concept, in effect not only creating an 'inside' to be juxtaposed to an 'outside' represented by other states but also creating an 'outside' on the 'inside' which was linked to the 'actual outside'. The creation of the homelands and the eventual sham independence granted to the Transkei, Ciskei, Venda and Bophuthatswana were but the logical conclusion of the policy began in 1913. But the usual distinction between inside and outside, the primary spatial image of the national state, did not apply in South Africa. The differences between Bophuthatswana or Venda on the one hand and Mozambique, at least southern Mozambique, Lesotho and Botswana on the other hand were academic at best.

Spaces of representation in Southern Africa

The production of such new spaces, however, requires the weakening of existing state (and spatial) structures for their success and it is here that I would like to return to the third leg of Lefebvre's conceptual triad, the spaces of representation. Although Lefebvre saw lived spaces primarily as passive or dominated spaces, such spaces also contain the lived experiences of inhabitants and contain therefore the possibility for the creation of counterspaces and subversive spaces, they are therefore 'a strategic location from which to encompass, understand and potentially transform all spaces simultaneously' (Soja, 1996: p. 68).

Such counterspaces at the regional level have existed for quite some time. Despite all efforts to impose the stamp of state control on the movement of migrant labour in the region, workers have evaded such controls. Even during the height of migration control through organization such as The Employment Bureau of Africa (TEBA), the number of migrants in the system was outweighed by those who crossed borders illegally. Newitt (1995: p. 489) estimates that besides the 80,000 officially recruited Mozambican workers in South Africa in 1967, some 300,000 were in the country illegally and thus had much larger degree of choice with regard to length of stay, place of work and control over pay.

Similarly, such migrants, both legal and illegal, created their own circuits of commodity flows which had not existed before. First (1983: pp. 126–7) describes the appearance of cement floors, brick houses and a variety of consumer items such as furniture, crockery, and even radios and bicyles. Today similar circuits exist. Hawkers and sidewalk traders from the SADC region who sell their wares in South Africa, for example, export a wide variety of goods. About 75 per cent of those who exported South African goods did so in amounts of R2,000 and above (Peberdy and Crush, 1998). Although there is not yet firm data, anecdotal evidence indicates that similar cross border trade exists throughout the region.

We can therefore imagine regions not only as spatial constructs which facilitate the exploitation of the subcontinent; we can also imagine them as counterspaces, as sites of resistance to such processes. One such imagination is to think of regions as spaces of rights rather than spaces of flows or spaces of places. A region so conceptualized constitutes an integrated space not because of trade flows or institutional apparatuses but because its inhabitants share a commitment to struggle for the same enforceable protections against abuses be they committed by states or corporations.

To conceive of regions as spaces of rights represents a direct challenge to the hegemonic consensus on liberalism. Such efforts transcend the traditional spatial organization by insisting that rights of persons be recognized outside and independent of the national state. They reject the position of the state as the sole arbiter of the rights of 'its' citizens and therefore create new spaces of reference. In some ways the human rights discourse has always represented such a challenge to the state and the spatial make-up of the globe. In practical terms, however, human rights has remained wedded to the state in that the state remains central as the arbiter of such rights. Southern Africa as a space of rights differs from this conception in that such a space envision rights as separate from the spatial confines of the state and, instead embed them in a new space.

A strategy for the creation of Southern Africa as spaces of rights if it aims to go beyond the current spatial/statist divisions cannot, in the end, rely for its success on the very state/spatial structures which were originally the basis for the authoritarian systems which created

Southern Africa in the first place. This is not to say that states have become irrelevant spatial categories. They remain rather crucial spatial layers for a wide variety of reasons. The regional layer, however, if it is to be a counter-hegemonic layer in today's global system, must transcend these spaces.

I propose here that the creation of a multiplicity of links between social movements as a result of which each of the social movements (including labor organizations) constitutes a node in a web can serve as the basis for a regional space of rights. Such a web would constitute an alternative conceptualization of the region because it represents an effort to curtail, at the regional level, the tendencies of globalizing capital to exploit the differences between various places. Exploitation of such differences represents a foundational aspect of global capitalism and a web of links between popular organization may well constitute the best tool to bring into the open this practice. However, this conceptualization of the region as a web constituted by various movements and organizations requires rather significant changes in organizational outlook within and among organizations that have traditionally carried the burden of organizing opposition to global capitalism.

Research into the activities of social movement has mushroomed during the past decade or so. Many of the insights developed have stayed outside mainstream IR literature. It is nevertheless crucial that the insights gained are brought to bear in the study of regionalization. 'Social movements have always arisen under conditions of social distress' (Walker, 1988: p. 26). Consequently, they are by definition local in that the causes which underlie their rise to visibility, while not necessarily local in nature, always manifest themselves in specific forms at various locales. This local nature of social movements is often viewed as their largest shortcoming, an inevitable weakness when it comes to confronting the state.[7]

However, place-boundedness of social movements does not necessarily imply an exclusively local focus. There are numerous examples of 'local' movements which nevertheless maintained links across state boundaries and viewed their mission as one which was not limited by such boundaries. The environmental movement with its focus on the ecosphere of the globe or particular regions is probably the best example. However, the anti-apartheid movements in the US and Europe are equally important examples of local movements with a transnational focus.

The paradox of globalization is that the ever decreasing protections offered by states and the questions of human rights (including both civil/political and economic/social rights) which are raised as a result are now broadcast around the entire world in real time. In other words, the impact of globalization, while local, nevertheless becomes global as a result of the increased flows of information. The ability to receive such information is, of course, not equally distributed, but there are few places left in the world without either direct or indirect access to means of communications through which social movements can link to others. It is this ability to link up with other like-minded organizations using information technology which makes possible the scenario of a multinodal network at the regional level envisioned here.

One such example can be found in the work currently done by the Southern African non-governmental organization (NGO) community which is attempting to build a network of various NGOs as a counterpoint to state efforts in the region.[8] In response to Article 23 of the SADC charter of 1992 which envisions the incorporation of voices from civil society, these NGOs began to set up their consultative structure in 1996 and became operational in February 1997 as the Southern African Human Rights NGO Network (SAHRINGON). Currently, some 64 organizations from 11 of the 14 member states belong the network representing a wide variety of interests in civil society. At an initial meeting in Malawi in September 1997, SAHRINGON decided to focus its attention on the key areas of policing practices, gender issues and questions related to the freedom of assembly and association. At the 1998 meeting in Zimbabwe, member NGOs determined that the initial focus areas were too narrow and decided to include issues related to persons with disabilities and the large complex of social and economic rights to the agenda. By late 1998, the network was in the process of developing a plan of action based on this agenda.

The general reception of the various states to SAHRINGON has been mixed. Representatives of the organization have been shunned at official SADC meetings and, provisions of Article 23 notwithstanding, consultation with the network has not taken place. A specific example is the launching of the SADC Organ on Politics, Defence and Security under the chairmanship of Robert Mugabe, President of Zimbabwe. Throughout the negotiations, no NGOs were consulted despite the fact that various interested organizations had prepared submissions on the training of police forces in human rights issues and related questions. Such obstacles are unfortunately predictable, especially in the early stages of the formation of such a regional network. They also point to the difficulties involved in any effort to overcome states as guarantors of security when one has little choice but to rely on the sympathetic ear of at least some of the states in the region in order to have an impact.

However, the network approach to constructing regions as spaces of rights faces significant problems. Inequality of resources between members of a network constitute one such drawback. As Macdonald (1995) has pointed out, the role of North American NGOs in Central America has had mixed consequences which, more often than not, were the result of poor information on their partners; combined with a fair degree of paternalism this has resulted in failed projects. Southern Africa has already witnessed this phenomenon to some extent where South African NGOs often engage in regional work with a similar attitude.[9] Furthermore, the view of NGOs as superior vehicles for regional links has to be tempered with the realization that the internal organization of such NGOs is often hierarchical (ibid., p. 35) and therefore can constitute a barrier to full grassroots engagement. In short, the barriers to creating regions as spaces of rights are formidable as are all efforts to produce new spaces.

Nevertheless, social actors, institutions and movements who wish to create counterhegemonic spaces which can provide an effective counterweight to the forces of global/regional accumulation should take advantage of the weakening of the state to create a network of critical social movements which transcends old boundaries in order to challenge those structural and institutional apparatuses whose fundamental purpose is to further accumulation from a location which they themselves created. Such lived spaces, spaces which represent solidarity across traditional boundaries, could represent networks of social movements which are linked in such a way as to avoid the exploitation of differences between various micro-regions. This would be a first step towards creating political community at a local level while avoiding parochial isolation. More generally, however, all efforts to construct and occupy strategic institutions at the regional level in order to counteract corporate power require a full understanding of all the levels of social spatiality at stake, the strength or weakness of the actors and processes located on those levels, and the typically conflictive/complicit nature of their relationship with a capitalism which is, by its very nature, simultaneously everywhere and nowhere at home.

Notes

1. There was clearly no space for women in any of the early modern philosophical constructs. The proto individual was a man and therefore had to display

the qualities deemed masculine then (and now). For an analysis of this gender bias see Di Stephano (1983; 1991), Sylvester (1994) and Tickner (1992).

2. See, e.g., the protracted negotiations and conflicts over the control of the *zuurveld* during 1780–1820 where Xhosa conceptions of space conflicted with white settler conceptions, therefore making coexistence difficult and leading to the forceful expropriation of the Xhosa territory by 1812 (Omer-Cooper, 1994: pp. 32–4, 44–7). A crucial difference in spatial conceptions was that for white settlers, ownership of land was deemed crucial. A young white man needed to have 'his own land' in order to be regarded as a man. The Xhosa, on the other hand, valued ownership of cattle similarly, measuring the wealth and social standing of a man by the number of cattle he owned which lead to a need for grazing land which in turn conflicted with white property claims. It was therefore impossible for a society whose spatial categories rested on the ownership of land as a means to accumulate to coexist with a society whose spatial categories rested in ownership of cattle as an expression of wealth.

3. I would like to thank Neil Parsons for pointing out this connection.

4. For some, a still viable option – see Holden in this volume.

5. See also Newitt (1995: pp. 127–46, 228–37) for his account of early spatial/racial relations in Mozambique along the Zambezi River.

6. See Mamdani (1996) on this issue. In this context I want to raise a further point not made by Mamdani but which ties into the analysis he provides. The transition from a 'civilizing mission' colonialism to a 'crowd control' colonialism must, in my opinion, be understood in terms of the Foucauldian concept of governmentality (Foucault, 1986). Only after the concept of population as an entity became accepted and European racisms became state racism based on biological notions of race does the abandonment of the civilizing mission colonialism make sense. The move towards indirect rule on the basis of 'customary law' is, in effect, the basis on which the entire apartheid construct was built since it implies separate spaces for different races.

7. See Adler and Steinberg (1999) for analyses of the role of NGOs in the political transition of South Africa since 1990.

8. The bulk of the information on the following paragraphs is derived from a personal interview on 28 June 1998 and ongoing communications with Corlett Letlojane, Africa Desk Coordinator of Lawyers for Human Rights, the South African country co-ordinator for SAHRINGON.

9. This experience has led some South African NGOs to take a back seat in regional efforts so as to avoid fostering such a paternalistic image. Personal interview with Vincent Williams, Project Manager, Southern African Migration Project, Cape Town, 15 June 1998.

References

Abu-Lughod, J. (1989), *Before European Hegemony* (New York: Oxford University Press).

Adler, G. and J. Steinberg (eds) (1999), *The South African Civics Movement and the Transition to Democracy* (London: Macmillan).

Agnew, J. (1994), 'Timeless Space and State-Centrism: The Geographical Assumptions of International Relations Theory', in S. Rosow, N. Inayatullah and M. Rupert (eds), *The Global Economy as Political Space* (Boulder, CO: Lynne Rienner).

Anglin, D. (1985), 'SADCC after Nkomati', *African Affairs* 84, 163–81.

Ashley, R. (1988), 'Untying the Sovereign State: A Double Reading of the Anarchy Problematique', *Millennium* 17/2: 227–62.

Bender, G. (1978), *Angola under the Portuguese* (Berkeley: University of California Press).

Bundy, C. (1979), *The Rise and Fall of the South African Peasantry* (Berkeley: University of California Press).

Couclelis, H. (1992), 'Location, Place, Region, Space', in R. Abler, M. Marcus and J. Olsen (eds), *Geography's Inner Worlds. Pervasive Themes in Contemporary American Geography* (New Brunswick: Rutgers University Press).

Davies, R. (1993), 'Emerging South African Perspectives on Regional Cooperation and Integration after Apartheid', in B. Odén (ed.), *Southern Africa after Apartheid* (Uppsala: Scandinavian Institute of African Studies).

Dear, M. (1988), 'The Postmodern Challenge: Reconstructing Human Geography', *Transactions of the Institute of British Geographers* 13, 262–74.

Di Stephano, C. (1983), 'Masculinity as Ideology in Political Thought: Hobbesian Man Considered', *Women's Studies International Forum* 6, 633–44.

Di Stephano, C. (1991), *Configurations of Masculinity. A Feminist Perspective on Modern Political Theory* (Ithaca and London: Cornell University Press).

First, Ruth (1983) *Black Gold: the Mozambican mines, proletarian and peasant* (Sussex: The Harvester Press).

Foucault, M. (1986), 'Governmentality', in G. Burchell, C. Gordon and P. Miller (eds), *The Foucault Effect* (Chicago: University of Chicago Press).

Frederikson, G. (1981), *White Supremacy. A Comparative Study of American & South African History* (Oxford: Oxford University Press).

Haas, E. (1958), *The Uniting of Europe* (London: Stevens & Sons).

Harvey, D. (1985), *The Urbanization of Capital. Studies in the History and Theory of Capitalist Urbanization* (Baltimore: Johns Hopkins University Press).

Johnson, P. M. and D. Martin (1988), *Frontline Southern Africa. Destructive Engagement* (New York: Four Walls Eight Windows).

Kern, S. (1983), *The Culture of Time and Space 1880–1918* (Cambridge, MA: Harvard University Press).

Kimble, G. (1996), 'The Inadequacy of the Regional Concept', in J. Agnew, D. Livingstone and A. Rogers (eds), *Human Geography. An Essential Anthology* (Oxford: Blackwell Publishers).

Lee, M. (1989), *SADCC. The Political Economy of Development in Southern Africa* (Nashville: Winston-Derek Publishers).

Lefebvre, H. (1991), *The Production of Space* (Cambridge: Basil Blackwell).

Libby, R. (1987), *The Politics of Economic Power in Southern Africa* (Princeton, NJ: Princeton University Press).

Macdonald, L. (1995), 'A Mixed Blessing. The NGO Boom in Latin America', *NACLA Report on the Americas* 28/5, 30–34.

Mamdani, M. (1996), *Citizen and Subject. Contemporary Africa and the Legacy of Late Colonialism* (Princeton, NJ: Princeton University Press).

Martin, W. G. (1986), 'Southern Africa and the World-Economy', *Review* X/1, 99–119.

Martin, W. G. (1987), 'Incorporation of Southern Africa, 1870–1920', *Review* 10/5–6 (Summer–Fall), 849–900.

Manzo, K. (1996), *Creating Boundaries. The Politics of Race and Nation* (Boulder, CO: Lynne Rienner).

Mitrany, D. (1966), *A Working Peace System* (Chicago: Quadrangle Books).

Morgenthau, H. J. (1960), *Politics Among Nations. The Struggle for Power and Peace*, 3rd edn (New York: Alfred A. Knopf).

Newitt, M. (1995), *A History of Mozambique* (Bloomington, IN: Indiana University Press).

Niemann, M. (1991), 'Regional Integration in the Periphery: The Case of Southern Africa', Unpublished PhD dissertation, University of Denver, Denver.

Ohlsen, T. and S. Stedman (1994), *The New Is Not Yet Born* (Washington: Brookings Institution).

Omer-Cooper, J. D. (1994), *History of Southern Africa*, 2nd edn (Portsmouth: Heinemann).

Østergaard, T. (1989), *SADCC Beyond Transportation* (Uppsala: Scandinavian Institute of African Studies).

Sally Pederdy and Jonathan Crush (1998) 'A Brief History of South Africa's Immigration Legislation', in J. Crush and R. Majapelo (eds), *The Aliens Control Act: A Review and Critique*, (Cape Town: IDASA).

Ruggie, J. G. (1993), 'Territoriality and Beyond: Problematizing Modernity in International Relations', *International Organization* 47/1 (Winter), 139–74.

Seidman, A. (1980), *Outposts of Monopoly Capitalism: Southern Africa in the Changing Global Economy* (Westport: Lawrence Hill).

Soja, E. (1993), 'Postmodern Geographies and the Critique of Historicism', in J. P. I. Jones, W. Natter and T. Schatzki (eds), *Postmodern Contentions. Epochs, Politics, Space* (New York: Guilford Press).

Soja, E. (1996), *Third Space. Journeys to Los Angeles and other Real-and-Imagined Places* (Oxford: Blackwell Publishers).

Sylvester, C. (1992), 'Feminists and Realists View Autonomy and Obligation in International Relations', in V. S. Peterson (ed.), *Feminist (Re) Visions of International Relations Theory* (Boulder, CO: Lynne Rienner).

Sylvester, C. (1994), *Feminist Theory and International Relations in a Postmodern Era* (Cambridge: Cambridge University Press).

Taylor, P. J. (1981), 'Geographical Scales within the World-Economy Approach', *Review* V/1, 3–11.

Taylor, P. J. (1982), 'A Materialist Framework for Political Geography', *Transactions of the Institute of British Geographers* 7, 15–34.

Taylor, P. J. (1994), 'The State as Container: Territoriality in the Modern World-System', *Progress in Human Geography* 18 sol 2, 151–62.

Taylor, P. J. (1996), 'On the Nation-State, the Global and Social Science', *Environment and Planning A* 28, 1917–28.

Thompson, L. (1995), *A History of South Africa. Revised Edition* (New Haven, CT: Yale University Press).

Tickner, A. (1992), *Gender in International Relations. Feminist Perspectives on Achieving Global Security* (New York: Columbia University Press).

Tilly, C. (1985), 'War Making and State Making as Organized Crime', in P. B. Evans, D. Rueschmeyer and T. Skocpol (eds), *Bringing the State Back In* (New York: Cambridge University Press).

Tilly, C. (1990), *Coercion, Capital, and European States AD 990–1990* (Cambridge: Basil Blackwell).

Vaitsos, C. (1978), 'Crisis in Regional Economic Cooperation (Integration) Among Developing Countries: A Survey', *World Development* 6/6, 719–69.

von Braunmühl, C. (1976), 'Die nationalstaaliche Organisiertheit der bürgerlichen Gesellschaft. Ansatz zu einer historischen und systematischen Untersuchung', *Gesellschaft Beiträge zur Marxschen Theorie* 8–9, 273–334.

Walker, R. B. J. (1988), *One World, Many Worlds: Struggles for a Just World Order* (Boulder, CO: Lynne Rienner).

Walker, R. B. J. (1993), *Inside/Outside: International Relations as Political Theory* (Cambridge: Cambridge University Press).

Waltz, K. N. (1959), *Man, the State and War. A Theoretical Analysis* (New York and London: Columbia University Press).

Waltz, K. N. (1979), *Theory of International Politics* (New York: McGraw-Hill).

Wilson, W. (1996), 'The World Must be Made Safe for Democracy', in J. Vasquez (ed.), *Classics of International Relations* (Upper Saddle River: Prentice-Hall).

Wionczeck, M. (1978), 'Can the Broken Humpty-Dumpty Be Put Together Again and By Whom? Comments on the Vaitsos Survey', *World Development* 6/6, 77–82.

5
Regional Cooperation for Security and Development in Africa

Björn Hettne

> Just as I was convinced that political freedom was the essential
> forerunner of our economic growth and that it must come, so
> I am equally convinced that African Union will come and pro-
> vide that united, integrated base upon which our fullest devel-
> opment can be secured.
>
> – Kwame Nkrumah (1963: p. 170)

Introduction: Africa and global social theorizing

International relations theory (IRT) has been called an American discipline, portraying the world order in a Cold War context from the US
national security perspective. In particular the Third World, as it was
called, was seen mainly as an arena for superpower or great power
rivalry, rather than as an actor in its own right. To some extent area
studies, among which African Studies has been prominent, sometimes
has been seen as a remedy to this Western ethnocentrism and mis-
placed universalism, since it focuses on the peculiar and contextual
rather than the general and universal. Both academic positions as
described here are likely to be exaggerated, and, to the extent they are
expressed in such doctrinaire terms, they probably signify a rather
non-principled struggle for academic resources.[1]

A useful way of overcoming whatever tensions there may exist
between 'globalism' and 'localism' is to focus on comparative regional
studies within a globalized framework; that is, to look upon a particular region in a world of regions, together constituting an emerging
world order. In terms of theoretical points of departure it is argued
that development theory as a state-centric concern lacks relevance
and, in order to regain its earlier importance, needs to be merged with

international political economy (IPE). IPE, on the other hand would be enriched by the more dynamic and normative concerns central to development theory. Such a merger may ultimately strengthen an emerging 'critical political economy', dealing with historical power structures, emphasizing contradictions in them, as well as change and transformation expressed in normative terms (Cox, 1996).

The study of world order can be said to constitute the distinct contribution of IPE to social science, and consequently to development theory. What shall one mean by world order? It can be defined as the rules and norms regulating international economic transactions. Disorder often refers to the turbulent interregnum between stable world orders, but one must also recognize the possibility of 'durable disorder' (Cerny, 1998).[2] We must, however, also assume that a conceived chaos provokes some countermeasures by some sort of agency in the direction of political regulation. Polanyi used to warn against what he called the 'hazards of planetary interdependence' associated with global market expansion (Polanyi, 1957: p. 181). His sceptical view on interdependence based on the market corresponds to the contemporary neo-mercantilist view of the market system as a fragile arrangement in need of political control. The postwar world economy was in fact a historic compromise between international economic *laissez-faire* and a certain level of domestic control. This essentially Keynesian approach was abandoned during the 1970s and in the subsequent decade neo-liberal principles grew increasingly dominant, a trend that culminated when the socialist world began to disintegrate. Disorder is therefore, among more radical theorists, often associated with economic globalization, the crucial question then being the return of 'the political' and what form this return will take.

Returning to the proposed marriage between development theory and IPE, the advantages of such a merger would be a two way traffic. It can be described as filling a theoretical vacuum constituted by at least two problematic gaps in development theory. The first is between the growing irrelevance of a 'nation-state approach' and the prematurity of a 'world approach'. The second is between immanence, that is a theorizing about development as 'inherent' in history, and intention, a political will to 'develop', which may breed unrealistic voluntarism, particularly as development has become globalized and out of reach for the main actor, that is the state (Hettne, 1996). The missing link here is the region; as a level of analysis and as a political actor.

Africa is both an appropriate and challenging case by which this approach can be tested and evaluated. It seems to be the continent with the greatest number of regional organizations and, furthermore, it has an impressive ideological tradition of pan-Africanism expressed by the pioneers in nation-building, indicating an inherent transnationalism or 'regional civil society' that is, political, economic and social networks of an inclusive kind that transcend national state borders. However, there is in spite of this impressive tradition and much current rhetoric so far not much of real regional integration going on. To what extent will Africa ultimately be affected by the new wave of regionalism, the New Regionalism?[3] My claim is that this new global wave will have an impact on all parts of the world, including Africa. I thus make a strong distinction between the current trend of regionalism, since about 1985, and what went on before, particularly in the 1950s and the 1960s. I shall also argue that this regionalism largely is a political response to the market-driven process of globalization and the social eruptions associated with this process. Furthermore, even if it is convenient to deal with regional organizations such as EU, NAFTA, Mercosur, SAARC or SADC, the real analytical focus is on the regional territory as such, even it if is hard to define and delimit, 'region' being a process rather than an object (see, also, Niemann's understanding of 'region' in Chapter 4 above).[4]

In our approach, and by 'our' I am referring to the United Nations University/World Institute for Development Economic Research (UNU/WIDER) project on the New Regionalism (see, for example, Hettne, Inotai and Sunkel, 1999), there are many more objectives than the stimulation of trade, which regionalism can achieve. This chapter analyses this promising worldwide movement in an African context with special emphasis on Southern Africa. It also tries to situate this particular region in the emerging world order, characterized by both globalization and regionalization, processes that in complex ways are related to each other.

Globalism and regionalism

Globalism and regionalism refer to ideologies, that is the normative content, whereas globalization and regionalization refer to real processes, which contain very different and not necessarily compatible trends, depending upon which actors are behind the driving wheel. Globalism as ideology can be defined as programmatic globalization: the realization of the vision of a borderless world, integrated by a global market. Globalization as process, primarily implying market expansion, was made possible by the political stability of the American hegemonic world order, which lasted from the end of the Second World War until the late 1960s or the early 1970s. Since then the global context has changed from bipolarity towards multipolarity, and due to this change, the process of political regionalization as a response to economic globalization has become intensified. This is because a multipolar world facilitates regionalization coming from within the region.

There are theorists who deny that globalization is such a new phenomenon, or even that it exists as a reality (Hirst and Thompson, 1996). The origins of globalization, in the sense of internationalization of local or national economies and increasing interdependence between them, may certainly be traced far back in history, but one could also argue that the process of economic internationalization reached a qualitatively new stage in the post-Second World War era. Globalization means a deepening of the internationalization process, strengthening the functional and weakening the territorial dimension of development. I therefore see globalization as a qualitatively new phenomenon that consequently warrants a new theory, a global social theory as was observed in the introduction. Globalization, thus, implies the growth of a functional world market, increasingly penetrating and dominating so-called 'national' economies, which in the process are bound to lose much of their 'nationness'. Economy is being delinked from both culture and politics, both of which are becoming intrinsically mixed in the new 'politics of identity', which came as a big surprise to the modernization theorists, since the modernization paradigm assumed the disappearance of ethnic variety, as society moved towards full modernity.[5]

States are now becoming spokespersons for global economic forces, rather than protecting their own populations and their cultures against these demanding and largely inexplicable changes (Cox, 1996). Therefore, the state is becoming alienated from civil society, defined as inclusive institutions that facilitate a societal dialogue over various social and cultural boundaries and, furthermore, that in this process of dissolvement, identities and loyalties are being transferred from the level of civil society, as defined above, to primary groups, competing with each other for territorial control, resources and security. This could be a morbid replay of the nineteenth-century Westphalian logic, but where the security dilemma now is faced by subnational social groups, forced to organize their own defence without the protection of a state. The contradictions involved may end up in a collapse of organized society, both state and civil society, as defined above. I shall here abstain from discussing other possible meanings of this contested concept (Tester, 1992).

For this reason, there will eventually emerge a political movement to modify, halt or reverse the process of globalization, in order to safeguard some degree of territoriality, civic norms, cultural diversity, and human security, principles that we traditionally associate with organized society. One way of achieving such a reversal of negative trends, that is some degree of 'deglobalization', could be through regionalization as a political project: the building of (suprastate) regional communities. The regionalist response can, as we shall see, take different forms depending on the interests of the dominant actors. If globalization can be seen as a 'first movement' in a second Great Transformation (*à la* Polanyi), regionalism, in a more or less neomercantilist form, may be said to form part of a 'second movement' together with other forms of resistance to globalization.[6]

The two processes of globalization and regionalization are thus articulated within the same larger process of global structural transformation, the outcome of which depends on a dialectical rather than linear development. It can therefore not be readily extrapolated or easily foreseen. Rather it expresses the relative strength of contending social forces involved in the two processes. They deeply affect the stability of the traditional Westphalian state system; and therefore they at the same time contribute to both order and disorder and, possibly, a future post-Westphalian world order of some sort.

By 'Westphalian system' (admittedly a Eurocentric concept) is implied an inter-state system constituted by sovereign states and the particular political logic that characterizes the external and internal behaviour of each of the states. Inside the single state are the citizens 'belonging' to it with particular obligations and rights defined by the rules of citizenship and allegiance to 'their' nation-state. The outside world is conceived by most of these citizens as anarchy, where there are neither rights nor obligations. This Westphalian political rationality takes a particular state as the given (and only) guarantee for security as well as for welfare. The identity of the security of the citizens and the security of the state is taken for granted. The increasing turbulence and uncertainties many people experience today come with the unpleasant realization that this guarantee, historically associated with the status as citizen of a state, can no longer be taken for granted. Increasing numbers of people are becoming international refugees without citizen rights, or a 'floating' domestic population, similarly without substantive rights and unwelcome everywhere. Africa provides many examples, and in South Africa even the concept of 'aliens' has been used with reference to migrants. As the state breaks down, pre-Westphalian structures are again emerging, for instance in the form of new warlordism or in the revival of more traditional 'chiefs'. Protection seems to be the essential function of the mafia/state (Tilly, 1985; for a different view, see Solomon in Chapter 3 above).

The basic problem with globalization, not unlike the historical process of colonization, is in my view its unevenness and selectiveness. External commercial interests are in search of specific resources in specific places. Exclusion is therefore inherent in the process, and the benefits somewhere are evenly balanced by misery, conflict and violence elsewhere. It is in this way that a 'new' Third World may be said to be emerging, of course in fact including much of the 'old' Third World, but not necessarily confined to that. However, poverty and violence are the crucial criteria in identifying this poor world, not the history of colonialism as such. These two criteria express a low level of what I call 'regionness'. In a situation of low regionness there is an acute lack of confidence and trust between neighbouring states, both in the fields of security and cooperation. The negative effects of this lack are ultimately incompatible with the survival of civil society and also the nation-state.

'Regionness' and regionalization

The awkward and frightening situation sketched above, raises the fundamental question of how essential security can be maintained in a world of eroding nation-state structures. Are there emerging local or transnational structures to compensate for the, if not vanishing, at least transforming nation-state? A post-Westphalian rationality would assert that the nation-state has lost its usefulness, and that solutions to problems of security and welfare therefore must be found increasingly in different forms of transnational structures, multilateral or, as this paper argues, regional. The 'world region' can, by maintaining the territorial focus and the stress on the role of 'the political', be said to constitute a compromise between Westphalian and post-Westphalian in the sense that the world region combines economies of scale and large markets (economic rationalism) with some degree of territorial control (the political imperative).

The new regionalism, I suggest, would, as it develops, include economic, political, social and cultural aspects, and it would go far beyond preferential trade arrangements, characterizing 'old' regionalism.

Rather, the political ambition of establishing regional coherence and regional identity, apart from security and welfare, seems to be of primary importance. This I call 'the pursuit of regionness', which can be compared to 'the pursuit of stateness' in classic mercantilist nation-building. What shall we then more exactly understand by 'regionness'? First of all it means that the point of departure is a geographical area, not a regional organization (on this point, compare both Niemann and Odén in this volume). Secondly, it means that a region can be a region 'more or less'. Region is a process. There are three generalized levels or 'stages' of 'regionness', which may be said to define the structural position of a particular region in terms of regional coherence. The 'region' can only be identified *post-factum* and it is therefore only potential in the first stage. The actual regionalization process happens in stage two, whereas stage three shows the outcome in terms of actual regional formations, such as the EU (so far the only one). Mostly when we speak of regions around the world we actually mean regions in the making, emerging from stage one. I elaborate briefly on each of these stages below.

The pre-regional stage

In the pre-regional stage, the potential region constitutes a geographical area, delimited by more or less natural physical barriers and marked by ecological characteristics: 'Europe from the Atlantic to the Ural', 'Africa South of Sahara', Central Asia, or 'the Indian subcontinent'. This level can be referred to as a 'proto-region', or a 'pre-regional zone', since there is no informal or formal organized translocal or international society in this very hypothetical situation. In order to further regionalize, this particular territory must, necessarily, be inhabited by human beings, maintaining some kind of translocal relationship. Region as social system implies ever widening translocal relations between human groups. Such relations of embryonic interdependence constitute a 'security complex', in which the constituent units (typically states), as far as their own security is concerned, are dependent on each other as well as on the overall stability of the emerging regional system (Buzan, 1991).

Thus the existing social relations may very well be basically hostile and completely lacking in cooperation. It still constitutes a regional complex of a primitive kind. The region, just like the larger international system of which it forms part, can therefore on this level of regionness be described as anarchic. The classic case of such a regional order in nineteenth-century Europe, where the constituent units were states. At this low level of regionness, a balance of power, or some kind of 'concert' between the nation-states, is the sole security guarantee. This is a rather primitive security mechanism, becoming of course even more primitive as the authority of the nation-state collapses. Similarly, the exchange system tends to be more based on symbolic kinship bonds rather than trust, and thus shrinking rather than expanding. We could therefore talk of a 'primitive' region, exemplified by some parts of Africa.

The regionalization process

The regionalization process, characterizing the second stage of rising regionness, starts with some type of transnational cooperation, organized (*de jure*) or more spontaneous and informal, in any of the cultural, economic, political or military fields, or in several of them at the same time – that is, multidimensional regionalization. In the case of more organized cooperation, region is defined by the list of countries which are the formal members of the regional organization in question. The more organized region could be called the 'formal' region.

In order to assess the relevance and future potential of a particular regional organization, it should be possible to relate the 'formal region' (defined by organizational membership) to the 'real region', which has to be defined in terms of potentialities, convergencies of different kinds and through less precise criteria. This is the stage where the crucial regionalization process takes place. The dynamics of this process can be described as a convergence along several dimensions, economic as well as political and cultural. This convergence may come about through formalized regional cooperation or more spontaneously. It is the result in terms of regionness that counts. At some point along this route, it becomes natural to talk about regional integration rather than regional cooperation.

Regional outcomes

The outcome of the regionalization process is region as acting subject with a distinct identity, institutionalized actor capability, legitimacy, and structure of decision-making. Crucial areas for regional intervention are organized conflict resolution (between and particularly within former 'states') and creation of welfare (in terms of social security and regional balance). This process is similar to state-formation and nation-building, and the ultimate outcome could be a 'region-state', which in terms of scope and cultural heterogeneity can be compared to the classical empires, but in terms of political order constitutes a voluntary evolution of a group of formerly sovereign national, political units into a supranational security community, where sovereignty is pooled in the interest of all. This is basically the idea of the European Union as outlined in the treaty of Maastricht.

It should be emphasized that conflict resolution, in order to properly reflect this third stage, implies the existence of institutions and mechanisms, not ad hoc interventions of the type that happen today. However, these repeated attempts at crisis management, often unsuccessful, underline the need for more institutional forms of conflict resolution at the regional level.

Region as civil society takes shape when an enduring organizational framework (formal or less formal) facilitates and promotes social communication and convergence of values and actions throughout the region. Of course the pre-existence of a shared cultural tradition (an inherent regional civil society) in a particular region is of crucial importance here, particularly for more informal forms of regional cooperation, but it must be remembered that culture is not only a given, but continuously created and recreated. However, the defining element here is the multidimensional and voluntary quality of regional cooperation, and the societal characteristics indicating an emerging 'regional anarchic society', that is, something more than anarchy, but still less than society. In security terms the reference is to 'security community'.

These three stages or levels may express a certain evolutionary logic. However, the idea is not to suggest a stage theory but simply to provide a heuristic framework for comparative analysis of emerging regions. Obviously, the second stage of regionalism is what is of interest in that respect. Since regionalism is a political project and therefore devised by human actors, it may, just like a nation-state project, fail. This, similarly, means decreasing regionness and peripheralization for the 'region' concerned. Changes in terms of regionness thus imply changes of the structural position in the centre-periphery order. A region in decline means decreasing regionness and ultimately dissolution of the region itself. It is obvious that the reference here is to the peripheralized regions. The struggle against peripheralization is the struggle for increasing regionness, from a very low level of potential or 'primitive' region. I shall return to this more activist dimension towards the end of the chapter.

The new regionalism is, as pointed out earlier, in different ways linked to globalization, and can therefore not be understood merely from the point of view of the single region in question, whether

Southeast Asia, South Asia, Southern Africa or the southern cone of Latin America. Rather, it also should be defined as a world order concept, since any particular process of regionalization in any part of the world has systemic repercussions on other regions, thus shaping the way in which 'the new world order' is being organized.

The emerging global power structure will thus be defined by the world regions, but by very different types of regions. To clarify this pattern, I shall fall back upon 'good old' dependency theory and, within the field of development studies, the familiar division of the world into centre (or core) and periphery. However, this is a dependency analysis at a stage of higher integration and interdependence of the world, where the 'delinking' option, whether on the national or regional level, is ruled over in any other way than unwanted involuntary marginalization.

In search of African regions

The bases for regional formations are many but not necessarily overlapping, which is a problem particularly in Africa, where ecological, cultural and political borders and boundaries rarely coincide (see Swatuk in Chapter 12 below). Looking for the potential new regional formations in Africa, and I confine myself to Sub-Saharan Africa, the first issue is that of geography and social system. Secondly, following the stairway of regionalization suggested above, we can identify formal regions in terms of organizational membership. African countries are grouped into more than 200 regional bodies. However, judging from the results of integration, it is not the number of regional organizations that counts. Apart from the formal regions, there are more important informal networks transcending state borders and these networks can be seen as embryonic regional civil societies (see the chapters by Vale and Niemann in this volume). To the extent that one can speak of a new regionalism in the African context, the trend should rather be from single issue organizations to consolidated, multidimensional regions, ranging from economic development to security. On the whole the level of regionness, like the level of 'nationness' is very low in Africa, and there are even some geographical areas which largely lack experience of regional cooperation. At the same time, there may be an 'inherent regionness' from precolonial times which form the basis for latent, informal regions transcending the current state system. In the absence of a clear principle for making a consistent demarcation of regions and to have a starting point, I am falling back on the rather conventional division into West, Central, East and Southern Africa. The actual subregions in the process of being formed can only be identified in retrospect by empirical research on concrete processes and actors of regionalization. They will probably differ from the conventional regions mentioned above.

In West Africa, where the major regional initiative, ECOWAS, had been more or less paralysed for a long time, partly due to Nigerian dominance, partly because of the modest level of communication between the French and British former colonies, there were unexpected signs of a somewhat more active regionalism, in terms of a regional security regime. Delinking of the state apparatus from elite interests may lead to a strengthening of regional as well as local levels: the regional because of development and security imperatives, the local because this is where the democratic forces are.

Central Africa, dominated by former Zaire, now the Democratic Republic of Congo (Kinshasa), is a region only in the sense of a geographical area and a social system (security complex), in which there has been a high level of violence in recent years. Efforts at external interventions have been confused and ineffective, and as far as regional initiatives are concerned, display deep contradictions. One can speak of a rather primitive regional security complex. It is quite correct to say that Burundi, Rwanda and Congo are fated to suffer the fallout of each other's social and political problems (Synge, 1997: p. 32). No effective efforts have been taken to control this situation through peacekeeping from within the region. Recent warfare and its consequences in terms of regional power structures however suggests that a new pattern of domination is emerging. This permanent disintegration of Congo, a vacuum drawing its neighbours into geopolitical rivalry, may be the end of the region as a political concept.

Eastern and Southern Africa can best be treated as one albeit not very coherent region. East Africa constitutes a traditional region formed by colonial bonds, but also culturally integrated through the Swahili language. In the northeastern subregion Horn of Africa the record of conflict is much longer than the record of cooperation. However, in recent years joint efforts have been made to combat one enemy that in the long run may prove more formidable than even war, namely the deteriorating environment. Thus, there is an urgent need for regional cooperation. Normally, there must be an embryonic regional framework to build upon. However, even in the Horn, a pattern of regional cooperation is slowly beginning to emerge. In January 1986, countries in the region (Somalia, Djibouti, Ethiopia, Eritrea, and Sudan) established the

Intergovernmental Authority on Drought and Development (IGADD). Unfortunately there are still internal conflicts, most conspicuous in Somalia, and inter-state conflicts, recently between Ethiopia and Eritrea, disrupting such efforts.

The Eastern group of Kenya, Tanzania and Uganda formed one area or historical integration by colonialism, later divided by national rivalries and even war (specifically, the Tanzanian invasion of Uganda under Idi Amin). Furthermore, Tanzania joined SADC and oriented itself towards the south. The 'old' and imposed regionalism that failed miserably is now being revived by a 'new', more spontaneous regionalism, albeit challenged by the old type of political leadership.

In Southern Africa, which is the regional area of main interest here, several important subregional initiatives in the context of the new regionalism, at least in terms of declared objectives, have been taken. One example is SADCC (Southern Africa Development Coordination Conference), now covering 14 countries. At its inception in 1980, the main function of SADCC (now SADC) was to reduce dependence on apartheid South Africa, a regional power with evident designs of regional control through the destabilization of 'hostile' regimes. Thus, it is at least on paper a fairly clear example of 'the new regionalism', since SADCC was not simply based on the common market concept but had wider political objectives. So far, however, the instruments have been lacking and no supranational powers conferred (for details, see Du Pisani in this volume). Nevertheless there is a strong regional quality and growing identity in this case. As Vale suggests in Chapter 2 above, it is rooted in the colonial background, particularly the various projects of Cecil Rhodes, projects that shaped the region.

Situating Africa in the world: regionalism and global structure

Despite the current wave of post-structuralist thinking in IRT, it still makes sense to conceive the world as a structural system, that is a system defined by certain regularities and rigidities in the relations among its constituent units. The point is not to exaggerate structural rigidities but to focus on the interaction between actors and structures. What is new with the world system today is that various structural positions, as a consequence of transnationalization processes and domestic changes, can increasingly be defined in terms of regions rather than nation states. This makes it important to understand the nature of the emerging regional formations in the North and in the South. A rough distinction can be made between three structurally different types of regions: regions in the core zone, regions in the peripheral zone and, between them, regions in the intermediate zone. The latter are situated in an ambivalent position, which means that they can move in both directions; they can achieve core status or become peripheralized. Regions transform in accordance with structural changes and thus move from one zone to another.

How do these types of regions then differ from each other in structural terms? There are two basic characteristics. The regions are distinguished by their relative degree of internally generated economic dynamics and by their relative political stability. These characteristics also reflect an underlying higher level of regionness, and thus constitute criteria by which regionalization at least in a qualitative sense can be measured. At the same time regional integration – in terms of development and security – becomes the obvious strategy to reduce the structural gap between periphery and core; that is, to move from the peripheral to the intermediate zone.

The core zone

Regions in the core zone, North America, Europe and East Asia centred on Japan, are thus economically more advanced and normally growing, and they also have stable – if not always democratic – regimes which manage to avoid interstate as well as intra-state conflicts. They organize for the sake of being better able to control and get access to the rest of the world, with respect to resources and markets. Thus, they have an impact rather than being impacted upon. The predominant economic philosophy in the core is neo-liberalism and 'free-tradism', which therefore also, with varying degrees of conviction, is being preached throughout the world as 'the only game in town'. As always has been the case, the stronger economies demand access to the less developed in the name of the free trade. We can thus speak of 'free trade regionalism', although the concept may sound like a contradiction in terms. This is the 'stepping stone' (rather than 'stumbling bloc') interpretation of regionalism with respect to its relation to globalization.

The intermediate zone

Regions in the intermediate zone are in many cases closely linked to one or the other of the core regions in the sense that they have strong economic relations with a particular core and try to imitate its policies. This is the case of South America, Central Europe and Southeast Asia. They are under 'core guidance'. They will thus, if they are lucky, gradually be incorporated into the core, as soon as they fully conform to the criteria of 'coreness', that is, sustained economic development and political stability. This means that although 'politics of distribution' probably has been thrown on the historical dustbin, praise for free trade is here somewhat more reserved. The expression used both in Southeast Asia and Latin America is 'open regionalism', which means open economies, albeit with some preference for one's own region, as well as a rather precautionary attitude as far as the core regions' assumed adherence to free trade is concerned. However, to this category I also count regions which are losing their comparative advantages in terms of robust economies and stable political regimes. Their level of regionness is decreasing, which means that they are threatened to become peripheralized.

The peripheral zone

Regions in the peripheral zone, in contrast, are politically turbulent and economically stagnant. War, domestic unrest, and underdevelopment constitute a vicious circle which make them sink to the bottom of the system, creating a zone of war and starvation. Consequently they have to organize in order to arrest a threatening process of marginalization and peripheralization. At the same time, their regional arrangements are necessarily as fragile and ineffective as their states, and – this weakness notwithstanding – they must first of all tackle acute poverty and domestic violence. Their overall situation thus makes 'security regionalism' and 'developmental regionalism' more important than the rather irrelevant creation of preferential trade regimens, or even adhering to the more cautious 'open regionalism', which becomes relevant only as some strength *vis-à-vis* the rest of the world has been achieved. They are necessarily more interventionist. This is what lies behind the protectionist ('stumbling bloc') interpretation of the new regionalism.

   How does Africa fit into this global structure? Africa is, on the whole, closer to the periphery than to the core and the subregions are either intermediate or peripheral. This is one possible meaning behind the so-called 'marginalization of Africa'. After an impressive record of conflict resolution, Southern Africa, or part thereof, shows potential for moving into the intermediate space. This is, however, under the condition that South Africa plays the role of regional hegemon and becomes the engine of regional economic development, as well as the guardian of regional peace. In West Africa, where there exists similar potential, Nigeria for various mixed reasons has intervened to stabilize the regional peace, but was for some time itself politically divided and internationally isolated. South Africa's role is, perhaps, somewhat more credible in this regard, even if most observers easily withhold their optimism (compare arguments made by Odén and Holden in this volume). North Africa, while a potential candidate for intermediate status, unfortunately appears more likely to sink into the periphery due to the excessive domestic unrest in Algeria (with spillover risks) that has been on the increase during the past couple of years. It is necessary to put an end to this destructive process in order to avoid sinking further into the periphery. The question is how this should be done without further violence. The rest of Sub-Saharan Africa, particularly Central Africa and the Horn of Africa, is clearly peripheral. One can also argue that West Africa belongs here despite a distinct potential to become intermediate.

In many countries in these regions the political structures called 'states' are falling apart, at the same time as new political economies are emerging. The conventional view has it that disintegration of the state leads to chaos and non-development (Kaplan, 1994). Anthropological analyses of 'real' substantive economies suggest a more complex, nuanced and basically novel picture of emerging 'local' (or rather 'glocalized') economies, delinked from state control, run by a new type of entrepreneur, supported by private protection, and with crucial international connections. All this is possible, since the state is unable to legally define and protect various assets situated within the 'national' territory (Duffield, 1998).

This distinction between intermediate and core regions in the case of Africa can thus certainly be questioned, and my purpose here is not classification, putting things in closed boxes, but comparative analysis of trends in terms of regional security and regional economic cooperation. However, to be stressed here are the observable changes in terms of changing regionness, and how such changes can be brought about by concerted political action coming from within the region. Thus, the peripheral regions are 'peripheral' because they are stagnant, turbulent and war-prone. This is of course no explanation of their status, merely a structural analysis of their relative positions in the world system. By 'positions' I certainly do not imply permanence, but rather a way of identifying trends, which means that the whole pattern is very tentative and floating. Trends imply positive as well as vicious circles. Underdevelopment for instance generates conflicts, and conflicts prevent necessary steps to get the economy in order. To the extent that structural criteria change by purposive state action, the region 'moves' from one structural position to another. The exact borderlines between the three zones are impossible to draw. The dividing line sometimes goes even within larger countries (South Africa, for instance). It seems likely that attempts by the most dynamic areas of larger countries to reach intermediate status by linking up to the world market will lead to deeper internal divisions with destabilizing consequences. There are also cases where individual countries avoid to commit themselves or are lingering between two structural positions, either between core and intermediate, or between intermediate and peripheral (South Africa as a region by itself or as part of Southern Africa).

The African continent is seen by many observers as becoming increasingly marginalized in the world economy (see Tsie, Chapter 6 below). The only way for poor and violent regions to become less peripheral in structural terms is, according to this analysis, to become more regionalized, that is, to increase their levels of 'regionness', particularly in the fields of security and development. Otherwise, their only power resource would rest in their capacity to create problems for the core regions ('chaos power'), thereby inviting or provoking some sort of external engagement. This mechanism can be seen in Southern Europe's concern for North Africa.

Pathways from the periphery: security and development regionalism

So far this chapter has dealt with the structural pattern. The definition of this pattern in terms of established and repeated behaviour among states and other actors in made purposely so as to avoid the image of a structural trap, which characterized much of earlier dependency theory. A behavioural change may thus involve also structural change. The structural problems are to a large extent internal and can thus be dealt with by changed policies in the various states, but a change that goes in the same direction among a group of neighbouring countries. This may either be through purposeful action or through more spontaneous convergencies along several dimensions. However, in the case of peripheral regions, one could argue that concerted, purposeful action is imperative. Let me therefore turn to the problem of change of structural positions, through the help of regional cooperation and integration. The issue I want to discuss here concerns the strategic value for various actors, this brief discussion being confined to state actors, of a conscious regionalization policy in the interrelated fields of security and development in peripheral areas. Violence and underdevelopment are the two most important problems characterizing 'peripherality'.

Security regionalism

Regional integration implies a security dimension, which is quite essential to the dynamics of the integration process. It does not make sense to distinguish the economics of integration, on the one hand, from the politics of disintegration, on the other. Integration and disintegration form part of the same dialectical process and should be dealt with within a single theoretical framework. To develop such a framework is a challenge to the social sciences. By security regionalism, I shall refer to attempts by the states in a particular geographical area – a region in the making – to transform a security complex with conflict-generating inter-state relations towards a security community with cooperative relations. Thus a higher level of regionness implies a lower degree of conflict whereas decreased regionness leads to security problems.

What are, first, the security problems to which regionalization may provide a solution? They can be summarized in what in UN terminology is referred to as 'failed states'. These constitute a problem for neighbouring states which for their international credibility rely on a stable regional environment. Therefore they are prone to intervene if something goes wrong in one particular state. Nigeria thus takes an interest in stabilizing the West African region despite being itself a rather shaky political construction. National disintegration seems to reinforce the process of regionalization by way of threats to regional security, provoking some kind of reaction on the regional level. National disintegration may even by said to form part of the process of regionalization, since the enlargement of political space provides opportunities for different subnational and microregional forces, previously locked into state structures, to (re)assert themselves in peaceful (as in the case of microregionalism) or violent (as in the case of ethnonationalism) ways.

The undermining effect of globalization on the Westaphalian state system and on the internal legitimacy of weak state formations was discussed earlier in the chapter. The collapse of political authority at one level of society (the nation-state) tends to open up a previously latent power struggle at lower (subnational) levels, and in a complex multi-ethnic polity the process of disintegration may go on almost indefinitely (see Brown 1993; Posen 1993). However, sooner or later there must be some reorganization of social power and political authority on a higher (transnational) level of societal organization, to my mind most probably the region. Why? Since most wars today are civil wars, and a region facing in one of its states a Hobbesian situation, must provide some substitute for the vanishing state authority.

This regional arrangement, however, is likely to be preceded by some form of external intervention with the purpose of reversing the disintegration process, threatening to become a regional security crisis. Again the region may play a role as an actor, but there are also other, and so far more important ones. In making an inventory of possible actors, a distinction can be drawn between no less than five different modes of external intervention in regional security crises: unilateral, bilateral, plurilateral, regional and multilateral (see Hettne, 1995b).

Unilateral intervention

The unilateral intervention can either be carried out by a concerned neighbour trying to avoid a wave of refugees, or by a regional/super power also having strategic interests in the region. In Africa there are a number of French interventions that come to mind.

Regarding neighbourly interventions, such as that of Tanzania in Uganda, it is interesting to remember that they have been highly controversial despite the fact that in some cases there might have been rather good reasons behind them.

Bilateral intervention

In the bilateral case there is some kind of (more or less voluntary) agreement between the intervenor and the country in which the intervention is made. An African case in point would be the role of Cuba in Angola.

Plurilateral intervention

The plurilateral variety can be an ad hoc group of countries or some more permanent form of non-territorial alliance, such as NATO or the Islamic Conference. Lesotho 1994 is a case where a number of neighbours (South Africa, Zimbabwe, Botswana), but not the regional organization, SADC, as such were active.

Regional intervention

The regional intervention is carried out by a regional organization through an accepted mechanism and thus has a territorial orientation. The SADC-sanctioned interventions in Lesotho in 1998 and in the DRC the same year are two such examples, highly contested and controversial though they may have been. Another, rather unexpected, intervention was the ECOMOG force in Liberia, organized within the framework of ECOWAS. I return to this below.

Multilateral intervention

The multilateral intervention, finally, normally means a UN-led or at least UN-sanctioned operation. One such spectacular but unsuccessful operation was the one in Somalia, while Rwanda illustrates the case of non-intervention.

These distinctions are not very clear-cut, and in real world situations several actors at different levels may be involved, the number usually increasing with the complexity of the conflict itself. However, it is my understanding that future external interventions will prove to be a combination of regional and multilateral operations, but with an increasingly important role for the former. Unilateral action lacks legitimacy and raises suspicion in the international community. In cases where there are sleeping regional organizations, such as the case of ECOWAS in West Africa, they may be revived and even find a new task for themselves by a regional crisis. Even when there are no regional organizations at all, regional initiatives are nevertheless taken. The legitimacy of such actions rests merely in the fact that no organized actor with sufficient legitimacy is prepared to get involved. This may, however, be a security imperative for neighbouring states, since inactivity may spell their own undoing. This also suggests a stronger regional interest in a durable solution. For a multilateral force the intervention is a task with a definite end (the soldiers move out), but for regional actors the problem remains unless it is solved in a more comprehensive way. Angola would be a case underlining this. A regional solution must be embedded into the larger regional power structure. A ceasefire agreement between belligerents is not enough. A stable solution demands a security regime and in the longer run the building of a regional security community.

The record of regional intervention in domestic conflicts and regional conflict resolution is a recent one, and therefore the empirical basis for making an assessment is weak. However, in almost all world regions, there have been attempts at conflict resolution with a more or less significant element of regional intervention, albeit often in combination with multilateralism (UN involvement). Perhaps the preferred future world order can be characterized as regional multilateralism? In contrast with the unpleasant 'clash of civilizations' scenario, this would be a world with largely introverted (but not closed) regions, in symmetric balance and involved in a multicultural dialogue and a constructive political relationship.

Disintegration on the level of the nation-state creates a power vacuum soon filled with violence among warlords sooner or later provoking some kind of external intervention. The significant issue is who does the inter-vening. Should it be the US, this would imply a low level of 'regionness'. Should it be the region itself, this would indicate a process of regionaliza-tion. Here there is a difference between the subregions of West Africa and the Horn of Africa, judging from the equally traumatic cases of Liberia and Somalia. Somalia represents a conflict in which the region was paral-ysed, Liberia one in which the region took action. In Somalia the UN had little choice but to intervene, but lost credibility and legitimacy.

The Liberian crisis can be said to have speeded up the process of regional cooperation in West Africa. ECOWAS, through the ECOMOG troops, and in a rather improvised way intervened with the explicit purpose of preventing a general massacre of the population. Although not fully backed by the whole region and, furthermore, not a highly successful operation in terms of conflict resolution, it was unprece-dented in the history of African regional cooperation. The shared view in the region was that 'the ECOWAS states cannot stand idly by and watch a member state slide into anarchy' (*West Africa*, 1–7 July 1991). The problem in this region, as in so many others, is the dominance of one state, Nigeria. Thus peace enforcement and peacekeeping on the regional level implies a significant role for the regional power with obligatory (and often realistic) suspicions that there is an imperialistic project behind the humanitarian intervention. The Nigerian role was diluted after the Geneva talks and the peacekeeping force made into an all-African force through the participation of Zimbabwe, Egypt and Botswana. At the same time, the OAU stepped in with blessing from the UN. Clearly there were efforts at increasing the degree of legitimacy by involving more and more international parties. In this particular case Nigeria was a dominant local actor.

This picture remains valid throughout the region. Through spillovers from Liberia, an even nastier internal war started in Sierra Leone, where 'such order as there is, comes from the West African peacekeep-ing force Ecomog' (*The Economist*, 28 November 1998). This is not to say that intervening forces do not tend to become parties to the local plunder going on. But what is the alternative? Ironically, a democratic Nigeria, more sensitive to the death of Nigerian soldiers, will be less willing to fight for democracy outside Nigeria. It may be hard, how-ever, to stand by watching the chaos grow. The third case of regionally destabilizing internal clashes so far is Guinea-Bissau, which also proves the point that neighbours are involved whether they like it or not.

In Southern Africa, SADC asked for trouble by including disintegrat-ing Congo in the organization. When a new internal war started, involving Uganda and Rwanda on the rebellious side, its rival leaders Mugabe (head of SADC security) and Mandela (former SADC chair) took different sides, and Mugabe, supported by Angola and Namibia, claimed to be acting on behalf of SADC. New patterns of amity and enmity cross over several countries and subregions. The traditional states are becoming less and less relevant as objects of reference. The internal rival forces are often evenly balanced and it is hard to see what emerging authority may rule the 'country'. It is thus impossible to make conventional 'national interests' the basis for analysis.

After the miserable Somalia operation the UN will be less eager to undertake peacekeeping, let alone peace-enforcing operations. The regions themselves will have to develop some emerging organization for this, perhaps in cooperation with and with support from the UN. Furthermore, this new kind of conflict, characterized by a complete breakdown of political order, necessitates some kind of organized governance imposed on the 'black holes'. This is best done by a regional authority, if there is any in the first place. If not, the best security policy for Africa would be to develop a structure of transnational governance in all the subregions.

A significant, but still largely inconsequential, development in this context is the OAU's recently established Division of Conflict which intends to deal with tensions between and within member states. The traditional principle of non-interference has thus been reconsidered. From now on, the more stable regimes within a certain region may feel obliged to interfere through regional institutions in countries en route toward anarchy. It need not be said that there are dangers in this as well. However, under the conditions that the intervention has a degree of legitimacy in comparison with the regime against which the intervention is carried through, the regional cause is strengthened. Integration and disintegration go together. The point is obviously not that a 'regional' political structure is inherently better than a 'national', which would be nonsense since all political communities are 'imagined', but that the shift in the relative importance of the levels, local as well as regional, has some significance in the emergence of a new world order.

Development regionalism

The new regionalism may also provide solutions to development problems. This can in fact also be seen as a form of conflict prevention, since many of the internal conflicts are rooted in development problems of different kinds. Under the old regionalism, free trade arrangements reproduced centre–periphery tensions within the regions, which made regional organizations either disintegrate or fall into slumber. By development regionalism I refer to concerted efforts from a group of countries within a geographical region to increase the efficiency of the total regional economy and to improve its position in the world economy.[7] Let me propose seven interlinked and partly overlapping arguments in favour of a more comprehensive development regionalism:

First, although the question of size of national territory might be of lesser importance in a highly interdependent world, regional cooperation is nevertheless imperative, particularly in the case of micro states which either have to cooperate to solve common problems or become clients of the 'core' (*the sufficient size argument*).

Second, self-reliance was rarely viable on the national level and has now lost its meaning, but a strategy of 'development from within' may yet be a feasible development strategy at the regional level, for instance in the form of coordination of production, improvement of infrastructure, and exploitation of various economic complementarities (*the viable economy argument*).

Third, economic policies may remain more stable and consistent if underpinned and 'locked in' by regional arrangements, which can't be broken by a participant country without provoking some kind of sanctions from the others (*the credibility argument*); this can be extended to political credibility (see also Holden in this volume).

Fourth, collective bargaining on the level of the region could improve the economic position of marginalized countries in the world system, or protect the structural position and market access of emerging export countries (*the effective articulation argument*).

Fifth, regionalism can reinforce societal viability by including social security issues and an element of social or regional redistribution (by regional funds or specialized banks) in the regionalist project (*the social stability argument*).

Sixth, ecological and political borders rarely coincide. Therefore few serious environmental problems can be solved within the framework of the nation-state. Some problems are bilateral, some are global, quite a few are regional, the latter often related to water: coastal waters, rivers, and ground water. Like a regional security complex, we can speak of a regional ecology complex (see Swatuk in this volume). The fact that regional resource management programmes exist and persist, despite nationalist rivalries, shows the imperative need for environmental cooperation or 'environmental regionalism' (*the resource management argument*).

Seventh, regional conflict resolution, if successful and durable, elimi-nates distorted investment patterns, since the 'security fund' (military expenditures) can be tapped for more productive use (*the peace dividend argument*).

In Sub-Saharan Africa (SSA) there has been little regional integration, simply because there is little to integrate, perhaps even less than at the time of independence. In discussing development regionalism, we are thus talking of future prospects and potentials. Only 5 per cent of the continent's trade in formal terms is inter-African. The need is rather for 'integrated economic development' on the regional level (Thisen, 1989), an element conspicuously lacking in Africa's structural adjust-ment programmes, supposed to be the answer to Africa's development problems in the 1990s. Promising efforts are being made, particularly in Southern Africa. Following Martin (1991), three scenarios can be out-lined: (i) 'regional restabilization' under South African dominance; (ii) regional breakup, peripheralization and bilateralization of internal and external relations; and (iii) a neo-regional alternative implying regional restructuring based on a symmetric and solidaristic pattern of develop-ment. The last one is probably a very optimistic scenario, but it is also realized that the fate of South Africa is intertwined with the fate of the smaller countries in the region. The question is how much attention South Africa can devote to its neighbours in view of its pressing prob-lems. The national imperative seems to have become stronger in recent years (see Odén's chapter in this volume). Much therefore depends on the future character of a post-apartheid (and post-Mandela) regime, not only for Southern Africa but for the whole of SSA. As suggested by Odén in Chapter 8 below, the South African government seems to give some priority to regional cooperation. This regional cooperation must, how-ever, include South Africa and move from a defensive alliance between former 'frontline states' to a real regional actor. This would necessitate a stronger economic base, without which regional cooperation at the most can play the role of a negotiating cartel.

As with all regional scenarios, it is ultimately the domestic politics of the constituent states which play the decisive role. There is little to show that they are prepared to sacrifice national sovereignty (McCarthy, 1996). To this must of course be added the international arena from which Southern Africa (including South Africa) has been increasingly marginalized. The prospects for regional cooperation, however, generally begin to look brighter, partly as a result of the weakening of the previ-ously so almighty nation states as the dominant political institutions.

I am referring to the 'inheritance elites' who, in Basil Davidson's terms, had 'not become their countries' first ministers in order to preside over the liquidation of their domestic empires' (Davidson, 1980: p. 289) This does not mean that a complete disintegration of the states in a region (for instance the Horn of Africa) can be seen as a path towards regionalism. The issue is rather how state power is used. Regionalism would in the shorter run strengthen state capacity, while in the longer run erode national sovereignty.

In Sub-Saharan Africa there is an urgent need for a broader and more dynamic concept of development, beyond 'stabilization'. Again this is considerably facilitated within a framework of regional cooperation. The 'dynamic approach' to regional integration (Robson, 1968) must be further developed. Above all, this must become a political imperative among African leaders as the only way to halt the continued marginalization of the continent. This also implies a more realistic view of political intervention in the economic process than has been the case during the last decade. If the great discovery of the 1980s was that political intervention is not necessarily good, the discovery of the 1990s has been that it is not necessarily bad either. The nation-state system is more or less dead in certain areas, and the concept of a national development process is dying with it. The cruel choice seems to be regionalization or recolonization.

Regionalism, however, has been a highly politicized issue in Africa. It tends to create suspicion in the national centres of decision-making. Of Nkrumah's pan-Africanism little remains today, but what was then a dream has now, nevertheless, become a necessity (Nkrumah, 1963). This is not only for economic reasons. Many ethnic conflicts, for instance, cannot be resolved within the nation-state framework, particularly as the unsuccessful nation-building project in fact is the main cause behind these conflicts. This is a strong argument for regional cooperation. Of importance here are the ongoing processes of democratization, the so called 'second liberation' in Africa, including South Africa, which, to the extent that there is a democratic political culture underneath the authoritarian model, will increase the political homogeneity of the region, although the political winds are unpredictable. In the longer run, foundations for an African security community may emerge. Similarly, economic polices are 'harmonized' due to the dramatically increased dependence on the IMF and the World Bank, as well as the donor countries which all tend to give the same advice. The new political conditionalities can be criticized from many points of view, but they undoubtedly harmonize the political cultures in the various nation-states. The problem is whether the externally imposed economic policies are consistent with internal political pluralism in poor and unstable states (compare Tsie's observations in Chapter 6 below).

At OAU meetings it has been repeatedly stressed that the ongoing integration of Europe calls for a collective response from member states in the form of an African Economic Community (AEC). The most common reason mentioned is the threatening marginalization of Africa, to which regionalism by many is then seen as the remedy. Many previous initiatives have of course been taken in this direction, for instance the 1980 Lagos Plan of Action, but undoubtedly the issue now has assumed a special urgency. The implementation of the AEC will take decades, and the first period will, realistically, be devoted to the strengthening of existing regional economic communities as building blocs in the creation of a continent wide unity.

Conclusion

In sum, security has become a regional issue in Africa and will continue to be so in the years to come. More difficult to grasp, however, are the actual patterns of the regionalization process. Since the 'nation-states' in reality are 'state-nations', where nations are slipping away from the states, it is hard to pinpoint the relevant political actors involved in the regionalization process. It is a grave mistake to assume that current formal regional organizations will play an important role. This would be to look at the wrong place. The transformation of Africa or its various subregions into a regional security community is a long process. One could even conceive 'glocalized' structures in which the regional dimension remains thin. Similarly, development regionalism is a relatively new phenomenon. It contains the traditional arguments for regional cooperation of various relevance for different actors, such as territorial size, population size, and economies of scale, but, more significantly, also add some which are expressing new concerns and uncertainties in the current transformation of the world order and world economy. There is a vicious circle, where conflict and under-development feed on each other. But the circle, if reverted, can also become positive. Regional cooperation for development would reduce the level of conflict. The resulting peace dividend would facilitate further development cooperation. Regional peace thus becomes a comparative advantage in an integrating but turbulent world economy, a factor usually disregarded by economists. In contrast, regional conflict

means disaster for millions and millions of non-combatant populations as the catastrophies in Central Africa and the Horn of Africa
show. Security and development form one integrated complex, at the
same time as they constitute two fundamental imperatives for regional
cooperation and increasing regionness. Thus, political will and political
action will play their part in breaking the vicious circle of uneven globalization, regional conflict, underdevelopment and human insecurity.

Among the African regions, Southern Africa currently appears to be a
promising case for regionalization of the 'new' kind discussed here.
However, it cannot be denied that national governments, including
that of South Africa, rarely transcend national interests and strategies.
Furthermore, the 1997 inclusion of Mauritius and, particularly, the
DRC in SADC makes it hard to see an underlying regionalist consistency, and may actually break up SADC. However, regionalization is
not primarily a state-centric process, but expresses a global and
regional logic influencing a large number of increasingly interdependent actors within a regional territory, thereby increasing its regionness. The state may not necessarily be the only initiator. A region is
ultimately a process carried forward by a large number of actors, not a
piece of paper on which non-committed governments make empty
promises (compare the definitions and understandings of 'region' put
forward by Niemann and Odén in this volume).

Why then a regionalist approach? With more porous borders, with
the weakening of the state-nations and with the actual disappearance
of some states, the political arena will not necessarily shrink to primary
groups, but rather expand to 'natural' regions and traditional areas of
communication, of course on the assumption that some forms and
arrangements of regional security can be created. The basis for such an
analysis must draw more upon historical and anthropological research
and rethink the role of the state and theories about inter-state
relations. But, still, it has to be within the project of global social
theorizing.

Notes

1. See the debate on African versus Global Studies in *Africa Today* 44/2
   (April–June 1977).
2. 'Order is whatever pattern or regularity is to be found in any social situation'
   (Cox, 1996: p. 48).
3. This concept has been used in many different ways. For the critics, the
   regionalist trend constitutes a threat to the multilateral economic system
   and it also violates the ideal of UN political multilateralism. At international

financial institution (IFI) conferences dealing with what is referred to as the new regionalist trend (often interpreted as 'protectionism'), the main focus has thus been on trading blocs; and regionalism and multilateralism have been compared and judged primarily with respect to effectiveness in promoting free trade and maximizing 'global welfare'. For the regionalist enthusiasts, on the other hand, the new regionalism might form the most important basis for an improved multilateral system, including a badly needed deal for the poorer regions of the world (this being a central assumption for most, if not all, of the contributors to this volume).

4. The acronyms standing for, in order, the European Union, North American Free Trade Agreement, the Common Market of the South (Latin America), South Asian Association for Regional Cooperation, and Southern African Development Community.

5. For an interesting discussion on ethnicity in the South African context, see Mare (1993). For a fuller discussion of the changing nature and role of the state in globalization, see Tsie in Chapter 6 below.

6. See the more detailed discussion on the Polanyi approach applied to the new global context in the introduction to Hettne (1995a).

7. Du Pisani in Chapter 9 of this volume rightly underlines the difference between an economic community and a 'development community'.

References

Brown, Michael E. (ed.) (1993), *Ethnic Conflict and International Security* (Princeton, NJ: Princeton University Press).

Buzan, Barry (1991), *People, States and Fear: An Agenda for International Security Studies in the Post-Cold War Era*, 2nd edn (Hemel Hempstead: Harvester Wheatsheaf).

Cerny, Philip G. (1998), 'Neomediavalism, Civil War and the New Security Dilemma: Globalization as Durable Disorder', *Civil Wars* 1/1 (Spring), 36–64.

Cox, Robert, with Timothy J. Sinclair (1996), *Approaches to World Order* (Cambridge: Cambridge University Press).

Davidson, Basil (1980), *Africa in Modern History* (London: Penguin).

Duffield, Mark (1998), 'Post-modern conflict: Warlords, Post-adjustment States and Private Protection', *Civil Wars* 1/1 (Spring 1998), 65–102.

Hettne, Björn (ed.) (1995a), *International Political Economy: Understanding Disorder* (London: Zed Books).

Hettne, Björn (1995b), 'The United Nations and Conflict Management. The Role of the New Regionalism', in Saul H. Mendlovitz and Burns Weston (eds), *Preferred Futures for the United Nations* (New York: Transnational Publishers).

Hettne, Björn (1996), 'Developmental Regionalism', in M. Lundahl and B. J. Ndulu (eds), *New Directions in Developmental Economics: growth, environmental concerns and government in the 1990s* (London and New York: Routledge).

Hettne, Björn, Andras Inotai and Osvaldo Sunkel (eds) (1999), *Globalism and the New Regionalism*, vol. 1 in the New Regionalism series (London: Macmillan).

Hirst, P. and G. Thompson (1996), *Globalization in Question* (Cambridge: Polity Press).

Kaplan, Robert (1994), 'The Coming Anarchy', *The Atlantic Monthly* (April).

McCarthy, Colin (1996), 'Regional Integration', in Stephen Ellis (ed.), *Africa Now* (The Hague: Ministry of Foreign Affairs with James Currey, London, and Heinemann, Portsmouth).

Maré, Gerhard (1993), *Ethnicity and Politics in South Africa* (London: Zed Books).

Martin, William G. (1991), 'The Future of Southern Africa: What Prospects After Majority Rule?', *Review of African Political Economy* 50, 115–34.

Nkrumah, Kwame (1963), *Africa Must Unite* (London: Panaf).

Polanyi, Karl (1957), *The Great Transformation* (Boston: Beacon Press).

Posen, Barry R. (1993), 'The Security Dilemma and Ethnic Conflict', in Michael E. Brown (ed.), *Ethnic Conflict and International Security* (Princeton, NJ: Princeton University Press).

Robson, Peter (1968), *Economic Integration in Africa* (London: George Allen and Unwin).

Synge, Richard (1997), 'World Dithers as Central Africa Erupts', *Africa Today*, (Jan.–Feb.).

Tester, Keith (1992), *Civil Society* (London and New York: Routledge).

Thisen, J. K. (1989), 'Alternative Approaches to Economic Integration in Africa', *Africa Development* XIV/1.

Tilly, Charles (1985), 'War Making and State Making as Organized Crime', in Peter B. Evans, Dietrich Rueschemeyer and Theda Skocpol (eds), *Bringing the State Back In* (Cambridge: Cambridge University Press).

6
International Political Economy and Southern Africa

Balefi Tsie

Introduction

This chapter has three interrelated concerns. First, it seeks to establish the scope and substance of International Political Economy (IPE) as a distinct field of study within 'the broad' discipline of international relations (IR). Second, it will attempt to distil or tease out the theoretical implications from this growing field of specialization for the study of international relations in Southern Africa, especially in relation to the changing role of the state *vis-à-vis* market forces in the regional political economy. Third, it will assess the prospects for Southern African development by examining the opportunities, constraints and options that might be available for the region to build its competitive advantage in the contemporary world economy. Here the main emphasis is on the possible role that South Africa might play in that envisaged project of regional structural transformation. The chapter contextualizes these issues by relating them to three main trends in the world economy which are of significance for Southern Africa, and indeed, for the study of IPE in general. These trends are globalization, regionalization and the marginalization of Sub-Saharan Africa (SSA) in world politics and trade. The chapter examines each of these interrelated processes and asks what are the relative roles of the state, capital and labour in this changing architecture of power and wealth in the modern world. Specifically, it closely examines the argument that the authority, power and autonomy of the state has been eroded to such an extent that it can no longer be regarded as a key actor in domestic and international politics, especially in matters of domestic economic policy. The conclusion offers a synthesis of the various strands of thought contained in the body of the chapter and suggest how IPE and its presumed parent discipline, international relations (IR), might be enriched.

The nature and scope of IPE: a synoptic overview

According to one of the leading scholars in the field, the study of IPE is in a state of unresolved disarray (Strange, 1995: p. 157). No one, it seems, is in a position to establish the boundaries of this otherwise flourishing field of study, much less say what are its substantive areas of concern. Consequently, there is considerable debate among scholars in the field of IR about the nature, scope and content of IPE. Some conceive it merely as the politics of economic relations between states in the global arena (Spero, 1977; Blake and Walters, 1987). As such, the impression is created that IPE is simply a marriage of convenience between economics and politics at a global level which allows one to explain certain events and processes in international politics that might otherwise be incomprehensible to economists and political scientists operating from their compartmentalized academic environments. But even if one were to agree that 'it is necessary to bridge the gap between economics and politics, to explore the interface between economics and politics in the international system' (Spero, 1977: pp. 1–2), they provide little clue regarding how to study IPE. There is, to return to Strange's perceptive observation, a state of confusion and uncertainty arising largely out of diverging perceptions of what IPE is all about. Thus, liberal-realist scholars such as Robert Gilpin (1987) see it as a composite of three hermetically sealed 'ideologies of political economy' or value systems articulated by states in their strategic interaction for power and influence in international politics.

He argues that these three ideologies are fundamentally different in their conceptions of relationships among society, state, and market so much that each controversy in the field of international political economy is ultimately reducible to differing conceptions of these relationships (Gilpin, 1987: p. 25). Although Gilpin makes an important point when he says that the study of political economy focuses on the market and its relationship to the state because the world market economy is critical to international relations in the modern era (ibid., p. 26), he is still unable to discern that economic structures and processes have their own reciprocal effects on power relations between states. More importantly, the critical issue of which actors determine the rules of power politics is not seriously considered by Gilpin. Here one has in mind the vital question of structural power which underpins relations between states and firms in the world economy. As defined by Strange, structural power refers to 'the power to decide how things shall be done and/or to shape frameworks within which states relate to each other, relate to people or relate to corporate enterprises' (Strange, 1987: p. 25). It is a critical variable in IPE and should therefore be taken seriously. An additional criticism that can be leveled at Gilpin is that since his analytical framework is steeped in the liberal-realist framework, he is unable to specify the nature and character of the state in the contemporary epoch. For Gilpin, as for the majority of neo-realist scholars, the state is a timeless ahistorical entity. As suggested by Solomon in Chapter 3 above, differences between states, if at all there, exist only in terms of their power capabilities.

Two pertinent points are worth making at this juncture in relation to the 'poverty' of realism and its descendant known as neo-realism. The first is that these theories falsely take the state as an unproblematic entity when, in fact, the state is a complex organization with its own internal divisions of interest, multiple contradictory policy goals and competing agendas (Pierson, 1996: p. 184). The second is that there is little awareness, if not total resistance, to the idea that change in the international system does not simply revolve around states but that it frequently occurs in the form of social revolutions from below over which states may have little control (Skocpol, 1979; Halliday, 1994). In making these observations, one is not necessarily denying the significance of the state in world politics. It is only to question the excessively statist orientation of the neo-realist paradigm. Indeed, as will be argued below, the state is an important actor in the global arena. However, one has to seriously consider the question of whether or not the state is still the primary unit of analysis in international relations and if so, in which particular domains. This is an important issue because, contrary to neo-realist thought, there may be other equally important or even more powerful actors in the international political arena than the state depending upon which issues are at stake. In fact, the neo-realist billiard-ball model of international relations is misleading because it conveys the wrong impression that states react to the actions or policies of other states. A more balanced view would consider the interplay between transnational forces such as multinational corporations (MNCs), organs of global civil society in the form of non-governmental organizations (NGOs) and inter-governmental organizations (IGOs) such as the United Nations (UN) and the European Union (EU) to name but two IGOs. To view the latter simply as arenas in which power politics takes place on the grounds that they are creations of states and depend on them for political and material support is a serious error. These entities frequently enjoy widespread legitimacy, have relative autonomy from states and also exercise significant authority on major world issues.

Similarly, pluralism or 'liberal political economy' in Gilpin's terminology, does not take us very far in terms of grasping the essentials of IPE except to sensitize us to the fact that there are other equally important actors in the global political arena in the form of MNCs and their descendants commonly referred to as transnational corporations (TNCs). Liberal political economy seeks to provide the political context of economic relations between states. Its distinctive hallmarks are a commitment to individual freedom, government through democratic representation, rule of law, sanctity of private property, equality of opportunity, cognitive progress and a competitive market system (Doyle, 1993: p. 54). It lays heavy emphasis on the market as the most reliable means of allocating scarce resources and therefore as the surest path to economic growth, prosperity, peace and stability. These supposed attributes of the 'free market' are taken to be the best antidotes against conflict and war; the fundamental pillars of a just and humane world order. That the market is an embodiment of inequalities and deep-seated political conflicts is frequently ignored in liberal political economy. This is not surprising because, as Stephen Gill reminds us, liberalism is more a doctrine of the primacy of market forces rather than a balanced account of the interactive relationships between states and markets in the international system (Gill, 1994: pp. 79–80).

There are two core assumptions of liberalism worth noting. The first is that relations between states are inherently harmonious provided the market mechanism is allowed to operate freely in both the domestic and international arena. The greater the amount of trade liberalization, the greater the benefit to all participants in the world economy – so runs the argument. In this view, interdependence will steadily ensnare states into cooperative relationships which, in turn, means that conflict can be managed, contained or even eliminated through appropriate international mechanisms of cooperation and coordination. The second is that the state is a neutral arbiter of conflicting interests in society. It responds to a diversity of interests in society because it is not a captive of any particular group or class. Since the state is internally divided with a series of constitutionally entrenched checks and balances, what matters most is the legitimacy and/or validity of the different demands placed upon it and not class, race, gender or any other consideration. Put differently, liberal political economy places a high premium on a limited, minimalist state which leaves as much space to civil society as possible. In liberal political thought, the role of the state is to provide those public goods that markets cannot provide and to remove all impediments to the free play of the forces of supply and demand. Liberals therefore posit the minimalist state and the world economy as creative partners in a virtuous circle of economic growth, prosperity and peace guided and founded upon free market forces.

Notwithstanding these claims, liberal political economy has several serious limitations. Only a few pertinent ones will be highlighted here. First, liberalism is too narrow as a conception of IPE because it confuses it with foreign economic policy. Second, liberalism emphasizes techni-cal/scientific manipulation to correct deficiencies that may crop up from time to time in the international system. In short, it is part and parcel of problem-solving theory. Like mainstream political theory, liberalism, founded on positivistic methodology, falsely draws a dichotomy between the world-of-fact-out-there and the realm of the-ory. Moreover, liberalism, like neo-realism, draws a false distinction between the economic and political domains in the untenable belief that the two have their own separate logics and dynamics. Yet, as demonstrated below, the dynamic interaction between states, firms and markets should actually be the central theoretical concern in the study of IPE.

In this regard, Polanyi's remark that the road to the free market was opened and kept open by an enormous increase in continuous, cen-trally organized and controlled interventionism is apposite (Polanyi, cited in Evans, 1995: p. 29). It invites us to consider the role of political power in the creation and functioning of markets. For, the market in both theory and practice did not emerge spontaneously (Boyer and Drache, 1996: p. 3). Instead, it is a culmination of a long historical process involving numerous political struggles and conflicts over how the economy, the state and society should be organized. Liberal politi-cal thought misses this historical dimension in its quest to bestow the market with an aura of naturalness. It simply takes it as given, thus requiring no further historical investigation.

It should be clear from this brief survey of neo-realist and liberal thought that both paradigms are severely inadequate for an in-depth and comprehensive understanding of the substantive concerns of IPE. Both perspectives suffer from an excessive reification of the state in the sense that they regard it as a unified actor capable of making rational decisions in support of its economic welfare and national security. They hardly consider the possibility that the state could also be a field of contestation between different social forces formed at the level of civil society and, as such, it may not always act in a rational manner from the point of view of some of those social forces. They also fail to locate the state within the social relations of production, distribution and exchange peculiar to the modern system of capitalist production. Both perspectives disregard the fact that political power becomes intelligible when located within the context of concrete accumulation processes and the struggles generated by these (Mamdani, 1996: p. 23). In other words, neo-realism and liberalism do not offer a coherent account of the nature and character of the state, especially its class character and the global processes of accumulation in which it is embedded. Above all, they are more concerned with continuity rather than transformation of the existing world order. Both fail to reflect on their complicity with the existing, and terribly unequal world order (Burchill and Linklater, 1996). If anything, they put more emphasis on identifying appropriate principles, rules, procedures and institutions for purposes of stabilizing, strengthening and preserving it. It is this fundamental concern with developing 'regimes' or systems of management to govern economic and political relations in a liberal international economy, rather than change, that has occupied the minds of many liberal institutionalist/neo-realist scholars (see Du Pisani in this volume; also, Keohane 1983; 1984; 1986; 1989; Gilpin, 1981; Krasner, 1983; 1985; Nye, 1990).

Given these concerns, both neo-realism and liberalism form part of what Robert Cox has referred to as 'problem-solving' theory as distinct from 'critical theory'. According to Cox, the main purpose of problem-solving theory is to solve problems arising in the various parts of a complex whole in order to make it function smoothly and effectively (Cox, 1983). In that vein, both perspectives are inherently conservative because they seek to justify, legitimize and sustain the prevailing world order. They are far more concerned with questions of order, stability and security for the benefit of dominant classes and groups in society and not so much with issues of justice and equality. As such, they cannot be relied upon in terms of constructing an alternative, emancipatory vision for humanity as a whole (see, also, Vale's critique in Chapter 2 above).

Critical theory is a better candidate for this role because, unlike problem-solving theory, its major objectives are first, to explain how the present order came into being and second, to offer historically feasible alternatives to it (Cox, 1995: p. 32). As shall be shown below, critical theory is also comprehensive, offers a coherent account and penetrating insights into the nature of the modern state including its relationship with civil society, how it is organically linked with the rise of the modern global market economy and directs our attention to prevailing disparities of wealth and power in the international system. Neither neo-realism nor liberalism satisfy these criteria in their entirety (see, also, Leysens in Chapter 10 below).

Having said that, one should appreciate the fact these two paradigms do provide some partial insights about certain aspects of the contemporary international system. For example, realism highlights the centrality of the state in IPE, the anarchic character of the state system or the strategic framework within which modern states exist. These are useful starting points for contextualizing IPE and are not ends in themselves as neo-realists assume. Liberalism, on the other hand, helps to bear in mind that the international economic and political order is one that is highly interdependent, market-driven and therefore transnational in character. States are embedded in this complex network of interdependence. None the less, both paradigms are poor candidates for generating a sound theory of IPE. A promising route in this direction is paved by the intellectual tradition that Viotti and Kaupi (1987) refer to as globalism, also known as structuralism. It is a broad paradigm embracing several offshoots and tendencies such as Marxism, neo-Marxism, dependency theory and world systems theory. What unites scholars writing from this perspective is a generally held belief that it is necessary to understand both the overall economic structure of the global political system within which states, firms and other entities interact and how it arose in the first instance, for it is not self-evident that it was always there. Specifically, Marxist-inclined structuralists insist, and quite correctly so, that this global system is underpinned by a capitalist mode of production which works in such a way as to generate inequalities between individuals, states and societies which make up the modern world system.

Structuralists contend that relations of exploitation, inequality, dependence and domination permeate the entire structure of global production, distribution and exchange of goods and services. This is so because under capitalism the means of production (land, capital, factories, technology, etcetera) are concentrated in the hands of a few people (that is, the capitalist class) who, by virtue of ownership and control of the means of production, extract surplus value (profits, dividends, rental and so on) from those whose main means of survival is the sale of their labour power or capacity to work (that is, the proletariat/working class assuming they have not yet been rendered superfluous by the dynamics of capitalist accumulation). In Marxist theory, class is the analytical point of departure; not the state *qua* state. Put another way, class structures constitute the central organizing principles of societies in the sense of shaping the range of possible variations of the state, ethnic and gender relations and thus historical epochs can best be identified by their predominant class structures (Wright, 1985: p. 31).

The state enters the picture as an apparatus of domination which defends and advances the interests of the economically dominant class in a given social formation. It mediates conflicting class interests in both the domestic and international arena. There is thus a strong link between class power and state power. The former is a form of structural power which defines the parameters of state action thereby setting limits on what those in charge of the state machinery can and cannot do. The significance of this point will become clearer when we look at relations between states and TNCs in the contemporary capitalist world economy. For now what should be stressed is that class conflict and class struggles over surplus product lie at the heart of Marxist IPE. In this view, class relations are also embodied and reflected at the levels of civil society, the state and the existing system of states. Marxists further argue that capitalism is riddled with serious contradictions such as the coexistence of ostentatious wealth and abject poverty and periodic economic crises or recessions. These contradictions render the capitalist system susceptible to change and transformation through political struggles of the dominated classes. In classical Marxist thought, the main purpose of class struggle is to replace capitalism with an alternative and, one hopes, better form of society. It should be clear from what has been said so far that Marxist theory is an integral part of critical theory as defined by Robert Cox (1987; see Leysens, Chapter 10 below).

Thus, in this tradition, conflict between states is not merely an outcome of the anarchic nature of the modern state system, as posited by neo-realists, although international anarchy is not completely irrelevant as a possible source of tensions and conflicts between states. Conflict could also be a consequence of the diverging or competitive material interests of dominant capitalist classes in an anarchical world market since they, more than the dominated classes, frequently have more power and influence on the content and direction of the foreign policies of individual capitalist states. Marxists also recognize or see distinct possibilities of cooperation between capitalist states if and when their common interests are threatened by, for example, communism,

new social movements or Islamic fundamentalism. Therefore, cooperation between states does not necessarily reflect a natural harmony of
interest arising out of existing patterns of interdependence, as argued
in liberal political economy. At root then is the point that conflict and
cooperation have to be situated within the prevailing patterns of capitalist accumulation. Admittedly, Marxist theory is not free of conceptual problems and ambiguities. Indeed, legitimate complaints have
been raised about, among other things, its deterministic or class-reduc-
tionist view of politics; its Eurocentricism; its gender blindness; its
indifference to identities other than class; its tendency to privilege
the proletariat as the only authentic agency of human emancipation;
and its failure to acknowledge the anarchical nature of international
politics.

Nevertheless, it can be argued that, in spite of these serious problems,
Marxism offers important insights about the nature and character of
contemporary capitalist societies, including the various ways in which
capitalism has been transformed – notably its accounts of the rise of
MNCs/TNCs, the emergence of global financial markets, the prevalence
of uneven development captured by the so-called North–South divide,
deepening class and gender inequalities within society, and the internationalization of the state in these interrelated processes. Indeed, there is
no doubt whatsoever that social relations of production constitute a
crucial explanatory category for a better understanding of IPE. So these
are important insights in and of themselves in the sense that they can
be deployed innovatively to arrive at a more unified and integrated
approach to the study of IPE. Thus, a compelling argument can be
made that critical theory, especially its Marxist variant, is far more consistent, coherent and comprehensive than any of the rival paradigms
discussed above. It has better scope than both neo-realism and liberalism and takes global inequalities seriously. In particular, the emphasis
that Marxist theory puts on the state, its relative autonomy and the
form of class power underpinning it is helpful in terms of directing
attention to the interface between the state and the market or the economic structure of production in the modern world.

From this perspective, it is easier to connect the economic and political domains together and thus have a better focus on what IPE is all
about. The fundamental issue at stake here is succinctly summed up by
Stubbs and Underhill (1994: pp. 34–7):

[T]he politics of the state mediates between the economic and political domains and between the domestic and international levels of

analysis. Understanding the state, what it is, what it does and where it fits in state-society complex is in a way the [fundamental] problem of international political economy ... [P]olitical articulation, or how interests are organized and institutionalized, is the link between the economic structure, on the one hand, and the politics of the state and international system on the other. The politics of the state is the principal linkage between these two levels or domains because politics constitutes a two-way relationship between structure and agents in a particular institutional setting.

These are pertinent observations and they go to the very heart of the substance of IPE as the study of the interplay between economics and politics in the world arena or the study of the politics of the world economy (Frank and Gills, 1993: p. 1). Put another way, IPE denotes a 'set of questions' around the social, economic and political arrangements affecting the global system of production, exchange and distribution (Strange, 1988: p. 18). Seen in this light, IPE rejects the presumed separability of economics and politics, the domestic and the international, and persuasively argues that these domains are inextricably bound together. Who benefits from the existing world economy, and at whose expense is the key question that IPE poses (Tooze, 1997: p. 218). Therefore, a reconstructed IPE is a critical, normative and historical materialist perspective which analyses the complex interaction between states, firms, civil society and international institutions in the global arena.

As such, its central task is to explore the dialectic of continuity and transformation in the existing global order with the avowed objective of making the world a humane place for all by challenging and exposing those theoretical perspectives which, implicitly or explicitly, sustain prevailing patterns of domination and dependence, exploitation and oppression. Taken to its logical conclusion, this comprehensive definition of IPE correctly implies that it is far wider than the field of IR which, for a long time, was taken to be the parent discipline of IPE. Thus, the problem identified at the beginning of this chapter regarding the appropriate boundaries of IPE is, in a fundamental sense, a false one. It basically emanates from the pedagogic value of separating international economics from world politics for purposes of clarifying intricate relationships which would otherwise be too complex for extant, orthodox forms of analysis in IPE. This false separation was taken as valid and continued by way of the dominance of realism in the newly emergent post-First World War field of IR. Moreover, because both realism and neo-realism preclude a serious analysis of the nature of the state, its social basis and the fact that state practices are profoundly influenced by structural imperatives emanating from within the world capitalist system, the separation of these interrelated disciplines was further reinforced and made to appear permanent and immutable by 'organic intellectuals' of American imperialism. To the contrary, these two disciplines are inseparable because the state and the market are, in both theory and practice, the central preoccupations of IPE. Integrating them into a unified, holistic field of study in the form of IPE is a methodologically and conceptually challenging task. A few hints about how to tackle this daunting task are provided by Cox when he says 'IPE is concerned with the historically constituted frameworks or structures within which economic and political activity take place' (Cox, 1995: p. 32). He adds that such structures, which are the object of IPE, contain both elements of coherence and contradiction, meaning that change and transformation and not just order and stability are inherent in them. The world capitalist economy is one such historically consti-tuted complex structure which displays both of these elements of coherence and contradiction. To study and unravel its contradictions and what they portend for the future of Southern Africa requires one to first examine the changing role of the state in this complex whole. An important question to ask at this juncture is whether or not the power of the state to shape outcomes has been irreversibly eroded and, if so, by what forces and in what specific areas of state activity. In other words, we should appreciate the fact that what we call a state is a com-plex of governmental functions and societal practices and also that states differ in terms of their forms and capacities for action (Cox, 1994: p. 37). The same state also differs over time. With these caveats in mind we may now proceed to look at the debate on the changing role of the state in the contemporary world economy.

State adaptation or state decline? The debate on the role of the state in the world economy

Controversies abound on the changing role of the state in the contem-porary world economy. It is therefore appropriate to closely examine the various positions that have dominated this debate. Such an excur-sion has the potential of providing a strategic entry point into the cur-rent state-of-the-art in IPE and its implications for theorizing IR in Southern Africa. There are four identifiable positions that have domi-nated the debate on the role of the state in the world economy at the close of the twentieth century. Each of these positions will be considered in summary form because they have already been extensively dealt with by several competent scholars (see, for example, Palan and Abbott, 1996; Hirst and Thompson, 1996; Panitch, 1994; 1996; Scholte, 1997; Weiss, 1997). The first position, commonly associated with the neo-realist school, claims that the power of the state has not been significantly affected by the process of globalization. While they accept the fact of complex interdependence, neo-realists are sceptical about the corrosive effects of globalization on the power of the state. They contend that globalization is the latest fad in political analysis because we are no where near a global society nor is the world economy more open than in previous epochs. This position is aptly summed up by Jackson and James when they write: 'The qualitative changes associated with globalization have not reduced the significance of sovereign statehood as the fundamental way in which the world is politically organized' (Jackson and James, 1993: p. 6).

They point out that everywhere around the globe people want to establish their own independent state if they do not have one already, identify with particular states of which they are citizens by, for example, the passports they carry and are quite prepared to fight and die for the sovereign statehood of their countries if necessary. They cite the creation of several independent states from the former Soviet Union, the secession of Eritria from Ethiopia and the struggle for the establishment of such sovereign entities in the former Yugoslavia as indicative of the powerful appeal of nationalism and self-determination in the post-Cold War period. For them states will continue to be the preferred 'communities of fate' just as they have been since the emergence of the modern state system in Europe and its subsequent spread to other parts of the world. The fact that every country in the world has its own national flag, anthem, central bank and currency proves beyond doubt that sovereign statehood will endure. In this view, everywhere around the world people continue to look up to the state for protection against external threats to their lives and property be they in the form of terrorism or aggression from other states.

Thus, this position insists that world politics is still characterized by 'the struggle of political entities for power, prestige and wealth in a condition of anarchy' (Gilpin; cited in Hall, Held and McGrew, 1992: p. 116). From this perspective, state power remains unchanged because there are no other loci of sovereignty to pose serious challenges to the state. NGOs, intergovernmental organizations, and MNCs exist at the behest of states, are creations of states or operate with the blessing and/or support of the state. It is states and states alone which are sovereign and which generally command the support and loyalties of their citizens. Solomon's chapter in this book offers eloquent testimony in support of this thesis from a Southern African perspective.

Some aspects of this position have a degree of validity especially if counterposed to the grossly mistaken view that globalization heralds the 'end of the nation-state' propounded by such writers as Ohmae (1990), Reich (1992) and Horsman and Marshall (1994). This second, triumphalist position, which conflates globalization with progress for all, amounts to 'the political construction of helplessness' in the face of transnational capitalist forces (Weiss, 1997). It is one-sided, teleological, insensitive to the contradictions of globalization and unduly dismisses potential oppositional forces to the harmful effects of globalization expressed, for example, by new social movements. Surely, countless examples can be given to sustain the view that the state is not about to wither away and to refute the allegation that globalization has created a 'borderless world'. If it was indeed true that globalization has created a 'borderless world' why have immigration laws in the North (and in parts of the South such as South Africa) become more stringent and that labour remains far less mobile in the world economy than capital? Furthermore, why is it that elections matter? Proponents of the strong globalization thesis cannot answer these questions satisfactorily. For instance, they fail to appreciate the fact that elections are increasingly seen by transnational elites, Western governments and their allies in the South as an important mechanism for manufacturing consensual domination as distinct from the less effective coercive domination. In other words, they legitimize prevailing power relations and preempt fundamental change geared toward meeting popular needs and aspirations.

The 'end of the nation-state thesis' is hardly a defensible proposition. At core, it is simply a celebration and forward defence of highly mobile speculative international finance capital and those who benefit from it at the expense and suffering of the poor and powerless. But that is not the same thing as claiming that the power of the state remains intact in the face of globalization. Those holding this position are wrong to dismiss globalization as a delusion. Such an 'ostrich response' is misleading and unwarranted. As shall be demonstrated below, globalization is a reality, not a fad or myth. And it has had a significant impact on the state including the form it is taking and the variety of its responses to globalization.

The problem is that propagators of the 'end of the nation-state' thesis have often failed to specify the domains in which the state has lost powers (Ohmae, 1995). Nor have they been sufficiently careful to delineate the changing forms of sovereignty in the era of globalization. With respect to the former, there is no doubt that the power of the state in the military and security sectors remains largely unscathed. If looked at from this angle alone, then the first, neo-realist, position appears to be correct. But surely, state power is not confined to the military-security domain alone. The economic, financial, social and cultural domains are also relevant. There is plenty of evidence to demonstrate that the power of the state has indeed been significantly eroded in these domains. To pretend otherwise on the grounds that international anarchy is a fact of life is to lose sight of important changes in the nature of state power and the way it is being exercised in the contemporary period.

Concerning the issue of sovereignty, all that can be said at this juncture is that the concept has multiple meanings and purposes. If we take the concept to mean 'the right of states to exercise complete jurisdiction within mutually exclusive territorial domains' (Kofman and Youngs, 1996: p. 19), then it is valid to regard it as an enduring fact of life because all states possess this attribute. So far, none of them is prepared to give away this attribute. In this strict sense, sovereignty will endure so long as citizens and their states continue to value and seek to consolidate it especially when it is inextricably bound up with authority and legitimacy in a specified territory.

But sovereignty is not the same thing as autonomy or capacity. In this wider sense, sovereignty is differentiated because states have unequal capacities in the same way as individuals are equal before the law but have unequal capacities in the exercise of their civil and political liberties. In this wider context, the first position is surely mistaken in asserting that state power remains unchanged. It should therefore be dismissed as too narrow and misleading because globalization had adversely affected state autonomy and capacity. Writers such as Held (1995) are correct in saying that states no longer have effective capacity to control events and processes within and outside their borders even though they remain *de jure* sovereign. But even then, it should be recognized that globalization has had a differential impact on the unequal capacities of states and in the different domains of their traditional powers. Some states have experienced a serious diminution of their sovereignty (notably those in SSA) while others (principally those in North America, Western Europe and Southeast and East Asia) have retained a substantial degree of theirs. In other words, globalization has had differential effects and consequences on the variety of states around the world.

The third position, which one might term the 'declinist thesis', argues that the power of the state has been substantially eroded to a point where decisions it used to make on major economic policy issues have now been surrendered to or taken over by international capital in the form of TNCs, international financial institutions (IFIs) and multinational banks (MNBs). Declinists attribute the diminishing role of the state to the process of globalization. In the South, especially SSA, this external pressure on the state took the form of structural adjustment programmes (SAPs). To fully appreciate this argument and others that follow, it is imperative to quickly unpack the notion of globalization. The first point to bear in mind is that globalization is an essentially contested concept which defies precise definition. It has been defined in different ways by scholars of different ideological persuasions. It is also a set of contradictory processes which simultaneously promote integration and disintegration, cohesion and fragmentation, inclusion and exclusion, growth and stagnation, peace and turmoil, empowerment and disempowerment. Above all, it has facilitated accumulation of ostentatious wealth for the already rich minority and deepening poverty and despair for the disadvantaged majority of the world's population. Since it is a contradictory process, globalization helps shape a terrain of political struggles between contending forces at local, regional and global levels. It simultaneously opens possibilities for emancipation while also entrenching and intensifying existing relations of domination and subordination.

Setting aside its contradictions and the ambiguities surrounding it, globalization can be defined as the economic, political, cultural and technological processes which generate a multiplicity of linkages and interconnections between states and societies which make up the modern world system (Held and McGrew, 1993: p. 262). There is no doubt that globalization is a qualitatively new process that is characterized by, *inter alia*, liberalization and integration of global financial markets, internationalization of production, trade liberalization and extensive use of digital information technology to facilitate fast flows of information and rapid or instant telecommunication. Seen in this light, globalization entails the compression of time and space, a ceaseless movement of people, goods, money, information and ideas across national boundaries. Above all, it is fundamentally about the intensification and extension of capitalist social relations on a global scale (see Hettne in Chapter 5 above).

The declinists, whether of liberal or radical persuasion see globalization as inexorably leading to the erosion of state power and authority.

In some liberal circles, it is even asserted that globalization spells 'the end of sovereignty', the withering away of the nation-state (Ohmae, 1995; Camilleri and Falk, 1993). James Rosenau, echoing this theme, informs us that it is no longer accurate to conceptualize states as possessing their traditional autonomy because they are enmeshed in a network of interdependence (Rosenau and Czempiel, 1992: p. 60). Held and McGrew concur that states are no longer in possession of effective capacity to control events and processes within and outside their borders, let alone formulate and pursue independent national policies and strategies (Held and McGrew, 1993). These writers emphasize the fact that states no longer control the flow of information. People see, hear and read what they want in electronic and print media. They also stress the unprecedented high mobility of capital across national boundaries. The fact that a genuine worldwide market in stocks, bonds, and currencies now exists tied together by data processing and communications technology lends powerful credence to the view that the power of the state is in irreversible decline. To drive the point home, there is widespread consensus that literally 'trillions of dollars in global derivatives operate in relative detachment from territorial jurisdiction' of states (Scholte, 1997: p. 443). The core of the argument of the declinists is that states in the age of globalization no longer have *de facto* sovereignty. They are only formally or *de jure* sovereign. A multiplicity of parallel supranational structures of power and authority such as the World Trade Organization (WTO), TNCs, and NGOs, are said to have emerged and are steadily outflanking the modern state. For example, the WTO has the power to force its member states to abide by decisions of its trade dispute settlement mechanism.

According to this view, states are now forced to comply with the demands of international capital in terms of trade liberalization, prudent financial management, first class infrastructure, a highly skilled and disciplined labour force, less regulation of economic activity and a variety of incentives to attract and retain private investment. There is therefore a growing tendency toward economic policy convergence among states. In particular, macroeconomic policy convergence has been reinforced by the fiscal crisis of the state in both developed and developing countries, the prolonged world recession which began in the late 1970s and the perceived mistakes and failures of inward-looking statist, developmentalist policies of the 1960s. Put differently, state policies and practices are increasingly being adjusted to the logic of world market forces because states are, to varying degrees, constrained by the structural power of international capital. TNCs, MNCs and

MNBs, as institutional expressions of world market forces are beyond the control of states.

The point is made more forcefully by Strange (1995: p. 14) when she asserts that 'the authority of all states, large and small, weak and strong, has been weakened as a result of integration of national economies into one single global market economy'. She is emphatic that 'the domain of state authority in society and economy is shrinking' (ibid., p. 82). Thus, in this view, states no longer control the course of international events. They are increasingly driven in one direction of unregulated capitalism by the growing power of international capital and its associated neo-liberal SAPs enforced by IFIs in the developing world. The thrust of the argument here is that a significant part of who gets what, when and how is now decided by corporate capital. Indeed, these are pertinent observations. They cannot be glossed over or dismissed as a delusion on the grounds that power politics remain resilient as ever as asserted by neo-realist scholars (Layne, 1993; Krasner, 1994).

However, some crucial qualifications are in order if the insights of the 'declinist' school are to remain informative and credible. First, the declinist school cannot adequately explain the East Asian miracle because the rise of the East Asian 'tigers' has little to do with globalization but more with effective state intervention (Amsden, 1989; Wade, 1990). Of course, their success helped facilitate and give substance to globalization. Second, organizations such as the WTO and the IFIs are creations of states. Indeed, there is an enduring organic link between the state and international capital by way of intergovernmental organizations such as WTO and the IMF. These state-centric organizations work very closely with private institutions which represent the interests of international capital. The point being made here is that the state continues to play an important role in the reproduction of capitalist property relations, including the political cohesion of the capitalist class itself.

A further qualification is that loss of autonomy by some states is not coterminous with loss of their political sovereignty. As indicated above, states are sovereign in a political sense. Many of them, however, may not be so in an economic sense. Hence the once popular idea of consolidating the political independence of newly independent African states in the 1960s and the 1970s in order to avoid subjection to foreign domination in the form of neo-colonialism (see the quotation from Nkrumah in Chapter 5 above). The import of this observation is that sovereignty, in its wider sense, is not an attribute that states acquire once and for all. It is a protracted process denoting the right of self-realization by states in the context of international anarchy.

A further qualification that needs to be made is that states have always been subject to external pressures even in terms of international law. In other words, sovereignty has never been absolute. Even more telling is the fact that states have never been in a position to effectively control capital movements ever since the rise of capitalism. The declinist school may therefore be overstating the traditional powers of the state. But what is probably distinct about external pressures on the state in the era of globalization is their intensity, scope and points of origin. In this era, states are confronted with a multiplicity of acute pressures on the economic, political, social and cultural fronts from above and below. Overall, these trends which have been underway since the early 1980s reflect the rise of neo-liberal hegemony in the world economy. As is well known, the thrust of neo-liberal economic reforms is to reduce the role of the state in the economy and to expand that of the private sector including the latter's role in macroeconomic policy formulation. Having said that, it should be recognized that states have not been passive victims of the erosion of their powers, at least not all of them. They have not been simply on the retreat on all fronts as the title of one of Susan Strange's books implies. Rather, some states have been active participants and, in some cases, facilitators of this process while others (notably those in SSA) have been passive spectators and are therefore likely to be further weakened by globalization. As Panitch (1994) correctly points out, an important aspect of globalization is primarily about reorganizing rather than bypassing the state in order to render it more serviceable to the material interests of capital and in the process, conferring new powers on it which it did not have before. For instance, the surveillance powers of the state have increased enormously as a result of the technological revolution associated with globalization. So too has its relative strength *vis-à-vis* that of organized labour. Besides, states continue to perform that important role of upholding and enforcing property rights without which a capitalist economy cannot properly function. In this regard, Scholte makes an important point when he remarks that 'states have been forced to retreat only with respect to ownership of the means of production via privatization' (Scholte, 1997: p. 441). He also convincingly argues that 'states still retain some crucial capacities for governance' (ibid., p. 427). Hirst and Thompson (1996: p. 190) endorse this view when they argue that states are still the primary sources of binding rules, key practitioners of the art of government, pivots between international agencies and subnational activities, prime centres of administrative regulation and, to the degree that they are credibly democratic, they are representatives of the citizens within their borders. Therefore, it is not just a case of state power being in irreversible decline across all domains as the declinist thesis implies.

Conceived in this way, the relative roles of the state and capital in the process of globalization are complementary even if one concedes that the relationship is fraught with contradictions. For example, the demand for a favourable climate of investment by international capital in the form of lower taxes, world class infrastructure, a skilled and disciplined labour force coupled with a host of austerity measures induces a 'fiscal crisis of the state' and undermines its legitimacy in the eyes of the population. Given these contradictory roles of the state in the modern world economy, it can be concluded that the declinist school is inadequate in so far as it captures only one aspect of an evolving complex relationship between the state and capital; one where the state is shedding some of its traditional functions and assuming new ones. States are responding to these powerful globalizing forces in a variety of ways.

It is this line of inquiry which informs what one might term the 'state adaptation school'. This fourth position argues that what is often regarded as loss of power by states actually amounts to state adaptation to changing circumstances and conditions in the world economy. The point being made is that despite profound changes in the world economy, states retain certain vital economic and political functions at both the domestic and international levels (Cerny, 1995: p. 618). Therefore, what we are witnessing are actually changing forms of state intervention to provide the necessary conditions for attracting both local and foreign investment thereby facilitating domestic capital accumulation.

It is not so much the decline of state power but its reconstitution or creative adjustment to new challenges brought about by globalization. This thesis of state adaptation argues that 'far from relinquishing their distinctive goals and identities, states are increasingly using collaborative power arrangements to create real control over their economies by building or strengthening power alliances: upwards by way of interstate coalitions at the regional and international level and/or downwards by way of state-business alliances in the domestic market' (Weiss, 1997: p. 24). In saying so, Weiss is sensitive to the fact that not all states have this high degree of adaptability and therefore some, especially the weaker ones, are likely to succumb to the pressures of neo-liberal globalization and be marginalized further in the world economy.

As indicated earlier, most of these weak states are found mainly in South Asia and SSA. Ravaged by economic crisis, deepening poverty, hunger, illiteracy, disease, precipitous decline in export earnings due to a variety of factors such as the dematerialization of the production process in their traditional export markets, escalating debt burden, poor governance, environmental degradation, and natural calamities such as drought, they appear to be caught in the quagmire of underdevelopment and dependence from which there is little prospect of escaping (Chege, 1995; also, see Hettne in this volume). They are performing poorly in the competitive game of attracting and retaining foreign capital and are far from being active participants in the globalizing world economy. This gloomy picture is reinforced by estimates that Africa accounts for less than 1 per cent of world trade (Cheru, 1996: p. 49).

One major reason why SSA is being marginalized in the world economy is that world demand for what it produces is 'growing slowly or even declining, while world supplies are being constantly expanded and many of the commodities in question are increasingly being produced several times more efficiently outside Africa under capitalist conditions of production, forcing prices steadily downwards towards levels at which Africans will no longer be able to survive on what they can get from a day's labour of producing them' (Leys, 1994: pp. 34–5). The other is that even in those areas of economic activity in which SSA had competitive advantage such as ostrich farming are being taken over by the North. No wonder then that SSA accounts for 32 of the least developed countries in the world and 28 of those that are severely indebted. To compound matters, less and less of what SSA produces is relevant to the skill-driven world economy but it is still subjected to a highly exploitative system of debt peonage superintended by the IFIs. This system of debt peonage is graphically illustrated by estimates that SSA's total external debt as a percentage of exports rose from 91 per cent in 1980 to 270 per cent in 1995 (Sparks, 1998: p. 13).

In simple terms, Africa has been bypassed by globalization, at least in its economic dimensions. Thus, the connection between Africa and the world economy seems to be because of its high level of indebtedness and acute need for aid. Consequently, African states lack the capacity to pursue meaningful strategies of development even if they wished to do so (Jackson and James, 1993: p. 23). These are 'quasi states' whose domestic economic situation, rather than their given policies, structurally discourage meaningful long-term investment, both domestic and foreign, in their economies (Palan and Abbott, 1996: p. 188).

This gloomy picture about the African state in the era of globalization has some degree of validity. Across the continent, numerous examples can be given about 'collapsed states' or those tottering on the brink of disintegration such as Angola, Chad, Lesotho, Liberia, Sierra Leone and Somalia. There is also some validity in the much acclaimed 'neo-patrimonial' character of the African state which has spawned a 'crisis of governance' in several parts of the continent. However, the problem with the neo-patrimonial thesis is that it is insensitive to the diversity of African states and their historical specificities. There are African states, few as they may be, which have not been afflicted by the malaise of authoritarian governance and whose development performance has been relatively good even during the difficult 'lost decade' of the 1980s. Among these are Botswana, Mauritius and to some extent, Zimbabwe before the introduction of SAPs in 1991. They have been joined by Namibia and South Africa in the 1990s. Some differentiation is surely warranted. It is hard to sustain the argument that these African states have not or are not going anywhere. They too have been adapting to changing conditions in the world economy by, for example, making their foreign investment legislation more attractive to international capital, and forming regional integration schemes and revamping them.

The major problem with the neo-patrimonial thesis is that it tends to see corruption and mismanagement as causes rather than symptoms of the crisis of underdevelopment and debt peonage (Szeftel, 1998). The main causes of the crisis are the weak social formations upon which African states preside and their extreme dependence on one or two export commodities for foreign exchange. Added to this is the fact that rural relations of production have not undergone any significant transformation since colonial days and, with few exceptions – notably South Africa and Zimbabwe – SSA is still, if ever, to make a transition to self-sustained industrialization. To sidestep these fundamental aspects of Africa's political economy by prioritizing neo-patrimonialism is tantamount to obscuring rather than illuminating the continent's predicament.

On the other hand, the negative sovereignty thesis propounded by writers such as Jackson (1990) and Clapham (1996) is that it frequently fails to locate the structural position of African states in the world economy. It is as if African states can attain positive sovereignty in isolation from the operations of the world capitalist economy and the mechanisms of domination that sustain it. Notwithstanding bad governance and its deleterious consequences, it is certainly important to recognize the multitude of external obstacles that impede the self-realization of

African states in the global political economy. These range from the pro-longed world recession, declining terms of trade, the new protectionism, the concentration of foreign direct investment in the advanced capitalist countries and a few select East Asian NICs to SAPs, debt peonage and political conditionalities. Therefore, a more nuanced analysis informed by a critical IPE as elaborated above is called for. Instead of dwelling on the so-called patrimonial character of the African state and reinforcing neo-liberal hegemony by painting a picture of total helplessness in the face of transnational capitalist forces, the proposed alternative analytical framework will attempt to examine the actual and potential social forces that might propel African states in a direction of transformation and renewal. The next section will attempt precisely that in relation to the Southern African region.

IPE and Southern African development: the dynamics and prospects for transformation of the regional political economy

A fundamental theoretical premise that informs this section is that the dynamics and prospects for Southern African development in the era of globalization can best be explored from the perspective of critical IPE. This claim is made on the grounds that critical IPE, unlike conventional IR, fully takes cognizance of neo-liberal globalization and its implications for developing regions such as Southern Africa. It thus puts the question of the 'new regionalism' on the agenda, an issue that is of immense importance to the peoples of Southern Africa since, for a long time, regionalism has been a preserve of states and governing elites at the expense of popular participation in regional integration schemes (see Hettne, Chapter 5 above and Du Pisani, Chapter 9 below). Moreover, critical IPE places 'development' at the centre of analysis by posing the question 'who benefits from the prevailing regional/world order?' It also seeks to unlock the social forces that might promote change and transformation in that regional/world order and expose those that resist or hinder such transformative/emancipatory projects. As such it serves as a guide to strategic action for bringing about an alternative order (Cox, 1996: p. 90).

   With this focus, critical IPE is better suited for analysing the dynamics and prospects for transformation in Southern Africa than conventional IR because it takes into consideration not just inter-state relations but also state–market relations, and the place and role of civil society in regional relations (including that of regional organizations such as SADC). In pursuing this line of inquiry, the analysis will build on preceding sections regarding the manner in which states in this region have been responding to the forces of globalization. Before looking at how states in the region have been adapting to changing circumstances in the world economy, it is imperative to lay out the regional political economy. Only the most salient features will be highlighted here because substantial work has already been done in this important area (Amin *et al.*, 1987; Saasa, 1991; Martin, 1992; Blumenfeld, 1991; Maasdorp and Whiteside, 1992; Odén, 1993; Thede and Beaudet, 1993; Davies, 1994; Venter, 1994; Tsie, 1996; Weeks, 1996; McGowan and Ahwireng-Obeng, 1998).

The most striking feature about the Southern African region is the economic dominance of South Africa. It has the most sophisticated manufacturing industry in SSA, the best infrastructure, a highly developed mining industry, a relatively advanced agricultural sector, all supported by a robust service sector in the form of banking and insurance services. Its gross domestic product (GDP) is four times larger than that of the remaining SADC economies. Its GNP per capita is roughly five times greater than that of the rest of the SADC countries. Even more telling is the fact that manufacturing value added (MVA) in South Africa is 'over five times larger than the sum of all other SADC member states' MVA, and nearly 15 times than that of the second biggest manufacturer, namely Zimbabwe' (Mayer and Thomas, 1997: p. 9; see also tables in Chapter 7 below). It is therefore no surprise that post-apartheid South Africa is often seen as the regional economic powerhouse which, once ignited (if ever), would serve as the locomotive of recovery, growth and development for the region and the rest of SSA (Odén assesses this argument in detail in Chapter 8 below).

Polarized patterns of accumulation inherited from the colonial period ensure that the rest of the SADC economies remain dependent on South Africa for trade routes, food imports, labour migration, foreign investment and a host of manufactured goods such as textiles and clothing, building materials, vehicles, machinery and transport equipment. Even Zimbabwe, the second largest economy in the region, is highly dependent on South African capital investment and as a market for its textile industry. The skewed economic integration between South Africa and the rest of the region has made it an almost foregone conclusion that intra-regional trade would be a one-way street. Thus, in 1993 South Africa's visible exports to the rest of the region exceeded imports by four to one (Davies, 1997: p. 110). If invisibles are included, the ratio may be as high as 8 : 1.

Although trade relations with the rest of the continent have improved significantly since 1992, most of South Africa's trade is with its Southern African neighbours, especially the BLNS states (Botswana, Lesotho, Namibia and Swaziland) with which it has been enjoined in a customs union agreement since 1910. Outside the customs union, Zimbabwe is South Africa's next important trading partner followed by Mozambique and Zambia. In overall terms, the SADC region accounts for roughly 90 per cent of South Africa's exports to Africa, the majority of which are manufactured goods. Its imports from the region consist mainly of unprocessed raw materials such as cotton, tobacco, gemstones but also textiles and garments, water, energy and for some time vehicles assembled in Botswana by Hyundai Motor Corporation. In contrast, South Africa's exports to overseas markets, principally the European Union (EU), comprise minerals (gold, diamonds, platinum, chrome among others) and agricultural products. These trade flows clearly reveal that South Africa is a semi-industrialized country juxtaposed to a backward, underdeveloped periphery which is nevertheless of paramount importance to its future growth and prosperity. More importantly, they reveal that the regional economies are characterized by competitive rather than complementary production structures wherein countries produce similar primary agricultural and mineral commodities for export markets, mainly the EU market. So, even South Africa, which is by far the largest economy in the region, resembles a developing country rather than a developed country. It is not hyperbole therefore to state that South Africa faces many of the same challenges as do its neighbours. Specifically, the daunting challenge to all SADC states is one of structural transformation. Whether or not South Africa can provide constructive leadership in that transformative project is a question that awaits further analysis (see Odén in this volume). For now, the analytical focus is on how SADC states have been responding to the challenges posed by globalization.

Although Southern African states are weak by international standards, they too have been individually and collectively adapting to the pressures generated by the processes of globalization. In some cases, this adaptation has been forced upon them as a result of the economic crisis confronting them and the debt crisis that ensued. Many states in the region such as Lesotho, Malawi, Mozambique and Zimbabwe, to name but a few, have been implementing SAPs under the tutelage of the IFIs. Others such as Botswana, Namibia and South Africa have also been adjusting their domestic economic policies in the light of changing conditions in the world economy without being compelled to do so by IFIs. The stated central thrust of these largely neo-liberal economic reforms – whether internally generated or imposed by IFIs – is to put the affected economies on the path to sustainable economic growth and development by improving their international competitiveness. Key components of these reforms are trade liberalization, privatization of public enterprises, currency devaluation, price decontrol, reduction of state expenditure to reduce and ultimately eliminate government budget deficits, achieving real interest rates and, above all, maintaining macroeconomic stability. Elements of these reforms are found in almost all SADC countries. For example, both Botswana and South Africa have declared their commitment to privatization and have been maintaining very high interest rates in order 'to fight inflation'. Essentially, these reforms, whether packaged as SAPs or implemented voluntarily on a piecemeal basis, are anchored on a 'back-to-the-future' strategy which encourages export-orientation in order to fully exploit the comparative advantage of each economy. Whether they will achieve their stated objectives is doubtful. But there is no doubt that their underlying current is to change the balance of state–market relations in the direction of market-led development as distinct from statist developmentalism which was so common in the region in the 1970s.

Market-led development is also the surest way of fully integrating the regional economies into the world capitalist system mainly as producers of primary commodities. Above all, private sector-led development is strategically refashioning state intervention in the SADC region away from direct involvement in the economy to the provision of propitious conditions for private capitalist accumulation in the form of first class infrastructure, skilled manpower, disciplined labour, extension of incentives to private capital and a central voice in domestic economic policy formulation. As a result, we are witnessing the rise of the 'competition state' in the SADC region whereby states in the region are locked in a fierce competition for foreign capital investment. For instance, Mozambique, Namibia, South Africa and Zimbabwe have or are in the process of setting up export processing zones (EPZs).

While no one would deny the importance of attracting and retaining foreign investment or for that matter, the need to maintain macroeconomic stability, there is a potential danger that the 'competition state' will undermine the objective of achieving equity in regional relations. In the absence of a coordinated, interstate investment code, foreign capital may gravitate toward the already stronger economies such as South Africa and Zimbabwe thereby aggravating existing disparities (compare the argument in Holden, Chapter 7 below). Even more frightening is the prospect of the state being gradually compelled by the logic of world market forces to abandon its social responsibility of alleviating poverty which is already rampant in the region.

The central thrust of the argument being offered here is that neo-liberal regionalism as expressed in, for example, the Cross Border Initiative (CBI) has little to offer in terms of how to diversify the regional production structure, how to avoid polarization effects, how to empower the poor and powerless and arrest the 'race to the bottom' unleashed by the so-called free market forces. Too often, it pays scant attention to critical obstacles to increased intra-regional trade such as poor and/or inadequate infrastructure, acute export dependence and the debt overhang. Instead, its focus is on rapid reduction of tariff barriers to trade, currency convertibility and liberalization of financial markets as if these are the principal obstacles to low intra-regional trade when in fact they are not. If indeed they were, the BLNS states would be exporting more of their products to South Africa since they belong to the same customs union rather than to the EU. The fact that they are not strongly suggests that there are fundamental factors at play which neo-liberal regionalism is not prepared to recognize. Moreover, neo-liberal regionalism is premised on the contestable assumption that what is good for local and foreign capital is good for society as a whole or in this specific instance, for the regional economies.

However, in this age of high mobility of international finance capital across borders, the evidence points to the contrary. International finance capital, which has now subordinated productive capital to its short-term profit calculations, is wreaking havoc on economies, especially those that are home to emerging financial markets or are close to them. For instance, the fall of the South African Rand in May 1997 is inexplicable without reference to speculative fund managers who, by simply changing millions of rands into US dollars and other hard currencies, put immense pressure on the rand thereby undermining investor confidence in the economy. The fact that the 'fundamentals' of the South African economy 'remained intact' during that period does not mean that its prospects for long-term sustained growth and those of the neighbouring economies were not compromised. In fact they were seriously compromised, contrary to the projections of mainstream economists. The point being made here is that neo-liberal regionalism is inappropriate for the region because it offers next to nothing regarding the critical question of structural transformation;

that is, how to modify or alter the inherited production structures so that they become more and more complementary rather than being competitive.

The project of structural transformation in Southern Africa is one that cannot be left to market forces alone. Market forces are more likely to reinforce the inherited lopsided development in which existing disparities between regional economies are reinforced rather than mitigated and in which the majority of the people are impoverished. Such a trend has two potential undesirable consequences. First, it has the potential to undermine SADC's stated objective of equitable regional integration and, in the process, foster competition and conflict between SADC states rather than collaboration and cooperation for mutual gain. Second, it is likely to provide political instability because people will not passively accept their immiseration. Instead, the likelihood is that they will withdraw their support from governing political parties and mount protests against 'democratic austerity'. With that, the legitimacy of the state itself is put in question. Recent developments in Lesotho and Zimbabwe attest to this. Democratic development, to which all SADC states are formally committed, cannot be sustained under such conditions. Stated bluntly, unregulated market-driven development is deeply inimical to democratization, poverty alleviation and equitable regional integration.

From the perspective of critical IPE, what is required in Southern Africa is a synergy between the state and the market in pursuit of a regional developmental project that is democratic, gender sensitive, equitable, environmentally friendly and conscious of the need to empower the poor and powerless through such measures as land reform, education and employment creation. Such a developmental project need not be the province of states alone but should involve the private sector and organs of civil society such as trade unions, the youth, women's organizations, peasant cooperatives and so on. In short, it is the 'new developmental regionalism' that is inspired by the notion of 'coordinated social market economies'. The key question that emerges at this juncture is whether such a regional development project is feasible or not. No doubt there will be those who will say it is utterly impossible given the power of predatory transnational globalizing forces, soft/weak states, weak civil societies, the escalating crime rate in South Africa, lack of 'political will', dire financial straits afflicting many economies in the region, aid/sympathy fatigue on the part of SADC's cooperating partners and the low level of foreign direct investment flows into the region compared with other regions of the world such as Latin America and South East Asia. Admittely, these are serious constraints and cannot therefore be glossed over.

Actually, the SADC programme of action is characterized by severe contradictions. As highlighted by Du Pisani in Chapter 9, the official policy stance is that SADC is seeking to achieve equity, balance and mutual gain through development integration. There is also an explicit understanding that market integration is not the most appropriate strategy for a developing region such as Southern Africa. But in practice virtually all SADC states have either enthusiastically embraced neo-liberal policies (for example, South Africa's policy of GEAR) or have been forced by IFIs to adopt them in the form of SAPs and the CBI. So, neo-liberal regionalism is on the ascendancy both by stealth and design in Southern Africa despite its deleterious consequences for the masses. What this suggests is that an alliance of material interests has been consummated between state elites and the dominant social forces in the region on the one hand and international capital on the other. It is this powerful configuration of social forces that is likely to undermine progressive developmental goals in Southern Africa because it has strong links with powerful external forces such as the IFIs and Western governments.

But there are opportunities as well. Only three critical opportunities are mentioned here. The first is the relative political stability which the region is enjoying (with the exception of Angola and the Democratic Republic of Congo) after decades of conflict and war. This 'peace dividend' could contribute to development provided there is a strategic vision regarding where the region ought to be in the next millennium. Ironically, the continuing troubles in the Great Lakes Region may serve as a catalyst in this regard. The second is the increasing convergence of macroeconomic policies among the SADC states and their stabilization over time. Maintenance of macroeconomic stability is one important mechanism for attracting and retaining foreign investment, especially if it is accompanied by removal of undue interference with people-friendly market forces. The third is the introduction of parliamentary democracy in almost all SADC countries. Should democratic governance be consolidated in the region (and that is possible only if economic reforms yield material benefits for the general populace), then prospects for transformation will be enhanced. Thus, in overall terms, Southern Africa is in relatively more propitious circumstances at the end of the millennium than was thought possible in the recent past. The region provides the best hope for halting and ultimately reversing the marginalization of SSA in the world economy. Apart from being richly endowed with a variety of natural resources such as minerals, oil, fisheries, good agricultural land and tourist attractions, two of the most diversified economies in SSA, namely South Africa and Zimbabwe, are in Southern Africa.

These opportunities can be exploited for the benefit of the region as a whole provided South Africa is prepared to play the role of a benign hegemon and is accepted as such by other SADC states (for a detailed analysis of the likelihood of this transpiring, see Odén in this volume). Such a leadership role necessarily entails the opening of the South African market to products other SADC economies produce more cheaply than South Africa. Some of these are textiles and garments, leather and footwear, tea, coffee, tobacco, potash, and maize in return for selling its intermediate and capital goods in the region. Even more vital for economic growth in South Africa itself is importation of water, electricity and natural gas from countries such as Congo, Lesotho and Mozambique. Such imports could be complemented by an extended use by South Africa of the rehabilitated regional transport infrastructure, specifically the Maputo Transport and Development Corridor and the Trans-Kalahari Highway. Use of the latter could significantly reduce transport costs for exports from the Gauteng Province destined to West Africa and the EU provided sufficient service stations are set up along this 600 km road and the Walvis Bay port is refurbished. In that way, complementarities between the regional economies could steadily be built providing South Africa with a growing regional market instead of it seeking to sell as much as it can to its neighbours without taking due regard of their economic interests.

South African mining companies could also contribute to improved intra-regional trade by increasing their investments in the region's mineral sector whose full potential is still to be realized. According to Jordan (1995: p. 23), almost all the minerals necessary for industrialization are already produced in the region or exist as unexploited resources. He adds that 'contrary to popular wisdom, there is a significant degree of resource complementarity' (ibid.). For example, further beneficiation of chromite ore could enable South Africa to produce stainless steel products for the region and overseas markets. The same applies to hydrocarbon by-products such as fertilizers. What this analysis implies is that there is need to purposefully build dynamic linkages between SADC economies and in the process create new comparative advantages wherein the region moves toward high productivity sectors thereby avoiding being permanently trapped in low productivity, low value-added products. It also implies the need to enhance the development of the private sector so that a constructive partnership between it and the state is forged.

The critical question that these observations raise is: what degree of openness should SADC retain with the world economy? Should it take the form of open regionalism advocated by IFIs and the TNC-driven WTO or should it be premised on strategic integration into the world economy? If it is premised on the former, then the kinds of outcomes being foreseen here are unlikely to materialize because external competition would wipe out nascent industries in the region. The fact is that the playing field in trade relations between Southern Africa and the North is not level as illustrated, for example, by the dumping of beef in the South African market by the EU. But if the form and degree of openness is informed by strategic integration, then such possibilities become more open and realizable (for a contrasting perspective, see Holden, Chapter 7 below). The major constraint, it seems, is at the level of policy development both in South Africa and the region at large. It would appear that SADC states have succumbed to open regionalism partly as a result of pressure from IFIs in the form of SAPs but also as a result a deliberate policy decisions most clearly exemplified by the SADC Free Trade Protocol. These policy decisions assume that there is some unique form or degree of openness to the world economy that is true for all countries at all times when in fact there is none (Singh, 1994: p. 18).

Of course, engagement with the global economy is unavoidable. What is at issue are the terms of that engagement. From a critical political economy perspective, the challenge for progressive forces is to pressurize SADC governments to adopt policies that limit the detrimental effects of neo-liberal regionalism, identify and promote complementarities in the regional economy, fortify its competiveness in the world economy and, above all, promote policies that seek to resubordinate market forces to societal needs. Regrettably, such forces are weak and have little influence on policy formulation compared to those that support neo-liberal regionalism. But that is not to say they are totally powerless. Organized labour in particular is quite strong in countries such as South Africa and Zimbabwe. So neo-liberal regionalism will not proceed uncontested.

Bearing this in mind, it would appear that SADC needs to rethink its trade protocol as well as its relations with the world economy in the direction of strategic integration rather than open regionalism because, in the long run, uncoordinated rampant competition will be ruinous for all SADC economies. Collaborative competition might be the best policy stance because it gives room for states to work together in creating the region's competitive advantage *vis-à-vis* the rest of the world. Of course, it could be argued that weak state capacity in the various SADC countries rules out the possibility of pursuing structural transformation despite the long term benefits inherent in it. However, weak state capacity is not a pervasive problem throughout the region. There is already a reasonable level of state effectiveness in Botswana, Mauritius, Namibia, South Africa, Swaziland and Zimbabwe. State capacity in the rest of the region is problematic and in some cases (for example, Angola, DRC and Mozambique) needs to be built from scratch. The challenge then is to build, improve and strengthen state capacity in the region because without that there is little prospect for equitable regional development, let alone structural transformation.

Given what was said above regarding the importance of the regional market for South African exports, the interests of South African business and large-scale agriculture dictate that the country should take the lead in promoting structural transformation and balanced regional development. Without that even GEAR will not succeed. Unfortunately, available evidence suggests that South Africa is reluctant to assume the role of a benign hegemon even though the ANC government has not been found wanting in public pronouncements about equitable regional relations (see especially Odén in Chapter 8). Of course, one major reason why this is so is that the ANC government is under immense pressure to address the legacies of the past: to deliver on housing, education, water and sanitation and above all, employment creation for the majority of its citizens who have been so grossly repressed and disadvantaged by successive apartheid regimes. Granted that such concerns are legitimate, there have been no concrete policy measures taken by the ANC government to promote balanced trade and integrated industrial development in the region. Instead, South Africa has increasingly displayed a neo-realist regional economic policy in which it uses its economic power to address domestic problems at the expense of the rest of the region (McGowan and Ahwireng-Obeng, 1998: pp. 189–90). Thus, there is a yawning gap between ANC policy declarations and actual practice in the domain of regional economic relations. As a result the previous neo-colonial pattern of regional economic relations is being reinforced, this time more and more by South African corporate capital.

Another reason underlying South Africa's reluctance is that dominant capitalist interests inside the country, principally corporate interests and their think-tank allies within and outside the state bureaucracy, seem to believe that cultivating closer relations with the EU and com-pradorizing the region are in the best 'national interest'. This neo-lib-eral position is favoured by the five conglomerates which dominate the South African economy, the white establishment in the top echelons on the public sector, South African finance capital in general and their external allies in the form of IFIs. It is a position that reflects existing power relations in the region and the global system itself. At present, it is given credence by the defeat of progressive forces in South Africa as demonstrated by the adoption of GEAR and the deteriorating eco-nomic and political situation in countries such as Angola, DRC and Zimbabwe. With the onset of aid fatigue and the continuing 'invest-ment drought' in much of the region beyond South Africa, dominant classes and state elites 'are prepared to endorse the neo-liberal strategy as long as it facilitates their personal economic enrichment' (Cheru, 1997: p. 239). But in pursuing this line, both the ANC government and South African capital miss the fundamental point that South Africa cannot prosper while its neighbours are sinking deeper into the quag-mire of poverty and dependence. Clearly, such a neo-realist policy regime is detrimental to structural transformation and equitable regional integration. In light of what has been said so far, it can be concluded that the prospects for balanced regional development in Southern Africa are dim.

Even if one puts South African reluctance aside, other SADC states seem to be too preoccupied with their domestic economic problems to the detriment of more constructive approaches to regional cooperation and integration such as those outlined above. Consequently, 'national interests' are often given priority over and above the interests of the region as a whole. So, unless a Polanyian 'second movement' orches-trated by a broad coalition of democratic forces in support of the poor and powerless takes off, the region's future is not as bright as was once thought in the aftermath of South Africa's transition to majority rule. It is here that civil societies in the region, weak as they currently are, might make a difference by thinking regionally and acting locally to put pressure on political leaders to come up with more constructive strategies for translating SADC's guiding principles of balance, equity and mutual gain in regional relations into practice.

Conclusions

This chapter has been concerned with identifying the scope and sub-stance of IPE in the age of neo-liberal globalization. It argued the case for a 'new' IPE underpinned by Coxian critical theory in the firm conviction that it is the most fruitful perspective from which to explore a complex set of issues such as the impact of globalization on state–market relations. In the course of that discussion, it demonstrated that IPE is a far broader field of study than conventional IR. First, the 'new' IPE problematizes the question of development which IR has long neglected. Second, it does not take the existing world order as given, immutable and unchanging. Rather, it seeks to identify the social forces that might promote change toward plausible alternative world orders to the prevailing one none of which is predetermined or given in advance.

The implications of this 'new' IPE for the study of IR in Southern Africa are many and varied. Therefore, only the most pertinent will be considered here. In future, IR in Southern Africa will increasingly have to confront the critical question of how to sensitize students to the 'multiple axes of exclusion' inherent in the existing regional order, how these came about, what mechanisms sustain them and what possibilities exist for overcoming them in order to build an alternative regional order that is more humane and just. Incorporating these complex 'sets of questions' into IR suggests a reorientation of the discipline away from a preoccupation with the anarchy problematique encapsulated in the debate between neo-realism and neo-institutionalism without neglecting important insights that can be gleaned from this debate. Equally important will be a grounding of IR on the dominant relations of production which exist in the region, the forms of state and civil societies that they have given rise to and how the state and civil society in the region are being affected by the process of globalization. In essence, this means that IR in Southern Africa may well have to transcend both the 'neo-neo' synthesis and mechanical Marxism exhibited by such notions as core–periphery and be prepared to engage with other perspectives such as feminism and environmentalism (see Chapters 11 and 12 below).

The chapter also examined at length the debate on the changing role of the state in the global political economy. While it conceded that states no longer possess their traditional powers, it rejected the claim that state power is in irreversible decline on the grounds that transnational capitalist accumulation still needs a strong and effective state albeit in a marketized form. Instead, it defended the thesis that state power is being refurbished so that it is more in tune with the demands of a globalizing world economy and that states are responding in a variety of ways to these pressures, including those that are commonly thought to be 'not in the game' at all, principally those in SSA.

This state adaptation thesis served as a strategic entry point into the analysis of the respective roles of states and market forces in Southern African development. The main issue at stake in that part of the discussion was how a post-apartheid Southern Africa could reposition itself in the world economy in order to avoid further marginalization. The picture to emerge was one where Southern African development in the form of structural transformation accompanied by equitable regional integration is at present seriously constrained by the lack of South African benign hegemonic leadership, the dominance of neo-liberalism in national development policy and its influence in laying the parameters for regional cooperation and integration. This, it was concluded, fosters narrow competitive conceptualizations of 'national interests' instead of collaborative competition in the interests of the region as a whole. The only potential source for long term progressive change in the region is seen to lie in a latent Polanyian 'second movement' generated by popular civil society across the region.

References

Amin, Samir, *et al.* (1987), *SADCC: Prospects for Development and Disengagement in Southern Africa* (London: Zed).

Amsden, Alice (1989), *Asia's Next Giant: South Korea and Late Industrialization* (Oxford: Oxford University Press).

Blake, D. H. and R. S. Walters (1987), *The Politics of Global Economic Relations* (Engelwood Cliffs, NJ: Prentice Hall).

Blumenfeld, Jesmond (1991), *Economic Interdependence in Southern Africa* (London: St Martin's Press).

Boyer, R. and D. Drache (1996), *States Against Markets: The Limits of Globalisation* (London: Routledge).

Burchill, Scott, and Andrew Linklater (1996), *Theories of International Relations* (London: Macmillan).

Camilleri, Joseph, and Richard Falk (1993), *The End of Sovereignty?* (London: Edward Elgar).

Cerny, Philip (1995), 'Globalisation and the Changing Logic of Collective Action', *International Organisation* 34/2.

Chege, Michael (1995), 'Sub-Saharan Africa: Underdevelopment's Last Stand', in Barbara Stallings (ed.), *Global Change, Regional Response: The New International Context of Development* (Cambridge: Cambridge University Press).

Cheru, Fantu (1996), 'Africa and the New World Order: Rethinking Development Planning in the Age of Globalisation', in Adebayo Adedeji (ed.), *South Africa and Africa: Within or Apart?* (London: Zed Books).

Cheru, Fantu (1997), 'Civil Society and Political Economy in South and Southern Africa', in Stephen Gill (ed.), *Globalisation, Democratisation and Multilateralism* (London: Macmillan).

Clapham, Christopher (1996), *Africa and the International System* (Cambridge: Cambridge University Press).

Cox, Robert W. (1987), *Production, Power and World Order: Social Forces in the Making of History* (New York: Columbia University Press).

Cox, Robert W. (1983), 'Gramsci, Hegemony and International Relations: An Essay in Method', in Stephen Gill (ed.), *Gramsci, Historical Materialism and International Relations* (Cambridge: Cambridge University Press).

Cox, Robert W. (1994), 'Global Restructuring: Making Sense of the Changing International Political Economy', in Richard Stubbs and Geoffrey R. D. Underhill (eds), *Political Economy and the Changing Global Order* (London: Macmillan).

Cox, Robert W. (1995), 'Critical Political Economy', in Bjorn Hettne (ed.), *International Political Economy: Understanding Global Disorder* (London: Zed).

Cox, Robert W., with Timothy J. Sinclair (1996), *Approaches to World Order* (Cambridge: Cambridge University Press).

Davies, Rob (1994), 'Approaches to Regional Integration in Southern Africa', *Africa Insight* 24/1.

Davies, Rob (1997), 'Promoting Regional Integration in Southern Africa', in Larry A. Swatuk and David R. Black (eds), *Bridging the Rift: The New South Africa in Africa* (Boulder, CO Westview).

Doyle, M. (1993), 'Liberalism and World Politics Revisited', in Charles W. Kegley (ed.), *Controversies in International Relations Theory: Neo-Realism and Neo-Liberalism* (New York: St Martin's Press).

Evans, Peter B. (1995), *Embedded Autonomy: States and Industrial Transformation* (London: I. B. Taurus).

Frank, Andre Gunder, and Barry Gills (eds) (1993), *The World System* (London: Routledge).

Gill, Stephen (1994), 'Knowledge, Politics and Neo-Liberal Political Economy', in Richard Stubbs and Geoffrey R. D. Underhill (eds), *Political Economy and the Changing Global Order* (London: Macmillan).

Gilpin, Robert (1981), *War and Change in World Politics* (Cambridge: Cambridge University Press).

Gilpin, Robert (1987), *The Political Economy of International Relations* (Princeton, NJ: Princeton University Press).

Hall, Stuart, David Held and Tony McGrew (1992), *Modernity and Its Futures*, (Oxford: Polity Press).

Halliday, Fred (1994), *Rethinking International Relations* (London: Macmillan).

Held, David (1995), *Democracy and the Global Order* (Stanford: Stanford University Press).

Held, David and Anthony McGrew (1993), 'Globalisation and the Liberal Democratic State', *Government and Opposition* 28/3.

Hirst, P. and G. Thompson (1996), *Globalisation in Question* (Cambridge: Polity Press).

Horsman, M. and A. Marshall (1994), *After the Nation-State* (London: Harper Collins).

Jackson, Robert H. (1990), *Quasi-States: Sovereignty, International Relations and the Third World* (Cambridge: Cambridge University Press).

Jackson, Robert H. and Alan James (eds) (1993), *States in a Changing World* (Oxford: Clarendon Press).

Jordan, P. (1995), *The Mining Sector in Southern Africa* (Harare: SAPES Trust).

Keohane, Robert O. (1984), *After Hegemony: Cooperation and Discord in the World Political Economy* (Princeton, NJ: Princeton University Press).

Keohane, Robert O. (ed.) (1986), *Neo-Realism and its Critics* (New York: Columbia University Press).

Keohane, Robert O. (1989), *International Institutions and State Power* (Boulder, CO: Westview).

Kofman, E., and G. Youngs (eds) (1996), *Globalisation: Theory and Practice* (London: Pinter).

Krasner, Stephen D. (ed.) (1983), *International Regimes* (Ithaca: Cornell University Press).

Krasner, Stephen D. (1994), 'International Political Economy: Abiding Discord', *Review of International Political Economy* 1/1, 13–19.

Layne, C. (1993), 'The Unipolar Illusion: Why Great Powers Will Rise', *International Security* 17/4, 5–15.

Leys, Colin (1994), 'Confronting the African Tragedy', *New Left Review* 204.

Maasdorp, Gavin, and Alan Whiteside (eds) (1992), *Towards A Post-Apartheid Southern Africa* (London: Macmillan).

Mamdani, Mahmood (1996), *Citizen and Subject: Contemporary Africa and the Legacy of Late Colonialism* (London: James Currey).

Martin, William G. (1991), 'The Future of Southern Africa: what prospects after majority rule?', *Review of African Political Economy* 50 (March), 115–34.

Martin, William G. (1992), 'Southern Africa and the World Economy: Regionality and Trade Regimes', in Sergio Vieira, William Martin and Immanuel Wallerstein (eds), *How Fast the Wind? Southern Africa 1975–2000* (Trenton, NJ: Africa World Press).

Mayer, M., and R. H. Thomas (1997), 'Trade Integration in SADC: Problems and Prospects', in L. Kritzinger van Nierkerdk (ed.), *Towards Strengthening Multisectoral Linkages in SADC* (Braamfontein: Development Bank of Southern Africa).

McGowan, Patrick J., and Fred Ahwireng-Obeng (1998), 'Partner or Hegemon: South Africa in Africa: Part Two', *Journal of Contemporary African Studies* 16/2, 165–95.

Nye, Joseph (1990), *Bound to Lead* (New York: Basic Books).

Odén, Bertil (ed.), (1993), *Southern Africa After Apartheid*, Scandinavian Institute of African Studies Seminar Proceedings No. 28 (Uppsala: SIAS).

Ohmae, Kenneth (1990), *The Borderless World: Power and Strategy in the Interlinked Economy* (London: Fontana).

Ohmae, Kenneth (1995), *The End of the Nation-State* (London: HarperCollins).

Palan, R., and J. Abbott (1996), *State Strategies in the Global World Economy* (London: Pinter).

Panitch, Leo (1994), 'Globalisation and the State', *Socialist Register* (London: Merlin Press).

Panitch, Leo (1996), 'Rethinking the Role of the State', in James H. Mittelman (ed.), *Globalisation: Critical Reflections* (Boulder, CO: Westview).

Pierson, C. (1996), *The Modern State* (London: Routledge).

Reich, Robert (1992), *The Work of Nations* (New York: Simon & Schuster).

Rosenau, James, and Ernst Otto Czempiel (eds) (1992), *Governance Without Government* (Cambridge: Cambridge University Press).

Saasa, Oliver (1991), *Joining the Future: Economic Integration and Cooperation in African* (Nairobi: Africa Centre for Techology Studies).

Scholte, Jan Aarte (1997), 'Global Capitalism and the State', *International Affairs* 73/3.

Singh, A. (1994), 'Openness and Market-Friendly Approaches to Development', *World Development* 22/12.

Skocpol, Theda (1979), *States and Social Revolutions* (Cambridge: Cambridge University Press).

Sparks, D. (1998), 'Economic Trends in Sub-Saharan Africa', *Africa South of the Sahara* (London: Europa Publications).

Spero, Joan (1977) *The Politics of International Economic Relations* (New York: St Martin's Press).

Strange, Susan (1987), 'The Persistent Myth of Lost Hegemony', *International Organization* 41/4.

Strange, Susan (1988), *States and Markets: An Introduction to International Political Economy* (London: Pinter).

Strange, Susan (1995), 'Political Economy and International Relations', in Steve Smith and Ken Booth (eds), *International Relations Theory Today* (Cambridge: Polity Press).

Strange, Susan (1996), *The Retreat of the State* (Cambridge: Cambridge University Press).

Stubbs, Richard, and Geoffrey R. D. Underhill (eds) (1994), *Political Economy and the Changing Global Order* (London: Macmillan).

Szeftel, Morris (1998), 'Misunderstanding African Politics', *Review of African Political Economy* 76.

Thede, Nancy, and Pierre Beaudet (eds) (1993), *A Post-Apartheid Southern Africa* (London: Macmillan).

Tooze, Roger (1997), 'International Political Economy in an Age of Globalisation', in H. Baylis and S. Smith (eds), *The Globalisation of World Politics* (Oxford: Oxford University Press).

Tsie, Balefi (1996), 'States and Markets in the Southern African Development Community', *Journal of Southern African Studies* 22/1.

Venter, Minnie (ed.) (1994), *Prospects for Progress: Critical Choices for Southern Africa* (Cape Town: Maskew Miller Longman).

Viotti, Paul, and Mark Kauppi (1987), *International Relations Theory: Realism, Pluralism and Globalism* (New York: Macmillan).

Wade, Robert (1990), *Governing the Market* (Princeton, NJ: Princeton University Press).

Weeks, John (1996), 'Regional Cooperation and Southern African Development', *Journal of Southern African Studies* 22/1.

Weiss, L. (1997), 'The Myth of the Powerless State', *New Left Review* 225.

Wright, E. O. (1985) *Classes* (London: Verso).

7
Is a Free Trade Agreement the Answer for Southern Africa? Insights from Development Economic Theory

Merle Holden

Introduction

Since the Second World War, the economies of the world have gradually integrated through increased trade. Over the past 20 years world merchandise exports have risen from 11 to 18 per cent of world GDP. Service exports have risen even faster increasing from 15 per cent of world trade to 22 per cent. Of all the trading on stock markets one in seven sales involve foreigners. These statistics provide a snap shot picture of the degree to which economies around the world have integrated, or to use the catch phrase of the moment the degree of globalization that has occurred.

This trend in trade and capital market liberalization, combined with the information revolution, has meant more goods becoming traded with capital in search of profitable investment opportunities. In this economic environment multinational firms have played an ever increasing role in the economies of both developed and developing countries. Nevertheless, as recent events in Asia have shown, policy makers now face a different set of constraints as a consequence of globalization. Sound economic policies have been shown to be essential in order to maintain confidence in both domestic and international markets.

However, globalization is not evenly spread throughout the world. Of 93 developing countries, the trade ratios of 44 actually fell over the last two decades (World Bank, 1996). Where trade ratios rose in developing countries, ten countries – mostly in East Asia – contributed more than three quarters of this increase. African countries, including South

Africa, failed to experience a rise in their trade ratios. The same distributional picture emerges from an analysis of the flows of capital to be directly invested in developing countries.

Despite the increasing integration of markets worldwide, preferential trading agreements in the guise of free trade agreements have also proliferated. In reaction to these agreements the countries in Southern Africa are hoping to avoid further marginalization by adopting similar forms of integration (see also Hettne, Chapter 5 above). Theoretical guidance as to the desirability of preferential trade agreements has in the past focused on the static costs and benefits of trade creation and diversion, only paying passing attention to the benefits from dynamic economies of scale or the problems of spatial location. More recently theory has developed to take into account location investment decisions and the distribution effects of these agreements. In the light of this theory the recent move towards the establishment of a free trade area by the Southern African Development Community (SADC) is evaluated and the major forms of integration in the region are reviewed. The economic performance of the countries in the region and the rationale behind the establishment of a free trade area within SADC is examined. The chapter concludes with two observations. First, certain of the institutional arrangements in the region can be justified on economic grounds. Second, it is likely that the new free trade protocol within SADC will impose more costs than benefits and divert the attention of policy makers from the merits of pursuing unilateral trade liberalization.

Agglomeration effects and trade diversion

Development economics has travelled a varied road over the past 30 years. The theories of Rosenstein-Rodan and Hirschman initially held sway by emphasizing the importance of a 'Big Push' in industrial development that would raise a country from a low income equilibrium trap. These theories were also used to justify import substitution policies as a route to industrialization.

While development theorists emphasized strategic complementarities and the attendant problems of coordination, their particular views faded in the theoretical literature for want of the required modelling skills to develop these ideas. Krugman (1996) attributes the neglect of these theories to an inability to model economies of scale and the resulting imperfections in the markets. The neoclassical economists' bag of tricks at this time only contained the limited but tractable tools of constant returns to scale and perfect competition. Hence Lewis's dual-economy models were in vogue.

Another gap in neoclassical economics was filled by Krugman (1991) in his book *Economic Geography*, where space is formally introduced into economic models through the explicit modelling of economies of scale and market structures. He shows that in the absence of economies of scale, but in the presence of transport costs, the production of goods would be evenly spread across the country. What is observed in the real world is a highly uneven distribution of activity.

Economic geographers did try to come to terms with reality in a number of ways through the use of gravity, cumulative causation and land rent-use models. Unfortunately these models failed to capture the effects of external economies and market structure.

Krugman (1991) reintroduces geographical considerations into economics. He elegantly points to the role played in location decisions through a combination of economies of scale and transportation costs. He also demonstrates that sufficiently low, but not too low, costs of transportation,[1] sufficiently strong economies of scale and a large share of 'footloose' industries can account for the rise of conurbations of manufacturing activity. This concentration of manufacturing leads to development patterns with cores and peripheries of economic activity. Furthermore, regions that have a head start are able to attract industry away from those regions that have a less favourable set of initial conditions.[2]

In the event of greater economic integration, how likely is it that industry in the smaller countries will be pulled into the larger cores of their more powerful neighbours? Krugman argues that such agglomeration is not inevitable as it depends on the size of the larger core, the level of transport costs, economies of scale and the share of 'footloose' industries. Krugman shows that in the event of polarization it is the immobile factors of production in the periphery which suffer.

Krugman and Venables (1990) have also argued that as regions become more integrated the possibility of perverse location effects arises. The more dominant country has higher wages and production costs but proximity to a large market. Low wage countries are further away from the major market. However when transport costs are reduced, the high wage country may paradoxically attract production away from a lower wage country. This can occur they argue because a reduction of transport costs will first, promote the location of production where it is cheapest, and second, promote a further concentration of industry in order to enjoy the economies of scale.

Krugman and Venables provide a numerical example that demonstrates that when transport costs are high production takes place in both countries. When transport costs are low, production takes place in the low wage country. Whereas, when transport costs are at an intermediate level, access to markets and the benefits of economies of scale outweigh the reduction in transport costs. Production therefore shifts to the high wage centre. They therefore hypothesize that the relationship between transport costs and output in the low wage country is U-shaped. Unfortunately, knowledge as to where the U-shape inverts has not been empirically established.

Krugman draws the strands of his theories together in *Development, Geography and Economic Theory* (1996), where he theoretically examines the forces that would either lead to agglomeration or militate against it. An economy that is specialized in agriculture would not experience centrifugal forces towards agglomeration. Whereas he shows that when manufacturing forms a significant part of an economy where transport costs are low and economies of scale are high, the forces of agglomeration are stronger.

It can be concluded from this research that the level of integration is important if polarization effects are to be avoided. If barriers to trade in the form of tariffs, quantitative restrictions and transport costs are substantially reduced, peripheral countries where wages are lower should not lose industry to the centre. However, if economic integration only partially opens economies there is a real possibility of greater agglomeration in the more advanced larger economies.

In addition to agglomeration effects, the literature suggests that when a larger less efficient country joins a free trade area, trade is often diverted from the rest of the world to the new partner (Bhagwati and Panagariya, 1996). The smaller countries in the Southern African region fear that in addition to trade diversion they may also experience a form of deindustrialization, or polarization, as their industry is sucked into the core of the larger South African economy (Robson, 1987). The dynamic benefits arising from a more rapid diffusion of technology throughout the region from South Africa should not be underplayed. In addition, economic growth in the advanced centre may spill over into the peripheral areas through growth in their exports. Improved infrastructural links will also decrease transport costs that are known to be particularly high in Africa (Amjadi and Yeats, 1995a). Nevertheless, despite these favourable dynamic effects, the smaller countries fear that the unfavourable polarization effects and trade diversion may exceed the benefits arising from the dynamic external economies of having access to the larger market.

Bhagwati and Panagariya (1996) have highlighted the distributional effects of preferential trade agreements. Schiff (1995) also concluded that in theory it can be shown that a country will benefit in net terms from the redistributive effects if it enters into a free trade agreement with a partner with high trade barriers and with whom it has a large trade surplus. Conversely, a country loses in a free trade agreement if imports are large and the tariffs on these imports are high. Support for Schiff's contention follows later.

Ongoing research on regional integration at the World Bank (1997) suggests that it is not possible to predict the net impact on welfare for any particular regional agreement. Their initial findings suggest if a country's neighbours are more open and large, and if the country is closer to major world markets and more open itself, it will grow more rapidly. Furthermore, if trading blocs maintain lower external barriers, they are shown to impose lower costs by minimizing the chances of trade diversion. The research therefore indicates that smaller developing countries would be advised to unilaterally liberalise rather than integrate with each other.

Regional groupings in Southern Africa

There are four major economic groupings in the Southern African region. These are the Southern Africa Customs Union (SACU), the Common Monetary Area (CMA), the Southern African Development Community (SADC), and the Cross-Border Initiative (CBI). Table 7.1 shows the country membership of the various groupings.

The Southern African Customs Union was formed in 1910 between South Africa, Botswana, Lesotho and Swaziland. On reaching independence in the late 1960s, Botswana, Lesotho and Swaziland renegotiated the agreement for implementation in 1969. Until its independence in 1990, South Africa administered Namibia as part of the customs union. The formalization of Namibia's membership of the union resulted in a union between South Africa and the smaller four countries now known as the BLNS.

The common revenue pool is administered by the South African Reserve Bank. The revenue is allocated to members according to a formula that enhanced the revenue share going to the smaller countries by 42 per cent. The enhancement factor was designed to compensate the smaller members for the disadvantages of forming a customs union with South Africa. This included a loss of fiscal discretion, increased prices which arose from South African quantitative restrictions and

Table 7.1 Membership of regional groupings

Country	Southern African Customs Union (SACU)	Southern African Development Community (SADC)	Common Monetary Area (CMA)	Cross-Border Initiative (CBI)
Angola		✓		
Botswana	✓	✓		
Burundi				✓
Comoros				✓
DRCongo		✓		
Kenya				✓
Lesotho	✓	✓	✓	
Madagascar				✓
Malawi		✓		✓
Mauritius		✓		✓
Mozambique		✓		
Namibia	✓	✓	✓	✓
Rwanda				✓
Seychelles		✓	✓	✓
South Africa	✓	✓	✓	
Swaziland	✓	✓	✓	✓
Tanzania		✓		✓
Uganda				✓
Zambia		✓		✓
Zimbabwe		✓		✓

polarization of economic activity in South Africa (Lundahl and Petersson, 1991). Fluctuations in revenue for the smaller countries led to the introduction of a stabilization factor that constrained revenues to an average rate of 20 per cent of the duty – inclusive value of imports and excisable production.

Prior to 1974, a *de facto* monetary union existed between South Africa, Botswana, Lesotho and Swaziland. In 1974 the monetary union was formalized in an agreement that recognized the Rand Monetary Area (RMA) between South Africa, Lesotho and Swaziland. Upon Namibia's independence in 1991, the agreement was revised to incorporate Namibia into the Common Monetary Area (CMA). As part of the overall agreement compensation for the loss of seignorage is paid by South Africa. In order to preserve its macroeconomic independence, Botswana declined to join the union and established its own central bank and currency in 1976.

Regional cooperation in Southern Africa occurred in response to opposition to the political policies of South Africa (see Vale and

Du Pisani in this volume). The original members of the community were Angola, Botswana, Lesotho, Malawi, Mozambique, Swaziland, Tanzania, Zambia and Zimbabwe. On its independence in 1991, Namibia joined the community and became the tenth member of what was termed the Southern African Development Coordination Conference (SADCC). It was hoped that the formation of SADCC would reduce the dependence of the Frontline states on South Africa and promote regional cooperation in regional projects (Maasdorp and Whiteside, 1992; also, Du Pisani in this volume). At this stage of its inception SADCC was not concerned with matters relating to trade integration. Initially the organization concentrated on transportation and communications projects. Issues of food security, energy, industry and trade followed.

The political changes that occurred in South Africa in the early 1990s spurred the members of SADCC to reassess the role of the community. In August 1992, the promotion of trade integration topped the agenda of the Treaty governing the newly renamed Southern African Development Community (SADC). The community planned to integrate trade by reducing tariff and non-tariff barriers between members, coordinate external tariffs and promote the mobility of capital and labour in the region. The treaty did not contain any scheduled reductions of tariffs. In 1994 South Africa elected to join SADC. Mauritius joined the community in 1995 followed by the Seychelles and the Democratic Republic of Congo in 1997.[3]

Two key agreements were signed in 1995. It was agreed to share river basins for the diversion of water in times of drought and to form a regional pool to facilitate the buying and selling of hydroelectric power (for details, see Du Pisani in Chapter 9 below). Initially a free trade agreement did not materialize, as South Africa convinced other members that integration may divert trade to South Africa. This would not be in the interest of the other member states. Despite these fears, in 1997 SADC members agreed to a Trade Protocol that would establish a free trade area to be phased in over a period of eight years. The details of the protocol including phase-in, sensitive products and exclusions and possible sector specific rules of origin are presently under negotiation. However, only three members have ratified the protocol. Other members, including South Africa, will only ratify once the details have been negotiated.

The most recent of the regional initiatives is the Cross-Border Initiative (CBI). The objective of this initiative is the promotion of cross border trade and investment in Eastern Africa and Southern

Africa. The CBI was proposed at the Maastricht Conference on Africa in 1990 and is funded by the World Bank, IMF, European Union and the African Development Bank. The 14 participating countries are Burundi, Comoros, Kenya, Madagascar, Malawi, Mauritius, Namibia, Rwanda, Seychelles, Swaziland, Tanzania, Uganda, Zambia and Zimbabwe. As both Namibia and Swaziland are also members of SACU, this dual membership creates the potential for complicating the control of goods across national boundaries. At the present time South Africa has not indicated an interest in joining the grouping, and its membership in SACU effectively precludes Namibia and Swaziland from participating.

Despite reservations from some members, the Second Ministerial Meeting of the CBI in March 1995 proposed quite radical plans for trade reform. The plan is to eliminate tariffs on intra-regional trade and converge the external tariffs of the participating countries to a trade-weighted average of 15 per cent with a maximum of 25 per cent by 1998. Those countries that have undertaken extensive reforms, namely Uganda, and Zambia will have little difficulty with compliance. The remaining countries are particularly concerned about the revenue implications of such large cuts in tariffs and have consequently delayed implementation.

Economic characteristics of SADC members

Aside from having many common borders, SADC countries represent an extraordinarily diverse economic grouping with South Africa the dominant economic power in the region. In 1993 South African GDP was more than four times greater than the total of remaining SADC GDP, and is two and half times greater than the CBI total GDP. A similar picture emerges when GDP per capita comparisons are drawn. South African GNP per capita was twice the size of per capita GNP in the CBI and seven times greater than per capita GNP in SADC countries (Table 7.2).

However, Table 7.2 also shows that per capita income in Mauritius exceeds that in South Africa. Income per capita in Botswana has also risen rapidly over the years to overtake South Africa.

Convergence in SADC and SACU

Using several different definitions of convergence in per capita GDP, Jenkins and Thomas (1996) show that for the period from 1960 to 1990 there is no evidence of convergence between the members of

Table 7.2 Economic characteristics of SADC states

Country	Population 1993 (millions)	GDP 1993 (US$ millions)	GDP per capita 1993 (US$)	Inflation 1994	Merch Exports (1991 US$ millions)	Budget Defict percent of GDP 1990–94
Angola	10.3	7800	600	972	n/a	−1000
Botswana	1.4	3813.4	2790	8.2	1903	+6.6
Lesotho	1.9	758.6	650	8.3	67.2	−6.4
Malawi	10.5	1973.7	200	22.8	475.5	−8.2
Mauritius	1.1	3279.8	3030	7.3	1215.1	−0.5
Mozambique	15.1	1467.5	90	52.5	162.3	−26.2
Namibia	1.5	2507.6	1820	10.7	1251.9	−5.0
South Africa	39.7	117433	2980	9.0	23289.2	−4.9
Swaziland	0.9	1037.9	1190	14.3	596.6	−3.5
Tanzania	28	2373.2	90	34.1	362.2	−3.8
Zambia	8.9	3685.2	380	52.3	1172.2	−3.6
Zimbabwe	10.7	5635.2	520	22.2	1693.8	−7.5

Source: Imani Development, various reports.

SADC. In fact, one of the measures suggests that there may have been divergence. However, within SACU marked convergence was established. Botswana and Lesotho caught up with Namibia, South Africa and Swaziland. Jenkins and Thomas also show that in terms of macroeconomic indicators such as inflation, deficits and interest rates there has been a convergence of policy between Namibia, South Africa, Swaziland, Botswana, Lesotho and Mauritius (see Table 7.2).

Jenkins and Thomas hypothesize that the convergence of GDP per capita in SACU may be due to the similarity in domestic policies followed and their openness in trade to each other. Given that SACU is such a long-standing institution, it is more likely that the explanation should be sought in the economic decline resulting from the apartheid policies in South Africa and the high price that Botswana has received for its diamond exports.

Economic growth in Sub-Saharan Africa

Theories of endogenous growth are based on the observation that there appears to be little convergence in income levels worldwide. These theories stress the growth enhancing effect of spillovers through skills development and the externalities caused by agglomeration of firms. These effects were seen to free an economy from the productivity of capital diminishing at the margin.

At the same time that non-convergence was observed worldwide, convergence appeared to be occurring between groups of countries. These groups were termed 'convergence clubs' and have been attributed to the trade openness that these countries have displayed to other members of the club (Sachs and Warner, 1995). Growth regressions drawing on the theories of endogenous growth now abound. In all these studies, however, the poor performance of African countries cannot be entirely explained by the variables in the models. This is referred to as the 'African dummy' effect.

On the basis of macro and micro data, Collier and Gunning (1997) dissect the reasons for this poor performance. Sub-Saharan African countries are shown to have had high barriers to trade and the disadvantage of operating in a risky business environment. Social capital and infrastructure is low and the financial sector remains for the most part undeveloped, apart from South Africa. Collier and Gunning (1997) attribute the 'African dummy' effect to poor government and the behaviour of firms and rural households. They suggest that to the detriment of the majority, governments have been captured by narrow constituencies. In addition the high risk natural environment has encouraged rural households to protect themselves by moving into non-taxed activities such as subsistence agriculture. Manufacturing firms have been less successful in adapting to the environment. Their failure to promote and develop the necessary social capital has been a severe impediment to vigorous growth and development.

Collier and Gunning (1997) conclude that the 'African dummy' largely can be attributed to omitted variables. Although recent democratizations in African countries should improve government performance, the increased demand for skilled government employees has shown how thinly spread are the skills to govern effectively. Capacity building in government has assumed an urgency that was not felt before.

Trade integration in SADC

It is against this background of differential economic performance and economic structure that the preferential trade agreement in SADC has to be judged. Many of the regional schemes in Africa that have promoted import substitution and maximized intra-regional trade have been described as singular failures (Elbadawi, 1995; Fine and Yeo, 1994).

The SADC trade protocol is no exception for it embodies many of the elements that would also predict disaster. Members are set to maintain their present external tariff structures that in some cases have been shown to be high. The protocol accordingly promotes import substitution *vis-à-vis* the rest of the world while attempting to maximize intra-regional trade with the elimination of trade barriers between members.

The direction of trade matrix shows that the majority of intra-SADC trade occurs between SACU and the other members reflecting the attractiveness and size of this major market (Table 7.3). The average tariffs levied on imports from SADC members are shown in Table 7.4. These were calculated by dividing the tariff collections of SADC goods by the value of imports. Tariffs are shown to be highest in Zimbabwe, Mauritius and Mozambique.

Redistributive effects of the trade protocol

It is estimated that the reduction of tariffs between the members of SADC will reduce customs revenue accruing to each member. The average tariff rate was applied to imports for each member and the resulting

Table 7.3 SADC direction of trade matrix: Average 1991–93 (US$000)

Imp/exp	Angol	Mala	Maur	Moz	SACU	Tan	Zam	Zim	SADC
Angola	0	0	9	0	27398	0	0	3914	31321
Malawi	0	0	1309	0	61657	0	0	27819	90785
Mauritius	0	6	0	0	247470	982	0	8892	257350
Mozambique	0	0	1120	0	100635	0	0	26026	127781
SACU	114	16270	5302	6147	0	2163	7735	221926	259657
Tanzania	3124	0	157	0	6072	0	0	2228	11581
Zambia	0	0	647	0	136103	0	0	31519	168269
Zimbabwe	0	1813	4914	3328	643720	2927	8394	0	665096
SADC	3238	18089	13458	9475	1223055	6072	16129	322324	1611840

Source: Industrial Development Corporation Report on SADC; Imani Development Country Reports.

Table 7.4   SADC average tariffs (percentage)*

Country	1993	1994	1995
Angola	14 (1990)		
Malawi	23	16	14
Mozambique	22 (1992)		
Mauritius		28	
SACU		17	17
Tanzania	9	12	
Zambia	27		5
Zimbabwe	23	19	32

*Average tariff rates on imports from SADC countries.
Source: Industrial Development Corporation; Imani
Development Country Reports.

Table 7.5   Tariffs and revenue losses

Country	Tariff rate (%)	Imports (US$000)	Revenue loss (US$000)	Loss as percent GDP
Angola	14	31321	4384	0.06
Malawi	14	90785	12709	0.63
Mauritius	28	257350	72058	2.2
Mozambique	22	127781	28111	1.92
SACU	17	259657	44141	0.04
Tanzania	12	11581	1389	0.05
Zambia	5	168269	8413	0.3
Zimbabwe	32	665096	212830	3.82

losses were computed as a proportion of GDP in Table 7.5. The major losers are shown to be Mauritius (2.2 per cent of GDP), Zimbabwe (3.82 per cent) and Mozambique (1.92 per cent).

As exporters in SADC will now have preferential access into each other's markets they will be able to price up to the extent of the external tariff in each market and hence enjoy a windfall gain. The gains in revenue that would accrue to the exporters in each SADC member country are shown in Table 7.6. The average tariff was calculated by assuming that exporters faced an average of tariffs in SADC that excluded their own country tariff. The table shows that export producers located in Zimbabwe (0.96 per cent), SACU (0.18 per cent) and Malawi (0.16 per cent) are the primary beneficiaries of the discriminatory liberalization.

The net distributional gains are shown in Table 7.7. The only net gainer is shown to be SACU. Also note that SACU is the only member

Table 7.6 Average tariffs, exports and revenue gains to producers

Country	Average tariff on exports	Exports (US$000)	Revenue gain to producers (US$000)	Gain as percent GDP
Angola	18.57	3238	601	0.01
Malawi	18.57	18089	3359	0.16
Mauritius	16.57	13458	2230	0.07
Mozambique	17.43	9475	1651	0.11
SACU	18.14	1223055	221897	0.18
Tanzania	18.86	6072	1145	0.04
Zambia	19.86	16129	3202	0.10
Zimbabwe	16.71	322324	53874	0.96

Table 7.7 Net gains accruing to SADC members and SADC balance of trade

Country	Net gain (US$000)	Balance of trade (US$000)
Angola	−3783	−28083
Malawi	−9350	−72696
Mauritius	−69827	−243892
Mozambique	−26460	−118306
SACU	177755	963398
Tanzania	−244	−5509
Zambia	−5211	−152140
Zimbabwe	−158956	−342772

that enjoys a positive balance of trade with the other SADC members, and has relatively high tariffs on imports from the majority of SADC members.

These redistributive effects could be alleviated by means of a compensating formula. For example the SACU agreement allows Botswana, Lesotho, Swaziland and Namibia to include imports from all sources in the formula base. The inclusion of South African imports takes into account the revenue diverting effect to South Africa from the smaller partners. The enhancement factor of 42 per cent is used to compensate the smaller members for the price raising effects of tariffs on consumers and the effects on the economy of what has been termed 'polarization'. South Africa's share of the common revenue pool is the residual. Nevertheless, the SACU agreement is being renegotiated as all members of SACU have expressed varying levels of dissatisfaction with their receipts under the formula. South Africa has indicated an unwillingness to conclude a similar agreement with the members of SADC.

In an attempt to ascertain whether the reduction of tariff barriers between the members of SADC is likely to stimulate trade between them a gravity model of trade was estimated. Gravity models typically propose that countries are likely to trade in greater volume with each other if they are closer together and if markets are large in terms of gross domestic product. These models have also found that size of population lowers the volume of trade. The distance between countries has also been found to lower the volume of trade.

In order to estimate the likely effect that a reduction in tariff barriers would have on the volume of intra-SADC trade the following model is proposed:

$$\ln T_{ij} = \beta_0 + \beta_1 \ln GDP_{ij} + \beta_2 \ln POP_{ij} + \beta_3 \ln DIST_{ij} + \beta_4 \ln TAR_{ij} + \mu_{ij}$$

where the dependent variables T are the exports of the ith SADC country to the jth SADC country's market expressed in US dollars. The gross domestic product of each country is represented by GDP expressed in US dollars. The population of each country is represented by POP. The distance from each capital city is measured in kilometres by the variable DIST. The level of tariff barriers is measured in per cent by the variable TAR.

The equation was estimated in logarithmic form. Since exports for a number of the SADC countries were nonexistent, ordinary least squares estimates are biased towards zero and inconsistent (Greene, 1981). Therefore, Tobit maximum likelihood estimation was used. The estimating equation was run for 56 observations on the SADC trade matrix for 1993. The t-statistics are shown in parentheses (See Table 7.8).

The results show the importance of the size of market within the SADC region in stimulating trade. The level of gross domestic product is a major determinant of the flow of goods within the SADC region. The size of population on the other hand failed to influence the

Table 7.8 Regression results for the gravity model

Dependent	Constant	GDP	POP	DIST	TAR
Exports T	12.2	1.66*	−0.5	−2.71**	−0.68
		(1.997)	(−0.42)	(−1.68)	(−0.39)

* significant at the 1 per cent level.
** significant at the 5 per cent level.

volume of trade. The distance between the capitals of SADC was found to impact negatively on trade flows. However, bearing in mind that many countries were contiguous to each other it is not surprising that the variable was found to be at a lower level of significance. Significantly, it was found that differential levels of tariff barriers had not impeded the flow of goods between SADC members. This raises the issue of the role played by non-tariff barriers between members of SADC in impeding trade and explains why many countries prior to the conclusion of the agreement raised tariffs.

It is therefore tempting to conclude that the formation of a preferential trading agreement is unlikely to stimulate trade between the members of SADC. If trade is stimulated between members it is more likely to be between SACU and the rest of SADC as trade is diverted from the rest of the world to SACU.

Conclusions

The deepest form of integration in Southern Africa has occurred in the tip of the continent. The Southern African Customs Union and the Common Monetary Area are the longest standing arrangements in the region and, despite the diversion of trade to South Africa, the SACU agreement is being renegotiated in the light of extreme interdependence of the members.

Agglomeration effects and the level of integration have been shown theoretically to be important determinants of locational decisions. The interplay of economies of scale, distance to the market and barriers to trade is critical. Peripheral countries further away from the core South African market should not lose industry to the centre if wage differentials are sufficiently large. It is more likely that as transport links are further developed in the region that industrial production will locate to take advantage of each country's comparative advantage as determined by relative factor endowments. The extent of polarization within the Southern African region and its likelihood when SADC countries adopt the free trade protocol is therefore uncertain.

When trade barriers were high worldwide, a large economy was much desired. The benefits of economies of scale through long production runs made the United States and the melding of the European Community economic powerhouses. Now that markets are more open and technology has reduced transport costs and eased communication a small market is no longer a liability. Alesina and Wacziarg (1997) show that population explains a third of a country's trade relative to

GDP. Small countries typically involve themselves heavily in trade in order to specialize.

In the face of such evidence, the members of SADC, which can all be characterized as small economies, have chosen to pursue a discriminatory trade agreement. The proposed SADC free trade agreement is no exception to previous integration efforts in the region. The protocol fails to allow for the adoption of a lower common external tariff and seeks to establish a preferential trade area at the expense of committed most favoured nation trade liberalization. The SADC proposal is also fraught with the difficulty of integrating a more dominant economy with smaller more vulnerable economies. Not only is it likely that trade will be diverted to South Africa's larger manufacturing base, but revenues redistributed from the poorer weaker countries in the direction of South Africa.

To conclude, the existing trading blocs in Southern Africa ought to be encouraged to harmonize and lower external barriers in order to minimize the chances of trade diversion. The CBI proposals should set a good example for the rest of the region, for if the SADC trade protocol were to follow the CBI, the worst effects of integrating with their stronger southern neighbour will be reduced. In an ideal world, the pursuit of integration in the broader Southern African region should have been limited to cooperative ventures such as uniform customs documents, harmonized trade procedures and cooperation between transport units while pursuing phased unilateral trade liberalization.

Notes

1. Transport costs can also be interpreted in the broader sense to include all barriers to trade.
2. Many centres of manufacturing started as accidents of history. For example, the discovery of gold on the Witwatersrand spearheaded the concentration of manufacturing industry in the Gauteng region of South Africa. Economies of scale in servicing a larger internal market and the fall in transport costs, as the infrastructure developed, provided an additional impetus to this concentration.
3. In the analysis which follows, data for these countries have not been included.

References

Alesina, A., and R. Wacziarg (1997), 'Economic Integration and Political Disintegration', *NBER Working Paper* (Boston, MA: National Bureau for Economic Research).

Amjadi, A., and A. Yeats (1995a), 'Have Transport Costs Contributed to the Relative Decline of African Exports? Some Preliminary Evidence', *International Trade Division* (Washington, DC: The World Bank).

Amjadi, A., and A. Yeats (1995b), 'Nontariff Barriers Facing Africa: What did the Uruguay Round accomplish and what remains to be done?', *International Trade Division* (Washington, DC: The World Bank).

Beaumont, T. (ed.) (1995), *Trade and Investment: Southern Africa '95* (Johannesburg: Sterling Publications).

Bhagwati, J., and A. Panagariya (1996), *The Economics of Preferential Trade Agreements* (Washington, DC: AEI Press).

Collier, P., and J. W. Gunning (1997), 'Explaining African Economic Performance', paper presented at the *Biennial Conference of the South African Economic Society* (Potchefstroom).

Elbadawi, I. A. (1995), *The Impact of Regional Trade/Monetary Schemes on Intra-Sub Saharan African Trade*, AERC Research Workshop (Harare).

Fine, J., and S. Yeo (1994), 'Regional Integration in Sub-Saharan Africa: Dead End or a Fresh Start?', paper prepared for the *AERC Project Regional Integration and Trade Liberalization in SSA* (Nairobi).

Greene, W. H. (1981), 'On the Asymptotic Bias of the Ordinary Least Squares Estimator of the Tobit Model', *Econometrica* 49/2.

Krugman, P. (1991), *Geography and Trade* (Cambridge, MA: MIT Press).

Krugman, P. (1996), *Development, Geography and Economic Theory* (Cambridge, MA: MIT Press).

Krugman, P., and A. Venables (1990), 'Integration and the Competitiveness of Peripheral Industry', in C. Bliss and J. Braga de Macedo (eds), *Unity with Diversity in the European Community* (Cambridge: Cambridge University Press).

Lundahl, M., and L. Petersson (1991), *The Dependent Economy: Lesotho and the Southern African Customs Union* (Boulder, CO: Westview Press).

Maasdorp, G., and A. Whiteside (1992), 'Rethinking Economic Cooperation in Southern Africa: Trade and Investment', *Occasional Papers*, Konrad Adenauer Stiftung (Johannesburg).

Robson, P. (1987), *The Economics of International Integration*, 3rd end (London: George Allen and Unwin).

Sachs, J., and A. Warner (1995), 'Economic Reform and the Process of Global Integration', *Brookings Papers on Economic Activity* (Washington, DC).

Schiff, M. (1995), 'Small is Beautiful: Preferential Trade Agreements and the Impact of Market Size, Market Share, Efficiency, and Trade Policy', *International Economics Division* (Washington, DC: World Bank).

World Bank (1997), *International Trade Division Research Summary* (Washington, DC: World Bank).

8
South African Benevolent Hegemony in Southern Africa: Impasse or Highway?[1]
Bertil Odén

Introduction

Why is it so difficult to find someone who believes in a benevolent South African regional hegemony emerging in Southern Africa? South Africa's superior production, technology and institutional capacity, compared with that of the rest of the region is well documented. Would it not create sufficient capabilities for the South African state to establish a hegemonic regime in the region?

And why should that hegemony not be benevolent? There are numerous policy statements by the South African government to the effect that its intention is not to dominate or use its strength towards its neighbours in an exploitative way but in a cooperative spirit to work for the benefit of the whole region. Would the smaller states in the region not gain if South Africa provided regional public goods, which they can use? In many policy documents from the Southern African Development Community, SADC, in which South Africa became a member in 1994, it is emphasized that South Africa is regarded as an equal participant.[2] With the much stronger capabilities it can be argued that in practice the South African influence will be stronger, and in particular that the capacity of regional institutions and regulatory frameworks will be highly dependent on South African support.

The reasons for the scepticism towards a benevolent hegemonic regime in Southern Africa are of different kinds. One is that people's definition of the hegemony concept differs widely, which they implicitly include in their judgements. With Snidal (1985b: p. 614) it can also be argued that 'the common presumption of recent analyses that hegemony is widely beneficial rests on such special assumptions that it should be rejected'. Still, the theory is so widely referred to and used in international relations, albeit mainly for analysis at the global level, that it should not be excluded in the context of this book.[3]

Also those accepting the relevance of the model *per se*, may argue that the assumptions on which the theory is based are not in place in Southern Africa. A general objection could also be that the hegemony concept is only relevant at the global level, as any regional hegemon which is not simultaneously also a hegemon at the global level will not be allowed to play a hegemonic role at the regional level. Or expressed differently: Global forces do not allow South Africa to function as a hegemon at the regional level in Southern Africa.

This chapter is organized around five of the objections I have met, when arguing for a hegemonic regime in Southern Africa. Two of these are linked to theoretical issues and three to the perception of capabilities in South Africa and the other countries in the region:

1. The hegemony theory model is not consistent with South African official policy, which strongly supports a cooperative regionalization in the region.
2. Hegemony theory is only applicable at the global level. The influence of global forces makes it impossible to create regional hegemony in Southern Africa.
3. South Africa's dominance is not strong enough to shape a hegemonic regime and provide public goods in the region.
4. While the South African economic and institutional strength may be sufficient, domestic political support is too weak for the South African state to pursue a hegemonic policy in the region.
5. A sceptical or negative attitude in the other countries in the region provides obstacles to establish South African hegemony in the region. Such hegemony is also contrary to the SADC policy of cooperative regionalization. The capacity for regionalization in most of the other countries and in SADC is weak.

These objections are partly overlapping and they are not consistently deduced from one specific theory of hegemony, but emerge out of differing perceptions and interpretations of the hegemony concept. Still they represent a critique which might be used as the point of departure to discuss the problematique of a benevolent South African hegemony in the Southern African region. For an investigation of these issues, the various hegemony concepts have to be analytically situated and a definition suggested for the purposes of this chapter. This is done in the following section.

What hegemony concept?

'Hegemony' is used in various IR schools of thought. The main ones are that of hegemonic stability emerging out of the realist and then neo-realist school and alternative approaches growing out of that school on the one hand and the hegemony concept used within critical theory on the other.

Within critical theory the hegemonic concept is different from that of hegemonic stability. The most influential theoretical discussion of this concept is that of Robert Cox (see for instance Cox, 1983), who in turn is firmly based on Gramsci (1971). To Cox (1983: p. 171), hegemony at the international level is not merely an order among states. 'It is also a complex of international social relationships which connect the social classes of the different countries. World hegemony can be described as a social structure, an economic structure and a political structure, and it cannot be simply one of these things but must be all three' (for details, see Leysens and Niemann in this volume).

The theory of hegemonic stability developed as part of the realism school, often used in a military-influenced perspective. The theory is based on two central assumptions: first, that order in world politics is typically created by a single dominant power; second, that the maintenance of order requires continued hegemony (Keohane, 1980). Thus, hegemonic stability theory presumes a close relationship between the relative strength of the hegemonic state and the stability of the regime in question. Fragmentation of hegemonic power is anticipated to result in regime disintegration, whereas concentration of hegemonic power is supposed to lead to regime strengthening.[4] As in realist thinking generally, this original strand of hegemonic stability theory is strongly state-centred and the states are assumed to be rational unitary actors in a strong systemic framework. The hegemonic regime is assumed to be in the long run interest of the system and therefore not only to the hegemon, but also to the other states.

The most influential alternative approach can be labelled institutionalist or neo-liberal. The most influential scholar introducing this approach is Keohane (1984). The main difference between the neo-realist and this alternate model is that in the former, hegemony is a necessary prerequisite for the emergence and maintenance of order and cooperation in world affairs, while in the latter, it is assumed that a leader may initiate and facilitate cooperation among states, but hegemony is neither a necessary nor a sufficient condition for the emergence or maintenance of cooperative relationships among actors in the world political economy.[5]

In both strands of the theory the concept of public or collective good, introduced by Kindleberger (1973), is important. The hegemon is supposed to provide the system with one or several public or collective goods, which must meet the standard criteria of non-rivalness and non-exclusiveness.[6] The subordinate states can obviously take advantage of this situation, and thus benefit from the hegemonic regime (the 'free rider' issue). For Kindleberger one main public good was the free trade system and the hegemon's role of guaranteeing such a system has been implicit in much of the hegemonic theory.

This view of Kindleberger and Keohane was challenged by, for instance, Krasner and particularly Gilpin (1975), who argued that the hegemon provides a free trade regime to its own advantage but not necessarily to all participants. In subsequent contributions Gilpin argued that international order is a public good, benefiting subordinate states and that the dominant power is not only the provider of public good, it is also capable of extracting contributions toward the good from subordinate states, which thus no longer are free riders (see, for example, Gilpin, 1981). The hegemonic power thus is effective in coercing other states. This distinction between coercive and benevolent leadership or hegemony is of significant analytical interest.

According to Grunberg (1990), mainstream hegemonic theory implicitly assumed benevolence on the hegemon's part. This issue was not problematized until Gilpin's contribution to the discussion in the early 1980s. As Snidal (1985b: p. 612) puts it, the theory has appealing normative implications for a great power: 'The appeal of the hegemonic stability theory is that it points out how dominance may be reflected in leadership rather than exploitation'. Leadership here is used to cover a benevolent behaviour.

One important contribution to the debate by Snidal (1985 a,b) is the distinction between benevolent and coercive leadership models within the hegemonic regime. He argues that in a benevolent leadership model a greater absolute size of the largest actor means it has greater interest in providing the good. The dynamic corollary is that the maintenance or growth of the largest actor is the key factor in regime stability. In the coercive model the relative size is most important (Snidal, 1985b: pp. 588–9). The key is the ability to force subordinate states to make contributions and this ability rests primarily on the relative power of states. The distinction between absolute and relative size and the implicit link between size and power is however not clear in Snidal's argument.

Snidal argues that in both benevolent and coercive models effective hegemonic leadership requires an interest in providing the public good as well as the capability to do so. The benevolent model focuses primarily on interest, implying that capability follows: because a hegemonic state has a dominant interest in a cooperative outcome it also has the capacity to ensure its emergence. In contrast, the coercive model focuses on capability, implying that interest in providing the public good follows from the distribution of capabilities.

What constitutes, then, 'benevolent hegemony'? As there are various strands and sub-strands, there is no established opinion on this. Snidal focuses on the provision of a public good in a way which leaves the hegemon with all or at least the main costs. This is easier with a greater absolute size on the side of the hegemon. In such a case all participants are more likely to be privileged. The dynamic corollary to this is that growth of the larger actor is most important to the regime stability. Another issue is the type of sanctions the benevolent hegemon typically will use.

Snidal (1985a) argues that a benevolent hegemon will typically rely on positive sanctions (rewards), whereas an exploitative hegemon will mainly resort to negative sanctions (threats) in order to create and maintain the regime. Hirsch and Doyle (1977: p. 27) have accurately characterized hegemonic leadership as involving 'a mix of cooperation and control'. It is clear that a benign leader in general will be cooperative, while an exploitative hegemon primarily will rely on control. Therefore, in a benevolent hegemonic regime the level of cooperation, mutual adjustment, and positive sanctions will be high, while the level of enforcement, negative sanctions and control will be low.

Setting aside situations where hegemonic states operate purely as exploiters of weaker states, hegemonic stability theory thus contains two differing perceptions of the role of hegemons in the international system. Both perceptions involve the provision of collective goods, although they differ in the form and degree of centralization that this provision will entail. Both predict 'cooperative' outcomes that make states better off than they would be without the hegemonic power, but they have significantly different distributive implications. The two models are not logically incompatible. A hegemonic state can be both benevolent and coercive.

In a more recent contribution, Lake (1993) argues that what often is called the theory of hegemonic stability is not a single theory, but two analytically distinct theories. One is leadership theory based upon the theory of public goods and focusing on the production of international stability, which can be redefined as the international economic infrastructure. The other is hegemony theory, which seeks to explain patterns of international economic openness, defined as the sum of free trade and protectionist elements in the foreign economic policies of, at least, the largest states within the system.

Lake uses the distinction between benevolence and coerciveness in both theories. In leadership theory the debate is lively on whether the leader acts benevolently or coercively. When benevolent, the leader provides the international economic infrastructure unilaterally or at least bears a disproportionate cost of providing the public good and thereby gains relatively less than others. When coercive, the leader forces smaller states to contribute to the international economic infrastructure and, at the extreme, to bear the entire cost. According to Lake, 'the answer to the question of whether leadership is benevolent or coercive lies not in the distribution of benefits from the public good, but – at least in part – in the efficacy of international leverage'.

The concept of benevolent hegemony used in this chapter is influenced by Snidal, although with some modifications. The benevolent hegemon thus must provide a collective or public good, characterized by jointness, while its exclusiveness can be restricted, as normally is the case in the real world. Hegemony is assumed to be beneficial to the system and to all states included in that system. A benevolent hegemon might convince or coerce the others to contribute to the provision of the common good, but the main responsibility falls on the hegemon. A hegemonic state can be and often is both benevolent and coercive. The level of benevolence depends on the share of total costs for the public goods taken on by the hegemon. Moreover, if positive sanctions are used rather than negative, subordinate states are more likely to voluntarily accept this hegemony.

Basically the analytical perspective is that of the neo-liberal institutionalism hegemonic stability theory strand, with its stronger emphasis on variables at the unit-level as compared with a more strictly neorealist strand. It can be argued, however, that the two strands within hegemonic stability theory during recent years have converged into something which can be compared with the 'neo-neo synthesis' between neo-realism and neo-liberal institutionalism within the broader discipline of international relations.

Definitions

The concept of *region*[7] is defined as a subset of nation-states locked into the same geographical context (Buzan, 1991). The region *Southern Africa* is defined as the 12 countries, forming SADC in 1995[8]: Angola,

Botswana, Lesotho, Malawi, Mauritius, Mozambique, Namibia, South Africa, Swaziland, Tanzania, Zambia and Zimbabwe (compare with Niemann's definition in Chapter 4 above).

The concept of *regionalization* refers to the strategies aiming at economic and social development and the creation and distribution of wealth within the region (organization), while the visions, values and objectives that supervise these strategies will be referred to as *regionalism*.[9] Regionalism thus represents the phenomena and regionalization the strategy used to create a regional system in Southern Africa.

There is a strong difference between the definition of the regionalization concept between various scholars. While Hurrell (1995: p. 39) equals it to 'informal integration' or 'soft regionalism', arguing that the most important driving force comes from the market, Haarlöv (1997) argues that it covers policy driven regional cooperation and regional economic (trade) integration. For Hurrell (1995: p. 40) 'regionalization is not based on the conscious policy of states or groups of states', and regional economic integration is a sub-category of regional cooperation. In this context my definition of regionalization is closer to Haarlöv (1997), with state policy as one important ingredient and covering both regional cooperation and regional economic integration, which then are sub-categories of regionalization.

Following Du Pisani in Chapter 9 of this volume, *international regime* is here defined as the principles, norms, rules and decision-making procedures of international behaviour (Krasner, 1983). In a *hegemonic regime* these principles are established and maintained by a dominant power, which through positive (rewards) or negative (threats) sanctions ensures adherence to this set of guidelines and constraints. The regime is accepted by all taking part.

The literature on hegemony is vast and provides several suggestions as to how the concept of *benevolent hegemon* should be defined. Mine is close to Snidal (1985a,b). I thus refer to a dominant actor, which acts in the long-run interest of a regime as a whole and guarantees the provision of collective goods, in a manner useful to all countries within the regime. The level of enforcement from the benevolent hegemon will usually be low although a benevolent hegemon must sanction free-riders and possibly also may convince the weaker partners to pay part of the costs for the collective goods. In doing so it normally relies on positive rather than negative sanctions.

Interdependence can most simply be defined along the lines of Keohane's and Nye's original as 'mutual dependence. Interdependence in world politics refers on situations characterized by reciprocal effects among countries or among actors in different countries' (Keohane and Nye, 1977: p. 8).

The concept of *commitment* and how to measure it is complex and many scholars avoid it, instead discussing the actual outcome of processes. The BBC English dictionary distinguishes between three meanings of the word commitment. One of them is: 'If you give a commitment to something, you promise faithfully that you will do it; a formal use'. This is close to my use of the concept, which means that 'commitment' is one level firmer than the more generally expressed 'political will' and one level less firm than 'actual behaviour'.

On the relation between *power* and *hegemony*, Russett (1985: p. 209) has pointed out 'part of the difficulty stems from a lack of agreement about how much power is necessary to produce "hegemony" ... There is always room for argument about whether a given degree of superiority is enough to produce particular (and also rarely well-specified) results'. This problem, as far as I have been able to find out, is not solved in the literature and has to be assessed on a case by case basis. After these analytical and conceptional preludes, let us move to the five objections articulated in the introduction.

Objection 1: the theory is not consistent with official South African policy

Official South African policy on Southern Africa is firmly committed to cooperative regionalization. The hegemony model is not mentioned in official documents and many policy statements strongly suggest that South Africa should not use its relative strength to dominate its neighbours. One example can be taken from the government's RDP White Paper (1994: p. 10):

A central proposal of the RDP is that we cannot build the South African economy in isolation from its Southern African neighbours. Such a path would benefit nobody in the long run. If South Africa attempted to dominate its neighbours, it would restrict their growth, reducing their potential as markets, worsening their unemployment and causing increased migration to South Africa.

Another can be taken from an often quoted 1993 article in *Foreign Affairs* by Nelson Mandela:

Southern Africa will, however, only prosper if the principles of equity, mutual benefit and peaceful cooperation are the tenets that inform its future. Reconstruction cannot be imposed on the region by outside forces or unilaterally by ourselves as the region's most powerful state. It must be the collective enterprise of Southern Africa's people. Democratic South Africa will, therefore, resist any pressure or temptation to pursue its own interests at the expense of the subcontinent.

One way of handling the discussion on this issue would be to stop here and conclude that South African policy and benevolent hegemony are not consistent. This, however, would be an oversimplification. The influence of a dominant actor in formally cooperative regionalization schemes and institutions is inevitably stronger, which makes it possible to problematize the issue a bit further.

The importance of avoiding South African dominance is more strongly emphasized in the documents published up to 1994, than in those published thereafter. To what extent this can be interpreted as a change of South African policy is unclear. The change after 1994 can also be explained by the fact that the new South African government since its establishment in 1994 has been involved in negotiations with its neighbours on a renewed Southern African Customs Union (SACU) agreement, various SADC protocols and bilateral preference trade agreements and that negotiation positions of the South African Government might be weakened by general statements.

If the trend since 1994 has any significance, it indicates a less firm cooperative position, and perhaps a more open attitude to hegemonic behaviour. The perception in neighbouring states, that the South African state in negotiations with its neighbours is very restrictive when it comes to providing any 'extra' resources or 'common goods', would support such an interpretation, according to which the level of benevolence in such behaviour is uncertain. What actually counts, however, is the actual outcome of negotiations and it is therefore too early to draw conclusions.

The cooperative regionalization policy is still in force, and the most interesting point to discuss is if South Africa in the case of Southern Africa may provide benevolent leadership on regional issues which formally falls within 'cooperative regionalization', but *de facto* is closer to an attempt to provide regional public goods, taking at least part of the resource burden and responsibility. Empirical material may here be taken from South African effort on SADC's sector protocols. Here it can be noted that South Africa accepted the responsibility for the finance and investment sector and immediately established a Finance and

Investment Coordination Unit (FISCU), responsible for ambitious efforts to develop a sector protocol. Human and other resources allocated to the unit have been modest, but certain progress has been made. South Africa has also put significant efforts into the work to finalize the trade protocol, which was signed in 1996 with figures on tariffs, time schedules, lists of sensitive products, etcetera. Also in the field of the water and energy protocols, South African activity is reported.

Formally, any SADC sector protocol or other document falls within cooperative regionalization. South African capability to prepare such documents, implement their recommendations and provide resources to regional institutions is superior to the other countries (see below). The relevant question in this context is if South Africa is prepared to carry the *de facto* 'burden of the hegemon' in order to provide necessary regional institutions, norms and regulations. As Russett (1985: p. 213) has pointed out, 'we must identify hegemony at least with success in determining and maintaining essential rules, not merely with power base or resource share. Hegemony is a condition, as Keohane and Nye recognize, in which "one state is powerful enough to maintain the essential rules governing interstate relations, and willing to do so"'. In principle this is possible to do also in an institutionally cooperative framework, such as that of SADC as well as outside the SADC structures.

At a policy level this issue, formulated as a benevolent hegemony issue, has as far as I know, not been discussed, neither in South Africa, nor in the other SADC countries. It can be assumed that one reason for this is that the concept of hegemony for many has a strong negative connotation, although the benevolent hegemony adhered to in this context, rather should have positive ones.

Objection 2: global forces do not permit South African hegemony in the region

In general, 'hegemonic stability' is linked to global level analysis. In contrast, it is seldomly used at regional level. To the extent that this is done in the literature, the concept of regional hegemony has been used mainly to characterize a superpower or a giant state situated outside the region itself, which has tried to establish or create the type of regional security complex best suited to its own national security interests.[10] However, in this context, it is used with respect to a state located within a particular regional sub-sytem. This type of regional hegemony has in the literature also for the most part been applied to security complexes.[11]

Does this mean that the concept is suitable to Southern Africa? Some would answer not at all, arguing that the influence of global forces, including the international regimes for trade, capital flows, investments, together with the strength of transnational market actors, as well as civil society networks, place overwhelming constraints upon any aspiring regional hegemon.

According to this argument, the role of such a hegemon would at most be limited to implementation of the regional interests of either the global hegemon or in accordance with various global forces. This role was labelled 'sub-imperialist' in the context of neo-Marxist analysis, and 'semi-periphery' in world systems analysis. The main point is that the global context reduces the scope for a strong regional state to such an extent that the concept of a regional 'hegemon' becomes meaningless.

I argue that this is not necessarily so. The room for manoeuvre of a regional hegemon depends on how important dominating global forces perceive the region to be both strategically and economically. In the case of Southern Africa the following factors should be considered when assessing the scope for a hegemonic role for South Africa.

The marginalization of Southern Africa as well as the rest of Sub-Saharan Africa, in the world economy over the last decades has increased the scope for regionally induced initiatives (see Hettne in Chapter 5 above). To this long term trend may be added the fact that the Cold War strategic importance of Southern Africa evaporated with the collapse of the Soviet Union. One implication of this is a lower external interest in how the region organizes its cooperation and integration.

In the very recent years the gradual marginalization trend has reversed as a renewed interest in Africa has emerged in the North, based on, *inter alia*, democratization in South Africa, new concepts launched such as 'the African renaissance' and 'the second liberation', a new generation of African political leaders and on continued trade and capital liberalization in most African countries. For the first time in twenty years, international mineral companies are interested to explore the continent.[12] Privatization of state owned companies and introduction of stock markets, however tiny, attract foreign interests. US and European trust funds do not totally avoid Africa in their search for 'emerging markets'. In international media, Africa has become not only a suffering, starving and war-ridden continent but also an object for analysis on the financial pages, despite the modest changes on the ground.

It can thus be argued that since the fall of apartheid, external interest in Southern Africa has increased, albeit modestly. As this interest is not strategic it does not take the forms it took during the Cold War, and therefore it does not put any strong external constraints on regional development, as long as it does not contradict international dogmas regarding trade liberalization (for a counter argument, see Tsie in Chapter 6 of this volume).

After the debacles in Somalia and Rwanda, the US and Europe are reluctant to become directly involved in wars and ecological disasters in Africa. This increases the scope for Africa to handle its own emergencies and security problems. African actions without external involvement can even count on external financial support for such activities. In Washington and some European capitals particular hope is linked to South Africa in this context. The United States has for instance put strong efforts into convincing South African leadership that South Africa should participate actively in the Washington-initiated African Crisis Response Force.

Some of the SADC countries are strongly dependent on aid. With or without formal structural adjustment programmes all are forced to follow IMF and World Bank macroeconomic and trade liberalization doctrines. The international aid environment has changed, with stronger political and human rights conditionalities, at the same time as structural adjustment programmes (SAPs) implicitly are taken for granted. New generations of SAPs were developed with increased consideration to social and distribution effects. The sometimes disrupting regional effects of national SAPs have also been noted and in recent ones some consideration is said to be taken to envisaged regional effects. Still the effects of uncoordinated SAPs, together with that of the global strategies of external transnational mineral companies, are main fragmenting factors in the region.

The Bretton Woods institutions have finally realized that significantly improved debt relief is a necessary prerequisite for development in some of the poorest and most debt-stricken countries. Action to implement this understanding within the HIPC[13] scheme has however been extremely slow and some major World Bank members, such as Germany and Japan, oppose entirely the principle of writing off any part of foreign debt.

With the ongoing implementation of the Uruguay Round and the WTO global trade regime, trade liberalization has become the hegemonic principle. This process can have both fragmenting and regionalizing effects in Southern Africa. Transnationalization of production and globalization of finance both fragment the regional economy and support those who argue for further regionalization (see Holden's argument in Chapter 7). The result of the post-Lomé EU-ACP negotiations will not be known for a few years and not fully implemented before 2015. They might create obstacles for regional integration, if they treat various categories of countries differently and if they are not prepared to accept South African inputs as part of cumulation under the Lomé agreement.

The conclusion from the discussion above is that despite some fragmenting factors, both political and economic forces at the global level on the whole widen the room for manoeuvre of, and in some domains even support, further regional integration and cooperation in Southern Africa, as long as these processes are consistent with global trade liberalization and market economy thinking. Whether a regional regime is hegemonic, with South Africa as the hegemon, or if it takes other forms are factors irrelevant to global forces. It can even be argued that South African hegemony is conducive to the continued trade liberalization that is on the World Trade Organization's (WTO's) agenda.

Objection 3: South African capability is insufficient

There are two variants of this argument. The first is that while South Africa is clearly the dominant actor in the region, it is still not strong enough to play the role of regional hegemon. Russett's (1985: p. 209) point on the lack of agreement about how much power is necessary to produce 'hegemony' is of relevance here. There is always room for argument about whether a given degree of superiority is enough to produce particular (and also rarely well-specified) results. In the wake of established criteria I will in this section provide a brief qualitative analysis, covering some of the major sectors in the region. Before doing so it should be noted that Hurrell suggests that declining power, especially *vis-à-vis* other regional actors, may press the hegemon towards the creation of common institutions in pursuit of its interests, to share burdens, to solve common problems, and to generate international support and legitimacy for its policies. The combination of still marked superiority but declining overall levels of power may be particularly conducive to the creation of regionalism, still with the hegemon strong enough to provide some sort of leadership. Such a development might create more support for benevolence among various interest groups in the hegemonic state. It might even develop into support for a more cooperative, horizontally based regime, rather than a hegemonic one.

This argument is also put forward by Snidal (1985b: pp. 587–8): 'Only weakness will constrain a despot to act benevolently'.

Economic capacity

It is well established that, despite serious domestic problems with reconstruction and development, South Africa's economic capacity is significantly stronger than the rest of the region in several important respects (for details, see the chapters by Holden and Tsie in this volume). South Africa's physical and financial infrastructure is superior to the rest of the region. The six biggest banks in SADC, for example, are South African. The assets of the fifth largest South African bank correspond to those of the 21 biggest non-South African banks in SADC. South African mining houses, too, have strong interests in the mining sectors of Botswana, Namibia, Zambia and Zimbabwe. They are also involved in most of the other SADC countries.[14] Mining projects often depend not only on financing but also technology and management from outside, which further strengthens the domination of South African companies.

Mining production in neighbouring countries provides an important part of the total earnings of some of South Africa's mining houses. This creates a type of interdependence that may be consistent with the argument developed in this paper. For instance, Jwaneng in Botswana is the largest single diamond mine in the empire of De Beers, with ownership divided equally between De Beers and the Botswana government. Such interdependence, in combination with South African hegemony, may in fact facilitate a balanced regional development through investments and technology transfer. In other cases South African mining companies are more dominant and the leverage of their partners is weak. In such cases the relation at the company level may very well be more coercive than benevolent.

Transport and communications is another sector in which South African capacity is superior, but where interdependencies may be mutually beneficial. South African ports handle 90 per cent of SADC's total cargo volume and 80 per cent of its containers. Spoornet, the South African railway company, owns 85 per cent of the rolling stock in the region. More than 85 per cent of the region's cars and trucks[15] and almost 90 per cent of SADC's telephones are South African (McGowan and Ahwireng-Obeng, 1998). Due to the South African entry into SADC there are now wide potentials for rationalization and cost reduction of the transportation and infrastructure network. For instance, it is possible that the Maputo corridor and harbour can experience a renaissance as an outlet for production in Mpumalanga. It is also possible that South African agencies, such as Portnet and Spoornet, could be involved in the management of transport corridors in Mozambique. If these contracts are well-defined and implementation well-managed, these activities may sustain benevolent hegemonic regionalization.

Although low economic growth and capacity utilization between the late 1970s and the early 1990s have created a temporary South African surplus of electricity, hydroelectric power is another area in which South Africa will be dependent on external supply in the future. Hydroelectric energy is a sector with traditionally strong involvement by the state. Consequently it is also a candidate for early cooperation along lines that can be beneficial to all participants. Seen from this perspective, it is interesting to note that for years the state-owned South African electricity supply company, Eskom, has argued for a plan to connect all main hydropower plants in a regional network; this was codified in the 1995 agreement on a SADC regional power pool (SAPP) and also covered in the SADC protocol on the Energy Sector in the following year (see Swatuk, 1996). As with the transport and communications sector case discussed above, Eskom and other South African-based semi-governmental agents may sustain benevolent hegemonic regionalization, although it cannot be excluded that it follows a more exploitative pattern.

Hurrell's and Snidal's previously related position that reduced hegemony might create increased interest to cooperate in a benevolent way is of particular interest in the area of regional water distribution and management. South African industrial dominance combined with increasing dependence on external, regional water supplies heightens its need for regional cooperation. The first main stage in this process is the Highlands Water Scheme in Lesotho, through which the Gauteng area in South Africa will receive water for industrial expansion. The first phase was completed in early 1998. When fully implemented the Highlands Water Scheme is estimated to cover sufficient water supply in the area until 2010. Then it will be necessary to tap further water resources, and one source now looked upon is the Zambezi river. Such projects will carry heavy environmental risks, which further strengthens the need for close regional cooperation and development of common perspectives. Successful regional water management will be crucial for the stability of the region, as many conflicting interests will have to be conciliated.

Without being able to suggest quantitative measures on what kind and degree of South African dominance is needed for hegemony,

I argue that at least in some important sectors, South African economic actors have sufficient economic capacity to create and maintain a benevolently hegemonic regional regime. South African interest in keeping, at minimum, a benign attitude is reinforced by the insight that its dependence on resources from neighbouring countries is increasing.

Institutional capacity

If coherence and autonomy are the keys to a state's capacity to intervene in its environment, then a crucial question is whether South Africa has the necessary institutional capacity to take on the role of a benevolent hegemon in the region. This is a difficult and complex question and the answer seems to vary with the specific sector. Economic and institutional capacity is often mutually reinforcing. South Africa's relative institutional capacity is high in many, and often the same, areas as those in which its economic capacity is high. However, the question as to whether absolute capacity is sufficient cannot be assessed against any established quantified criteria. As in the case of economic capacity there has to be a qualitative assessment.

One instrument aimed at improving the homogeneity of the South African position is the National Economic Forum, NEF, with representatives from government, business and labour. NEF has contributed to a more coherent South African state in the sense that it has been instrumental in getting the main interest groups to pull in the same direction. To the extent that this has been successful, NEF has contributed to increasing state autonomy from the multitude of interest groups by restricting participation to the main groups.

So far, leading members of the business sector seem to be willing to strengthen their ties with government, particularly after introduction of the Growth, Employment and Redistribution (GEAR) macroeconomic policy, which in many fields mirrors private sector views. COSATU[16] initially was positive but has later become gradually more critical, particularly when GEAR replaced the Reconstruction and Development Programme. The initial homogeneity between the main interest groups thus is weakening.

Institutional capacity must also be analysed at sector level. Hydroelectric power appears to be of particular interest. This is so because despite its relatively superior energy capacity, South Africa is dependent on external supply for further industrial, agricultural and household use.[17] To be sure, the necessary economic capacity seems to be present and the magnitude of South Africa's (and Eskom's) institutional capacity within this sector is indisputable. Similarly, superior South African capacity obtains in the transport sector, occasional bottlenecks notwithstanding. The relative strength of South African institutional capacity thus is higher, generally and in many issue areas, both in the public and private sector, while institutional capacity is high also in absolute terms in some areas. This often actor and sector specific superiority may lead to hegemonic regimes. Without South African institutions and companies taking the lead, it can be argued that very little regionalization will take place. Is there sufficient support for such activities and government policy in South Africa? That is the topic of the next section.

Objection 4: support for a hegemonic regime is too weak in South Africa

This argument can be divided into three sub-issues. The first is that regional issues in general are low on the South African policy agenda. The second is that to the extent that regional issues are on the agenda, they do not focus on how the South African state should develop its role as benevolent hegemon in the region, but on more narrow issues, related to trade and investment. The third is that the South African formal policy of cooperative, non-hegemonic, regionalization has important political support. I will discuss the three arguments from the perspectives of political commitment and level of nation-building respectively.

Political commitment

As mentioned above, the ANC has in numerous statements declared that regional policy will be geared toward developing relationships without South Africa imposing its will on neighbouring countries. The decision to become a member of SADC in August 1994 and acceptance of responsibility for the coordination of the Finance and Investment sector in February 1995 are indications of the importance of regional matters for the new government. However, both before and after the elections in 1994, representatives of the ANC and of the new government emphasized that serious domestic problems inherited from the apartheid era restrict the capacity to focus on regional issues. Similarly, the private sector has given ambiguous signals on this issue, but the rapid expansion of South African exports to and direct investments in the region since 1990 should have some positive impact on perceptions in the private sector (see Swatuk, 1997: pp. 130–8).

The unrestricted play of market forces implies a risk of exploitative hegemonic regionalization, in which the South Africa-based players seek to maintain and create bilateral links with counterparts in various individual neighbouring countries. This tendency is strengthened by bilateral governmental agreements between South Africa and individual neighbouring countries, creating a 'hub-and-spokes' pattern in the region (see also Tsie, in this volume).

The concept of regional security has changed post-apartheid, from a strict state-centred, military perspective into a broader perspective, in which competition for natural resources, transnational environmental effects, uncontrolled migration, organized crime, drugs etcetera are important factors besides strictly military ones. SADC's Organ for Politics, Defence and Security was formed in 1996. Regional cooperation in the military field under, for example, the Interstate Defence and Security Committee, ISDSC, seems to develop more smoothly than for instance trade integration. South Africa's military resources are superior to those of other member states, but militaries in strong and weak countries alike have a common interest in keeping their capacity at a high level. In the weaker countries they see potential to increase their own strength through cooperation with South Africa. Military people also seem to accept each other as professionals, despite being enemies some years ago, although at the political level significant suspicion is left (compare the very different argument made by Thompson in Chapter 11 below). These rather brief illustrations show that so far the picture is rather diffuse, and as pointed out in a recent publication (Solomon, 1997) the process of defining foreign policy on regional terms remains unfinished business in South Africa.

To the extent that it underscores the necessity for balanced development and mutual adjustments, official policy in South Africa is consistent with the model of benevolent hegemonic regionalization. As previously mentioned, more cautious voices have also been raised both before and after the 1994 elections. However, these expressions of doubt do not necessarily point in the direction of the exploitative model of hegemonic regionalization, but may rather be understood as concerns regarding whether South Africa in fact has the capacity – economically and institutionally – to play the role of a benign or benevolent hegemon. Experiences so far lead to the conclusion that there is significant, although not united, political commitment in South Africa, consistent with the development of a benevolent hegemonic regime in Southern Africa. In general, however, regional issues are low on the South African political agenda, shadowed by domestic issues and the perception by certain business and old guard political circles that South Africa economically and politically should try to link to the North, rather than to southern or other parts of Africa.

Objection 5: scepticism and low capacity in other countries; weak institutional capacity in SADC

The economic capacity of individual SADC countries differs widely as does the degree of integration with South Africa. As highlighted in Chapter 7 above, the SACU countries are highly integrated with South Africa in a number of important fields, such as trade, infrastructure, transport and communications, distribution networks and financial services. As a result the (modest) modern infrastructural sectors in the SACU countries are of a similar standard to that in South Africa. Furthermore, Zimbabwe has a reasonably developed infrastructure, as well as mining, manufacturing and commercial agricultural sectors. There is also potential for increased interdependencies. In the other SADC countries, however, the economic and institutional capacity to participate in regionalization, be it hegemonic or otherwise, is poor.

Any South African dominating behaviour is regarded with strong reservations by most SADC member governments. In particular, it seems as if various interests in Zimbabwe, including the government, have great difficulty accepting it. In the poorer countries the position seems to be ambiguous. On one hand there is hope for investment and employment as a result of increased links with South Africa. There are also expectations that South Africa will take the lead and improve the situation of the whole region, even its situation towards the rest of the world. On the other hand, there is a reluctant attitude towards the penetration of South African companies with superior economic power and sometimes also with records of strong relations with the previous apartheid government.

The attitude towards South African-led integration varies between various interests in the neighbouring countries. Few governments seem to welcome such a regional regime. Concerning the attitude towards South African leadership another perspective may also play a role. If you are too weak to compete at all (as in the cases of Mozambique and Lesotho), a strong and dynamic unit could help you out of this situation, while if you are more competitive (for example, Zimbabwe) you may have something to fear from still stronger competitors. For the weaker states the benefits of common goods provided by a regional hegemon appear attractive, thus improving the chances for a positive attitude from those countries.

Since 1994 several conflicts related to bilateral trade issues have emerged, mainly between South Africa and Zimbabwe, South Africa and Zambia, South Africa and Swaziland, but also for instance between Zimbabwe and Zambia. The South African government is also accused of dragging its feet in the renegotiations of the SACU agreement and of a protectionist policy continuing from the apartheid era.

One major challenge of a workable hegemonic regime is to ensure all participants visible benefits, otherwise sufficient political will cannot be created. Equally important, a sustainable hegemonic regime cannot be built on the unrealistic expectations of weaker partners and free-rider policies. Again, it is important to stress the fundamental difference between different sectors. It is quite clear that visible mutual gains for all participants are much more easily created and distributed within 'regional' goods sectors than within 'international' or 'national' sectors which makes it easier for the states to define their national interests in a way that sustains benevolent hegemonic regionalization (Balassa and Stoutjesdijk, 1976). As a consequence, the political will to participate in a hegemonic regime is often higher within 'regional' goods sectors.

In general the institutional capacity of the individual SADC countries is poorly developed. In most of these countries the ability to influence the international agenda and the negotiation process connected to it is poor, as is the capacity to implement agreements and commitments, to achieve compliance from fellow partners, and to adjust to contextual changes.

The nation states of Southern Africa are entities of deliberate political actions undertaken during the colonial era. They consist of culturally heterogeneous populations, which had to be convinced by their leaders during and after the liberation struggle that they ought to think of themselves as members of their respective states and therefore ought to give these entities their primary loyalty. Furthermore, part of the state administrative capacity developed during the first decades of independence was eroded as a result of the first wave of structural adjustment programmes during the 1980s. The autonomy of the state is also weak in many SADC countries. However, except for a few minor cases, Southern Africa has not experienced problems of irredentism or secession.

From this perspective it is relevant to ask whether the rest of the SADC countries have the necessary institutional capacity to take part in a benevolent hegemonic regionalization. Although a general state-ment would be that state authorities are weak in many SADC coun-tries, this does not mean there are no promising sectors upon which to build a benevolent form of hegemonic regionalism. 'Promising' is here defined as sectors which contain both South African superiority, mutual interdependence and with some capabilities in the rest of the SADC countries as well as within the SADC framework.

For the time being, the sector with the strongest capacity in this respect is probably transport and communications, but hydro power and water management may be other starting points. For instance, it is possible that relevant SADC institutions or SADC governments with coordinating responsibility for SADC sectors could team up with South African counterparts to embark on regional strategies, for example SADC's Southern Africa Transport and Communication Commission in cooperation with Spoornet and Portnet.

If such a strategy is to emerge, there is need for organizational changes within the SADC framework. In 1997, a consultancy report, the *Review and Rationalization Study*, commissioned by SADC, was finalized. One of its aims was to assess the relevance of existing SADC institutions and the SADC programme of action for the new roles of SADC. One main recommendation of the study was that the seventeen existing Sector Coordination Units, located in member states' line ministries, should merge into five Coordination Directorates, located at the SADC headquarters. The study also concluded that only a minor part of the projects included in the Programme of Action were genuinely regional, while most of them were national. The study was discussed before the 1997 SADC Summit Meeting, but it was decided that further national and regional consultations were necessary and decisions were post-poned. Many countries were critical of the study's recommendations.

If member states are not prepared to accept radical reforms of SADC institutions, the requirements to reach the objectives of the organiza-tion are significantly weakened. These objectives are along the lines of cooperative regionalization rather than in support of a benign hege-monic regional regime. At the same time, the position of South Africa is ambiguous, as it is strongly in support of effective institutional reform, but not in a direction in which SADC institutions become more autonomous.[18]

There is a potential contradiction between a successful new and reformed SADC and the introduction of a hegemonic regime. With a strong SADC, and following from its mandate, the mode of regional-ization should be cooperative and not hegemonic. However, many international institutions in which the formal position of all member states is equal, *de facto* are driven by interests and capabilities of the strongest member, which provides a common good. The other members accept this situation as long as they perceive net gains to derive from it.

Conclusions

Following this chapter's organization around the five objections articulated above, the following tentative conclusions can be drawn.

Objection 1: South African policy

Official South African regional policy emphasizes cooperative regionalization rather than hegemonic. However, the relative and absolute strength of South Africa virtually ensures some kind of regional 'leadership'. Clearly, real South African regional policy, both public and private, is more hegemonic than the officially stated one, particularly in specific issue areas. To the extent that hegemonic regimes are created within the political realm, they can be characterized as benevolent. There are, however, also interests in South Africa that have a low interest in the region, arguing either that it is in South Africa's interest to link itself economically and politically as much as possible to the North or that domestic issues have to be handled with priority, or both.

Objection 2: global forces

In the case of Southern Africa, it can be argued that global forces leave significant space for the construction of a hegemonic regime, as long as it is consistent with international trade, capital liberalization and a neo-liberal market economy.

Objection 3: South African capability

South Africa has the capability to provide common regional goods in a number of issue areas. The South African state at the rhetorical level is committed to cooperative regionalization and supportive of a SADC with the same cooperative policy. The *realpolitik* is however more ambiguous, like South Africa's foreign policy in general (see also Solomon in Chapter 2 above).

A failure to reform and strengthen SADC and its institutions may result in a more hegemonic regional regime (see also Du Pisani in this volume). The benevolence of this hegemony may differ between various issue areas. South Africa's capability is there, while there most likely is a low level of acceptance of such a regional regime in the other countries of the region. A reformed SADC will be dependent on South Africa to provide resources, a kind of institutional common good. A successful reformation and strengthening of SADC is therefore closely connected to a situation in which South Africa provides common goods in the form of SADC institutions. In such a case it will not be 'common good', defined in line with the original hegemonic stability theory, as the other member states also will be supposed to contribute to the cost of the institutions.

In a few areas South Africa will be increasingly dependent on good relations with other countries. This situation is an important factor which most probably will strengthen the forces in South Africa that are interested in a more cooperative regional regime or possibly a benevolent hegemony in areas where this is difficult to avoid, due to the strong South African dominance.

Objection 4: weak domestic support

The issue of domestic political support for the South African government can be divided into two sub-issues. The first is that in general regional issues are low on the political agenda in South Africa and therefore there is limited support for them. The second is that among those interested in regional issues, a cooperative approach from South Africa is the ideal (see, for instance, Davies, 1997; 1994; 1992). With South Africa holding superior capability in many areas, however, it might be necessary to take on the role of a benevolent hegemon or, at least, clear leadership in SADC and other regional organizations. Public statements on the commitment of the South African government to the goal of improving the regional balance and to use SADC as an instrument for this process are common. As demonstrated above, however, when it comes to implementation the picture is more ambiguous.

Objection 5: other SADC countries and SADC itself

Any South African hegemony or hegemonic behaviour is regarded with strong reservations by most other SADC member governments. Within the region, national and SADC institutional capacity is weak as is interest in radically reforming SADC institutions. Even where there is support for SADC reform, as in South Africa, this is given on condition that the reform does not move decision making power from the national (that is, the political bodies of SADC) to the regional (that is, SADC institutions as such, particularly the SADC secretariat). This means that the field is open for market operators to continue their activities, creating selected economic dynamics and further increasing South African dominance.

The recent focus on trade integration in Southern Africa is unfortunate, as it concentrates the efforts of the member countries on issues where the potential and short term negative effects on the national economy easily enter the central stage, while the positive effects are more long term and less easily defined (see Chapter 7 above). Bilateral trade and investment conflicts also reduce cooperative spirit in other areas. Trade integration among unequal partners has to include compensatory mechanisms in order to be sustainable. The negotiations of such mechanisms tend to be very time consuming and easily generate ill will, particularly if the dominant economic actor is perceived as not being prepared to accept that it has to compensate the weaker partners.

However, regarding functional cooperation around physical and financial infrastructure, mutual benefits for the participating countries are more easily identified. This does not imply that the benefits of functional cooperation automatically are equally allocated among the participants. In the case of Southern Africa it is easy to sketch scenarios in which already dominating South African operators, such as Portnet, Spoornet, Rennies and Eskom will be the main beneficiaries.

Thus, some factors, notably political commitment, economic and institutional capacity in South Africa, together with obvious mutual interests in sectors like water management, hydroelectric supply, transportation and communication supports the establishment of a benign hegemonic or cooperative regionalization. Obstacles to such development are lack of commitment in some SADC member states, lack of economic and institutional capacity at both national and regional level and unfinished nation-building in many SADC countries. There is therefore little evidence supporting the hypothesis that SADC in the short term perspective will emerge as a strong instrument to provide improved regional balance. Due to ambiguous action at the political level, market forces instead will continue to develop further polarization in the region. These conclusions seem to be in line with those obtaining in the chapters by Tsie and Du Pisani.

The probable outcome is that a market driven, spontaneous regionalization will take place, in which concern for regional balances and sustainability is limited or nonexistent. In other words, effects similar to what would take place under coercive regional hegemony. Ironically, such a development would be the effect of the lack of hegemony, rather than enforcement and control by a dominant state. The possible, albeit not likely, alternative might not be benevolent regional hegemony but cooperative regionalization, along the lines of South African and SADC official regional policy. Such a strategy, however, has to accommodate the dominance of South Africa and South African actors. Without constituting a highway for regionalization in Southern Africa, then, a benevolent South African hegemony might not be an impasse either, if it can be contained in a cooperative regionalization framework.

Notes

1. I am grateful to Björn Hettne, Peter Vale, Fredrik Soderbaum and all partici-pants at the workshop for helpful comments on earlier drafts of this chapter.
2. 'SADC does not accept proposals that seek in practice to enhance develop-ment polarization in the region in favour of South Africa, such as the "nat-ural entry point" to Southern Africa, or the unmandated representative of the Region in a continental axis of "power point" countries. Democratic South Africa is expected to take its place in SADC as an equal participant in the re-ordering of region relations and cooperation post-apartheid' (SADC, 1994: pp. 32–3).
3. Compare, e.g., Arrighi (1982); Gill (1986; 1990); Gilpin (1975; 1981; 1987); Kennedy (1988); Keohane (1980; 1984); Kindleberger (1973; 1981; 1986a, b); Krasner (1976); Stein (1984); Webb and Krasner (1989). For critical overviews, see for instance Snidal (1985a,b); Grunberg (1990); Lake (1993).
4. Compare, e.g., Gilpin (1975); Keohane (1980); Kindleberger (1973; 1981; 1986a,b); Krasner (1976).
5. The implication of this difference between the two models is far reaching. The most important consequence is that the alternative version is no longer a systems theory, but it acknowledges also the importance of variables at the unit-level.
6. By non-rivalness is meant that one's enjoyment or consumption of a good does not diminish the amount of the good available to anyone else; by non-exclusiveness, that it is not possible to exclude any party from enjoyment of the good, as a result of which many actors may be 'free-riders' unwilling to pay any of the costs for providing the good. It should of course be noted that, in reality, few goods fit these criteria perfectly.
7. For a more detailed discussion on the concept of region, see Russett (1967) and Hettne (1992).
8. Since then, the Democratic Republic of Congo and the Seychelles became members in 1997. While the integration of the DRC and the Seychelles into the SADC structures can be assumed to take a long time, their membership, and also that of Mauritius in 1995, makes it more difficult to stick to the territorial definition as the organizational one which, I would argue, still is the most logical.
9. Although this study mainly focuses on the political economy dimension of regionalism and not in particular on the security dimension of the concept, I adopt a broader understanding of the concept compared with, for instance, Bhagwati (1992) who reserves regionalism solely for trade policy. For a more

detailed discussion on regionalism and regionalization, see Hettne (1994) and Odén (1996; 1994).

10. For instance, Orén (1990) and Binder (1982) have analysed the British and US attempts to establish regional hegemony in the Middle East, respectively. Likewise, Vanden and Morales (1985) have examined the US strategy to achieve regional hegemony in Central America. Furthermore, US efforts aiming at regional hegemony in the Americas have been investigated by Mares (1988).

11. For instance, Iyob (1993) has analysed Ethiopia's role in the Horn of Africa. Turner (1991) has investigated the case of Brazil in South America. Ross (1991) has evaluated the regional hegemony of China in South East Asia. Kamalu (1991) has analysed the role of Iran–Iraq in the Middle East. The regional hegemony of South Africa in Southern Africa has been examined by Price (1985), Shaw (1977) and Thompson (1991).

12. The oil companies have always been interested.

13. HIPC stands for highly indebted poor countries. This scheme gives an opportunity for around 20 poor and highly indebted countries to obtain better debt relief conditions, provided they during a period of 3 plus 3 years follow strict structural and stabilization programmes negotiated with the IMF. The first country to try the HIPC scheme is Uganda.

14. Some examples are the interest of Gencor in the Moatize coal mine in Mozambique, Alusaf and Gencor in the Mozal aluminium project in Maputo, ISCOR in iron production, De Beers in expansion of diamond exploitation in Namibia, use of Kudu gas for stainless steel production. AAC is involved for instance in plans for a new platinum mine in Zimbabwe, gold mines in Tanzania and the privatization of the copper mines in Zambia.

15. All transport sector comparisons are based on statistics in SADC, 1997 *Transport and Communications*. Windhoek, 9–10 Feb.

16. The Congress of South African Trade Unions, with its 1.3 million members, is the most powerful labour organization in South Africa.

17. Of the estimated 7.3 million households in South Africa, 55 per cent do not have access to electricity; of the estimated 22,000 schools in the country, 87 per cent are not electrified; and of the estimated 4000 larger clinics, 75 per cent do not have electricity.

18. Some would argue that this disagreement was at the heart of the matter leading to the September 1999 resignation of SADC's Executive Secretary, Kaire Mbuende.

References

Arrighi, Giovanni (1982), 'A Crisis of Hegemony', in Samir Amin *et al.* (eds), *Dynamics of Global Crisis* (London: Macmillan).

Balassa, Bela, and A. Stoutjesdijk (1976), 'Economic Integration among Developing Countries', *Journal of Common Market Studies* 14, 37–55.

Bhagwati, Jagdish (1992), 'Regionalism vs Multilateralism', *World Economy* 15.

Binder, Leonard (1982), 'United States in the Middle East: Toward a Pax Saudiana', *Current History* 81/471.

Buzan, Barry (1991), *People, States & Fear. An Agenda for International Security Studies in the Post-Cold War Era*, 2nd edn (London: Westview Press).

Cox, Robert (1983), 'Gramsci, Hegemony, and International Relations: an essay in method', *Millennium* 12/2.

Davies, Rob (1992), 'Integration or Cooperation in a Post-Apartheid Southern Africa? Some Reflections on an Emerging Debate', *Southern African Perspectives: a working paper series 18* (Bellville: Centre for Southern African Studies).

Davies, Rob (1994), 'Creating an Appropriate Institutional Framework', in Minnie Venter (ed.), *Prospects for Progress. Critical Choices for Southern Africa* (Cape Town: Maskew Miller Longman).

Davies, Rob (1997), 'Promoting Regional Integration in Southern Africa: An Analysis of Prospects and Problems from a South African Perspective', in Larry A. Swatuk and David R. Black (eds), *Bridging the Rift: the new South Africa in Africa* (Boulder, CO: Westview Press) pp. 109–26.

Gill, Stephen (1986), 'US Hegemony: Its Limits and Prospects in the Reagan Era', *Millennium* 15/4.

Gill, Stephen (1990), *American Hegemony and the Trilateral Commission* (Cambridge: Cambridge University Press).

Gilpin, Robert (1975), *US. Power and the Multinational Corporation: The Political Economy of Foreign Direct Investment* (New York: Basic Books).

Gilpin, Robert (1981), *War and Change in World Politics* (Cambridge: Cambridge University Press).

Gilpin, Robert (1987), *The Political Economy of International Relations* (Princeton, NJ: Princeton University Press).

Government of South Africa (1994), *RDP White Paper* (Cape Town: CTP Book Printers).

Gramsci, Antonio (1971), *Selections from the Prison Notebooks* (London: Lawrence & Wishart).

Grunberg, Isabelle (1990) 'Exploring the Myth of Hegemonic Stability', *International Organization* 44/4, 431–78.

Haarlöv, J. (1997), *Regional Cooperation and Integration within Industry and Trade in Southern Africa*, (Aldershot: Avebury).

Hettne, Björn (1992), 'The Regional Factor in the Formation of a New World Order', *Padrigu Working Papers No. 26* (Göteborg: Göteborg University).

Hettne, Björn (1994), 'The New Regionalism: Implications for Development and Peace. Analytical Framework, Overview and Areas for Research', in Björn Hettne and András Inotai, *The New Regionalism. Implications for Global Development and International Security*, (Helsinki: WIDER).

Hirsch, Fred, and Michael Doyle (1977), 'Politicization in the World Economy: necessary conditions for an international economic order', in D. Hirsch and M. Doyle *et al.* (eds), *Alternatives to Monetary Disorder* (New York: McGraw-Hill for the Council on Foreign Relations).

Hurrell, Andrew (1995), 'Regionalism in Theoretical Perspective', in Louise Fawcett and Andrew Hurrell (eds), *Regionalism in World Politics: Regional Organization and International Order* (Oxford: Oxford University Press).

Iyob, Ruth (1993), 'Regional Hegemony: Domination and Resistance in the Horn of Africa', *The Journal of Modern African Studies* 31/2, 257–76.

Kamalu, Ngozi Caleb (1991), 'Regional Conflicts and Global Tensions: The Iran–Iraq War', *Conflict* 10/4, 333–46.

Kennedy, Paul (1988), *The Rise and Fall of the Great Powers* (London: Allen & Unwin).

Keohane, Robert O. (1980), 'The Theory of Hegemonic Stability and Changes in International Economic Regimes, 1967–1977', in Ole Holsti *et al.* (eds), *Change in the International System* (Boulder, CO: Westview Press).

Keohane, Robert O. (1984), *After Hegemony: Cooperation and Discord in the World Political Economy* (Princeton, NJ: Princeton University Press).

Keohane, Robert O. and Joseph Nye (1977), *Power and Interdependence: world politics in transition* (Boston: Little Brown).

Kindleberger, Charles P. (1973), *The World in Depression, 1929–1939* (Berkeley: University of California Press).

Kindleberger, Charles P. (1981), 'Dominance and Leadership in the International Economy: Exploitation, Public Goods, and Free Rides', *International Studies Quarterly* 25/3, 242–54.

Kindleberger, Charles P. (1986a), 'Hierarchy versus Inertial Cooperation', *International Organization* 40/4, 841–7.

Kindleberger, Charles P. (1986b), 'International Public Goods without International Government', *American Economic Review* 76, 1–13.

Krasner, Stephen D. (1976), 'State, Power and the Structure of International Trade', *World Politics* 28 (April), 317–47.

Krasner, Stephen D. (ed.) (1983), *International Regimes* (London: Cornell University Press).

Lake, David A. (1993), 'Leadership, Hegemony, and the International Economy: Naked Emperor or Tattered Monarch with Potential', *International Studies Quarterly* 37, 459–89.

Mandela, Nelson (1993), 'South Africa's Future Foreign Policy', *Foreign Affairs* 72 (Nov.–Dec.).

Mares, David R. (1988), 'Middle Powers under Regional Hegemony: To Challenge or Acquiesce in Hegemonic Enforcement', *International Studies Quarterly* 32, 453–71.

McGowan, Patrick J., and Fred Ahwireng-Obeng (1998), 'Partner or Hegemon? South Africa in Africa, Part Two', *Journal of Contemporary African Studies* 16/2, 165–95.

Odén, Bertil (1994), 'Southern Africa and the Global Arena', *Forum for Development Studies* 1–2.

Odén, Bertil (1996), *Regionalization in Southern Africa*, World Development Studies 10 (Helsinki: UNU/WIDER).

Orén, Michael B. (1990), 'A Winter of Discontent: Britain's Crisis in Jordan, December 1955-March 1956', *International Journal of Middle East Studies* 22/2, 171–84.

Price, Robert M. (1985), 'Southern Africa Regional Security: Pax or Pox Pretoria?', *World Policy Journal* 2/3, 533–54.

Ross, Robert S. (1991), 'China and the Cambodian Peace Process: The Value of Coercive Diplomacy', *Asian Survey* 31/12, 1170–85.

Russett, Bruce (1967), *International Relations and the International System* (Chicago: Rand McNally).

Russett, Bruce (1985), 'The Mysterious Case of Vanishing Hegemony: or, Is Mark Twain really dead?', *International Organization* 39/2, 207–31.

SADC (1994), *Regional Relations and Cooperation Post-Apartheid: A Strategy and Policy Framework* (Gaborone: SADC).

SADC (1997), *Transportation and Communications* (Windhoek, 9–11 Feb.).

Shaw, Timothy M. (1977), 'International Stratification in Africa: Sub-Imperialism in Southern and Eastern Africa', *Journal of Southern African Affairs* 2/2, 145–66.

Snidal, Duncan (1985a), 'Hegemonic Stability Theory Revisited', *International Organization* 39/3.

Snidal, Duncan (1985b), 'The Limits of Hegemonic Stability Theory', *International Organization* 39/4, 579–619.

Solomon, Hussein (ed.) (1997), *Fairy God-Mother, Hegemon or Partner? In Search of a South African Foreign Policy*, ISS Monograph Series, No. 13 (Halfway House: Institute for Security Studies).

Stein, Arthur A. (1984), 'The Hegemon's Dilemma: Great Britain, the United States, and the International Economic Order', *International Organization* 38/2, 355–86.

Swatuk, Larry A. (1996), 'Power and Water: The Coming Order in Southern Africa', *Southern African Perspectives: a working paper series 58* (Bellville: Centre for Southern African Studies).

Swatuk, Larry A. (1997), 'The Environment, Sustainable Development and Prospects for Southern African Regional Cooperation', in Larry A. Swatuk and David R. Black (eds), *Bridging the Rift: the new South Africa in Africa* (Boulder, CO: Westview Press) pp. 127–51.

Thompson, Lisa (1991), 'Of Myths, Monsters and Money: Regime Conceptualisation and Theory in the Southern African Context', *Journal of Contemporary African Studies* 10/2, 57–83.

Turner, F. C. (1991), 'Regional Hegemony and the Case of Brazil', *International Journal* 46/3, 475–509.

Vanden, Harry E., and Waltraud Q. Morales (1985), 'Nicaraguan Relations with the Nonaligned Movement', *Journal of Inter-American Studies and World Affairs* 27/3,

Webb, M. C., and Stephen D. Krasner (1989), 'Hegemonic Stability Theory: An Empirical Assessment', *Review of International Studies* 15, 183–98.

9
New Sites of Governance: Regimes and the Future of Southern Africa

Andre du Pisani

Introduction

Namibia draws 50 million cubic litres of water per annum from the Orange River, its southern border, with neighbouring South Africa. Elsewhere in Southern Africa, the Zambezi River Authority regulates the use of water from an international river according to the provision of the Helsinki Rules. Once considered 'low politics', the global environment is now firmly positioned as one of the primary issues – along with the global economy and security – that will determine the future of the region. What we are witnessing is the rise and functioning of issue-based regimes and their growing importance as new sites of governance, alongside states and other agencies.

The study of international regimes has emerged as a major field of research in world politics. Three principal approaches have shaped and continue to shape the debate: realism, which coalesces around power relations and the state as its core concerns; neo-liberalism, which anchors its analysis in interest-based networks; and, more recently, cognitivism, which underlines the significance of knowledge, communications and identities. Each of these approaches advance distinct views on the origins, coherence, role and importance of regimes for the international system.

The Southern African Development Community (SADC) provides the case study for this chapter. As a state-based regime, SADC constitutes an evolving site of transnational governance in a post-Cold War region and world. An analysis of SADC offers useful avenues for theoretical reflection, notably in the domains of agency behaviour, the nature of interest bargaining and the formation of behavioural and jurisdictional norms.

Conceptual issues

At the time of the Cold War, theoretical interest in regimes coincided largely with Western political and economic concerns, more especially with ensuring Western political and economic dominance. Consequently, as Strange (1995: p. 159) reminds us, 'the bulk of analytical work in international political economy, following the Nye and Keohane lead, had concentrated on the area of regimes – regimes for trade, for exchange rates, for the management of foreign debt and foreign investment, for environmental protection, for the regulation of air and sea transport, etcetera'. Now, deep changes in the global security structure continue to provide one of the principal reasons for studying regimes: their role in coordinating matters of defence, peace-building, security, human rights and regional development.

Two decades after scholars of world politics began to ask questions about 'international regimes', scholarly interest in the 'principles, norms, rules and decision-making procedures' (Krasner, 1983: p. 2) that govern state behaviour in specific issue areas of international relations persists (cf. Strange, 1982). While aware of some of the difficulties to which Krasner's definition has given rise, it is important to point to two significant implications. First, international regimes are international institutions and should be studied as such. Second, the terms 'international regime' and 'international organization' do not carry the same meaning, nor do they refer to the same entities, even though in many cases regimes will be accompanied by organizations designed or employed to support them in various ways (Young, 1989: pp. 25–7). Perhaps one of the most important differences between regimes and organizations – both of which can be seen as representing a special type of international institution (Keohane, 1989: p. 3) – lies in the fact that regimes, being no more than sets of principles, norms, rules and procedures accepted by states, do not possess much capacity to act, whereas organizations can respond to events (even when their space to act is circumscribed). Notwithstanding these conceptual distinctions, regime theorists such as Kratochwil and Ruggie (1986: p. 771) have warned against artificially separating the academic study of regimes from research on formal international and subregional organizations.

In a recent offering, Hasenclever, Mayer and Rittberger (1997: p. 1) argue that while the term 'regime' might have lost some of its earlier potency, nevertheless, 'the substantive questions that define the regime-analytical research agenda – whether couched in terms of "regimes", "institutions" or otherwise – still count among the major foci of international relations scholarship in both Europe and North America'.

Typically, the regime research agenda concerns itself with some of the following core theoretical questions: What accounts for the rise of rule-based cooperation in the international system? How do international institutions such as regimes shape the behaviour of state and non-state actors in the issue areas for which they have been designed? Which factors, within and without a regime, determine its success and coherence? How can we explain the particular institutional architecture of a specific regime? What is the nature of bargaining within a regime framework?

Susan Strange (1995: pp. 158–63) justifiably restates her earlier 1982 critique of the study of regimes, namely that regimes are 'value-laden in favour of order over justice and autonomy'. She proposes, instead, an alternative focus on the 'bargains – domestic and international, political and economic, corporate and inter-state' that underpin regimes, rather than a preoccupation with their structures and decision-making procedures. This chapter takes a leaf from Strange's book and is, therefore, not a comprehensive exploration of regime theories as such.

Various theories have been used to analyse some of these questions. Based on the explanatory variables that these theories use, they may – on the analysis of Hasenclever, Mayer and Rittberger (1997) – be classified as 'power-based', 'interest-based' and 'knowledge-based' approaches respectively. These authors refer to these as distinct *schools of thought* within the study of international regimes, implying that each has a distinct ontological status and clear analytic focus.

Realists focus on power relationships and their connection to the state. Neoliberals are interested in uncovering the interests that drive regimes, while cognitivists emphasize knowledge dynamics, communication, and identities. The use of the term 'schools' does not imply that there are no significant differences among the scholars themselves. It does imply, however, that 'the disagreements between members of different schools of thought are of a more fundamental nature' (Hasenclever, Mayer and Rittberger, 1997: p. 2).

One of the most important differences separating the three schools of thought is the degree of 'institutionalism' that power-based, interest-based, and knowledge-based theories of regimes advance. 'Institutionalism' refers to the view that institutions matter and that they create over time their own dynamics and interests. Analytically, regimes (as specific kinds of institutions) can be significant in two respects. They may be more or less *effective*, and they may be more or less *robust/resilient.* Regime robustness refers to the 'staying power of international institutions in the face of exogenous challenges and to the extent to which prior institutional choices constrain collective decisions and behaviour in later periods' (ibid).

Institutions that change with every shift of power among their members or whenever the more powerful members find that their interests are no longer well served by the current regime, lack institutional coherence. 'Change' in this context may mean either a fundamental alteration of the regime's normative domain or a drastic change (such as a decline) in the extent to which the regime's rules and norms are actually complied with by its members.

For the purposes of this chapter, Krasner's (1983: p. 1) working definition of 'regimes' is used: 'Implicit or explicit principles, norms, rules and decision-making procedures around which actors' expectations converge in a given area of international relations'. This understanding of regimes implies patterned behaviour, modes of cooperation, norms and sites of governance that go beyond ad hoc interaction, international treaties or international organizations.

Oran Young proposed a definition of regimes that has much in common with that of Krasner. Writing in 1982, Young conceptualizes regimes as social institutions within which there is a 'conjunction of convergent expectations and patterns of behaviour in practice'. Later, in 1989, he defined regimes as 'social practices consisting of easily recognized roles coupled with clusters of rules or conventions governing relations among the occupants of these roles'.

Other regime theorists such as Puchala and Hopkins (1982: p. 246) expanded on Young's earlier definition by adding an attitudinal dimension. For them, regimes come about and exist because of the participants' understandings, expectations or convictions about what constitutes legitimate or moral behaviour. Such understandings or expectations are bound to the rules, principles, norms and decision-making procedures which govern a particular regime.

Regime analysts have, by and large, concentrated principally on international cooperation in issue areas such as banking, trade, human rights, armaments, nuclear proliferation, chemical weapons, transportation and communication, Antarctica and the environment. This focus has rarely been applied to regional and subregional security concerns, including disarmament and arms control at that level of analysis.[1]

Regime analysis is not a fully fledged theory, but rather a conceptual framework and a research agenda. Most studies of regimes have indeed harnessed several theoretical ideas and concepts, in particular, structural approaches (such as hegemonic stability theory), game theory, public choice theory, functional theory, integrative theory and cognitive approaches. None of these theories should be seen *a priori* as superior. Every theory has its peculiar strengths and weaknesses in selecting, organizing, explaining and relating what we study and observe in the real world. Elsewhere (Du Pisani, 1998), I have provided a succinct theoretical overview of most of the dominant approaches in regime analysis. Since the categorization of theoretical approaches is not unproblematic and since there is no agreed typology in the literature on regimes, it serves little purpose to trawl the same waters here.

At this point it is appropriate to point to the confluence between 'regimes' and 'governance'.[2] One of the principal strengths of regime analysis is its potential to explain the possibility, conditions, patterns and consequences of international governance beyond anarchy but short of supranational government in a given issue area. Regimes are sites of governance and, if properly constituted, can complement states and influence their actions. Weak states, however, undermine the effectiveness of state-based regimes such as SADC. Within the framework of regimes, 'governance' acquires direction, normative and constituent meaning, regularity and takes institutional shape. That is why SADC as a state-sponsored site of governance can usefully be analysed from a regime perspective.

SADC as a regime: the weight of history

The seed that spawned SADC's precursor, the Southern African Development Coordination Conference (SADCC) came from the vision of former Zambian president, Kenneth Kaunda, who as early as 1974 and within sight of the independence of Angola and Mozambique spoke of the 'day when the independent state of Southern Africa could meet to discuss liberation. Not liberation from political dependence, but liberation from poverty'. Kaunda called for the creation of a 'transcontinental belt of independent and economically powerful nations, from Dar es Salaam and Maputo on the Indian Ocean, to Luanda on the Atlantic' (quoted in Mandaza and Tostensen, 1994: p. vii).

The seminal Arusha Conference of July 1979 and the founding Lusaka Summit of April 1980 constituted the first resolute steps on the journey towards the realization of this vision. On 1 April 1980, in Lusaka, the heads of state and government of what used to be called the 'majority-ruled countries' of Southern Africa adopted the Lusaka Declaration which culminated in the founding of SADCC.[3]

The genesis, norms, values, institutional habits, practices and evolution of SADCC have to be understood in the context of time: geographic contingency, common history, common economy, colonial inheritance, the corrosive force of apartheid and racism, the politics of nation-building, economic asymmetry and dependence and patrimonial rule and presidentialism, among others, all played their part.

In addition to the above, and as Vale points out in Chapter 2, it did matter that the Frontline States (FLS) – as a distinct diplomatic and political grouping – provided the principal inspiration for the formation of SADCC. The genesis and behaviour of this grouping, acting as the principal rear base in support of primarily state-based liberation struggles in Southern Africa, was, in itself, an important aspect of regime formation in the region. It also left a distinct legacy in the security domain, especially since 'security' was (unavoidably) elevated to the realm of 'high politics', carried a distinct 'hardware' connotation, and became intimately connected to the affairs of state (see also Thompson in this volume). This is but one illustration of how earlier choices shaped the later behaviour of present-day SADC.

While the history of the diplomacy and politics of the Frontline States falls outside the scope of this chapter, Gwaradzimba (1993: pp. 51–9) argues that the FLS gave a distinct political, personal and state-centric character to SADCC. To this must be added the norm setting value of the celebrated Lusaka Manifesto of 1969 and its formative influence on the regional diplomacy of the FLS.

In a departure from a preoccupation with trade-based and market integration, the founding members of SADCC signed a Memorandum of Understanding (MOU) in Lusaka, effectively creating a regime that was built on the conflictual relations between minority-ruled South Africa and the independent countries of the region. A further significant political feature of SADCC was that it granted observer status to the liberation movements of South Africa, the African National Congress (ANC) and the Pan Africanist Congress (PAC), a decision that anticipated eventual membership of a free South Africa in SADC. It also meant that liberation movements became important agencies within the SADCC framework and that their interests and values (which at times coincided with or diverged from those of the FLS) were reflected in the preoccupation of the regime, notably on the then-unresolved issues of South Africa and Namibia.

Political and diplomatic intercourse under the aegis of the FLS necessitated a level of economic cooperation which hitherto did not exist. Consequently, one of the core objectives of SADCC was to reduce dependence, particularly but not only, on minority-ruled South Africa through effective coordination of the respective strengths and resources of its member states. The Lusaka Declaration (SADCC, 1980: p. 1) embraced four interrelated objectives:

- reducing economic dependence, particularly but not only, on South Africa;
- forging links to create a genuine and equitable regional organization;
- mobilizing resources to promote the implementation of national, interstate and regional policies; and
- acting in a concerted fashion so as to secure international cooperation within the framework of SADCC's strategy of economic liberation.

It is commonly argued that four articles of faith anchored the SADCC regime (Gwaradzimba, 1993; Mandaza and Tostensen, 1994; and Odén, 1993). Firstly, that cooperation prevents and mediates conflict (a neo-functionalist precept). Secondly, that SADCC, as an attempt at such cooperation, would evolve its own capacity for the resolution and prevention of conflict. Thirdly, that collaboration on smaller issue areas would provide a basis for cooperation in larger spheres, and finally, that cooperation would produce greater internal cohesion and – over time – a regional identity (see also Hettne in this volume).

From a theoretical perspective, the above is interesting, for it underlines that SADCC, as the antecedent to SADC, implicitly reflected interest-based, power-based and knowledge-based approaches to regimes. The convergence of interests around a common desire to reduce economic dependence was motivated by both political and economic self-interest of the members concerned. Considerations of power, particularly as this related to regional asymmetries, too, played their part. From its inception, SADCC displayed a certain preoccupation with enhancing intra-state communication and forging a regional identity. Thus, it always had certain cognitive strands to it. Admittedly, these became more tangible after the 1994 transformation in South Africa.

The global and regional settings, too, spawned a need for closer cooperation. The rise of global capitalism and its attendant structure of hegemony, as well as drought, debt and destabilization, forged interest networks and neo-functionalist modes of collaboration. These and other factors meant that one of SADCC's primary concerns was to bring about a realignment of economic relations among and between its members and reconfigure their pattern of asymmetrical relations with South Africa to which they were historically linked as a periphery.

Hence much emphasis was put on the creation of transport infrastructure and the mobilization of donor assistance.

The programme of action: more programme than action

The agenda of the inaugural 1980 SADCC Summit included not only
the adoption of the Lusaka Declaration but also an item called the
'Programme of Action'. The latter embodied various programmes and
activities, and was intended to guide the operational work of the
regime. Significantly, the Programme of Action was intended to
advance the national interest of the member states, as much as it was
meant to advance regional concerns. This is characteristic of loosely
state-based regimes of the neo-functionalist variety (Lubbe, 1989).

The policy dimensions that followed from the Programme of Action
were anchored in a number of national projects rather than an ambitious regional project of economic integration. The failure of the earlier
East African Community as well as the vulnerabilities of the individual
member states and the sectoral philosophy championed by the late
President of Botswana, Sir Seretse Khama, all worked in support of this
approach to development and cooperation. The approach was to
address national concerns and to engage in the consolidation of
national power (not least for reasons of sovereignty and national prestige associated with newly acquired statehood) through regional
action. National and regional projects were not seen as incompatible,
yet national concerns superseded regional ones. This approach to
development led some critics of SADCC to conclude that it had no programme of its own, but instead promoted national projects and mobilized donor support for such projects (Maasdorp, 1992: p. 4).

The underlying principle for allocating sectors is that a member is
more likely to successfully coordinate and promote activity in an issue
area, if that issue area is also important to it nationally. The funding
arrangements for projects, as well as the legal ownership of assets, have
been approached innovatively. Under SADCC, the regime did not hold
legal ownership over the project or the assets created through cooperation. They remained the property of the member state(s) on whose territory the project was located. Regional projects were, therefore, not
defined in terms of joint or common ownership, but rather in terms of
the common benefits to member states. This has changed in certain
respects under the 1992 SADCC Treaty (see below).

Most analysts agree that prior to SADCC's 1992 mutation into a
'development community' it was most successful in the more functional

issue areas of transportation, communications and energy (see, for example, Maasdorp, 1992; Ostergaard, 1989; Odén, 1993). These priorities have also been reflected in the institutional fabric of the regime, for example, in the creation of the Southern African Transport and Communications Commission (SATCC), established to coordinate the use of existing systems and the planning and financing of additional regional transport and communications infrastructure. In the areas of intra-regional trade, reducing economic dependence on South Africa, environmental protection, food security, industrial policy, culture, gender and human rights, SADCC has been rather less successful (Du Pisani, 1998). Inherent state-centrism, weak institutional and non-governmental organizational (NGO) capacity, donor dependence and absorptive capacity constraints, among others, militated against according issues of low politics higher priority. These and other issue areas such as human resources development and institutional capacity became important regime concerns after the transformation of SADCC into SADC in August 1992.

Institutional structure

The sectoral philosophy and nascent state institutions significantly shaped the institutional fabric of SADCC, as well as its decision-making processes. It is important to remember that SADCC operated on the basis of a MOU. The regime came into being with neither formal treaty nor clearly-defined legal status. This in no way, however, detracted from it as a negotiated – rather than imposed – regime, even though it was decidedly 'loosely knit' and highly decentralized. For in the language of regime analysts, SADCC did embody principles, norms, rules and decision-making procedures around which actors' expectations converged.

The practice of establishing institutions was informed by the view that benefits had to outweigh costs. This reflected a crude application of game theoretic and public choice approaches. Exceptions to this principled approach, however, were to be seen in the case of the aforementioned SATCC and the Southern African Centre for Cooperation in Agricultural Research (SACCAR), where benefits came long after establishment of the institution.

In such cases, SADCC resorted to its cooperating partners to bridge the gap between the initial cost and the flow of benefits. Member states, however, had to meet the core costs of maintaining such institutions. To cover programme costs, SADCC sought outside technical and financial assistance. This in turn, made for excessive dependence on external resources, undermined local mobilization and favoured bilateralism over regionalism. For example, by 1989, SATCC with a portfolio of $4.8 billion accounted for 64 per cent of the total SADCC portfolio of $7 billion. Of this amount, $2.4 billion was pledged by foreign donors (Hanlon, 1989; p. 17).

Institutionally, SADC/C was and remains a decentralized regime. The intended effect of decentralization was that member states became the primary actors within the regime. This, in turn, bolstered the state-centric character of the regime and complicated coordination at regional level. In line with this approach to institutional development, each member state was assigned a specific sector to coordinate. Hence, each member state created a Sector Coordinating Unit (SCU), as part of its structure of governance to carry out its regional mandate. As seen in Table 9.1, by 1990 the Programme of Action was coordinated by 10 member states across 14 sectors.

The principal organs of SADC/C were established by the MOU signed by heads of state and government in July 1981. These include, the annual summit which is the supreme body responsible for overall policy setting of the regime; the Council of Ministers which consists of one minister from each of the member states, meets at least twice a year and is accountable to the Summit for overall implementation, coordination and supervision of the programmes of the regime; the Standing Committee of Officials which consists of senior civil servants,

Table 9.1   SADCC sectors and coordinating countries

Sector or sub-sector	Coordinating country
Culture and information	Mozambique
Energy	Angola
Food, agriculture and natural resources	Zimbabwe
Agricultural research and training	Botswana
Food security	Zimbabwe
Inland fisheries, forestry and wildlife	Malawi
Livestock production and animal disease control	Botswana
Marine fisheries and resources	Namibia
Environment and land management	Lesotho
Human resources development	Swaziland
Industry and trade	Tanzania
Mining	Zambia
Tourism	Lesotho
Transportation and communications	Mozambique

normally acts as the 'national contact point' of each member state, and meets at least twice a year. It is responsible to the Council of Ministers. Sectoral Committees or Sectoral Commissions may be established for programmes in specific functional domains. Commissions are constituted as separate legal entities by means of a convention ratified by member states (see Mandaza and Tostensen, 1994 for details). The budgets of the Commissions are jointly funded by member states on an equal basis. To date, there are only two commissions: SATCC based in Mozambique, and SACCAR based in Botswana.

Sectoral Committees are serviced by Sector Coordinating Units (SCUs) which are created by the member state responsible for each respective sector. Sectoral Commissions, on the other hand, are supported by Technical Administrative Units (TAUs) under the oversight of the member coordinating the sector.

The Secretariat is headed by an Executive Secretary who acts as Chief Executive Officer of the regime. The Executive Secretary is answerable to the Council of Ministers for the implementation of the Council and Summit decisions, and the coordination and execution of the work of the regime, custodianship of SADC property, amongst other functions. The Executive Secretary also prepares an annual report, and is the principal diplomat of the regime. These functions are undertaken with the support of, and in close liaison with the sector coordinators, in association with the diplomatic missions of member states.

In addition to these formal structures, there is a proliferation of various working groups and technical committees responsible for project planning, design and execution in their respective domains. Presently, the most active working groups are in the energy, transport, communcations, investment and trade sectors.

Finally, there is the Annual Consultative Meeting, brought into being by the Lusaka Declaration. The ACM has evolved more into a donor conference, with competing projects often detracting from the original intention of the founders, namely to engage in wide-ranging dialogue and to assess results and future plans of the regime (Hawkins, 1992: pp. 105–32).

Decisions are taken by consensus, a mechanism meant to recognize the equal sovereignty of member states. Some critics have argued that this gives the slowest and least committed member states disproportionate influence to frustrate progress (Gwaradzimba, 1993: pp. 52–6). Given the power asymmetry within the regime and that power is necessarily implicated in all forms of action whether cooperative or conflicting, consensus decisions tend to give equal weight to the views of all members, and by and large, have worked in support of greater internal cohesion and conflict avoidance.

Given the decentralized nature of its institutions, most of the operational work is done in the SCUs and in the member states. The effectiveness of the SCUs has been debated extensively. Similarly, the debate on the most appropriate organizational framework rages on within SADC with the adoption of the 1992 Treaty adding new urgency. So, too, the 1995 Draft Protocol on Capacity Building. Unlike its predecessor, SADC adopted a policy on the creation of institutions that is informed by two domain principles. These are

• institutional structures of the Community must provide for the active involvement of member states in the formation of polices, strategies and programmes, and the implementation of the activities of integration, and
• Community institutions and procedures should be independent of and outside the control of any individual member state.

These principles reflect some inconsistency, calling for 'active involvement' and 'independence' at the same time. There is need to establish more effective working relationships between national decentralized structures and transregional structures with sufficient capacity to carry out the increasingly complex task of building SADC. There are, of course, some institutional arrangements, for example SATCC and SACCAR, which could provide the basis for genuine transregional institutions. They are not under the control of an individual member state but they remain under the sector coordination of member states. This arrangement seems to have worked reasonably well; in any event, there is no inherent reason why it should not work in other sectors.

The future pattern of regime governance, however, will increasingly depend on the content of the specific arrangements and protocols in the various issue areas relevant to integration. Moreover, it is clear that more space will have to be created for other agencies such as organized labour, NGOs and community based organizations (CBOs). There is a growing need for transregional governance in the issue areas of population and migration, trade, transport, education, human resources development, gender, accounting, law, medical practice, health, water and other natural resource management, to name but several.

SADC: from a 'conference' to a 'community' (1992–99)

The Southern African Development Community was formally established with the adoption of the Windhoek Declaration of August 1992.

Unlike its antecedent, SADC is based on a legally binding treaty ratified by all member states. Its principal goal is to bring about a common market through development integration rather than extant and more limited neo-functionalist cooperation in specific issue areas. Building a 'community' became the clarion call, but what kind of community is envisaged for Southern Africa? How will it be realized? Moreover, an economic community does not equal a development community.

In more conventional economic literature, establishing an economic community is seen as essentially a linear undertaking that starts with trade liberalization and culminates in political union. In considering SADC, conventional economic theory may not be very useful for an understanding of the workings of a 'development community' (see Holden's chapter above). For, a development community denotes an attempt at effecting structural change which favours both national and regional development and which activates all sectors of the population to participate in the development process. Typically, the specific objectives of a development community include greater social equity, including the achievement of an equitable distribution of income and wealth, and the development of human potentials such as employment creation and meeting basic social needs (see Hettne in Chapter 5 above).

In considering the above, it needs to be pointed out that the core economic structures and relations of the region have remained virtually unchanged over the past few decades. As discussed in some detail by Tsie in Chapter 6, the region remains largely a producer and exporter of primary agricultural and mineral products, and an importer of capital and manufactures. Further economic difficulties arise from incompatible production and trade structures. Hence, the prevailing trade liberalization approach to integration (much favoured by the World Bank, the International Monetary Fund (IMF) and many neo-classical development economists – see Holden in Chapter 7), does not easily fit the regional reality. In adopting a development integration approach each member is allowed, at least in theory, to define the pace, scope and sectors of integration.

The core elements of 'development integration' have been described by the Executive Secretary of SADC, Kaire Mbuende: 'The coordinated development and integration of basic infrastructure, investment and production systems to yield enhancement of material production, service and exchange sectors of the regional political economy' (personal communication, Windhoek, 13 July 1995). Closer scrutiny of the SADC Treaty as well as its projects shows the envisaged project of development integration to be informed by notions of balance, equity and mutual benefit. Thus, trade integration, for example, must be accompanied by appropriate measures aimed at assisting the least developed members. In this scenario, the establishment of a bigger and more effective regional market and trade liberalization becomes but one aspect of a more encompassing project of regional integration.

The notion and ideal of 'integration' itself is widely understood to follow linearly from two preceding modes of interaction: 'coordination' and 'harmonization'. The first, coordination, constitutes the lowest level of economic integration. It suggests a voluntary alignment of specific national projects whether public or private in various functional domains. It may also involve the alignment of policies at the 'meso' or sector level in such issue areas as energy, transport, communications and natural resources management. This level of interaction characterized SADCC. According to the African Development Bank (1993: p. 10), harmonization is seen as 'the next level of integration that normally involves the adoption of common legislation … which might be regionally agreed but nationally controlled and applied'.

'Integration' usually means the assignment of responsibility for formulating regional policies, developing rules and regulations, and applying these policies to the functioning of all markets (capital, labour and factor) at the regional level. It means, as de Wilde (1991: p. 27) points out, ceding sovereignty over particular economic and fiscal authority or institution which exercises its power at the regional level. At this point in its evolution, SADC seems to favour neo-functionalist and nascent structuralist modes of cooperation over more integrative interdependence. This is reflected in the state-centric nature and importance attached to national concerns that characterize the regime.

In interrogating the chemistry of regional integration within the SADC regime, it needs to be kept in mind that SADC emerged out of a fundamentally changed and changing regional and global context (see, in particular, the chapters by Tsie and Hettne in this volume). Of particular importance is the fact that popular impulses from below for greater public accountability, pluralism and democracy are presently at work in the body politic of every member state. Almost without exception post-independence politics is being interrogated by governing parties, opposition formations and civil society. Against the backdrop of these and other regional and global changes, Mandaza and Tostensen (1994: p. 102) ask whether political solidarity at the regional level will fall victim 'to the absence of the common rallying point provided by the common struggles against colonialism, apartheid and racism'.

While the struggle against apartheid did erode the national sovereignty of the FLS, the new community project of SADC will deepen this project. Seen against the bitter struggle for national sovereignty, it is not strange that member states are hesitant to unreservedly embrace the wider project of community building. Hence the need for a more foundational basis and framework for deepening regional cooperation and enhanced governance. In this the rules, norms, institutions and projects of SADC need to be explored to determine whether the present regime provides an adequate framework for transregional governance.

Objectives, rules, institutions and projects

The core objectives of SADC are contained in Article 5(1) of the 1992 Treaty. These are to

- achieve development and economic growth, alleviate poverty, enhance the standard and quality of life of the peoples of Southern Africa and support the socially disadvantaged through regional integration;
- evolve common political values, systems and institutions;
- promote and defend peace and security;
- promote self-sustaining development as a basis of collective self-reliance, and the interdependence of member states;
- achieve complementarity between national and regional strategies and programmes;
- promote and maximize productive employment and utilization of resources of the region;
- achieve sustainable utilization of natural resources and effective protection of the environment; and
- strengthen and consolidate the long standing historical, social and culture affinities and links among the people of the region.

Article 5(2) embodies ten strategies and various projects in order to achieve the above. These range from harmonizing the political and socio-economic policies and plans of the member states, to cementing cultural ties across the region, to human resources development, to improved management and coordination of the foreign relations of member states.

SADC's stated objectives, strategies and projects reflect the negotiated nature of the regime, as well as its preoccupation with neo-functionalist concerns, primarily through the promotion of regional development and integration. The emphasis placed on the values of 'balance, equity and mutual benefit' reflects not only regional realities, but also a philosophy securely anchored in national states as the principal agencies of the regime. This philosophy is reaffirmed in Article 6 of the Treaty that bind member states of the regime's objectives and norms.

The 1992 Treaty that established SADC expanded the former SADCC's role and power of the Secretariat in three significant domains:

- SADC has been given responsibility for developing policies establishing a common market through the progressive elimination of barriers to the free movement of capital, labour, people, goods and services.
- SADC's operational terms require it to be fully involved in the design and process of regional integration. Its institutional capacity has been modestly strengthened, though it still remains a decentralized regime with specific sector-coordinating functions allocated to member states, and
- SADC's concerns and agenda now include post-Cold War issues such as 'good governance', human rights, gender and democratic practice – all issues of low politics.

Institutions

Article 9 of the Treaty lists the following principal institutions: (i) the Summit of Heads of State and Government; (ii) the Council of Ministers; (iii) the Commissions; (iv) the Standing Committee of Officials; (v) the Secretariat; and (vi) the Tribunal. Other institutions may be established as necessary.

The powers and functions of the principle institutions, save for the proposed Tribunal, mirror those under the former SADCC. They are, once again, marked by a commitment to state-based consensual decision-making.

The Tribunal will be responsible for the proper interpretation of the provisions of the Treaty and its subsidiary instruments. The Tribunal adjudicates upon disputes referred to it and functions under a Protocol of the Summit (Article 16, 1–5). Its decisions will be binding. While the Tribunal has not yet been established (agreement on a Draft Protocol was reached in April 1998), it may become an important instrument of governance and norm setting, two key activities of regimes. Under Article 17 (1–2) member states are called upon to respect the international character and responsibilities of SADC and are called upon not to seek to unduly influence the staff (notably the Secretariat) of the regime.

Before reflecting on the institutional architecture of the regime in more theoretical terms, one other institution needs to be introduced – the SADC Organ on Politics, Defence and Security. The establishment of this Organ early in 1996 illustrates some of the politics of institutions particularly well. The guiding principles of the Organ are set out in Article 4 of the SADC Treaty, and include the following:

- sovereign equality of all member states;
- respect for the sovereignty and territorial integrity of each state and for the inalienable right to independent existence;
- achievement of solidarity, peace and security in the region;
- observance of human rights, democracy and the rule of law;
- promotion of economic development in the SADC region in order to achieve for all member states, equity, balance and mutual benefit;
- peaceful settlement of disputes by negotiation, mediation and arbitration;
- military intervention of whatever nature shall be decided upon only after all possible political remedies have been exhausted in accordance with the Charter of the Organization of African Unity (OAU) and the United Nations.

The SADC 'Organ' as it is often called is meant to work in support of 16 objectives among which are: (i) to protect the people and safeguard the development of the region against instability arising from the breakdown of law and order, inter-state conflict and external aggression; (ii) to promote peacemaking and peacekeeping in order to achieve sustainable peace and security; and (iii) to address extra-regional conflicts which impact on peace and security in Southern Africa (SADC, 1996a).

The Organ operates at Summit level, and functions independently of other SADC structures. It also operates at Ministerial and technical levels, while the Chair of the Organ rotates on an annual and a troika basis. The Summit elects the chairperson of the Organ after wide consultation. The Organ is meant to operate in a flexible and informal manner. The Inter-State Defence and Security Committee (ISDSC) functions as one of the institutions of the Organ, while the Organ may establish other structures as the need arises.

The ISDSC provides a fulcrum where ministers of SADC states responsible for Defence, Home Affairs, Public Security and State Security, discuss matters relating to individual and collective defence and security. Originally established in 1983 under the aegis of the Frontline States, the ISDSC initially included seven member states, with South Africa, Lesotho, Malawi and Swaziland joining in November 1994.

The legacy of the ISDSC, with its narrowly state-centric conception of security, while somewhat diluted within the framework of the Organ, nonetheless lingers on. In the absence of a truly multilateral defence and security secretariat, the Organ is bound to serve bilateral and national interests over regional ones. Moreover, while new thinking on security and its relationship to development, for example, is evident in the Organ, its present structure does not fully support common security; instead, it favours collective defence. The relationship between security cooperation, economic integration and social development, too, needs to be brought into sharper relief.

From the above exposition it is clear that SADC, compared to its antecedent, offers more space for bargaining and negotiated interaction. Unlike the former SADCC, it is guided by a treaty and a Secretariat that is both more empowered and anticipating development of mechanisms to ensure that decisions are implemented. There are also provisions for imposing sanctions on any of the member states which persistently fail, without good reason, to fulfill obligations assumed under the Treaty or pursue policies which undermine SADC's principles and objectives (Article 33, 1–2). Sanctions are to be determined by the Summit on a case-by-case basis.

New dimensions of governance

Like the world of NGOs, governance implies the absence of a central authority and the need for collaboration among a raft of agencies which seek to develop common institutions, norms and goals in addressing common concerns (Weiss and Gordenker, 1996: p. 17). Since governance is about norm setting, policy setting, policy execution, mediation and bargaining, South Africa's accession to SADC in 1994 has had several important implications for the functioning of the regime: first, growing competition between post-apartheid South Africa and Zimbabwe – the only two industrial economies within SADC – for regional hegemony (see Odén, Chapter 8 of this volume). Second, the allocation to South Africa of the strategic financial and investment sector within SADC further enhanced that country's dominance and changed the nature of bargaining within the regime. Third, competition between the Secretariat and member states regarding determination of key projects within the regime is likely to intensify. Finally, the institutional habits and culture associated both with the former FLS and with apartheid South Africa may well endure into the forseeable future. From an epistemic point of view, it is hardly surprising that old habits and diplomatic practices endure, for example in the wrangling over the remit and relationship of the Organ to the other institutions of SADC.

The recent accession of Mauritius, the Democratic Republic of Congo (DRC) and the Seychelles to SADC raises the broader question as to the future relationship between SADC and the 23-member Common Market for Eastern and Southern Africa (COMESA). Integration between SADC and COMESA is still on the agenda and it is increasingly clear that competition rather than cooperation between these two subregional regimes will characterize their future relations. Tanzania's July 1999 decision to withdraw altogether from COMESA, while maintaining full SADC membership, is suggestive of one possible means of resolving the issue.

SADC is evolving nascent sites of transregional governance. These include, *inter alia*, the 1992 Treaty which provides both the legal and normative framework of the regime; Early Warning Systems on agriculture, drought and food security; several Protocols including those on shared watercourse systems, education and training, and mining; several Draft Protocols including those in the area of trade and combatting illicit cross-border drug trafficking; an intergovernmental MOU establishing the Southern African Power Pool (SAPP) which is to guide the development and operation of a region-wide energy grid; a Charter for the Regional Tourism Organization of Southern Africa; and a Declaration by the Heads of State and Government on Gender and Development. Additional Protocols, notably on the contentious issue of the 'free movement of persons' in SADC, are planned. The latter protocol will be of special importance to governance, for it will impact more deeply upon state sovereignty and the human rights of migrants. It will also provide for a normative framework in respect of the rights of citizens and migrants and the obligations of member states in respect of these (on this, see also Niemann in Chapter 4 above).

The July 1996 establishment of the SADC Parliamentary Forum in Windhoek provides yet another site of transregional governance (see SADC, 1995). This forum, which comprises three parliamentarians from each of the fourteen SADC member states, has both normative and developmental objectives. The former include promotion and consolidation of parliamentary democracy as well as safeguarding human and people's rights. The latter include, among others, promoting linkages between democracy and human development in SADC, working in support of regional cooperation and integration and harmonizing legislation in crucial areas such as cross-border movement, passport and border control, trade, crime prevention, import/export regulations and investment (SADC, 1996b). The SADC Electoral Commission, established in 1997, involves itself in norm and policy setting with a view towards making elections more transparent and free. This Commission observes – rather than 'monitors' – elections in SADC countries with the express purpose of ensuring the overall integrity and fairness of the process.

In addition to these sites of governance, SADC inherited from its SADCC antecedent two neo-functionalist modes of interaction and cooperation: SATCC and SACCAR. The 1995 theme document, entitled 'SADC: Resources, Institutions and Capacity for Integration', develops the theme of neo-functionalist integration further with reference to financial and capital markets, as well as cross-border investments. Both of these have taken on added importance following South Africa's 1994 accession to SADC.

The overall effectiveness of SADC as a regime will impact upon the success or other wise of the different protocols shaping and molding the behaviour of its members. Following Young (1982: pp. 160–94), a regime is effective 'to the extent that its operations impel actors to behave differently than they would if the institution did not exist or if some other institutional arrangement were put in its place'. Young is quick to point out that a significant complication concerning individual actor behaviour arises from the fact of states, which are often the principal agencies of regimes – as indeed they are in the case of SADC. In assessing the effectiveness of regimes, therefore, we must analyse the behaviour of states not only in implementing and respecting the provisions of regimes in such a way as to ensure that those operating under their jurisdiction (for example, NGOs, and even individuals) comply with institutional requirements as well. Under the 1992 SADC Treaty (Article 22, 1–3), protocols are seen as integral for structuring cooperation and enhancing governance (see SADC, 1992). Protocols define the domain objectives, scope and institutional arrangements for cooperation and integration. From a governance perspective, protocols also embody core regime principles, norms and values. Their importance for regime formation and consolidation is clear. The different protocols give direction and institutional form to issue regimes in domains as diverse as migration, human rights, water and other natural resources management, trade and investment.

There is a further theoretical caveat regarding 'collective behaviour'. Young (1982: p. 162) reminds us that, 'collective behaviour is not simply a term used to describe the behaviour of the members of inter-national society in the aggregate. Rather, it refers to the outcomes of interactive processes involving two or more members of international society'. Examples of such 'collective behaviour' include inter-state alliances, exchange relationships under conditions approaching perfect competition, unregulated uses of common property resources, harmo-nization of legislative and legal instruments in the domain of human rights and agreements reached through explicit negotiations or out-comes arrived at through open bargaining. While members of a regime may – and often do – differ on the net effects of a particular form of collective behaviour (as is evident in the case of the SADC Organ and the wrangling over the proposed Draft Protocol on the Free Movement of Persons in SADC), none of this alters the fact that collective behav-iour is properly understood as a concept referring to the outcomes of interactive process in contrast to the results of individual or unilateral behaviour or action.

These somewhat abstract considerations are pertinent to SADC as well, for as a loosely knit, state-based regime, SADC is often preoccu-pied with 'high politics', at times at the expense of collective behaviour and regime consolidation. At bottom, the various protocols would only become effective once they become a product of such interactive and collective behaviour.

Regime analysts, however, often find it helpful to approach the issue of effectiveness in more concrete terms, posing a number of focused questions about specific institutional arrangements. Typically, such questions include: Has the operation of the regime solved or alleviated the concerns or problems that led to its formation? Have the partici-pants been able and willing to implement the regime's principle provi-sions with respect to activities taking place within their jurisdictions? Do the members ordinarily comply with the regime's core rights, norms, principles and rules? Can the regime adapt to changing circum-stances without losing its capacity to deal with ongoing problems and concerns?

In the case of SADC, the ideal and the actual often diverge sharply with respect to regime performance in different settings. For example, SADC continues to accord much weight to the project of trade and eco-nomic integration (for understandable reasons) and the mobilizing of foreign assistance, and rather less weight to regime consolidation, com-munity building, transregional civil society and the advancement of a culture of human rights. Member states also continue to direct their energies into nation-building and reconstruction projects, which in some respects, invariably detract from regional concerns. Reliable implementation and perfect compliance, however, are unrealistic. But, as these and other questions suggest, the effectiveness of regimes, like their domestic counterparts, can be assessed in terms of their success in the domains of implementation, compliance and persistence.

Conclusions

While few state-based regimes have succeeded in realizing all of their original expectations and objectives, SADC could become one of the most robust in Africa. At the same time, however, without democratization, legitimate states and the protection of human rights, SADC would reap a bitter harvest of human insecurity.

Since socio-economic development and human security are indissolubly linked, SADC will have to simultaneously achieve democratic consolidation, economic growth and stability. Factors which will contribute to achieving the above will include the reinforcement of transregional civil society; the institutionalization of democratic civil–military relations; the countering of hegemonic ambitions by South Africa; development of peacekeeping and peace-building capacities without including unnecessary rearmament; the broadening of confidence-building in the region rather than bloc-building; and appropriate defensive restructuring.

In addition to these considerations, SADC will have to build joint policy-making and implementation capacity in domains such as migration and human rights, gender, human resources development, technology and the financial sector. There is also a need to strengthen jurisdictional norms through the work of the proposed Tribunal (see SADC, 1998). The overall dependence on foreign capital and technology, too, will have to be reduced by means of a programme of local research and development.

Finally, the future for SADC may well lie in the choice between two broad ideological paths. Down one path lies capitulation to the orthodoxy of the IMF and the World Bank with the regional hegemony of South Africa playing a key disciplinary role (see Odén above). Down the other path, SADC may find enough internal cohesion and political will among its members to negotiate the terms of its subordinate integration, maintaining a modicum of autonomy for national economies in relation to South Africa and defining an appropriate role for the state in regional and national development.

Notes

1. Despite this limitation, notable exceptions, rich in insights of broader security considerations are to be found in the work of, e.g., Jervis (1983); Rittberger (1990); Smith (1987) and Nye (1987).
2. 'Governance' is used here to mean the recognition of the existence of normative obligations and a willingness to honour them in the behaviour of states and other agencies.
3. Founding members were Angola, Botswana, Lesotho, Malawi, Mozambique, Swaziland, Tanzania, Zambia and Zimbabwe. (See also Vale in Chapter 2 above.)

References

African Development Bank (1993), *Economic Integration in Southern Africa* (Oxford: Oxprint).

de Wilde, J. (1991), *Saved from Oblivion: Interdependence Theory in the first half of the 20th Century: A study on the causality between war and complex interdependence* (Aldershot: Dartmouth).

Du Pisani, Andre (1998), 'Regimes and the challenge of transregional governance in Southern Africa', in J. Whitman (ed.), *Citizens and the State in Africa* (London: Macmillan).

Gwaradzimba, Fadzai (1993), 'SADCC and the Future of South African Regionalism', *Issue* 21/1–2, 51–9.

Hanlon, Joseph (1989), *SADCC Projects and Prospects. The Trade and Investment Future of the SADCC* (London: Economist Intelligence Unit, Special Report No. 182).

Hasenclever, Andreas, Peter Mayer and Volker Rittberger (1997), *Theories of International Regimes* (Cambridge: Cambridge University Press).

Hawkins, T. (1992), 'A mere magnet of funds', *Die Suid-Afrikaan*, (Oct.–Nov.) 13–14.

Jervis, Robert (1983), 'Security Regimes', in Stephen D. Kraser (ed.), *International Regimes* (Ithaca, NY: Cornell University Press).

Keohane, Robert O. (1989), *International Institutions and State Power: essays in international relations theory* (Boulder, CO: Westview Press).

Krasner, Stephen D. (ed.) (1982), 'Structural Causes and Regime Consequences: Regimes as intervening variables', *International Organization* 36/2.

Krasner, Stephen D. (ed.) (1983), *International Regimes* (Ithaca, NY: Cornell University Press).

Kratochwil, Friedrich and John G. Ruggie (1986), 'International Organization: The State of the Art on the Art of the State', *International Organization* 40, 753–75.

Lubbe, Ingrid Lisa (1989), *The Southern African Development Coordination Conference (SADCC): part of a whole or a cover?*, unpublished MA thesis, Rhodes University (Nov.).

Maasdorp, Gavin (1992), *Economic Cooperation in Southern Africa: prospects for regional integration* (London: Research Institute for the Study of Conflict and Terrorism).

Mandaza, Ibbo, and Arne Tostensen (1994), *Southern Africa in Search of a Common Future: From the Conference to a Community* (Gaborone: SADC).

Nye, Joseph S. (1987), 'Nuclear Learning and US-Soviet Security Regimes', *International Organization* 41, 371–402.

Odén, Bertil (1993), *Southern Africa after Apartheid* (Uppsala: Nordiska Afrikainstitutet).

Ostergaard, Tom (1989), *SADCC Beyond Transportation: the challenge of industrial cooperation* (Uppsala: Scandinavian Institute of African Studies).

Puchala, Donald and R. F. Hopkins (1982), 'International Regimes: lessons from inductive analysis', *International Organization* 36/2.

Rittberger, Volker (1990), *International Regimes in East-West Politics* (London: Frances Pinter).

SADCC (1980), *The Lusaka Declaration* (Lusaka, April).

SADC (1992), *Treaty of the Southern African Development Community* (Windhoek, August).

SADC (1995), *SADC Parliamentary Forum: The Constitution* (Windhoek, May).

SADC (1996a), *The SADC Organ on Politics, Defence and Security*, mimeo (Gaborone, January).

SADC (1996b), *SADC Parliamentary Forum*, mimeo (Gaborone, July).

SADC (1998), *Draft Protocol on the Tribunal of the Southern African Development Community*, mimeo (Swakopmund, April).

Strange, Susan (1982), 'Cave! Hic Dragones: A Critique of Regime Analysis', *International Organization* 36/2.

Strange, Susan (1995), 'Political Economy and International Relations', in Ken Booth and Steve Smith (eds), *International Relations Theory Today* (London: Polity Press).

Smith, R. K. (1987), 'Explaining the Non-Proliferation Regime: Anomalies for Contemporary International Relations Theory', *International Organization* 41, 253–82.

Weiss, Thomas G., and Leon Gordenker (1996), *NGOs, the UN and Global Governance* (London: Lynne Rienner).

Young, Oran (1982), 'Regime dynamics, the rise and fall of international regimes', *International Organization* 36/2.

Young, Oran (1989), *International Coordination: Building Regimes for Natural Resources and the Environment* (Ithaca, NY: Cornell University Press).

10
Critical Theory, Robert Cox and Southern Africa[1]

Anthony Leysens

The success or failure of the critical theory of international relations will be determined by the amount of light cast on present possibilities and not just by its performance in the spheres of philosophy and historical sociology alone.

– Linklater (1990: p. 172)

Introduction

The first phase of the 'return to the fold' of South Africa, one could argue, was formally set in motion in 1990 with the release of Nelson Mandela and ended in 1994 after his inauguration as the country's first democratically elected president. In the same year South Africa became a member of the Southern African Development Community (SADC). During this time Southern Africa has, deservedly, received a substantial amount of attention, most of it focusing on regional security issues[2] and the dynamics of regional integration/cooperation.[3] The scholarly output has come mainly from within the fields of international political economy and economics, and can be divided into orthodox/traditional and critical approaches.[4]

In this chapter an attempt is made to indicate the relevance and potential use of critical theory (CT) as an approach with which to view and study the Southern African region. More particularly, I focus on Coxian critical theory (CCT) and try to illustrate that it offers a coherent, consistent, and comprehensive theoretical framework which has the potential to act as an explanatory and heuristic tool for regional analysis. The reasons for choosing CCT are that it is flexible, reflective, and change-oriented or 'transformative' (see also Tsie, in Chapter 6 above).

The flexibility of CCT is to be found in the way it offers the analyst various 'points of entry'[5] which do not interact deterministically. These are: social forces related to production, the state, and the prevailing world order. To these we could add a regional point of entry. Coxian critical theory thus transcends the traditional state-domestic division of neo-realism and addresses the agent-structure problem which both neo-realism and world system theory do not resolve. This problem takes the form of what Wendt (1987: pp. 342–6) calls 'ontological reductionism'. In the case of neo-realism the structure of the system is (ontologically) defined in terms of the characteristics of its agents (states); in the case of world system theory the action of agents (states and classes) are derived from the characteristics of the (capitalist) system.[6] Second, in its focus on the nature of the relation of social forces to production, CCT emphasizes the importance of production in society: 'Production creates the material basis for all forms of social existence, and the ways in which human efforts are combined in productive processes affect all other aspects of social life' (Cox, 1987: p. 1). However, production is not ontologically viewed in a deterministic manner, even though it can enhance state power. The relationship is one of reciprocity: 'It has no historical precedence; indeed, the principal structures of production have been, if not actually created by the state, at least encouraged and sustained by the state' (Cox, 1987: p. 5).

Coxian critical theory is reflective because it acknowledges the indivisibility between subject and object. This premise leads to a willingness to reflect on the origin and nature of theory (Cox, 1986a: p. 207). This means that we have to reflect critically on the use of theory and its relation to broader politico-economic agendas. Theory, in other words, must be evaluated in terms of its consistency, comprehensiveness and coherency, but also in terms of whether it reflects upon itself, its historical development and origin within a particular social context. This leads one to CCT's transformative agenda and its orientation to (feasible) changes of the status quo. CCT does not accept that a given configuration of power relations are necessarily static. The analysis undertaken, particularly the focus on contradictions in prevailing orders, attempts to identify sites where change is likely to occur, and also to identify whether there are social forces which can be mobilized to present a counter-hegemonic challenge.

At this point, an initial caveat needs to be made. There is no hidden hegemonic agenda in my argument which aims to offer CT as 'the next stage in the development of International Relations Theory' (Hoffman, 1987: p. 244). While I am obviously in agreement with the underlying assumptions which inform CT, I am also motivated by the need for critical regional analysis to develop a link between theory and practical research. On this point I agree with Keohane's (1995) observation that critical, or reflective approaches[7] as he calls them, need to develop 'research agendas'.

In this regard I find Lapid's challenge – in an article commenting on the 1988 CT debate between Hoffman and Rengger – to be a reasonable one: 'To make critical theory more accessible and acceptable to mainstream scholar (*sic*) in international relations, proponents of critical theory must demonstrate that the core elements of the critical perspective can be fruitfully applied in innovative international relations studies' (Lapid, 1989: p. 85).

Herein lies the rub in 'going critical' (Rengger, 1988). In the remainder of the chapter, I first briefly differentiate between CT and postmodernism, both of which are often generically referred to as 'critical approaches' (compare, for example, George, 1994). I then set out the premises of Cox's critical theory. This is followed by a section in which I argue that, although much 'thinking space' has been opened up by critical approaches to regional analysis, some of the assumptions which have been made and prescriptions offered need to be located within an explanatory framework which is historically sensitive. In this respect, the admirable advocating of 'bottom up' perspectives needs to be followed by 'bottom up' research. Finally, I try to show what a critical, region-specific research agenda might look like.

Critical theory and postmodernism

The roots of the debate between CT and postmodernism lie in the philosophy of social and political theory, from where it has also gradually penetrated through to international relations and finds itself somewhat on the margins of enquiry. It is impossible to address this debate with any form of sophistication within the space constraints of this chapter.[8] The purpose of my comments here is to show a sensitivity and awareness of the difference between the two forms of enquiry, and to locate Cox's framework within CT.

The modern intellectual genealogy of CT is usually traced back to the members of the 'Frankfurt School'. This group of intellectuals – Adorno, Horkheimer, Fromm and later Habermas – were members of the Institut für Sozialforschung which was loosely attached to the University of Frankfurt. Horkheimer's distinction between 'critical' and 'traditional theory' is reflected in Cox's (1981) reference to 'critical' and 'problem-solving' theory. At the heart of traditional theory lies the modern version of Cartesian rational 'man'. Horkheimer, specifically refers to the positivist methodology of the natural sciences and its use in the investigation of social phenomena. Furthermore, this application of a universal, ahistorical 'set of tools' predicates *inter alia* a separation between subject (scientist) and object (reality) (Held, 1980: p. 29; Bernstein, 1976: pp. 179–80).

Critical theory, in contrast, posits a link between knowledge and interests/power. It, in other words, locates theory within a historical power matrix. Theory itself needs to be reflected upon. Neufeld (1995: p. 103) argues that within the positivist framework of enquiry, which professes value neutrality, lies the kernel of control: the ability to predict, gives one the option to prevent, or to exercise control.

Cox (1981: pp. 129–30) acknowledges the link between theory and interests/power, when he states that 'theory is always *for* someone and *for* some purpose'. Furthermore, when discussing CT and problem-solving theory, he sees the latter as operating within the power relations of a particular framework which is accepted as a given and does not need to be questioned. In effect, however, this approach maintains the prevailing order by focusing on 'problems' which, when resolved and/or controlled, ensure the maintenance of existing relations and institutions. Cox (1981: p. 130) concludes that, 'this aim rather belies the frequent claim of problem-solving theory to be value free... It is value-bound by virtue of the fact that it implicitly accepts the prevailing order as its own framework'.

For Cox, CT, in contrast, focuses on the nature and origins of the existing order itself. Institutions and power relations are investigated historically to build up a broader picture. In addition, contradictions within the contemporary order are identified to indicate possible future change and transformation. Critical theory also has a definite value component in that it 'allows for a normative choice in favour of a social and political order different from the prevailing order, but it limits the range of choice to alternative orders which are feasible transformations of the existing world' (Cox, 1981: p. 130). Cox's critical theory therefore can be said to have a distinct non-utopian character.[9]

The connection between a particular, modernist form of knowledge and power is, of course, also emphasized by postmodernists. Subject and object are regarded as constructs which are the result of 'historical practice'. By using methods such as deconstruction, textuality and genealogy postmodernists have illustrated how orthodox versions of reality (for example, realist conceptions of, among other things, sovereignty, diplomacy, and foreign policy) can be problematized when they are placed within historical, primarily-Western, context.[10] Far from being objective accounts of the real world, they lead to 'closure' and an account of the world which is ahistorical, universalist and based on the foundationalism of the post-Enlightment project. The postmodernist critique of CT is based on the accusation of the latter's foundationalism, in particular its refusal to delink from modernism, and its aspirations to develop a universalist explanatory framework (George, 1994: pp. 158–61, 191–2).

It is particularly Habermas who has borne the brunt of this criticism. His concern to emancipate critical social theory from the domination of 'technical-cognitive', problem-solving, positivist knowledge by, again, linking the three knowledge bases (technical/positivist; practical/ historical interpretative; emancipatory/critically reflective) to each other and human interests, is deemed to be foundationalist and universalist. Whereas Habermas sees room to manoeuvre within modernity, post-modernists do not. There is no promise in the rationality of the Enlightenment; its foundations have not been distorted, they were distorted 'in the first instance' (George, 1994: pp. 154–5, 160; Bernstein, 1976: pp. 192–3).

I am in agreement with George (1994: pp. 161–6) when he warns against a too simplistic reading of Habermas's work by some postmodernists. The crude position of simply detaching oneself from modernity, of 'throwing the [modernist] baby out with the bath water' (Habermas quoted in George, 1994: p. 159), in itself leads to closure and disconnection from political practice. On the issue of rationality and its connection to the modernist project Hoffman (1988: p. 92), arguing from within a CT perspective, makes the point eloquently:

> The difficulty is not with rationality *per se* but its distorted and partial development through the universalization of a single form of rationality, namely instrumental, economic and administrative reason ... Critical theory ... seeks to critique the development of certain forms of rationality but does not accept the radical interpretivist renunciation of reason itself.

Critical Theory thus engages in the process of inquiry by attempting to substantiate the claims it makes through the presentation of evidence, while it accepts that the principles of any theory are not cast in stone and that theory can and has been used as a legitimating narrative. As Cox (1981: p. 129) states: 'Because it deals with a changing reality, critical theory must continually adjust its concepts to the changing object it seeks to understand and explain'. Essentially this does not differ from the point which Lyotard (1992: p. 28) makes when he reflects on whether the modernist project can be sustained:

> The question suggests that to be sustained, such a project would call for strength and competence, and that these things may have failed us. Such a reading would have to spark an inquiry, an inquiry into the failing of the modern subject. And if this failing should be a matter of dispute, then we must be able to produce evidence for it in the form of facts or at least signs.

There is therefore, it seems to me, room for debate and engagement between CT and postmodernism. The alternative is closure.

Coxian critical theory: a framework for analysis

Cox's framework incorporates the interaction and mutual effects between social forces, states and world orders. State forms are the result of social forces within the state and the nature of their incorporation within the world order.[11] The investigation of the relations between social forces, states and world orders, that is their 'configuration', must take place within the context of a specific historical structure (Cox, 1981: pp. 133–5, 137).

Before going on to consider the elements of a historical structure I need to briefly point out two important aspects of historical material-ism which Cox takes from the historical, not the 'scientific' Marx. The first relates to *dialectic* which for Cox, at the logical level, means look-ing for contradictions, in the sense that concepts must continuously be measured against the reality they represent, and, at the historical level, an awareness of the possibility of the transformation of historical struc-tures due to tensions arising between contending social forces. The sec-ond is his focus on the links between power relations in *production processes*, the state, and the global order.

Within historical structures three 'forces' dynamically interact in a non-deterministic manner; actors can either accommodate themselves to these forces or resist. They are ideas, institutions and material capa-bilities. How these forces are configured is not a matter of abstraction but is determined by a study of the particular historical epoch within which they are located. Secondly, it also requires a focus on tensions which can lead to the emergence of 'rival structures'.

Ideas are divided by Cox into inter-subjective meanings, that is shared notions about for instance the nature of the state and its role, and the relations between states, and different perceptions by social groups about the 'legitimacy of prevailing power relations' which he calls 'collective images of social order'. Institutions are used to maintain a specific order; they reflect power relations and promote 'collective images' which are in tandem with these power relations. Material capabilities include technology, wealth, industries and armaments (Cox, 1981: pp. 136–7).

It is within historical structures that the three levels – social forces related to production, forms of state and world orders – can be viewed/explained in terms of the configurations between ideas, institutions and material capabilities. The meaning and use of the concept hegemony is crucial to understand the dynamics of this schema.

Cox's conceptualization of hegemony is Gramscian in origin (Cox, 1986b). This has several implications. First, it conceives of the state not just in terms of its traditional/realist apparatus – bureaucracy and executive – but includes those aspects of society which assist in maintaining the hegemony of the dominant social forces, specifically those related to production. Second, the means by which these forces maintain dominance is through the achievement of consensus. Thus, a hegemonic order, or hegemony, is characterized not only by coercion through the use of material power capabilities; it 'brings the interests of the leading class into harmony with those of subordinate classes and incorporates these other interests into an ideology expressed in universalist terms' (Cox, 1983: p. 168). Cox (1983) then goes on to apply Gramsci's concept of hegemony to 'international relations', incorporating his three levels and the components of historical structures.

At the level of world orders, hegemony – for example, *pax britannica* or *pax americana* – is the consequence of a 'fit' between ideas/ideology (support for 'free' trade), institutions (International Monetary Fund) and material capabilities (military, productive, technological). A hegemonic order, moreover, provides 'rewards' to ensure consensus and in order to incorporate potential resistance: so, among other things, preferential trade arrangements at the level of the state, and development assistance for rural 'self-reliance' at the sub-national level (Cox, 1981: p. 141; Cox, 1983: p. 171).

A hegemonic world order is not only an inter-state system. States can be seen as reflections of local configurations of social forces, which bring to the mix, among other actors, local capital/manufacturing; established, skilled, corporate, unionised labour; and non-established, semi- or unskilled, temporarily employed labour. Each of these groups may have links with transnational social forces (for example, global corporate managers, social movements). In terms of these configurations, forms of state – mercantilist, liberal, hyperliberal – and how they are incorporated within a particular world order can be identified (Cox, 1981: pp. 141, 148).

Moreover, social forces are related to specific modes of production. Cox (1987: p. 32) identifies twelve modes of production which have developed historically during pre-capitalist and capitalist phases. It is important to note that some of the premodern modes of production which have disappeared in core states, coexist with modern modes of production in peripheral states and regions. To illustrate how these may obtain in and shed light upon the Southern African region, I will refer to only three: primitive labour market, tripartism and state corporatism. The last two are modes of production which Cox locates within modern capitalist development, while the first is located in the pre-capitalist, simple reproduction phase.

Historically, changes in hegemonic world orders have been brought about by a change in the configuration of social forces related to production in the core states. For example, the cost of incorporating manufacturing workers in late nineteenth-century Britain, through the provision of welfare benefits, led to increased calls for protectionism and the decline of the free trade regime (Cox, 1981: pp. 141–2). Lastly, the hegemonic order, which has historically expanded from the core states after undergoing 'a thorough social and economic revolution' is 'laden with contradictions at the periphery'. This can be seen in the responses of local configurations of social forces – labour, capital and bureaucracy – in the periphery to the globalization of production, and the 'internationalisation of the state' (Cox, 1983: p. 171; Cox, 1981: pp. 146, 151). The necessary analytical 'building blocks' are therefore: social forces related to modes of production, states (and the particular form of those states), and the nature of the current world order.

Implications for Southern African regional analysis

In this section I offer some suggestions as to how the Coxian framework might be used as an approach to understanding and developing regional relations. The aim here is not to undertake a fully detailed empirical analysis, but rather to illustrate the heuristic potential of his theory and how the shift in focus gives us new insights and alternative avenues for research. I start by pointing out some theoretical implications, particularly related to reflexivity.

The first implication of using Coxian critical theory (CCT) is that we must look for contradictions in the concepts we use. Put differently, those concepts employed must be measured against the reality they are said to represent. This means that we must be historically sensitive when importing terminology from one space and time bound location to another. For instance, did advocacy of a regional security institution for Southern Africa based on the 'basket' approach of the former Conference for Security Cooperation in Europe (CSCE) critically take into account the vast historical differences between the security problems of Europe and the region (see Baynham, 1994)? The historical structure wherein concepts are developed and used to describe that particular structure should be of primary concern to the critical scholar, before they are applied to different historical settings. The attempt by Van Aardt (1997a) to evaluate the utility of the concepts 'regime' and 'community' to describe the security structure in Southern Africa marks one attempt to import concepts first developed to describe, explain and *prescribe* order within a particular historical context at the global, and not the regional level.[12]

Second, using CCT means being aware of the difference between 'problem-solving' and 'critical' approaches. This means not looking at security issues (migration, poverty, arms smuggling, drug trafficking, population growth, and the environment) in the region as being problems which need to be 'technically' resolved or 'controlled' within the prevailing framework (compare Cilliers, 1996). It also means accepting that there is an indivisible link between political and economic – read 'development' – security.

Some mainstream approaches to the region, in contrast, advocate 'divorcing' development from traditional, political security issues in the region (see, for example, Malan, 1998). Critical theory means looking at the historical structure of which the 'problems' are mere symptoms. Attempts to control the symptoms translate into maintaining the power configurations which cause them. We therefore have to perceive of these security problems as being signs of tensions which may lead to or require the transformation of the historical structure itself.

At this point, I want to issue a caveat. My use of CT does not warrant a rejection of 'problem-solving' approaches[13] as such. It does, however, recognize that the dominance of this approach and its use of a positivist rationale to evaluate what form of knowledge production is acceptable, has led to the drowning out of hermeneutic and critical approaches, Habermas's other two knowledge-constitutive bases (Habermas, 1972). The point, however, is not to replace one form of hegemonic knowledge with another, but to recognize the contribution which all three forms of knowledge creation can make. To this effect, critical theorists need to remain aware of the link between problem-solving approaches and practice, as well as their normative goal of wanting to 'control'. This does not mean, however, that the results of problem-solving research can be ignored or discounted, but rather that we have to critically and historically account for them in our own explanations.

A concrete example of this is the assumption made by critical scholars who focus on the region that migration in Southern Africa 'has further undermined the viability of states and the integrity of borders' (Booth and Vale, 1997: p. 351). While it can be argued that states in Southern Africa can be classified as weak states, including South Africa, the inter-subjective perception of the state in the eyes of the people of the region may be altogether a different matter. In their eyes states may still seem to serve some purpose. For instance, the findings of a recent IDASA national survey undertaken in Lesotho, Zimbabwe, and southern Mozambique indicated that 62 per cent of the respondents agreed 'that it is important to have a border that clearly differentiates their country from others', while 51 per cent agreed 'that borders do, in fact, differentiate people'. These sort of results cannot be ignored. On the one hand, they may be an indication that cross-border migration cannot be equated summarily with 'doing away' with *de jure* borders and states. However, they cannot be uncritically accepted, or ahistorically explained either.

I now turn to the heuristic potential of Cox's framework for regional analysis. Although many critical scholars have stressed the importance of a 'bottom-up' approach or perspective for regional analysis, much of the subsequent work has focused on the institutional or 'high political' aspect of regional relations, particularly the developments around the creation of the SADC Organ on Politics Defence and Security (see Thompson in this volume). This may be understandable given the fact that scholars often follow the path of events. A Coxian framework, however, leads us to focus not only on institutions, but also on ideas and capabilities. His framework, of course, does not include the regional level but I believe that it lends itself to the incorporation of this level. After all, the region consists of social forces and states, and is located within a world order. Leaving the issue of regional ideas, institutions, and capabilities aside for the moment, where might we start?

Regional enquiry, in terms of a Coxian framework, should begin with an analysis of the configuration of social forces related to production within the member states of the SADC,[14] and an investigation of trans-border linkages between them. The focus on social forces related to production does not undermine the notion of a broader conceptualiza-tion of security, because most of the non-traditional security issues (for example, migration) are the result (in terms of being excluded or mar-ginalized) of the power configurations between labour, capital and the state, and how they are incorporated within the contemporary world order.

For example, returning to the three modes of production identified earlier – primitive labour market, tripartism and state corporatism – we should look historically at social forces within and between states in the region to determine where the contradictions lie in the regional historical structure. In peripheral societies the primitive labour market still forms a large component of the population. The primitive labour market, according to Cox (1987: pp. 44–8), exists on the margins of the formal economy. It is an unskilled 'reserve pool of labour' which main-tains social cohesion through kinship and ethnic ties to the rural areas and through a clientelistic relationship with the state. This is particu-larly so in the African case. Support for the legitimacy of the state and the accumulation of capital is given in return for the provision of basic amenities. In South Africa, for instance, this is the group Simon Bekker labels the 'other half', those who were not privy to the elite bargain which enabled South Africa's transition to go ahead, and which do not form part of 'civil society' (Bekker, 1997: p. 69).

Tripartism is described by Cox (1987: p. 74) as an institutionalized arrangement where the state takes direct interest in shaping those agreements reached between labour and capital. This is normally found when trade unions are well organized and accept 'the continued orga-nization of the economy through the capitalist mode of development and recognition by capital that this acquiescence must be acquired by some concessions to labour' (Cox, 1987: p. 78). This coalition is widely attributed as having historically underpinned the welfare state form in Europe, and is deemed by some analysts as descriptive of the present alignment of forces within the National Economic, Development and Labour Council (NEDLAC) in South Africa. Whether NEDLAC will in the long run effectively promote the consolidation or 'rooting' of either tripartism or corporatism in South Africa is, however, a moot point (compare, for example, Pretorius, 1996).

The relations between state, capital and labour are, in contrast, quite different in the other Southern African states. This arrangement can be more accurately described by what Cox (1987: p. 79) calls 'state corporatism'. State corporatism occurs under conditions where one party dominates or where open party competition exists in name only. The state class dominates both labour and capital and the latter groups 'seek satisfaction mainly through direct relations with the officials either of the state bureaucracy or of the ruling political party' (Cox, 1987: pp. 80–1). Industrial peace is regarded as being in the national interest and any disturbances are dealt with severely by the state security apparatus. This form of state control runs into trouble, however, when the system is no longer perceived as legitimate by (organized and primitive) labour and capital because of a crisis in accumulation. The process of state cooptation/domination of labour in Zimbabwe after independence can be cited as an example. Sachikonye (1995) describes how a weakly organized Zimbabwe Congress of Trade Unions (ZCTU), which was initially coopted by the state, turned into a well organized labour movement prepared to challenge the state on the issue of economic liberalization (a condition of the IMF Economic Structural Adjustment Programme). The ongoing crisis is rooted in the inability of the Zimbabwean state class to maintain distributionist policies in the form of welfare measures, for instance the scrapping of the minimum wage guarantee, which are the quid pro quo for continued support.

Having determined and located historically the specific configuration of social forces within member states, we would next have to investigate regional linkages between them, and to place each state–society complex and the region within the contemporary global order. Currently, this is an order which, to emphasize an earlier point, is being shaped by the changes within the state–society complexes of the core states.

Important, in this regard, are the mostly successful attempts to break down the welfare state in Europe and the anti-welfare bill which was initiated by the Clinton administration and passed by the US legislature in 1997. The notion of a global market 'disembedded' from global society inhibits the abilities of peripheral states to address the needs of the 'marginalized', in particular the peasantry and urban unemployed. This is a major area of tension and potential change in the region.

In terms of Cox's framework one would, thus, expect to find a link between the dominant social forces (manufacturing capital with global links and their established labour force) in member states of the SADC and the global order. Furthermore, one would also expect to find that the hegemonic order in the region reflects the ideas/ideology – free trade and market competitiveness – of the global order. In Southern

Africa this manifests itself most overtly in the form of both formal and *de facto* structural adjustment programmes.

Hegemony in the Gramscian sense, it will be recalled, does not depend on coercion but on consensus. The question of whether South Africa is a 'partner or hegemon' therefore should be recast (see, for example, Ahwireng-Obeng and McGowan, 1998). In order to maintain a hypothetical regional hegemonic order, South Africa would have to be a partner and/or acquire partners in the region. Partners are acquired by making concessions, extending rewards and building institutions which espouse ideas and values (a universalist language) acceptable to subordinate social forces/states. To illustrate how this might work in the region we need to return to the concept of 'historical structure', the notion of ideas, material capabilities and institutions, and the 'fit' which is required between them to ensure a hegemonic order.

South Africa's material capabilities *vis-à-vis* the region are well documented. In fact, as Holden shows in Chapter 7 above, the region has become the main export market for South Africa's manufactured products (see also Ahwireng-Obeng and McGowan, 1998; Davies, 1997). When it comes to ideas, the universalist language in which South Africa's regional agenda is couched – 'equity', 'mutually beneficial', and 'non-hegemonic' political-economic order – is crucial to the establishment of a climate of consensus. These ideas, specifically the notion of mutually beneficial trade and cooperation which takes cognizance of developmental needs, are also reflected in and supported by SADC as an institution. My contention would be, however, that this 'universalist' language hides a very real hegemonic order of the Gramscian type. Moreover, it is a regional order which replicates the ideas/ideology of the current global hegemonic order.

Tsie (1996: p. 85) expresses surprise at the SADC Protocol on Trade which runs counter to the expressed developmental goals of the organization. Historically, however, there are reasons as to why a 'market oriented approach' (Davies, 1994) to regional integration is being followed. Martin (1990) shows how South Africa's position as a 'core' state within a peripheral region was established during the inter-war years, when it used the instability caused by the changeover from a British hegemonic order to an American one in order to implement protectionist policies in its regional trade relations. Before, regional trade was, for the greater part, free. Today, South Africa, as the political-economic hegemon, can afford to open its market to regional trade albeit with reservations expressed by traditionally protected sectors of the economy such as textiles. Primarily as a result of IMF SAPs, a number of states in the region have already opened their markets to extra-regional trade. Furthermore, regional free trade is in the interests of specific sections of South African capital and labour, that is those who are globally integrated and connected. The universalist language used in SADC documents is there to compensate, reward or simply placate the subordinate/marginalized social forces.

Concluding remarks

It is my contention that the major problem for future regional relations lies in the exclusion of these marginalized, subordinate social forces. They are not part of the dominant social forces which make up the present society–state–regional complex and are therefore a potential area of tension and transformation within the current historical structure. I have argued that a Coxian explanatory framework has the potential to productively investigate the contradictions found in the Southern African region. This, in sum, requires a focus on dominant social forces related to production in member states and the regional linkages between them; the nature of regional hegemony and its global links; the identification of marginalized regional social forces; the characteristics of the current global order; and the contradictions that manifest themselves there. Above all, a 'reflective' approach to theory should underpin the investigation.

Notes

1. A revised version of this chapter appears as 'Critical Theory and the Southern African Region: A Framework for Discovery', in *Journal of Contemporary African Studies*.
2. The concept security is used here in the 'broader' sense. This means that the traditional focus, which equates state security with individual security and emphasizes external threats to sovereignty, is rejected for an approach which recognizes that states can themselves be sources of insecurity (see, e.g., Krause and Williams, 1997). This approach also emphasizes issues which, in the past, have not been regarded as part of the security agenda. Swatuk and Omari (1997: pp. 90–5) identify a number of these issues in a regional context: poverty and economic marginalization, refugees, population growth, the environment, and AIDS.
3. See, for instance, Booth and Vale (1995; 1997), Carim (1995), Davies (1992; 1994; 1997), Cilliers (1996), Du Pisani (1992), Hull (1996), Keet (1994), Leistner (1995) Maasdorp (1994), Martin (1990), Mills (1995), Swatuk (1997), Thompson (1995), Tsie (1996), Vale (1996; 1997), Vale and Daniel (1995), Van Aardt (1993; 1995; 1997a,b), and Van Nieuwkerk (1995). This is by no means an exhaustive list, but it does point to some of the various

approaches which have been used in analyses of the Southern African region.
4. I return to this distinction below. See also Chapters 5 to 9 in this volume.
5. As opposed to 'levels of analysis'. I am grateful to Larry Swatuk for suggesting this term to me.
6. For further elaboration of these approaches, see Solomon, Hettne and Tsie in this volume.
7. A reference to the premise of critical approaches that theory itself must be theoretically reflected upon, and historically located within political, economic and social power structures (Neufeld, 1995: p. 20).
8. For an edited volume on the debate, with original contributions by Foucault and Habermas, see Kelly (1994). Also, see Thompson in Chapter 11 of this volume.
9. 'Critical theory ... would be over-stepping its competence if it undertook to project desirable forms of life into the future, instead of criticizing existing forms of life' (Habermas quoted in Hoffman, 1988: pp. 92–3). See also Cox (1987: p. 393): 'Critical awareness of potentiality for change must be distinguished from utopian planning, i.e., the laying out of the design of a future society that is to be the end goal of change'.
10. On sovereignty see Ashley and Walker (1990), on diplomacy, Der Derian (1987) and on foreign policy, Shapiro (1987).
11. Cox's (1986a: p. 242) view of the relationship between individuals and institutions is one in which the latter are the outcome of 'collective (human) responses to a collectively perceived problematic (the physical material context) that produce certain practices'. Furthermore, the state as an institution, response and practice does not exist in the same sense as the individual, but only exists through the shared intersubjective meaning with which individuals perceive it.
12. For an account highlighting problems associated with the concept 'regime' in the Southern African context, as well as its ideological connotations see Thompson (1991). See also, Du Pisani in Chapter 9 of this volume.
13. For an example of a 'problem-solving' approach to military security in Southern Africa see Hull (1996).
14. This is a point well made by Tsie (1996: pp. 81, 87–8), although I do not agree with his rather ahistorical reference to the potential of an 'autonomous' (along the lines of the Asian NICs) 'populist' state as having 'the greatest potential for promoting development in the region' (Tsie, 1996: p. 96). Autonomous from the prevailing world order, or autonomous from 'civil society'? There seems to be a contradiction here, whichever way one wants to answer the question.

References

Ahwireng-Obeng, Fred, and Patrick McGowan (1998), 'Partnership or Hegemon? South Africa in Africa: Part One', *Journal of Contemporary African Studies* 16/1 (Dec.–Jan.).
Ashley, Richard K., and R. B. J. Walker (1990), 'Reading Dissidence/Writing the Discipline: Crisis and the Question of Sovereignty in International Studies', *International Studies Quarterly* 34/3.

Baynham, Simon (1994), 'Regional Security in the Third World with Specific Reference to Southern Africa', *Strategic Review for Southern Africa* 16/1 (March).

Bekker, S. (1997) book review of H. Adam, F. Van Zyl Slabbert and K. Moodley, 'Comrades in Business: Post-Liberation Politics in South Africa', in *Politikon* 24, 2.

Bernstein, Richard (1976), *The Restructuring of Social and Political Theory* (Oxford: Basil Blackwell).

Booth, Ken, and Peter Vale (1995), 'Security in Southern Africa: After Apartheid, Beyond Realism', *International Affairs* 71/2 (April).

Booth, Ken, and Peter Vale (1997), 'Critical Security Studies and Regional Insecurity: The Case of Southern Africa', in Keith Krause and Michael Williams (eds), *Critical Security Studies* (Minneapolis: University of Minnesota Press).

Carim, Xavier (1995), 'Critical and Postmodern Readings of Strategic Culture and Southern African Security in the 1990s', *Politikon* 22/2 (Dec.).

Cilliers, Jakkie (1996), 'The Evolving Security Architecture in Southern Africa', *Africa Insight* 26/1.

Cox, Robert W. (1981), 'Social Forces, States and World Orders: Beyond International Relations Theory', *Millennium* 10/2.

Cox, Robert W. (1983), 'Gramsci, Hegemony and International Relations: An Essay in Method', *Millennium* 12/2.

Cox, Robert W. (1986a), 'Postscript 1985', in Robert O. Keohane (ed), *Neorealism and its Critics* (New York: Columbia University Press).

Cox, Robert W. (1986b), 'Social Forces, States and World Orders: Beyond International Relations Theory', in Robert O. Keohane (ed.), *Neorealism and its Critics* (New York: Columbia University Press).

Cox, Robert W. (1987), *Production, Power, and World Order: Social Forces in the Making of History* (New York: Columbia University Press).

Davies, Rob (1992), 'Emerging South African Perspectives on Regional Cooperation and Integration after Apartheid', *Transformation* 20.

Davies, Rob (1994), 'Approaches to Regional Integration in the Southern African Context', *African Insight* 24/1.

Davies, Rob (1997), 'Promoting Regional Integration in Southern Africa: An Analysis of Prospects and Problems from a South African Perspective', in Larry A. Swatuk and David R. Black (eds), *Bridging the Rift: The New South Africa in Africa* (Boulder, CO: Westview Press).

Der Derian, James (1987), *On Diplomacy: A Genealogy of Western Estrangement* (Oxford: Basil Blackwell).

Du Pisani, Andre (1992), 'Security and Peace in Post-Apartheid Southern Africa', *International Affairs Bulletin* 16/3.

George, Jim (1994), *Discourses of Global Politics: A Critical (Re)Introduction to International Relations* (Boulder, CO: Lynne Rienner).

Habermas, Jurgen (1972), *Knowledge and Human Interests* (Boston: Beacon).

Held, David (1980), *Introduction to Critical Theory: Horkheimer to Habermas* (Berkeley: University of California Press).

Hoffman, Mark (1987), 'Critical Theory and the Inter-Paradigm Debate', *Millennium* 16/2.

Hoffman, Mark (1988), 'Conversations on Critical International Relations Theory', *Millennium* 17/1.

Hull, Adrian (1996), 'Rational Choice, Security, and Economic Cooperation in Southern Africa', *Africa Today* 43.

Keet, Dot (1994), 'International Players and Programmes for – and against – Economic Integration in Southern Africa', *Southern African Perspectives*, no. 36 (Bellville: Centre for Southern African Studies).

Kelly, Michael (ed.) (1994), *Critique and Power: Recasting the Foucault/Habermas Debate* (Cambridge, MA: MIT).

Keohane, Robert (1995), 'International Institutions: Two Approaches', in James Der Derian (ed.), *International Theory: Critical Investigations* (London: Macmillan).

Krause, Keith and Michael Williams (1997), 'From Strategy to Security: Foundations of Critical Security Studies', in Keith Krause and Michael Williams (eds), *Critical Security Studies* (Minneapolis: University of Minnesota Press).

Lapid, Yosef (1989), '*Quo Vadis* International Relations? Further Reflections on the "Next Stage" of International Theory' *Millennium* 18/1.

Leistner, Erich (1995), 'Considering the Methods and Effects of Regional Integration', in Greg Mills *et al.* (eds), *South Africa in the Global Economy* (Johannesburg: South African Institute of International Affairs).

Linklater, Andrew (1990), *Beyond Realism and Marxism: Critical Theory and International Relations* (London: Macmillan).

Lyotard, Jean-François (1992), *The Postmodern Explained: Correspondence 1982–1985* (Minneapolis: University of Minnesota Press).

Maasdorp, Gavin (1994), 'The Future Structure of Regional Trade Integration and Development Cooperation in Southern Africa', *Africa Insight* 24/1.

Malan, Mark (1998), 'SADC and Sub-Regional Security: Unde Venis et Quo Vades?', *ISS Monograph Series*, no. 19 (Halfway House: Institute for Security Studies, Feb.).

Martin, William (1990), 'Region Formation under Crisis Conditions: South vs Southern Africa in the Interwar Period', *Journal of Southern African Studies* 16/1 (March).

Mills, Greg (1995), 'The History of Regional Integrative Attempts: The Way Forward?', in Greg Mills *et al.* (eds), *South Africa in the Global Economy* (Johannesburg: South African Institute of International Affairs).

Neufeld, Mark (1995), *The Restructuring of International Relations Theory*, (Cambridge: Cambridge University Press).

Rengger, N. J. (1988), 'Going Critical? A Response to Hoffman', *Millennium* 17/1 (March).

Sachikonye, Lloyd M. (1995), 'State and Social Movements in Zimbabwe', in Lloyd M. Sachikonye (ed.), *Democracy, Civil Society and the State: Social Movements in Southern Africa* (Harare: SAPES Books).

Shapiro, Michael (1987), *The Politics of Representation: Writing Practices in Biography, Photography and Policy Analysis* (Madison: University of Wisconsin).

Swatuk, Larry A. (1997), 'The Environment, Sustainable Development, and Prospects for Southern African Regional Cooperation', in Larry A. Swatuk and David R. Black (eds), *Bridging the Rift: The New South Africa in Africa* (Boulder, CO: Westview).

Swatuk, Larry A., and Abillah H. Omari (1997), 'Regional Security: Southern Africa's Mobile Front Line' in Larry A. Swatuk and David R. Black (eds), *Bridging the Rift: The New South Africa in Africa* (Boulder, CO: Westview).

Thompson, Lisa (1991), 'Of Myths, Monsters and Money: Regime Conceptualisation and Theory in Southern Africa', *Journal of Contemporary African Studies* 10/2.

Thompson, Lisa (1995), 'Beyond Borders and Between States: (Re)visions of Development and Security in International Relations – A Southern African Perspective', *Southern African Perspectives*, no. 48 (Bellville: Centre for Southern African Studies).

Tsie, Balefi (1996), 'States and Markets in the Southern African Development Community (SADC): Beyond the Neo-Liberal Paradigm', *Journal of Southern African Studies*, 22/1.

Vale, Peter (1996), 'Regional Security in Southern Africa', *Alternatives* 21/3.

Vale, Peter (1997), 'Backwaters and By-passes: South Africa and "Its" Region', in Larry A. Swatuk and David R. Black (eds), *Bridging the Rift: The New South Africa in Africa* (Boulder, CO: Westview).

Vale, Peter, and John Daniel (1995), 'Regional Security in Southern Africa in the 1990s: Challenging the Terms of the Neo-Realist Debate', *Transformation* 28.

Van Aardt, Maxi (1993), 'In Search of a More Adequate Conceptualisation of Security for Southern Africa: Do We Need a Feminist Touch?', *Politikon* 20/1 (June).

Van Aardt, Maxi (1995), 'Back to the Future?: Women and Security in Post-*Apartheid* Southern Africa', *Strategic Review for Southern Africa* 17/2 (Nov.).

Van Aardt, Maxi (1997a), 'The Emerging Security Framework in Southern Africa: Regime or Community?', *Strategic Review for Southern Africa* 19/1 (May).

Van Aardt, Maxi (1997b), 'The SADC Organ for Politics, Defence and Security: Challenges for Regional Community Building', *The South African Journal of International Affairs* 4/2 (Winter).

Van Nieuwkerk, Anthoni (1995), 'Big or Small, Open or Closed? A Survey of Views on Regional Integration', in Greg Mills *et al.* (eds), *South Africa in the Global Economy* (Johannesburg: South African Institute of International Affairs).

Wendt, Alexander (1987), 'The agent-structure problem in international relations theory', *International Organization* 41/3.

11
Feminist Theory and Security Studies in Southern Africa: Yet Another Faddish Trend?

Lisa Thompson

As the necessity to incorporate a gender focus into analyses of security has gradually permeated the discipline of international relations (a need mainly stressed, unsurprisingly, by women), so too have the murmurs of 'mainstream' (primarily, but not only, male) voices risen as to what the benefits would (or possibly could) be of feminist approaches or 'theory'. Even in the context of the latest theoretical flutter in the discipline, between advocates of an orthodox (realist or neo-realist) approach and advocates of the benefits of critical theoretical and/or postmodern approaches to international relations,[1] the insights of feminist approaches remain marginal, in spite of a burgeoning field of 'feminism and international relations' literature (Enloe, 1989; Peterson, 1992a,b; Tickner, 1992).

It is not an exaggeration to state that, with few exceptions, in the Southern African context even those academics and practitioners sympathetic to 'feminism' do not seem to have a clear idea of what precisely feminist theory or approaches could offer in the international relations context. This is especially so in relation to questions such as: Is there *a* feminist approach to international relations? How does feminism (re)vision security at the level of the individual, the state, the region, globally? These questions remain largely unexplored in mainstream and even critical analyses, bar for the general rhetorical (but politically correct) textual and conference reference to the 'need to incorporate women'.

Needless to say the above refrain highlights a crucial aspect of what could be broadly termed the 'gender subject/object dilemma'. It may be that elsewhere, particularly in states where gender analysis is at a more advanced stage (that is, the US, Canada, some states in Western Europe) that this dilemma does not feature as prominently. In the Southern

African context, academics (men and women) raised on a steady diet of orthodox political and international relations theory tend to take the idea of feminist *theory* as somewhat esoteric. Is it women who need to analyse? Or women who should be the focus of analysis? Do women (as opposed to men) define security differently? Do they experience (in)security differently? Without much fear of over-generalization, it can be said that mainstream theorists (and their theories) using the concept of security as their main prism through which to interpret regional events, tend to assume that gender (as a conceptual category) is supposedly inconsequential to the transcendental quality of positivist reasoning and the search for universal truths. Thus women's studies must be a 'normative' field of study about women.

Stated differently, the mainstream logic is that women's studies are for women (subjects), and about women (objects). While this, as a generalization, is true of some strands of feminism, particularly certain psychoanalytical approaches developed in the US, the irony of it is that *the same can be said about so called 'mainstream' analyses* in a number of social science disciplines. This is glaringly evident in the context of discussions of security, especially, but not only, in the international relations context. Since the establishment of the discipline, Institutes for Strategic Studies have abounded, in both the North and South. These institutes dealt with one conceptual definition of security: the military/political security of states based in essence on a reified masculine metanarrative: realism (Chapter 3 of this volume presenting a fine example in this regard).

The central problem hinges on the fact that in the international relations discipline much has been written recently of the need to challenge dominant knowledge, and corresponding legitimating metanarratives, but most of this has not taken on a sufficiently gendered perspective. As a result, even what I referred to as the 'critical flutter' has provided sustenance to what has been termed the 'view from nowhere' which anticipates that gender is not key to understanding the dominant metanarratives, as these are (ostensibly) based on humanity, not men. The error of this assumption is overwhelmingly evident to anyone even vaguely familiar with feminist deconstructions of philosophy as well as social and political theory. As Bordo (1991: p. 137) points out, 'the "view from nowhere" may itself be a male construction of the possibilities for knowledge'.

Metanarratives and narratives in Southern Africa

In the Southern African context, the dominant discourse on security remains caught up in its stereotypically 'male moment', reinforced, wittingly and unwittingly, by analysts who have bought into the spin-offs of operating as quasi-government 'think tanks' on security. At the level of the metanarrative, the presumptions of realism portray a state-centric view of political/military security; this then predominates as the most important referent by which governments should measure their legitimacy as states, and their status as states in the region. Even while the metanarrative is largely an internationally derived one which is further distorted by the vestiges of colonialism, socio-spatially as well as socio-economically, it is also fortified by overlapping forms of discrimination at the socio-economic level which are derived from a variety of culturally derived social patterns of behaviour (see Thompson, 1991; 1996).

Another, equally important, difficulty is that gender critiques tend to be absorbed and neutralized by national (state-led) discourses on development (see both Holden and Odén in this volume). These discourses, which are profoundly influenced by the dominant neoliberal metanarrative on development as it is enforced by international non-governmental organizations and development agencies, as well as certain local academic and research institutions, reinforce the distinction between 'development' and 'security'. The former concept revolves around assuring growth, with some attention to socio-economic security, the latter to a more 'traditional' view of security which is still primarily political/military and grounded in the socio-spatial demarcation of the nation-state (Crush, 1995; Thompson, 1997). Nowhere is this more clearly evident than in the evolution of the security debate within the Southern African Development Community (SADC), especially since South Africa joined in 1994. The predominance of political security matters, especially since the establishment of the *Organ on Politics, Defence and Security*, within the SADC organizational framework, has led to a further deemphasis on the linkage between political, social and economic security.

Thus at the analytical level, in the Southern African and African contexts, the result of the superficial acceptance of the need for gendered analyses has reinforced business as usual. The chapter on feminism in the latest book on security, and the obligatory conference panel on gender, development and security, remain all that is to be seen in the arena of 'mainstream' political studies (encompassing development studies, international relations and strategic studies). The consequence of this is that dominant metanarratives on security and development remain gendered. The view from nowhere remains gendered while ostensibly being gender neutral, as will be highlighted again at the end of this chapter.

Challenging dominant discourses

Gramsci (1971), Cox (1987), Strange (1987; 1991), Fraser and Nicholson (1991), Bordo (1990), Lyotard (1993), Crush (1995) and others have pointed out in various different ways, and using various different conceptual terms, such as hegemonic knowledge (Gramsci; Cox); 'dominant discourses' (Crush; Watts); legitimating metanarratives (Lyotard); (phallocentric) philosophical metanarratives (Fraser and Nicholson; Bordo) that the metanarrative (dominant knowledge) has a conditioning relationship on the narrative (historical explanations). The point made is that the way that events are explained will always contain a normative dimension. More seriously, the way that events are explained and predicted, as well as conditioned, may have more to do with whose knowledge is said to count (that is, legitimate knowledge) than with the superiority of one form of metanarrative over another. This can be the case even where there is no explicit metanarrative (for example, in newspaper articles, where say, neo-liberal economic assumptions are the prism through which international and national economic events are interpreted).

The first to call himself a postmodernist, Jean-François Lyotard, has gone so far as to say that to be truly *post*modern, we should do away with the search for universal explanatory metanarratives and concentrate instead on localized narratives (Fraser and Nicholson, 1991; Benhabib, 1991). Feminists who have begun to explore the potential of postmodern approaches have pointed out the drawbacks of dealing solely with localized narratives, the call for which is a kind of metanarrative all on its own, as well as the lack of cognizance by Lyotard and others, of structural influences on the content of localized narratives. The linkage between larger legitimating metanarratives and localized narratives, I will argue here, is in fact critical, especially in the so called 'developing' world, which by the very term is conditioned and disciplined by dominant knowledge to a standard set by the 'developed'. I wish also to discuss the ways in which certain feminist analyses have tended to contribute to this process of neutralization, often by over-hasty importations of certain feminist analytical frameworks (especially from the US), to underline the necessity of properly contextualizing the interplay between legitimating metanarratives and narratives. I then turn to examining a little more closely the various assumptions that feminists have made on gendered security, particularly in terms of their analyses of the relationship between the state and society. I argue that the prism through which gendered insecurities are channelled, by a wide variety of feminisms, is still based on logocentric thought, and on the mechanistic Descartian worldview (see Chapter 12 below). Feminist approaches will not influence mainstream metanarratives (and thus narratives) on security in Southern Africa, and arguably elsewhere, until the basis of the thought structure – logocentric metanarrative construction which informs gendered dichotomies – is deconstructed.

Dominant (mis)understandings of 'feminism' in Southern Africa

There is a common misperception which reinforces the mainstream view of 'women's studies' in both the developed and (Westernized) 'developing' world, one which extends to academics, to politicians, and to people in the street, who assume that feminism or feminist approaches have 'a women's perspective', *which is equivalent* to a 'culture of care' to contribute to our understandings of political and social life – both analytically and practically – in the 'real' world.[2] Thus it assumed that in a world where more women are 'added' to the public spheres of politics and economics, so too the more 'caring' such a world will become, and hence, secure. Of the few feminist contributions to the analysis of security in the Southern African region, this view has gained some prominence (Van Aardt, 1993; 1995). According to this view, the 'women's touch' would balance the harsh masculinity of the public political terrain. While some feminists have maintained this position, it should be noted that in a broader context it is one contested strand of feminist thought, and one which tends (perhaps by popular default since it corresponds with dominant patterns of socialization) to downplay the breadth and force of transdisciplinary feminist analyses. 'Difference' or psychoanalytical approaches to gender (as opposed to sex) differences have explored the question of socialization processes versus the biological predisposition to 'caring' in the female and male sex. This approach has been made popular by particularly Nancy Chodorow and Carol Gilligan, two US feminists, and continues to cause considerable controversy in feminist debates (Chodorow, 1978; Gilligan, 1982). Also, critics, feminist and otherwise, have pointed out that, while not denying that women have been assigned predominantly caring roles in society, that is, as child-carers, nurses, teachers, housewives and so on, to assume that feminist theoretical approaches amount to a sociology of caring is to grossly oversimplify, and also leads one into the nature versus nurture debate which centres on the highly contestable assumption that since women are supposed to be biologically and/or socially more caring, or bound to see 'care' differently (relationally), that men are, on the same grounds, in some way disposed to care less, or to see 'care' differently (individually).[3] Even more seriously, as Fraser and Nicholson have pointed out, the psychoanalytical approach tends to reinforce the essentialist categories of male/female, and can 'import' badly to other cultural contexts where gendered roles configure differently (Fraser and Nicholson, 1991).

How then, can feminist analyses make a difference to our understandings of security? A brief discussion of the central approaches feminists have used shows that what I call critical feminist approaches (note lower case c and f), while (generally) not denying the search for metanarratives which shed greater analytical clarification by virtue of their ability to adequately explain an aspect of social reality, are nonetheless deeply suspicious of essentializing and totalizing discourses, be these dominant or otherwise.

Gendering the security discourse in international relations

Feminist approaches to international relations (both as practice and as a discipline) are extrapolated from political philosophy/studies and sociology, and follow, to some extent, the same basic approaches as much of Western political philosophy. Broadly speaking, there are six central strands of feminist thinking: liberal, Marxist, radical, socialist, Third World and postmodernist feminism. Critical and ecofeminist approaches also exist, but are usually linked to one or other of the above six strands, with the exception of ecocentric feminism. There is a burgeoning body of literature drawing on one or more of the above approaches to bring fresh insights to subject matter sacred to both the 'hard' and 'soft' sciences. There is also an ongoing theoretical and methodological debate among the various approaches, and to date no consensus on a homogeneous feminist approach or feminist standpoint. Diversity is, overall, not perceived as a disadvantage, and the common goal of the emancipation of women is a strong unifier. The price for such easygoing diversity is, unfortunately, some incoherence with regard to 'a feminist perspective' on specific issues – security being one of them.

Feminism and mainstream theories

The dominant conceptualization of political and economic systems within and between states is linked to the trivialization of gender relations. These conceptualizations have, to a large extent, excluded a differentiated focus on women's participation in the public sphere of politics and in social relations of production. Okin (1979), Peterson (1992b) and Coole (1993) point out that these conceptualizations pre-date capitalism and can be traced back to the classical Athenian texts and Athenian state-making. Peterson (1992a: p. 370) describes the sep-aration of man as a political (reasonable) being from the oikos (house-hold). The household, as the realm of necessity, was distinguished from the political life of men. This gave rise to the first dichotomous repre-sentation of irrational/female/personal from rational/male/public. This representation has informed Western understandings of politics well into the twentieth century.

In addition to criticizing the ways in which dominant political phi-losophy and theory is gender biased, feminists interrogated the possibil-ities of 'reframing' theories, for example, liberalism, Marxism and socialism. In fact, with the exception of radical feminism, all feminist approaches have, at base, the essence of an already existing, classical, Western, theory. Liberal, Marxist and socialist feminism all draw heavily on the ontological and epistemological presuppositions of liberalism, Marxism and socialism, the difference being that feminist approaches try to point out the ways in which each of the theories has been biased towards women, and thus are flawed in terms of the universalistic stan-dards of truth, justice, equality and liberty on which they are based. Subsequent feminist analyses within the various 'strands' have then been concerned with eliminating that discriminatory edge. As the analysis below indicates however, the limitations of 'reframing' are that the essential structure of dominant metanarratives remain unchanged.

Liberal feminism

Liberal feminism does not attempt to break with the fundamental assumptions of liberalism and the Enlightenment tradition. What lib-eral feminists have tried to do is to incorporate a women's perspective into liberal theory.[4] As such, liberal feminism places the emphasis on the individual and draws on the epistemological underpinnings of lib-eral analysis. These underpinnings focus on the rational atomistic indi-vidual pursuing knowledge for his (or her) own ends. As Jaggar (1988, pp. 355–6) points out, the evolution of this approach culminated in positivism, the dominant disciplining framework for analyses in most of the social sciences. The primacy attached to empirically validated research is explicit, as Harding (1986; 1987) has illustrated. For this reason feminist liberalism has been closely linked with empiricism, and has also been labelled 'feminist empiricism'.[5]

Liberal feminism meets the standards of the positivistic interpretation of objectivity by pointing out how men *have been biased in terms of their own liberal framework*. But other feminists such as Harding (1987) and Hartsock (1985; 1987) have made considerable headway in showing that standards of objectivity and value free analysis in the social sciences *and* in the physical sciences and biology are not consistent. All three can be shown to be laden with the value beliefs of the (mostly male) scientists. Harding (1987: p. 136) points out that,

> ...the androcentric ideology of contemporary science posits as necessary, and or as facts, a set of dualisms – culture versus nature; rational mind versus pre-rational body and irrational emotions and values; objectivity versus subjectivity; public versus private – and then links men to the former and femininity to the latter in each dichotomy.[6]

While liberal feminism has successfully highlighted biases in 'neutral' liberalism, historically liberal feminism has failed to take sufficient account of the differences between women, in terms of class, race, gender and socio-economic position. Gaidzanwa (1992: p. 95), for example, states that Wollstonecraft's position on the rights issue should be set within the context of her background, in particular her class and race. Furthermore, critics of liberal feminism say that it is precisely because women are simply 'absorbed' into the ideology that women become an 'issue' in terms of economic security and development. However, this criticism, as will be discussed, is also applicable to Marxist feminism. In both cases the theoretical discourse changes very little. As such, the inherent societal biases which both approaches previously reaffirmed do not break down (Jaggar, 1988; Fraser and Nicholson, 1991; Meena, 1992; Mbilinyi, 1992; Gaidzanwa, 1992). It appears that in order to change the reality of women one needs a different, more appropriate way to explain women's oppression.[7]

Marxism and feminism

Early Marxist and post-Marxist approaches deny that women's oppression is epistemologically different from the oppression of workers or the proletariat. Thus the standard of 'truth' for Marxist theory is that those classes which wish to overthrow the existing order and to recreate the knowledge structure most closely represent the dominant body of repressed peoples in that society. Thus 'only a classless society will produce an undistorted and genuinely scientific representation of reality' (Jaggar, 1988: p. 359). Here, 'false' and 'distorted' knowledge is seen as the result of bourgeois, ideologically infused understandings of politics, economics and the role of the state (which functions to support dominant social relations of production). Marxist theory and praxis, however, are seen as 'true', 'undistorted', materially based understandings of social relations of production.

However, feminists working both within and outside the Marxist tradition, for example, Hartmann (1981), Eisenstein (1979), Harding (1987), Mackinnon (1982), Jaggar (1988) and Coole (1993) have shown that, while the goal of the Marxist approach is societal emancipation, the simplification referred to above causes the oppression affecting *women of all classes* to become obscured. Because the oppression of women differs both within and between classes, it is not reducible to the oppression of the proletariat and/or the peasantry. Women who are workers and/or peasants suffer from different and overlapping forms of oppression.

Most feminists who still use aspects of Marxist analysis also challenge the assumption that the 'proletarian revolution' would lead to an eradication of discrimination against women. As was pointed out earlier, feminists point out that discrimination predates capitalism, and therefore the eradication of capitalism, and of class, would not necessarily lead to women's emancipation. As a result of these adaptations to original Marxist theory, while some feminists still employ the term 'Marxist' to describe their work, their perspectives tend to approach more closely the socialist feminist perspective (Mackinnon, 1982; and 1987). Socialist feminism aims to bring women's standpoint into emancipatory theory. The standpoint is not conceptualized as all inclusive and applicable to all women, rather it is a rejection of the liberal viewpoint and a revision of the Marxist notion of a universal proletarian standpoint.

Socialist and 'Third World' feminism

Socialist feminism shares many linkages, in terms of its epistemological assumptions, with Third World feminism.[8] Socialist feminism also links up with Marxist theory in accepting that it is the material conditions of existence which determine or shape consciousness. In order to move away from false consciousness women need to understand themselves in relation to the world as projected by men and their ideas, that is, the discourse as it is initiated, shaped and regulated by the domination of men's beliefs of the nature of women and men. According to this approach women need to be made aware of how the material conditions of their existence shape their consciousness, their understanding of reality, and their understanding of others in relation to themselves. This consciousness is not universal. There may be common experiences shared by black African peasant women and white Western women, but there will be obvious, substantive differences (Sen and Grown, 1987; Meena, 1992; Mbilinyi, 1992 and Gaidzanwa, 1992).

The attempt to create a women's standpoint must be seen in the context of Western conceptions of history and the development of knowledge that has excluded women. Jaggar points out in this regard that 'historians commonly view classical Athens, Renaissance Italy and 18th century revolutionary France as periods of progressive change – in spite of the fact that women lost significant power and status during those periods' (Jaggar, 1988: p. 372). In terms of socialist and Third World feminism this is placed in the context of the dominance (or the perceived ideological superiority) of Western liberal approaches to knowledge, and its related impact on science and social science. This approach shares linkages with dependency and Marxist world systems theorists like Gunder Frank and Galtung who also refer to cultural imperialism in the Third World. Third World feminists also point out that on the whole the achievements and contributions made by women frequently get ignored or are represented in discriminatory ways.

Gaidzanwa gives two excellent examples of the above in her analysis of women's empowerment in Zimbabwe. Nehanda Nyakasikana, a militant spirit medium who was killed by the colonial administration has been immortalized by government by renaming a *maternity* hospital after her. This negates her decidedly 'non-domestic', 'politico-spiritual role'. Another good example is the monument the government erected after the war to honour the freedom fighters. Over and above the fact that the North Korean sculptors gave all the fighters Asiatic features, all the women are portrayed wearing skirts. Gaidzanwa concludes 'it is clear that the redomestication of women in Zimbabwe began immediately after the (liberation) war' (Gaidzanwa, 1992: pp. 116–17).

Radical feminism

'Radical' feminism, as indicated by its name, assumes a much more hardline stance towards the 'patriarchal' system (and men) (Daly, 1978). Patriarchy and its social and political manifestations are seen as responsible for women's oppression and false consciousness. This emerges clearly in the work of Mackinnon (1987: p. 137): 'Male dominance is perhaps the most pervasive and tenacious system of power in history ... It is metaphysically nearly perfect'.[9]

According to radical feminism, this all pervasive, nearly perfect, system of dominance requires 'radical' approaches in order for it to be eradicated. For this reason Jaggar (1988: p. 368) states that 'their view contrasts most clearly with the atomistic world view of classical Newtonian physics, liberal politics and positivist epistemology'.

But critics of the radical approach point out that the key problem area in radical feminism is the acceptance of male-projected views of women. Radical feminists absorb that which is projected. This tendency, to accept the characterization of women as more 'organic', 'natural', 'earthy', 'intuitive' (even psychic) helps reinforce the dualisms posited by liberalism, or patriarchy, as the radical approach defines it.

In modernist theoretical terms, radical feminism's acceptance of 'irrationality' is problematic, in that on these grounds, and by the standards of the dualisms of positivism, women cannot be equal because they are not as rational or responsible as men. Radical feminists reject this view, stating that there is no reason why women cannot be 'different but equal'. It is at this juncture that radical approaches meet with research done on the psychological aspects of sex/gender differentiation, for example the work of Chodorow and Gilligan referred to earlier.

Radical feminism's focus on 'women's experience' is also rather problematic given the obvious differences of class, race and geographical location. But one of the most problematic aspects of radical feminism is its alienation of both women and men. It is partly because radical feminism tended to catch the eye of the Western media that the impression has been conveyed that feminism *per se* is 'weird' (Jaggar, 1988: p. 382). However, despite the hostility which this approach has evoked, it has nonetheless played an important and valuable role both in terms of research and 'consciousness-raising'.[10] Radical feminism has also drawn attention to the pervasiveness of patriarchy.

It should be clear that, with the exception of radical feminism, the intellectual tradition of feminism has drawn extensively on ideological assumptions and theoretical constructs of the mainstream 'modernist' theories with varying levels of success at eliminating gender biases. It is in this context that postmodernist and critical approaches have recently opened up further possibilities for the structuring of gender analyses.

Feminisms and the 'realities' of socio-spatial dimensions

The problem of overgeneralization manifests itself in the attempt to create an all encompassing women's standpoint. Critical theorists, postmodernists and feminist postmodernists maintain that the problem of overgeneralization stems from the modernist theoretical urge to achieve universalistic understandings about the nature of social reality (Walker, 1989; 1995; Peterson, 1992b; Mbilinyi, 1992). In this sense the problem of achieving a common standpoint rests on knowledge. Socialist and Third World feminists, together with feminist postmodernists, emphasize that women in different classes and societies will have different realities, not only by virtue of geographical location, but also in terms of how the dominant or hegemonic discourse relating to power and knowledge is entrenched within their particular society. Similarly the difference between First World women's interpretation of reality and those in the Third World will be different. For example, the experiences of Latin American women or Southern African women would be different in terms of the knowledge structure in each society and/or region. For this reason Third World feminism tries to relocate questions of gender discrimination, in order to make the questions more appropriate. Third World feminism represents a break with modernist theory, and is closer to postmodern and critical approaches, in the sense that the approach deliberately avoids generalizing about 'women' as a universal category in the social (not biological) sense. Instead, there is a tendency to discuss women as a social category in a regional, or socio-spatially specific, context, as the following discussion makes clear. Third world feminism thus adds to emancipatory theory in the sense that it deliberately challenges relations which are enforced and entrenched through structural aspects of power.

The perspective of Third World feminism, by virtue of the political and economic position of women in the 'Third' World, tends to emphasize the economic hardship of women caused by capitalism and 'hangovers' from colonialism (Sen and Grown, 1987; Brydon and Chant, 1989). Meena points out that women in Southern Africa have to contend with *both* the remains of various forms of African patriarchy *and* Western patriarchy. She also emphasizes that while it is dangerous to generalize about African culture, 'as Africa presents cultural diversities which have been exposed to a variety of external forces' we cannot ignore the tendency of both the political and economic structures of society in Africa to perpetuate a bias towards African women (Meena, 1992: p. 8). She quotes Fanon in trying to define the situation: 'Decolonization is quite simply the replacing of a certain "species of men" by another "species of men"' (Meena, 1992: p. 9). The emphasis on African culture with regard to women has mystified and mythified women's roles (Sen and Grown, 1987; Brydon and Chant, 1989;

Meena, 1992; Gaidzanwa, 1992).[11] While this point will be taken up again later, it must also be seen in context of Western attitudes towards African women and the way in which women have been incorporated into the 'development' of Africa. This occurs both in terms of the formulation of state policy and development policies implemented through NGOs: 'Repressive policies against women were further reinforced by the fact that the *mainstream critiques of the postcolonial state either deliberately or otherwise ignored the dynamics of gender oppression'* (Meena, 1992: p. 19) (emphasis added).

Women's economic insecurity in Southern Africa

Third World feminists point out that women's roles as farmers, for subsistence and cash, remain trivial to 'mainstream' theory and also in terms of government policy. Both orthodox liberal and Marxist approaches fail to sufficiently take into account the importance of women's productive and reproductive roles, including production for subsistence. The economic (in)security of rural women has, as a result, received insufficient attention, theoretically and in practice. Brydon and Chant (1989: p. 48) spell out the problem:

> It is when we come to consider rural areas in particular that we become aware of the fact that what goes on in households cannot be relegated simply to the sphere of reproduction, as in conventional Marxist analyses, or left unanalyzed, as non-work, or at least not productive work... It is because Marx himself and early Marxists assumed that a division of labour into productive and domestic relations, with women predominating in the latter, was 'natural' and therefore outside the parameters of any social analysis, that categories of domestic reproductive work and subsistence production have largely been ignored.

Part of the reason for this is that the capitalist system, both in its internal and international manifestations, does not regard labour which does not have 'exchange value' as particularly important to the functioning of the market (Mackinnon, 1987). Supply and demand, while having the labour component built into the equation, does not regard the reproduction of labour, and labour for use value or informal markets as a fundamental economic component of the national or international economic system. It is for this reason that the role of women in agriculture both for exchange (market) and use (subsistence) value has not been adequately addressed by any of the mainstream approaches examined thus far (see, for example, Holden in Chapter 7 above).

From the above discussion it is evident that the need to incorporate women into mainstream theories of security and development requires both a deconstruction and a reconstruction of ideas, not simply the absorption of women into existing frameworks, particularly but not only the liberal framework. The emphasis on the Truth (deliberate uppercase) tends to enforce 'disciplining' metanarratives. As Mbilinyi (1992: pp. 39–40) emphasizes, the dominant discourse in Southern Africa is entrenched in terms of the hierarchical nature of truth, which in this case is a predominantly Western, liberal 'truth':

> The traditional/modern dichotomy ... continues to inform much gender research, in spite of its neo-colonial roots. The traditional/modern paradigm promotes a set of value judgments about the 'backwardness' and oppressive nature of pre-colonial indigenous society, and the progressive liberating nature of the present capitalist society ... Critical research on pre-capitalist gender relations ... has shown how gender relations in many classes and/or societies became more oppressive and exploitative during and after colonial rule.

The influence of liberal theory in shaping security and development debates has meant that, even when the explicit reliance on dichotomies is rejected, there is still a tendency to see development in terms of the tradition/modernity, internal/external dichotomies. Furthermore, the tendency of liberalism to conceptualize and spatialize women within the context of the home, or hearth, leads to an underemphasis on their personal and economic (in)security.

Gender analysis or analyses?

Possibly the only aspect on which feminists agree is that women are generally more insecure economically, politically and socially, than men – although some feminists argue that class, race and geographic locality should be figured in to differentiate and de-reify the category 'women'. Incoherence arises from the differing theoretical presuppositions of the six approaches and, more specifically, from how each approach constructs a gendered understanding of the social contract, that is, a gendered understanding of the relation between society and the state, and more particularly, why and how such a relation arises and is maintained. This understanding is crucial to security analyses. The understanding of the social contract further defines what is understood as 'international relations' (as such relations happen, so to speak), and even more specifically, the issues which dominate those relations (at the level of both interaction and understanding).

What contract?

The faultlines and essentialism in 'modified mainstream' approaches have led to considerable interest in postmodernist and critical theory discourses from feminists and gender analysts.[12] Postmodernism criticizes mainstream and related 'hooked on feminist' approaches for their failure to grasp the fact that the ways in which Western thought was initially constructed will always prevent the full eradication of discriminatory tenets from classical approaches. As discussed, the central problem is the logocentric nature of Western thought, which centres around conceptions of light/dark, rationality/irrationality, public/private, polis/oikos – where men are identified with rational/public/polis and women with irrational/private/oikos. Postmodern feminists argue that the male/female dualism is in fact pivotal to logocentric thought (Peterson, 1992b: pp. 1–24). Political philosophy and theory are constructed on this dichotomous way of thinking, which has become over time a reified hegemonic thought structure upon which we construct our theories of reality, thus excluding and oppressing certain groups (which include women as a category as well as different 'sub'-categories of women, the latter giving rise to varying layers of exclusion and oppression). Moreover, since modernist approaches aim at uncovering universal truth, justice and so on, the abilities of oppressed groups to delegitimize dominant discourses is rendered inoperative. Attempts to reconstruct the theories are thus futile, according to feminist postmodernists and critical theorists, since logocentric foundations hold the edifice of classical thought together.

Dominant discourses and critical feminism

The contesting of positivistic dualisms, and the examination of theory which serves hegemonic class or group interests, is a theme which dominates the work of critical feminists. This helps to illustrate the ways in which dominant conceptualizations of security are narrowly defined, and how they serve specific interests. For example Walker (1989; 1990), Peterson (1992b), and Tickner (1992) maintain that insecurity cannot be understood only within the context of the state, despite the fact that this is generally the context within which societal security is discussed. These analysts refer to the influence of positivistic dualisms on the discipline to illustrate how security has come to be understood in terms of an undifferentiated societal security which legitimates state structures, rather than focusing on the ways in which state structures may increase societal insecurity. This can occur both in terms of the internal as well as externally oriented policies of states, for example, in terms of economic policies which are implemented. These may be perceived of as rational within the context of a state being able to compete in international economic markets. But a policy perceived of as rational may *engender* economic policy in such a way that the consequences are gender-biased, in the sense that they lead to greater economic and political insecurity for women (Peterson, 1992; on this point, compare Niemann with both Solomon and Holden in this volume).

In or out?

Critical theorists such as Ashley and Walker (1990), Linklater (1992) and Walker (1992) have also focused on societal insecurity within and between states in terms of the dynamics of inclusion and exclusion. This dynamic operates on both theoretical and practical levels. As pointed out earlier, the conceptualization of states themselves is centred upon this dynamic, and is closely related to understandings of individual political identity. Linklater (1992: pp. 82–3) clarifies the ways in which the dynamic operates at both theoretical and practical levels:

> Elaborate and at times conflicting forms of inclusion and exclusion permeate all levels of society and politics, and all social actors know that their lives are interwoven with them ... In all societies human beings learn how to deal with the normative, sociological and praxeological aspects of systems of inclusion and exclusion.

Linklater emphasizes that modes of inclusion and exclusion are both materially manifest in societies, and also present in explanations and interpretations of relations within and between societies. Feminists and feminist postmodernists such as Di Stefano (1990), Bordo (1990), Tickner (1992) and Peterson (1992b) also concentrate on the dynamic of inclusion and exclusion in terms of how gender relations have given rise to modes of inclusion and exclusion within societies, and also in the ways in which theories which aim to explain reality tend to exclude women.

Feminism and postmodernism: on the road to nowhere?

The feminist postmodernist approach has been taken to task by other feminists who emphasize that the deconstructionist edge of postmodernism threatens to obliterate the category 'women' altogether. Even worse, some strands of what has come to be known as postmodernism, such as Barthian notions of 'the death of the author', where text relates only to text, and Derrida's notion of intertextual 'freeplay' render the practical emancipatory project void and meaningless – a theoretical indulgence which women the world over, but more especially those in the 'developing world', cannot afford.[13] While feminists who call themselves postmodernists would argue that it is not necessary or possible to break entirely with modernism (thereby validating the need to retain a focus on women) 'feminist postmodern' and 'postmodern' approaches are sometimes characterized by an 'analysis paralysis' – an inevitable part of trying to work out where modernism ends and postmodernism begins – particularly when the universality and/or particularity of the analytical object, or subject, or both, are in dispute (Nicholson, 1990). It is at this theoretical juncture that the emancipatory project is at its most vulnerable. Postmodernists' rejection of transcendence and acceptance of difference is all very well, but there are no answers as to how to avoid potentially paralyzing 'category' fragmentation analytically and in practice. Conversely, Critical Theorists *à la* Habermas, who accept the notion of transcendence, run the risk of 'totalizing' alternative (and competing) discourses. This amounts to replacing or attempting to replace the dominant discourse with another.

Critical feminism and dominant knowledge

In this writer's view, the most important contribution of what could be termed critical feminist approaches to the unpacking and challenging of dominant metanarratives, especially in the developing world, is the way in which notions of difference and discrimination are brought to the fore, not only in terms of our localized narratives, but also in terms of more global legitimating metanarratives. In other words, one of the main contributions of critical feminists working at the theoretical level is to bring into question the legitimacy, as well as the linguistic construction of metanarratives. It is for this reason that critical feminists such as Peterson, Fraser and Nicholson, Flax, Harding, Bordo, Meena, Mbilinyi and others have turned their attention to the postmodern 'promise'. However, most critical feminists draw synthetically on a variety of theoretical understandings.

Critical feminist approaches tend to be characterized by a gendered deconstructionist edge at the level of the metanarrative and its legitimating role in reinforcing narrative interpretation. As Peterson has pointed out, logocentric constructions of metanarratives are integrally related, *and arise from*, socialized masculine/feminine divisions (Peterson, 1992b: pp. 31–64).

Thus, critical feminist approaches have criticized, from the uncomfortable perspective of the 'strange' and the 'other' in the context of the evolution of classical Western thought, the very foundations of Western political philosophy and theory – and by extension the contributions of (neorealist) international relations theorists who have based their conceptualization and theory of security on those foundations. Critical feminist accounts have emphasized the necessity of emancipation at the level of Western knowledge structures, an integral, if not the integral, part of the roots of gender discrimination and oppression.

Critical feminists point out that the linguistic dualisms underpinning dominant metanarratives represent a reified thought structure, while radical and difference feminism (as well as many men and women in the street) have tended to link this dominant metanarrative to the narrative or 'explanations of the world as it is around us'. The fact that there are some grounds for generalization about 'men's' characteristics versus 'women', as a result of processes of socialization and through the institutionalization of gender discrimination, has created space for Western feminist narratives based on current role differentiations. It is when these 'generalized truths' form the predominant feminist basis for challenging dominant metanarratives, however, that one runs the risk of contributing to sustaining reified mainstream approaches. Since the overriding goal of feminist thought thus far has been to challenge hegemonic knowledge structures,[14] it is self-evidently crucial to ensure that the emancipatory edge is not cancelled out by initial assumptions which tend to partially unpack only the narrative.

What distinguishes critical feminism from critical theory is the explicit and central focus on gender relations and the impact of these relations on knowledge structures, especially the ways in which the knowledge structure manifests itself in global discourses. It is postmodern in its challenge to the structure and content of dominant discourses. Both critical feminism and critical theory further do not rule out consensus on 'truth(s)', but then neither do they pitch at one (upper case) 'Truth' as their 'end-goal' – thus explicitly breaking with the positivist ideal of a linear knowledge progression. The specificity of localized narratives, which take place within the context of community groupings and their gendered relations, is linked to larger scale and structurally generated dominant metanarratives. Critical feminism is thus characterized by fluidity; it amounts in practice to critical *feminisms*. However, these approaches show an overwhelming awareness of the need to be self-conscious to the dangers of 'thought-policing' at the level of the construction of alternative metanarratives (see, for example, Pettman, 1996).

Inside out: critical feminist approaches to the state

According to realists, while the social contract prevails inside the state, outside the state the 'known disposition' to war creates a state of eternal anarchy.[15] As argued by Solomon in Chapter 3 above, in this state of anarchy states are the unique preservers of security. Critical feminist approaches emphasize that the naturalized 'state as protector' conception legitimizes state violence, thus leading them to reject the connection between state-centric notions of security and sovereignty, a contradictory connection eloquently described by Walker (1990: p. 12):

> Orthodox security policy is not just a matter of external threat. It is also the site at which particular political communities become aware of the limits to their own claim to pursue universalizing standards of conduct. It is the point at which democracy, openness and legitimate authority must dissolve into claims about realpolitik, raison d'état and the necessity of violence ... The principle of state sovereignty denies both the possibility and the desirability of talking about humanity as such.

Critical feminism further questions the extent to which democracy, openn-ess, and/or legitimate authority apply to different groups inside the state, and draws attention to the fact that 'outside' can also be inside the state, and that self and other may have multiple meanings within and between states, and between groups sharing various allegiances. Moreover, critical feminism insists on talking about 'humanity as such', especially in terms of emancipation from oppression and discrimination, political and economic. The ways in which discrimination is entrenched theoretically and practically through dominant discourses on politics and economics is the key area of critical analysis. Deeply entrenched global gender inequality perforce renders a critical feminist approach to security borderless: focusing on the interplay between politics and economics within, and between, states and markets.

Critical feminists believe that the state is 'male', that is certainly not, in the first instance, a defender of the particular intrastate threats to women's security: economic discrimination and physical abuse (especially rape) are two prime areas of neglect. As Peterson (1992b: pp. 45–6) has put it,

> The State is … a 'bearer of gender' by reference to male domination of the top personnel of states and to the cult of masculinity among these personnel … The state is complicit 'directly' through its selective sanctioning of non-state violence, particularly in its policy of 'nonintervention' in domestic violence. It is complicit 'indirectly' through its promotion of masculine, heterosexist and classist ideologies – expressed, for example, in public education models, media images, the militarism of culture, welfare policies and patriarchal law.

It is clear that feminist approaches, and specifically what has been discussed here as 'critical feminism' leads us back to the community, to the individual in relation(s), with regard to reconceptualizing security. Feminist approaches highlight the oppression of women, and attempt to redress the (implicit and explicit) chauvinism of previous theoretical approaches to security.[16]

Feminism equals women?

Although the question of 'empowering women' is in itself a much needed goal, it cannot be achieved fully until logocentric thinking itself is deconstructed so as to render the negative gendered dimension thereof inoperative, that is when the question of gender equality is no longer thought of in terms of a women versus men power struggle. Integral to the notion of critical feminism should be the understanding that 'I am not truly free, until everybody is free', that is to say, both women *and* men.[17] While feminists have been at pains to point out that state notions of security have, on average, caused great insecurity for many women, emphasis could also be put on the ways in which state-bound notions of security have affected men – cannon fodder in the name of masculinity, honour and national loyalty – who frequently have taken part in wars for little reason other than through state motivated demands to prove their 'manhood' in the context of state psychological manipulation. Men who refuse(d) to fight are invariably derogatively described as women, weak, wimpish, and worse still in the age of nationalism, disloyal to the state. The flip-side of this is that women in war situations have frequently identified with the war experience in ways similar to men, that is, with a good deal of fear, but with courage under fire (Grant, 1992; Elshtain, 1992; Pettman, 1996). Critical feminism, to be truly emancipatory, must embrace gendered notions of insecurity that *deconstruct* the socialized dichotomy of 'male versus female', without totalizing the discourse in such a way so as to undermine the seriousness of existing patterns of gender discrimination in theory and in practice.

What is vital, as Eckersley (1992: p. 69) and others have pointed out in reference to the Eastern concept of dualisms (complementary and indivisible), is that what are perceived of as *feminine characteristics* must come in out of the conceptual and analytical cold, and become socialized and valued within each and every community, as part of all social, economic and political interactions, and of *all individuals*. In such a world, notions of security would truly take on a different meaning, as the notion of 'care' becomes communal, not exclusively a 'female' characteristic, and one which extends to understandings and attitudes of the non-human world as well as the human. This would indeed revolutionize international relations as we know it today, and profoundly reshape metanarratives as well as narratives. It is of course also as distant an ideal as a vision of universal peace, and the role of critical feminists is perforce a long one, as a brief (critical) glimpse of the dominance of realist metanarratives in Southern Africa emphasizes.

South Africa, SADC and security: whose security? whose reality?

As alluded to at the beginning of this chapter, in Southern Africa the narratives on security have, pre-1994, been conditioned by the international and regional realist security metanarrative which prioritized a conceptualization of security as state security 'from' (fill in South Africa; the US; the West; the communists; the Soviet Union as applicable), thus entrenching a rigid disciplinary inclusionary/exclusionary framework.

Initially the demise of offical apartheid and the end of the Cold War were seen as signals that South Africa, as hegemon in the region, would

forego its previous militarist profile. The military state played a fundamental part of (at least) the white population's construction of gender
differences, to the extent that the white male was constructed as protector of the white female, the protected, against the *swart gevaar*,
or 'black peril'. However, since South Africa joined SADC in 1994, a
disturbing trend towards the prioritization of military over economic
concerns has begun to emerge, albeit without its previous racist connotations. The 'Organ on Politics, Defence, and Security' which was
institutionalized within SADC as a replacement to the anti-apartheid
Frontline States (FLS) grouping, is a clear indication (Swatuk and Black,
1997). This 'high-political', military aspect to SADC was endorsed not
only by state leaders but more importantly, with the help of academics
specializing in strategic studies. The South African Department of
Foreign Affairs has also 'workshopped' with academics on how to make
the 'Organ' more effective. The Organ, as it is conventionally and
somewhat unfortunately called, is now considered to be the most
important institution within SADC.[18] The military metanarrative has
thus conditioned the narrative to the extent that it has become 'the'
regional priority among a host of 'others'.

The prioritization of a political/military horizontally-focused approach
by the South African state, even in its supposedly 'transformed' context, is transparent. The Organ and attached, militarily-oriented institutions such as the ISDSC (Inter-State Defence and Security Committee)
have been promoted so as to provide an outlet for the aspirations of
South African (combined new and old) political/military leadership.
The Organ, according to South Africa's proposal, was to be steered by
the heads of Foreign Affairs in the region. In other words, it was to
have a base at the Council of Ministers level within SADC and defer
to state leaders where necessary. As it has turned out a second Council
of Ministers was against SADC's Treaty rules, and so it fell to the Heads
of State to constitute its leadership. Robert Mugabe of Zimbabwe
became president of the Organ in 1996 at about the time Nelson
Mandela became President of SADC as a whole, and now SADC, hydra-
like, has two heads, two summits, and, ostensibly two main goals,
political and economic/developmental, with the political/military
aspect fast gaining prominence and threatening to undermine the previous orientation on economic cooperation (see Du Pisani in this volume). In light of this, it is ironic that Mugabe has stalled on regional
coherence when it has been needed on political/military matters, for
example in the case of leaving South Africa in the lurch over Nigerian
human rights violations in 1996 and more recently on the instability

in the Great Lakes region, especially in what is now known as the Democratic Republic of Congo (formerly Zaire).

The rivalry between Mandela and Mugabe has been sustained since 1996, with the South African head of state sending a tersely worded letter to the 'Chair of the Organ' towards the end of 1997 stating that in the event of the dual summit issue being resolved unsatisfactorily, South Africa would feel it necessary to step down from the SADC chair (Senior DFA Official, interview, 12 February 1998). The debate (ostensibly) revolved around split leadership within SADC, but the root-cause is undoubtedly the perception from other states in the region that South Africa is attempting to prevail as regional hegemon and should be prevented from doing so. The matter of the Organ thus lies unresolved, with the leaders in the region caught between their past loyalties to each other as part of the 'struggle' and the fear of political/military domination by South Africa (see also Odén in Chapter 8 above).

As of August 1998, the threat to Mobuto's successor, Laurent Kabila, brought the rivalry and hostility between Mandela and Mugabe into the public domain. Mugabe openly snubbed Mandela's peacekeeping efforts, instead sending troops to support Kabila in defiance of Mandela's requests. It has also divided the organization into two camps, with Tanzania, Namibia, Angola and Zambia supporting Mugabe, and other SADC states supporting Mandela. The Organ's functioning has effectively undermined the one strong point of the SADC organization since its inception – the ability to behave cohesively if only at the level of regional platforms like SADC. For some, the most disturbing outcome of the establishment of the Organ is that SADC's previously more important developmental role, weak as it was, is further undermined (cf. Vale, 1996; Van Aardt, 1997; and Malan and Cilliers, 1997).

In short, the state in Southern Africa is characterized by an overwhelming adherence to a logocentrically constructed conception of security, where politics is military state power. This is no different since the end of the Cold War. The global metanarrative of security remains realist and state-centric. It should further be clear that, viewed from a critical feminist perspective, the priorities of SADC, especially institutionally with the establishment of the Organ, are structured along lines which reflect a prioritization of gendered patterns of thought as Western classical theory and overlapping forms of socialization have enforced them. State and societal violence, both physical and structural, against women, and the characteristics which they are supposed to embody, continues. Caring remains a solely 'feminist' issue.

The extent to which states and state leaders decide on political, economic and societal priorities is largely determined at the centres of political power, and in relation to the ways in which social groups with relational power *vis-à-vis* the state manage to influence state behaviour. As argued effectively by both Vale and Niemann above, state structures themselves limit the ability to conceptualize a coherent or comprehensive regional social identity. The state centre after all, acts in a disciplinary manner towards social groups within the state, and towards those who wish to enter, as to the boundaries of social identity. This disciplinary power buttresses state legitimacy, and in its worst form can lead to the stirring up of anti-foreigner sentiment (witness South Africa's current heated debates on migration and refugee policies) and/or racial and cultural differences within and between societies in the region so as to enforce or build up state power.

The establishment of the Organ also institutionalizes a separation of political and economic security, effectively displacing the importance of emphasizing the interconnections between the two. It also conjures up nineteenth-century notions of security and the protection of state sovereignty. It is glaringly evident that, despite all the hot air on gender equality (including SADC's Declaration on Gender endorsed in 1997), notions of regional security have not been influenced by critical academic discourses, least of all feminism. At the same time, the socio-economic security of many marginal groups in the region remains precarious. The deconstruction of hegemonic knowledge structures, particularly in terms of reified notions of security in the region, remains at the margins of theory and practice.

Notes

1. The post-Cold War disciplinary debates have focused on the challenges of critical theory, feminism and postmodernism, but have also been marked by the staunch defence of the 'integrity of their territory' by stalwarts of the Realist School, specifically those within the Strategic Studies fold. For a good example of this debate in action, compare the chapters by Vale, Solomon and Niemann in this volume.

2. Another common misperception among many men and women across the social spectrum in Southern Africa (and arguably elsewhere) is that feminism is coterminous with the West, and/or with lesbianism and/or being aggressive (unfeminine). While some feminists do (proudly) remain true to some aspects of the stereotype, a great many others spend a great deal of time grappling with their various identities and social roles (for example, what does it mean to be a wife, an income earner, a mother, and still be

liberated? What in fact does liberation mean?). Among African women labelling oneself a 'feminist' may also bring the charge of emulating (white) Western women; this insinuates yet another 'disciplining' aspect into trying to work out what 'women' are trying to achieve through gender analysis.

3. Fiona Robinson (1999) uses the distinction between relational and individual based notions of care in her book 'Globalizing Care: Ethics, Feminist Theory and International Relations'. Although such a distinction deliberately tries to avoid the essentialism I am referring to, it nonetheless remains fuzzy and therefore open to misinterpretation. Also the coupling of 'feminist theory' to 'care' and 'ethics' regroups women/subject/object/care together.

4. Classical examples of liberal feminism include Wollstonecraft and J. S. Mill, whose views are discussed below.

5. See also the work of Bordo (1990) and Di Stefano (1990) where the connections between feminist liberalism and feminist empiricism are explored.

6. In this context, Marxist and socialist feminists also point out that science, as it historically originated, posited the objective separation of mind and body for a political purpose, that is to allow science to develop unhindered by the church and state (Jagger, 1988: p. 360).

7. For a clear and extremely well argued discussion of this see Okin (1979). Okin's central point is that 'adding' women to liberal theory is not effective, not only because it does not lead to equality in practice, but more importantly because the original theories are based on the justification of women's centrality in the private and not the public sphere. For true equality and freedom in both spheres, the notion of liberalism would have to be radically revised and would probably require the restructuring of society.

8. The term 'Third World' is kept as feminists in the developing world have 'coined' it themselves. This is despite my ambivalence towards the usefulness of the term, especially in terms of the derogatory connotations it embodies with relation to socio-economic development.

9. MacKinnon also uses aspects of Marxism in her work.

10. Catharine MacKinnon and Andrea Dworkin are but two examples of radical feminists who have had a substantive impact on feminist research in the United States. MacKinnon's extremely controversial article 'Feminism, Marxism, Method and the State: Toward Feminist Jurisprudence' (1987) shows the benefits of the radical approach clearly. She shows that the male 'point-of-viewlessness' of the legal system renders the concept of justice farcical when it comes to rape cases, precisely because *men* have defined what rape is.

11. Western feminists emphasize that the same has occurred in the context of Western culture. See, e.g., Daly (1979).

12. Critical theory is used here in the context of emancipatory approaches to analyses, i.e., by examining the ways in which dominant knowledge operates logocentrically, especially in relation to who is included and who is excluded. It does not refer specifically to Habermasian Critical Theory (note: capital 'C' and 'T') since a discussion of Critical Theory versus critical theory is an article in itself (at the very least). The central difference is that critical theory has been more receptive to postmodernist debates, whereas Habermasian Critical Theory retains more of a modernist edge. Note, however, that there are feminist writings which draw (often eclectically) on Habermas directly.

13. It should be noted that this is one 'moment' (as they call it) of poststructuralist postmodern thought. The second 'moment' is derived from the work of Foucault and Lyotard, and is much more practically orientated in the sense that the 'representation' (that which represents reality) may be emancipatory in the way that it challenges hegemonic connections between power and knowledge. It is to this second moment that feminist postmodernism belongs (Bertens, 1995: pp. 5–6).
14. As already mentioned, the conceptualization of hegemonic knowledge derives from Gramsci (1971) and has been extended by, among others, Robert Cox (1987) and Susan Strange (1987).
15. R. B. J. Walker (1990; 1995) has repeatedly pointed out that this conceptualization of anarchy between states is based on a misreading of Hobbes who did not perceive the international state system to be a mirror image of his theoretical construct of a state of nature where all men are equal, and equally disposed to do harm to each other. See also Thomas Hobbes, *Leviathan* (1968: especially p. 187).
16. Note the highly gendered language used by Solomon in Chapter 2.
17. Booth (1991: p. 322) uses this expression to refer to the input of critical theory to international relations.
18. This point was made by senior DFA personnel at an 'Advanced SADC Workshop for Academics' held by the DFA in January 1997, to which academics, including myself, were invited.

References

Andima, J. (1991), 'The Integration of Women into the Rural Development Process', *NEPRU Working Paper No. 4* (Windhoek).

Andima, J. (1993), 'Women's Role in the Development Process with Special Reference to Factors of Production', *NEPRU Working Paper No. 17* (Windhoek).

Ashley, Richard and R. B. J. Walker (1990), 'Speaking the Language of Exile: Dissident Thought in International Studies', *International Studies Quarterly* 34 3, pp. 259–68.

Barber, James, and John Barratt (1990), *South Africa's Foreign Policy: The Search for Status and Security, 1945–1988* (Johannesburg: Southern Book Publishers).

Benhabib, S. (1991), 'Epistemologies of Postmodernism: A Rejoinder to Jean-Francois Lyotard', in L. J. Nicholson (ed.), *Feminism/Postmodernism* (London: Routledge).

Bertens, H. (1995), *The Idea of the Postmodern* (London: Routledge).

Booth, Ken (1991), 'Security and Emancipation', *Review of International Studies* 17/4 (October).

Booth, Ken (1994), 'A Security Regime in Southern Africa', *Southern African Perspectives, a Working Paper Series 30* (Bellville: Centre for Southern African Studies).

Bordo, S. (1990), 'Feminism, Postmodernism, and Gender Scepticism', in Linda Nicholson (ed.), *Feminism/Postmodernism* (London: Routledge).

Brydon, Lynne and Sylvia Chant (1989), *Women in the Third World: Gender Issues in Rural and Urban Areas* (New Brunswick: Rutgers University Press).

Buzan, Barry (1983), *People, States and Fear: The National Security Problem in International Relations* (Brighton: Harvester Wheatsheaf).

Chodorow, Nancy (1978), *The Reproduction of Mothering: Psychoanalysis and the Sociology of Gender* (Berkeley: University of California Press).

Coole, Diana (1993), *Women in Political Theory: From Ancient Mysogyny to Contemporary Feminism* (London: Harvester Wheatsheaf).

Cox, Robert W. (1987), *Production, Power and World Order* (New York: Columbia University Press).

Crush, Jonathan (ed.) (1995), *The Power of Development* (London: Routledge).

Daly, Mary (1978), *Gyn/Ecology: The Metaethics of Radical Feminism* (Boston: Beacon Press).

Davies, Rob, Dot Keet and M. Nkuhlu (1993), *Reconstructing Economic Relations with the Southern African Region: Issues and Options for a democratic South Africa* (Bellville: MERG/Centre for Southern African Studies).

Der Derian, James, and Michael Shapiro (eds) (1989), *International/Intertextual Relations: Postmodern Readings of World Politics* (Massachusetts: Lexington Books).

Di Stefano, Christine (1990), 'Dilemmas of Difference: Feminism, Modernity and Postmodernism', in Linda Nicholson (ed.), *Feminism/Postmodernism* (New York and London: Routledge).

Eckersley, Robyn (1992), *Environmentalism and Political Theory: Towards an Ecocentric Approach* (Berkeley: University of California Press).

Eisenstein, Zillah (ed.) (1979), *Capitalist Patriarchy and the Case for Socialist Feminism* (New York: Monthly Review Press).

Elshtain, Jean Bethke (1992), 'Sovereignty, Identity, Sacrifice', in V. Spike Peterson (ed.), *Gendered States* (Boulder, CO: Lynne Rienner).

Enloe, Cynthia (1989), *Bananas, Beaches and Bases: Making Feminist Sense of International Politics* (London: Pandora).

Fraser, N., and L. J. Nicholson (1991), 'Social Criticism without Philosophy: An Encounter between Feminism and Postmodernism', in L. J. Nicholson (ed.), *Feminism/Postmodernism* (London: Routledge).

Gaidzanwa, R. (1992), 'Bourgeois Theories of Gender and Feminism and their Shortcomings, with Reference to Southern African Countries', in Ruth Meena (ed.), *Gender in Southern Africa: Conceptual and Theoretical Issues* (Harare: SAPES Trust).

Geldenhuys, Deon (1990), *Isolated States*, 2nd edn (Johannesburg: Jonathan Ball).

Gilligan, Carol (1982), *In a Different Voice* (Cambridge, MA: Harvard University Press).

Gramsci, Antonio (1971), *Selections from the Prison Notebooks* (London: Lawrence and Wishart).

Grant, Rebecca (1992), 'The Quagmire of Gender and International Security', in V. Spike Peterson (ed.), *Gendered States* (Boulder, CO: Lynne Rienner).

Harding, Sandra (1986), *The Science Question in Feminism* (Ithaca, NY: Cornell University Press).

Harding, Sandra (ed.) (1987), *Feminism and Methodology* (Bloomington: Indiana University Press).

Hartmann, Heidi (1981), 'The Unhappy Marriage of Marxism and Feminism: Towards a more progressive union', in Lydia Sargent, (ed.), *Women and Revolution: A Discussion of the Unhappy Marriage of Marxism and Feminism* (Boston: South End Press).

264   *Theory, Change and Southern Africa's Future*

Hartsock, Nancy (1985), *Money, Sex and Power* (Boston: Northeastern University Press).

Hartsock, Nancy (1987), 'The Feminist Standpoint: Developing the Ground for a Specifically Feminist Historical Materialism', in Sandra Harding (ed.), *Feminism and Methodology* (Bloomington: Indiana University Press).

Hobbes, Thomas (1968), *Leviathan* (Harmondsworth: Penguin).

Jaggar, A. M. (1988), *Feminist Politics and Human Nature* (Trenton, New Jersey: Rowman and Littlefield).

Linklater, Andrew (1992), 'The Question of the Next Stage in International Relations Theory: A Critical-Theoretical Point of View', *Millennium*, 21, 1.

Lyotard, Jean Francois (1993), *The Postmodern Condition: A Report on Knowledge* (trans Geoff Bennington and Brian Massumi) (Minneapolis: University of Minnesota Press).

Mackinnon, Catharine A. (1982), 'Feminism, Marxism, Method and the State: An Agenda for Theory', *Signs: Journal of Women in Culture and Society* 7(3) Spring, pp. 515–544.

Mackinnon, Catharine (1987), *Feminism Unmodified: Discourses on Life and Law*, (Cambridge, MA: Harvard University Press).

Malan, M. and J. Cilliers (1997), 'SADC Organ on Defence and Security: Future Development', *ISS Papers, no. 19* (March).

Maphunye, K. J. (1996), 'Gender Politics in the Bureaucracy? Botswana's Experiences', in *Governance in Southern Africa: An Occasional Paper Series 4* (Bellville: School of Government, University of the Western Cape).

Mbilinyi, Marjorie (1992), 'Research Methodologies in Gender Issues', in Ruth Meena, (ed.), *Gender in Southern Africa: Conceptual and Theoretical Issues* (Harare: SAPES Trust).

Meena, Ruth (1992), 'Gender Research Studies in Southern Africa: An Overview', in Ruth Meena (ed.), *Gender in Southern Africa: Conceptual and Theoretical Issues* (Harare: SAPES Trust).

Mills, Greg, and Christopher Clapham (1991), 'Southern African Security after Apartheid: A Framework for Analysis', *South African Perspectives, a Working Paper Series* (Bellville: Centre for Southern African Studies).

Nicholson, Linda (ed.) (1990), *Feminism/Postmodernism* (New York and London: Routledge).

Okin, Susan Moller (1979), *Women in Western Political Thought* (Princeton: Princeton University Press).

Peterson, V. Spike (1992a), 'Security and Sovereign States, What is at Stake in taking Feminism Seriously', in V. Spike Peterson (ed.), *Gendered States, Feminist (Re)Visions of International Relations Theory* (Boulder, CO: Lynne Rienner).

Peterson, V. Spike (ed.) (1992b), *Gendered States* (Boulder, CO: Lynne Rienner).

Pettman, Jan Jindy (1996), *Worlding Women: A feminist International Politics* (London: Routledge).

Robinson, Fiona (1999), *Globalizing Care: Ethics, Feminist Theory and International Relations* (Boulder, CO: Westview Press).

SADC (1992), *Towards Economic Integration*, proceedings of the Annual Consultative Conference (Maputo, Mozambique).

Sargent, Lydia (ed.) (1981), *Women and Revolution: A Discussion of the Unhappy Marriage of Marxism and Feminism* (Boston: South End Press).

Sen, Gita and Caren Grown (eds) (1987), *Development, Crises and Alternative Visions: Third World Women's Perspectives* (New York: Monthly Review Press).

Seymour, Vernon (1996), 'Global Dialogue, Human Rights and Foreign Policy: Will South Africa Please Lead', *Southern African Perspectives: a Working Paper Series 55* (Bellville: Centre for Southern African Studies).

Strange, Susan (1987), *States and Markets: An Introduction to International Political Economy* (London: Pinter Publishers).

Strange, Susan (1991), 'An Eclectic Approach,' in Craig Murphy and Roger Tooze (eds), *The New International Political Economy* (Boulder, CO: Lynne Rienner).

Swatuk, Larry A., and David R. Black (eds) (1997), *Bridging the Rift: The New South Africa in Africa* (Boulder, CO: Westview Press).

Thompson, Lisa (1991), 'SADCC: Part of a Whole or Whole of a Part?', *International Affairs Bulletin* 15/1.

Thomspon, Lisa (1996), *Strictures or Structures: Societal Security and the State in Southern Africa*, unpublished PhD Thesis, University of the Western Cape.

Thompson, Lisa (1997), 'Is the Dream Dreaming us? Developing Development Discourse in Southern Africa', *Africanus* 27/2.

Tickner, J. Ann (1992), *Gender and International Relations: Feminist Perspectives on achieving Global Security* (New York: Columbia University Press).

Tuana, N., and R. Tong (1995), *Feminism and Philosophy* (Boulder, CO: Westview Press).

Vale, Peter (1996), 'Regional Security in Southern Africa', *Alternatives* 21/3.

Van Aardt, Maxi (1993), 'In Search of a More Adequate Conceptualization of Security for Southern Africa: Do We Need a Feminist Touch?', *Politikon* 20/1.

Van Aardt, Maxi (1995), 'Back to the Future? Women and Security in Post-Apartheid Southern Africa', *Strategic Review of Southern Africa* 17/2.

Van Aardt, Maxi (1997), 'The SADC Organ for Politics', *South African Journal of International Affairs* 4/2 (Winter).

Walker, R. B. J. (1989), 'The Prince and the Pauper: Tradition, Modernity and Practice in the Theory of International Relations', in James Der Derian and Michael Shapiro (eds), *International/Intertextual Relations: Postmodern Readings of World Politics* (Lexington, Massachusetts: Lexington Books).

Walker, R. B. J. (1990), 'Security, Sovereignty and the Challenge of World Politics', *Alternatives* 15/1.

Walker, R. B. J. (1995), 'International Relations and the Concept of the Political', in Steve Smith and Ken Booth (eds), *International Relations Theory Today* (London: Polity Press).

Watts, M. (1995), 'A New Deal in Emotions: Theory and Practice and the Crisis of Development', in Jonathan Crush (ed.), *The Power of Development* (London: Routledge).

12
Southern Africa Through Green Lenses

Larry A. Swatuk

> We know that environmental degradation is dangerous. We know that we cannot go on as before. But how to go on, how to live individually and collectively, how to make the transition soon and how to persuade the intransigent, the selfish, the powerful and the uninterested? These are the questions that neither classical socialism [n]or contemporary social theory have provided sufficient intellectual or moral resources to answer. We shall have to equip ourselves.
>
> – Goldblatt (1996: pp. 202–3)

Introduction

International relations (IR) is a relatively new social 'science', a branch of political science, itself cleaved from an older, more inclusive, political economic base.[1] Similarly, ecology – concerned with studying the relations of organisms and species to their environment – in particular, conservation biology, are young offshoots of the biological sciences. Each, in its own way, takes the whole world as its 'bounded realm' or 'domain' of inquiry. Each seeks to explain, through theory formation and empirical analysis the interrelationship of the parts to the whole.[2] Whereas mainstream IR takes like and unvarying 'sovereign states' to be the fundamental units functioning within a constellation of interrelating states, ecologists attempt to explain the interrelationship of myriad and dissimilar parts in the workings of the whole, be it a biotic community, an ecosystem, or the biosphere – that is, Earth, *Gaia* – itself.

Traditionally, IR has been concerned with understanding the causes of war and the conditions of peace between and among states. Peace is deemed to be the ideal condition of the system. Balance of power is thought to be the mechanism bringing about such homeostasis. In other words, system maintenance is thought to be the ultimate end goal of IR theory (IRT) and practice. System maintenance, too, is the ultimate goal of ecology. However, while IR seeks to explain how and why states, and states alone, should and can continue to exist, ecology privileges no such particular units within a given system: at its grandest, all elements of the biosphere are accorded equal rights to existence. So, whereas IR is state-centric in its ontology, ecology goes far beyond the privileging of these social constructs, toward not androcentrism but eco- or biocentrism. A 'sustainable' world, then, constitutes a much more complex and difficult problematique for ecologists than for international relations specialists.

This is not to suggest that IR theorists have had an easier time of it, or that their work has borne more explanatory fruit. To the contrary, while IR theory is embattled on all fronts (Burchill and Linklater *et al.*, 1996; Rosenberg, 1994), ecology – including global political ecology – has moved, in my estimation, from both theoretical and analytical strength to strength. Most central to this chapter is the fact that these different worlds, and world views, have now collided. Global warming, population growth, species loss are now seen to be global political concerns; to some observers they constitute 'new threats' to 'human security'. At the same time, there are numerous local and regional environmental issues which have taken on enhanced political relevance: for example resource depletion and despoliation, pollution, energy production. Whether IR as presently constituted can get beyond its state-centric and power-as-domination political framings and contribute meaningfully to ecologically-nuanced, global 'system maintenance' is, in my estimation, doubtful.

The task of this chapter, therefore, is twofold. First, using examples specifically taken from the Southern African region, the chapter locates the 'environment' in traditional IR framings with a particular focus on realism, neo-institutionalism and structuralism. Second, the chapter provides a Green critique of IR in theory and practice in Southern Africa. It resists the urge to prescribe 'ways forward', however strong that urge may be.

Wholes and parts: the environment and established IR theory

Realism[3]

In a survey of the environment in political theory, Hurrell (1995) highlights just how uneasily the new environmentalist baby rests in the cradle of traditional IR. Clearly, its cries for attention are most readily heard – and most persistently ignored – in the house of Realism. Among Realists, the environment 'fits' into IR thinking in three ways: first, as a component of power[4]; second, as an essential aspect of myth-making and thereby nation-building; third, as a potential source of conflict in inter-state relations. Each of these factors is discussed in turn.

As a *component of power*, 'nature' is constituted as 'natural resources' (Paterson, 1995: p. 266), the absence or presence thereof determining both state behaviour and a state's likely position in the international pecking order. For example, Japan's lack of natural resources meant that for it to 'succeed' in the international system, Japanese state makers had to pursue aggressive, expansionist political and economic policies. At the same time, large states like Russia, China, Canada and the US are said to be 'rich' in natural resources and to enjoy several advantages of geography, like the presence of long coastlines or having temperate climates (Crosby, 1986), so having advantages over other states not so well endowed.

In Realist parlance, Southern Africa is said to be a *region* that is well-endowed with natural resources. Indeed, the region's insertion into the international states system was a function of this resource endowment: in the late-nineteenth century 'scramble for Africa', European state makers divided up the region on the basis of each territory's perceived potential contribution to European state power. This completed a process of European penetration of the region begun several centuries earlier by the Portuguese and the Dutch. Economic development of these territories was geared toward satisfying the colonizing state's desire for economic growth set within the twin contexts of inter-European rivalry and early modern industrialism (see Vale and Niemann in this volume).

Realist IRT, its protests to the contrary notwithstanding, is little concerned with history, with the 'why' of contemporary state forms. Rather, it takes states as givens and attempts to slot them neatly into power-oriented categories: strong or weak, large or small, new or old, developed or developing, North and South, West and the rest. In doing so, Southern Africa appears as a collection of small, weak states with varied resource endowments.

'Science' primarily in the form of statistics is brought to bear in such analysis. For example, according to the UNDP *Human Development Report 1997*, eleven of SADC's[5] member states are ranked as having 'medium' or 'low human development', with only relative newcomers Seychelles (admitted 1997 along with Congo-Kinshasa) and Mauritius (admitted 1995) having 'high human development'.

The World Bank's *World Development Report* for 1997 describes SADC's member states as being low-income (Mozambique, Tanzania, Malawi, Zambia, Angola, Zimbabwe in order of most to least of the poorest) or middle-income economies (lower-middle: Lesotho, Namibia, Botswana; upper-middle: South Africa, Mauritius). While World Bank data primarily focuses on macro- and micro economic factors, it also includes tables on 'population and labor force', 'land use and urbanisation', 'commercial energy use', and 'forest and water resources'.

The 'map' of Southern Africa which emerges according to this data is one of 14 small, mostly weak states lacking the capacity to diversify their economies, develop their human and natural resources and to manage their natural environment. Indeed, only those member states that are 'offshore' – Mauritius and Seychelles – fare any better. However arbitrary and incomplete these data may be, the world of state makers considers this evidence as fact with those richer states offering 'development aid' and financial assistance on a primarily country-by-country basis. In Realist terms, then, save for South Africa with its historically specific industrial and military development, the region gives stronger states little pause for consideration. Africa's only value, it is often said, is its nuisance value.

This framing of SADC as a collection of small, weak, divided states in a fragmented and mostly marginal region serves to stunt the collective regional imagination concerning alternative, potentially more fruitful and sustainable futures. SADC state-makers have, by and large, internalized this image and tend to form policies as though they are self-seeking states in a world of similarly constituted, self-regarding and highly unsympathetic entities. Moreover, within the context of this power-obsessed hierarchy, the environment is slave to mimicry: the road to development must be a technologically assisted, industrially driven, paved road. Nature, in this context, must be subdued and harnessed in a national effort to catch up with the so-called developed world (see Harris, 1986; Swatuk, 1998).

Nature also has long played a central role in *myth-making* and the construction of a *national identity*. Animals are chosen as symbols of particular qualities thought to obtain in a state form's peoples: the indomitable Russian bear, the majestic American bald eagle, the industrious Canadian beaver. Geography, too, plays an enduring role in identifying the 'heartland': mountain ranges and other compelling geomorphic formations; lakes, rivers and forests; the rolling wheat fields of the Canadian and American prairies, the 'bread basket' of the Ukrainian Steppe, the 'iron rice bowl' of China; even weather patterns, from snow to rain. These images are invariably manipulated by state makers as images of durability, strength, and prosperity. They are meant to appeal to those 'inside' the state and to define those inside from the 'other', those outside its borders. Seen in this light, nature becomes a totem, or an 'idol of the tribe'.

What is interesting for Southern Africa is the extent to which the natural environment is a shared environment. One finds it difficult to imagine constructing a persuasively exclusive South African identity based around the uniqueness of its fynbos, or in Lesotho of the Drakensberg mountains, particularly when so much of Basotho history physically extends deep into what is presently called South Africa, or of Victoria Falls – known locally as 'the smoke that thunders' – which, as part of the Zambezi River, is meant to divide Zambia from Zimbabwe, but belongs equally to each. Similarly, though state makers in Botswana may trumpet the fact that the Okavango Delta has been declared a 'world heritage site', the Delta stands very far both from the lived experience and the social imaginary of most Batswana. The simple facts of the natural environment, then, preempt state-centric identity construction in the region.

Among Realists, the *potential for conflict* over natural resources is unsurprising. According to Keegan (1994: p. 73), throughout history the zone of organized warfare tends to coincide with what geographers call 'the lands of first choice'. But these historical struggles over plenty are thought to be giving way to struggles over scarcity. Over ten years ago, the World Commission on Environment and Development (1987: p. 7) stated:

> The deepening and widening environmental crisis presents a threat to national security – and even survival – that may be greater than well-armed, ill-disposed neighbours and unfriendly alliances. Already in parts of Latin America, Asia, the Middle East, and Africa, environmental decline is becoming a source of political unrest and international tension. The recent destruction of much of Africa's dryland agricultural production was more severe than if an invading army had pursued a scorched-earth policy. Yet most of the affected governments still spend far more to protect their people from invading armies than from the invading desert.

In Southern Africa, the potential for violent, inter-state conflict is thought to be acute. Pallett (1997: pp. 44–5) point out that Botswana, Malawi and Namibia exist in conditions of 'absolute water scarcity', with South Africa and Zimbabwe suffering 'water stress'.[6] They also suggest that by 2020, and based on current population growth rates, both South Africa and Zimbabwe will be in conditions of absolute water scarcity, while Lesotho, Swaziland and Tanzania will have all entered conditions of water stress. It is unfortunate, however, that the authors of this study choose to use such alarmist figures.[7] This is not to suggest that the Southern African region will not face problems of resource scarcity in future. Rather, it is to question the point of using such crude statistics which ultimately are latched onto by narrowly focused 'think tanks' and policy making elites for questionable purposes. For example, a recent study (Solomon, 1996) takes as its starting point the idea that, among other factors, population growth and climate change will lead to absolute water scarcity in the region thereby raising the possibility for inter-state conflict over this so-called 'white gold'.[8] This regional perspective complements a large 1995 World Bank study examining environmental stress and conflict potential in a number of African environmental 'zones'.

Clearly, resource scarcity is a pressing issue. However, Realist analysis, supported by questionable assumptions and flimsy statistics, too often encourages framing of the issues in binarist terms: to wit, 'we must secure *our* water supplies and, if necessary, do so at the expense of *them*'. Might it not be more fruitful to portray water as a regionally held common property, the successful conservation of which could lead to a strong regional identity, and a climate and culture of regional cooperation?

Realists identify potential inter- and intra-state problems developing out of conflicting visions of resource use. The Chobe River area presents one such case, where Botswana and Namibia are presently contesting the ownership of Sedudu Island. At present, Botswana Defence Force troops occupy the island. Sedudu stands between contrasting uses of a common resource: land. On the Namibian side, there is smallholder farming and cattle ranching. On the Botswana side, there is the Chobe National Park (see Swatuk and Vale, 1999, for a more detailed discussion; more generally, see Swatuk 1996a).

VanDeveer and Dabelko (1999) highlight ongoing 'securitization', that is 'militarizing the environment rather than "greening" the military'. To be sure, 'securitization' is underway in both South Africa and Botswana, the two states most capable of maintaining the myth of 'state-building' in the region. At the same time, militaries in the region have been very resistant to change. The military 'ego' cannot conceive of a regional peace dividend whereby trained 'fighters' become ditch diggers and city park maintenance people (see Swatuk and Omari,

1997: pp. 95–100). Better to turn the environment, for example the Sedudu wetland area, into a potential site of conflict than to rethink the importance of environmental health to human security.

The media plays no small part in the 'securitization' process. For example, *The Botswana Guardian* under a banner headline 'WAR CLOUD' and with cropped photos of Presidents Nujoma and Mogae 'facing off', highlighted the contents of a 'confidential report' purporting to assess the likelihood that the two countries would go to war following a 'winner takes all' International Court of Justice (ICJ) decision on Sedudu. The contents of the report clearly did not merit such alarmist rhetoric.[9] The newspaper, without a trace of irony, stated:

> The first problem towards resolving the problem has been the propaganda war between the two countries. The report notes that the depth and sophistication of the pleadings by the two countries at the ICJ, 'demonstrated that the media, particularly the Namibian side which had been outrightly hostile to Botswana, had never appreciated the Botswana view in any detail as the Namibian media had simply been fed to feast on half cooked Namibian assertions'.

It appears that the Botswana newspaper will do its best to right the balance in the 'half cooking' of 'facts'. More seriously, however, is the way continued emphasis on conflict and the framing of environmental issues in unhelpful binaristic terminology seeps into the regional consciousness. To say 'Sedudu' is to conjure an image of conflict rather than cooperation over resources in the popular imagination. At the same time, in both Botswana and South Africa, state security, feeding on these characterizations of 'threat' and 'enemy', is more and more equated with militarization. The protection of domestic resources – 'our diamonds', 'our animals', 'our water' – in Botswana has resulted in the purchase of, among other things, very expensive jet fighters, tanks and patrol boats. Namibia's President Nujoma has publicly questioned the wisdom of this traditional IR reading of the means to Botswana's security in Southern Africa

Neo-institutionalism

Neo-institutionalist approaches to IR and emerging arguments in favour of sustainable development and the management of the global commons seem to fit together like hand in glove.[10] As Paterson (1995: p. 253) states, 'most writers within IR who write on environmental problems and who are clearly motivated by the normative concerns adopted by environmentalists, adopt liberal institutionalist positions'. Neo-institutionalism builds on the idealist tradition in international relations: from Kant's 'perpetual peace' to Mitrany's 'working peace' to the Carlsson and Ramphal Commission's 'global neighbourhood'. There are countless strands to neo-institutionalist thought in IR. For the purposes of this chapter, and in the context of Southern Africa, I will simply point to three: first, the burgeoning of inter-governmental organizations concerned with the multilateral management of the environment; second, the countless linkages developing between state, non-state, sub-state and transnational actors, many of which are leading in progressive and hopeful directions, in particular toward a consensus around the community based management of natural resources; and third, the revaluation of local knowledge and processes in 'development'.

Regimes and institutional development

Power is shifting to institutions above the level of the state, driven by the need to solve common problems in an increasingly interdependent world. As a result we are seeing a fundamental shift in the balance of rights and duties between the particularist claims of nominally sovereign states on one hand, and the authority of international society on the other. Regimes and international institutions are coming to form new centres of authority that challenge the authority of national governments

(Hurrell, 1995: p. 137).

For sure, state-makers continue to cling jealously to 'sovereignty'. In the Southern African context, however, the fallacy of state 'sovereignty' is exposed daily as goods, people, capital (mostly US dollars) and resources flow freely and continually throughout the region: informal sectors flourish; taxes are evaded; borders are ignored; and families are united. For all intents and purposes, Southern Africa is a united region. Yet, colonial boundaries and bureaucracies continue to impede more creative approaches to the utilization of the region's resources.

Beyond the Cold War, Southern Africa's state-makers continue to take many of their cues from developments outside the region. They remain 'recipients' of development (Graf, 1996). At state level, 1992's Rio Summit on Environment and Development (UNCED) concentrated the minds of SADCC's member states enough so that the organization could produce a special report to the UNCED secretariat entitled *Sustaining Our Common Future* (1991). Similarly, each SADC member state now has a department and/or ministry devoted to environmental issues.[11] In cooperation with UNEP, other intergovernmental organizations, bilateral donors, and NGOs, SADC is pursuing a number of regional-focused, multilateral projects designed to address some of the more pressing environmental problems and developmental needs of the region (for example in the areas of River Basin Management and hydroelectric development including establishment of a region-wide energy grid) (see Swatuk, 1996b and 1996d for an overview of these issues). In addition, most SADC states are signatories to the major international treaties, conventions and protocols which centre on environmental issues: from the Montreal Protocol on ozone depletion to the Basle Convention on trade in toxic waste.

South African state-makers are actively participating in the region and in the world at large.[12] For example, South Africa's former Minister of Water Affairs, Kader Asmal, is the Chair of the Global Commission on the World's Dams. South Africa, through SADC and in association with the European Union, has also been centrally involved in regional cooperation on river basin management. While the Commission and other water resource management activities are fundamentally state-centred – along the lines of the Commission on Sustainable Development which seeks non-governmental input from time to time – regional approaches to water cooperation are increasingly and deliberately pluralist and multi-level in nature.

More recently, several SADC states banded together to lobby the world community at the June 1997 CITES meeting held in Harare. This united front was successful in its main aim: the downlisting of the region's elephants from Appendix One (which bans all trade in their products) to Appendix Two (which allows limited, controlled trade by Botswana, Namibia and Zimbabwe to Japan).[13] The renewed trade in elephant products, however limited, is something of a watershed agreement in regional development: it suggests that Northern states and interests are on occasion willing to devolve power to Southern states, and to defer to the 'authority' and 'expertise' of peoples historically treated as backward and primitive (see also, Adams and McShane, 1992).

Community-based development: toward epistemic community?[14]

While the non-governmental community is both diverse and divisive – witness the heated debate over the downlisting of elephants – in the region there seems to be an emerging consensus around the inherent value of community based development, at state, sub-state and non-state levels. In the region, international NGOs such as the IUCN,

International Rivers Network, Conservation International, and the World Wide Fund for Nature are developing linkages with previously dis-empowered Community Based Organizations (CBOs) to assist them in the identification and articulation of needs and interests (Hasler, 1996).

For much of Southern Africa's post-colonial history, 'conservation' has been a dirty word (Swatuk, 1996c), too often associated with the exclusion of indigenous Africans from both their land and resources. This type of exclusion is typical of modernist, state-led development. It was most often justified in terms of the upliftment of backward peoples.

Recently, 'rethinking' has centred on the notion of 'proprietorship'. That is to say, rural peoples will develop an interest in conserving only those resources which they perceive to be theirs. In the absence of communal ownership of a resource, individuals are compelled to maxi-mize their (household) benefit from the immediate and necessary use of that resource. Cutting trees for firewood, clearing land for agricul-ture, hunting animals for meat, and killing problem animals which threaten lives and destroy crops are rational survival strategies pursued by inhabitants of rural communities. To abandon these practices, rural peoples need to see that changes in their attitudes and behaviour – par-ticularly toward large mammals – result in tangible and sustainable, that is real, socio-economic rewards.

Zimbabwe was the first country to embark on projects designed specif-ically to take these factors into account. They were followed soon after by, among others, Tanzania and Zambia. At first these projects were gov-ernment initiated, but later NGOs as well as communities themselves came to be involved in all stages and at all levels of the projects.

Most projects focus on conservation through the sustainable utiliza-tion of natural resources for commercial use. This concept is taken from the private sector, which, since the 1960s, has increasingly recog-nized the economic potential in different kinds of natural resource uti-lization. The Southern African region remains one of the few regions in the world, 'where abundant quantities and varieties of wild animals roam the wild', also outside protected areas (Mukute, 1994: p. 157). This resource is attractive to foreigners who are willing to pay for the opportunity to observe, study or hunt these animals. At the same time, however, the region is characterized by large, often exceedingly poor, rural populations. As Africa's crisis of development has deepened over the last 20 years (see SADC, 1998), these natural resources have come under increasing pressure from overuse by rural peoples.

The concept of community based management of natural resources involves a wide range of policies and concepts. At the heart of CBMNR, however, are two notions: (i) that popular participation and people's empowerment at village level are fundamental to sustainable utilization; and (ii) that the devolution of power, particularly with regard to property rights, from the centre to the periphery will buttress this empowerment and facilitate the realization of shared benefits from natural resource use. I look briefly at each of these factors.

One of the cornerstones of CBMNR projects is the empowerment of people living in (particularly rural) communities. In theory, CBMNR projects help empower local people in four ways. First, by devolving 'appropriate authority' over natural resources to affected communities, rural peoples are legally empowered to manage their natural resources as they see fit. Second, CBMNR projects provide an immediate supplementary source of income to the household. Third, the socio-economic situation of the community as a whole is improved. Fourth, all people in affected communities participate in the choice and implementation of CBMNR projects.

Community empowerment, with few exceptions, can only be achieved through decentralization of state power and the devolution of authority. Thomas (1991: p. 2) writing about CAMPFIRE – the communal areas management programme for indigenous resources – the CBMNR programme in Zimbabwe and perhaps the most extensive to date in Southern Africa, states that

> The success of CAMPFIRE will hinge on the will of central government to decentralise full control over the wildlife resource to local communities, and the willingness and capacity of rural communities to adopt and further this concept of devolution. The legitimacy of the local institutional arrangements which develop will be critical to this success.

Clearly, 'decentralization' bears elements of Green political philosophy: that indigenous communities should have power over their resources; that violent interventions into sensitive biotic systems may do more harm than good. At the same time, however, it is clear that the path toward a state structure with a high degree of decentralization and popular participation is fraught with obstacles. Often this process is marred by central government's unwillingness to give up power. According to Moyo *et al.* (1993: p. 302),

> The continued emphasis on the physical and technical aspects of development has underplayed the importance of the human factor.

As a result, programmes are designed for the rural population without due regard to their participation. A long-lasting solution that ensures sustainable development can only be guaranteed with the willing and active participation of the people, not only in the sharing of the benefits of development, but also by participating in the task of creating these benefits.

So far, projects have emerged all over the Southern African region, especially in the cases of tourism activities such as game viewing, trophy hunting and wilderness experiences. Participating communities also engage in other activities, for example cultural services, small scale wildlife harvesting, and commercial timber production (Mukute, 1994: pp. 172–3; Jones, 1995: p. 3).

Respecting and sharing local knowledge in the global village

Many of these projects are linked to international patrons and protagonists so combining Kantian ideals of 'cosmopolitanism', perhaps most closely associated with the global 'environmental movement', with E. F. Schumacher's 'communitarian' ideals of localization of development processes. These positions, it seems to me, are not antithetical ones. To the contrary, epistemic thinking on sustainable development seems to emphasize that the 'global village' is made up of many, diverse households. Moreover, positive experiences on the ground in Southern Africa are translatable to other regions of the world: community based management regimes are a fungible global currency.

All of this neo-institutionalist activity is heartening. What its long-term impact will be is debatable, as will be seen in the *Green Critique* below. Precisely because the environmental movement is so amorphous, and transnational civil society so diverse and ill-organized, much of the sub- and trans-state activity occurring in the world today focuses on two things: first, the gathering and disseminating of scientific evidence, that is, countering destructive modernist practices with constructive ones; second, the promotion of a universalist ideology centred on human rights, that is, challenging the myth of state 'sovereignty' (see, also, Niemann in this volume).

In response, states are eager to maintain the intellectual high ground. A flurry of new 'multilateralist' and regime-ist activity has emerged around issues of the 'global commons'. In most cases, state-makers are involving NGOs in the policy-making process. For instance, the 53-member Commission on Sustainable Development permits any NGO accredited at the Rio Summit to sit in on its proceedings.

In Southern Africa, SADC is attempting to formalize (and in all likelihood, control) NGO participation through the formation of an NGO-desk. South African state-makers seek to maintain popular participation through, among other things, citizens forums.

What remains problematic, however, is both the pace of policy-making and the ability to enforce those policies once made. SADC states are busy formulating protocols in many areas of cooperation – water, electricity, transportation, communication – but almost none are ratified. At the international level the process is even more difficult: it took 14 years to arrive at a Convention on the Law of the Sea (UNCLOS); five years to achieve the Montreal Protocol. Neither of these documents are being applied to any discernible practical effect. Both are still highly contested. At local level in Southern Africa, while the notion of CBMNR is laudable, devolution of real power from the central state to village, ward or district is still mostly myth.

Structuralism

The persistent principle of state sovereignty can only partly explain these conditions. The structuralist critique argues that state-makers, in fact, act in these ways due to structural, political economic factors, operating at state and world system level. I will focus on two aspects of the structuralist argument, restricting my examples to Southern Africa: (i) the contribution of global capitalism to poverty and environmental degradation; and (ii) the nature of the state in the evolving world system.

Structuralist quarrels with Realism, neo-Realism and neo-institutionalism were for many years intra-modern but inter-paradigm debates (see Swatuk, 1991: pp. 75–133). In both cases, states were taken as givens, as was industrialism. Indeed, industrialization was and remains the 'jewel in the crown' of development and state power. But in the latter, there were attempts to illustrate the relationship between state and class; to shift the 'dependent variable' from war and peace to economic inequality; to articulate the role of trade and finance capital in embedded inequality; and to identify, as 'organic intellectuals', strategies for getting 'out from underdevelopment'.[15]

Rather than rehearse the well-known aspects of the various strains of structuralism, I will simply make this point: each were and remain fundamentally concerned with the history and contemporary manifestations of global capitalism, in particular the unequal terms of trade that derive from Europe's headstart and the ensuing economic enslavement of much the rest of the world in the industrialization of Europe.

The environment figured marginally in these theories: it was regarded simply as a matter of resources: the Periphery being rich in raw materials; the Core being rich in technological capacity and industrial production.

In the case of Southern Africa, South Africa's early industrial development, its hegemonic position in the region, and its status as the regional state most approximating the Westphalian model all derive from its vast mineral wealth (for a detailed discussion, see the chapters by Niemann and Vale above).

Over time the development and persistence of underdevelopment throughout the region began to manifest itself in what UNICEF describes as the PPE Spiral: high rates of population growth make it difficult to overcome poverty on limited resources; widespread poverty results in increasing environmental degradation as poor people ravage the land in the attempt to make a living; environmental degradation means that poor people are made to depend on ever more meagre resources and so the spiral continues.

The World Commission on Environment and Development (1987: pp. 37–41) made the link between underdevelopment and environmental degradation very clear:

> Failures to manage the environment and to sustain development threaten to overwhelm all countries. Environment and development are not separate challenges; they are inexorably linked. Development cannot subsist upon a deteriorating environmental resource base; the environment cannot be protected when growth leaves out of account the costs of environmental destruction. These problems cannot be treated separately by fragmented institutions and policies. They are linked in a complex system of cause and effect.

The historical development of centre–periphery linkages and the ensuing skewed pattern of economic growth has resulted in countries of the North facing quite different environmental challenges from those in the South. The North is primarily concerned with the consequences of high consumption and overdevelopment: pollution of lakes, rivers and streams; acid rain; global warming; depletion of the ozone layer; the production of toxic and nuclear waste. The South, on the other hand, is primarily concerned with forms of environmental degradation resulting from the struggle for survival: soil degradation and erosion, deforestation, desertification, declining biodiversity including the unseemly illegal trade in endangered species.

These are all issues central to the developmental problematique in Southern Africa. According to SADCC (1991: p. 8), 'Dealing effectively with our many environmental problems will require tackling the underlying domestic and external causes of underdevelopment and population pressures'. Domestically, widespread poverty, particularly among rural and peri-urban populations, contributes significantly to the persistence of the PPE spiral. The links between apartheid and environmental degradation throughout the region are well known (Ramphele, 1991).

Clapp (1995: pp. 7–8) highlights the role played by external economic factors in Africa's environmental and developmental crisis. While acknowledging that reducing poverty and policy 'distortions' is a key to ending the PPE spiral,

> This analysis...fails to take full account of the external factors which have also been very important contributors to the environmental and poverty problems facing Africa. These external factors are largely determined by the continent's status in the global political economy, which has been characterized by extremes of both marginalization, and incorporation...But at the same time that Africa is largely marginalized in the world economy, it is these very debt, trade, investment, and aid relationships which loom large within African economies – and affect them profoundly in a number of ways.

South Africa's pariah status in the world of states resulted in a number of pernicious economic developments that will impact on the regional environment and challenge even the most creative development planner for many years to come: State supported industrial and agricultural development in the context of 'total onslaught' led to the creation of dirty industries, widespread soil erosion, ill-fated investments in questionable industries (nuclear power; oil from coal programmes), and the indiscriminate use of scarce resources, in particular water. Apartheid social engineering created bantustans and townships that are, for all intents and purposes, environmental wastelands. And regional destabilization led to, among other things, trade in the products of endangered species (rhino horn, elephant tusk, in exchange for weapons), the spreading of millions of landmines, and hundreds of thousands of deaths: what might rightly be called a scorched earth policy.

At the same time, the debt crisis and subsequent adoption of (*de jure* and *de facto*) structural adjustment programmes throughout the region meant that few resources were available for environmental monitoring, human resource development in the field of environmental science, among other things. It also meant both a privileging of 'comparative advantage' and a prodding toward Lockeian forms of state policy: what Hasler (1996) terms the 'limited state in service of unlimited appropriation'. In both cases this meant putting more land under cash crops, encouraging the overstocking of beef, and pushing peasants and remote area dwellers on to ever less fertile land, all in the hope of earning foreign exchange so that states may pay their debts. The results were predictable: greater social inequalities in combination with increasing rural poverty and environmental stress. It has also been encouraging South African state-makers to frame the production of weapons of mass destruction in terms of 'niche development' and 'competitive advantage'.[16]

What is to be done? structuralist insights

How to address these problems? Short of world revolution – a modernist project in itself – structuralist analyses, although sharing the social ecologist's perception of the link between global capitalism and environmental degradation (Bookchin, 1980; 1982), have been notoriously weak on strategies for action. Realists waffle between denial and reactionism, marshalling 'cornucopians' and 'market-friendly' intellectuals as the need arises. Neo-institutionalist positions, while sensitive to environmental 'problems', are overly dependant on the 'power of the lab-coat' and work within time-lines and organizational frames that may be too long and too slow to address problems which need attention now (McKibbon, 1998).

More recently, structuralist analyses have grown both more sophisticated and admitting of action. Coxian analysis, for example, combines a focus on the structures of power in the global political economy with state structures and situates both within their particular spatio-temporal contexts (see Tsie and Leysens in this volume).

This school takes as its starting point the fundamental assumption that development is determined by production. The mode of production determines both the state form and the pattern of accumulation. 'Development', then, centres on strategies of accumulation and the rational allocation of resources within society.[17] 'Underdevelopment' derives from a particular structural impasse (for example, timing of incorporation into the global economy and the vested interests which develop around that position) which prohibits the rational allocation of surplus in a society. Prospects for 'development' are determined by a mix of external and internal factors.

How the hierarchy of social forces are arrayed within a state form differs both within particular states over time, and between states over space and time. States, although the dominant structure in global society, are not static, but highly changeable. Different 'historic blocs' emerge depending on the configuration of social forces. The social relations of production determine how successful an historic bloc will be in maintaining itself in power domestically and internationally in terms of other states, financial institutions, companies and militaries. State forms and the international system itself are understood to be shaped by different structural factors – economic, political, environmental, gender, race, etc. – and these patterns of power should be mapped out in order to understand (i) the character and content of hegemony in the international system; (ii) the nature of the historic bloc within specific state forms; and (iii) the differential impacts of particular social relations of production and power within a society and across state forms more generally. According to Cox (1987: p. 357)

> The importance of this kind of social mapping is to better understand the composition of existing historic blocs and the elements available for the formation of new historic blocs – and hence the potential for change in the form of state, in the interstate system, and in the future organization of production.

Cox points out that hegemony will manifest itself differently, indeed incompletely, at the margins of the system than at the centre. In terms of the global economy, Southern Africa is clearly marginal. It remains tied to the world economy by ever more tenuous strands: debt; gold and various other minerals, many of which are declining in global demand. The region enjoys special preferences by way of Lomé, but these too may soon disappear, to be replaced by an ever more hegemonic free trade regime monitored by the WTO. At the same time, however, South Africa in particular, but also Southern Africa, occupies a central place in the varied agendas of G-7 state-makers. The region, it appears, is the high-consumption countries' last hope for 'success' in Africa; indeed, the *Economist* considers South Africa to be an 'emerging economy'. To borrow from Chege (1995), Southern Africa appears to be 'modernization's last stand' in the continent.

Interestingly, this modernist project hopes to build an economic house which rests on an environmental foundation: the tourist 'industry', specifically high-cost, low-volume eco-tourism. Equally interesting, this foundation is not necessarily to be confined to the juridical Southern African state: transnational parks; adherence to the convention on highly migratory species; river basin management; trans-border CBMNR projects are all aspects of the 'new regionalism' in Southern Africa (Swatuk, 1996b; more generally, see Hettne, 1997). Two questions immediately come to mind. First, given the emerging linkages between 'marginal (post)modernists' – feminists, environmentalists, indigenous peoples organizations – might there not be the kernel of a progressive, emancipatory form of development emerging in Southern Africa linking the environment and development in a sustainable way? Second, in applying a Coxian framework to the analysis of power in Southern Africa, what sorts of strategies might be most effective in advancing a rearticulated, progressivist, regional or subregional historic bloc? These are complicated questions demanding further research.

A Green critique

As compelling as Cox and company may be, the Green critique, particularly its 'deep ecology' variant, remains sceptical of all anthropocentric, but not necessarily modernist, theorizing.[18] As such, its adherents would regard IR theory in almost all its variations as unequal to the task of theorizing a sustainable future for the planet

At the heart of Green political theory (GPT) are 'environmental ethics'. According to Leopold, 'an ethic, ecologically, is a limitation on freedom of action in the struggle for existence' (in Zimmerman *et al.*, 1993: p. 95). For Taylor (ibid., p. 69), all living things have the right to existence. They are the 'appropriate objects of the attitude of respect' and should be regarded as 'entities possessing inherent worth'. Much Green political theorizing rests on Leopold's understanding of the 'land ethic'. Writing in 1949, Leopold argued that for human behaviour to be sustainable, land must not be judged on its use value alone; land, in other words, is more than soil. To Leopold, the land ethic 'simply enlarges the boundaries of the community to include soils, waters, plants, and animals, or collectively, the land' (ibid., p. 96). Leopold encouraged us to think of ourselves as being part of an organic whole of functionally interdependent parts, as part of a land pyramid or biotic community. Land, he said, is a 'fountain of energy flowing through a circuit of soils, plants and animals … it is a sustained circuit' (ibid., p. 103). In terms of ethics, Leopold suggested, 'A thing is right when it tends to preserve the integrity, stability and beauty of the biotic community. It is wrong when it tends otherwise' (ibid., p. 108).

This notion of a self-sustaining circuit, of a condition of 'homeostasis', has more recently been extended to the entire planet by Lovelock (1979: p. 11) in his notion of 'Gaia':

> [Gaia is a] complex entity involving Earth's biosphere, atmosphere, oceans and soil; the totality constituting a feedback or cybernetic system which seeks an optimal physical and chemical environment for life on the planet.

For deep ecologists, then, human behaviour is unethical in the extreme: in privileging human activity above all others, it is partial as opposed to holistic; in considering all of nature for its 'use value', it has led to environmental degradation of planetary proportions. Greens differ as to the root cause of this unfortunate condition. For deep ecologists, it is both anthropocentrism and modernity in all its forms: the state and other large scale bureaucratic and administrative structures of social organization; private property, in particular the binary distinction between public and private; the dominance of secular, materialist, rationalist and individualist cultural values (see Hall *et al.*, 1992). For social ecologists it is political, in particular the inequalities which inhere in the global capitalist system. For ecofeminists, the root cause is androcentrism, in particular its post-Enlightenment variant whereby modernism and scientism managed to elevate man *qua* humanity, and man *qua* man above all other 'known' objects, organic and inorganic.

The legitimacy of this enterprise came from its very success. Advances in technology improved life in the European world. Modernism became internalized, unquestioned and, ultimately, the purported driving force in human history. 'Progress' was its mantra and scientism its tool. There emerged a belief that the diligent application of rational and objective thought would reveal universal truth. At the same time, there developed an unselfconscious trust that science would provide solutions to problems as they arise.

To the contrary, according to Berry (in Zimmerman *et al.*, 1993: p. 175), we now find ourselves 'caught in a profound cultural pathology'. Our propensity for over-consumption has resulted in the creation of a 'new Earth', what McKibbon labels 'Earth 2'. More than anything else, the production of carbon dioxide, resulting in global warming, has altered global climate patterns. Earth 2 is both wetter and drier, there are more storms, glaciers are in massive retreat everywhere, there has even been rain in Antarctica. To McKibbon, '... global warming will be like a much more powerful version of El Nino that covers the entire globe and lasts forever, or at least until the next big asteroid strikes' (McKibbon, 1998: p. 70).

For Greens, 'today's environmental threats are the accumulated consequences of our technological society's neglect of its natural context' (Yearley, 1992: p. 130). All strands of GPT, then, agree that there are limits to growth. Dobson (1990: p. 205), for example, suggests that in future the 'good life will involve more work and fewer material objects':

> Fundamentally, ecologism takes seriously the universal condition of the finitude of the planet and asks what kinds of political, economic and social practices are (a) possible and (b) desirable within that framework.

Where, then, does this Green theorizing about sustainability and limits to growth leave Southern Africa? In other words, from a Green perspective, what is good and bad about the theory and practice of international relations in Southern Africa? It seems to me a Green critique of IR in the region would focus on three ontological problems: (i) the state as predominant and 'legitimate' social organization; (ii) the continuing equation of 'development' with catch-up industrialization; and (iii) the overwhelming hegemony of neoliberalist discourse as unproblematic narrative in regional relations.

With regard to the state, as Paterson suggests the 'state is not only unnecessary from a Green point of view, it is positively undesireable' (1995: p. 238). This is more so the case in Southern Africa. Here, Greens find some sympathy for the insights offered by structuralism outlined above. The juridical state as constituted in Southern Africa is little more than an arbitrarily imposed social construct. To identify with the 'state', to speak of a Zimbabwean or South African 'nationalism' runs against the grain of locally generated histories, narratives of the liberation struggle notwithstanding (see Vale, Chapter 2 above). Moreover, Southern Africa's states are non-viable economic entities. They cannot compete in the global capitalist system; in the region, truck and trade often ignores these borders. For Greens, then, the constellation of sovereign states in the region clearly stands in the way of a more viable approach to sustainable development.

In terms of the last two items – development as catch-up and global discourse – Greens would criticize these positions as being anthropocentric not ecocentric. The global neoliberalist discourse continues to place use values on nature, particularly in terms of its contribution to capitalism. It values, above all, industry as the means to 'development'. Within this context, 'failure' is equated with bad government. So, the continued poor economic performance of, among others, Zambia, Swaziland, and Tanzania is due not to their historic insertion into the global capitalist system. Rather, their poor performances stem from anti-democratic and/or anti-market governments. Again, there is some sympathetic overlap with structuralist critiques of this state-centric, neoliberal analysis.

What would a Green 'strategy for action' look like in the region? Is there any evidence of a 'greening' of Southern Africa? While GPT is long on critique, it is short on action. In this way, it shares similar problems with other emancipatory philosophies, like critical theory, feminism, and post-modernism. For Greens, in general, a sustainable world would be one in which there existed 'a global network of self-reliant communities' (Paterson, 1995: p. 258). As stated previously, the state is both too small and too big to be of much use to Greens. GPT counsels the decentralization of power and supports grassroots democracy. In Paterson's estimation, GPT envisions 'small scale democratic communities [as] most likely to produce sustainable practices with limits set by a finite planet' (ibid., p. 268).

In Southern Africa there is some evidence of a nascent greening of political organization and social practice, itself suggestive of an ontological shift. As many of the examples provided above suggest, organization is both *bigger* and *smaller* in the region. There are transnational global and regional linkages developing around issues such as wetlands, river basin and (trans)national parks management. At the same time, CBMNR with its focus on sustainable utilization of resources suggests a viable form of sub-state organization and community building, albeit one vigorously resisted and/or coopted by vested interests in the region. Both of these bigger and smaller forms of social organization draw from a similar, environmental ethical base, one which places ecosystems, water resources, animals and plants at the centre of community development. To be sure, these are small gains but they are gains nonetheless.

Conclusion: muddling through

The overwhelming complexity of the issues to hand (global warming, acid rain, deforestation, depletion of fish stocks) makes it difficult to

know where first to begin to look for solutions. Over-simplified explanations are attractive in such a situation, as is the parsimony of (neo)
realist and/or some (neo)institutionalist theories. To wit, in Southern
Africa, inefficient state bureaucracies need to be trimmed to enhance
efficiency and reduce bottlenecks in the economy; in Southern Africa
the unwillingness of the state to devolve power to local and village
level stunts entrepreneurial spirit and inhibits development; in
Southern Africa, regional cooperation can be enhanced by focussing on
functional, low political issues: three simple statements admitting of
action.

These perspectives, as demonstrated in this chapter and throughout
this volume, are ultimately unsatisfying. Technical-cognitive approaches
too often seem to create as many problems as they purport to solve. At
the same time, they simply do not get to the heart of the matter. State-
centred thinking and approaches to resource management and environmental security cannot solve problems in a region where the state itself
is a fundamental part of the problem. This is a point made by almost
every contributor to this volume, but it is a point that bears repeating.

It appears we are back to Dickens' *Hard Times* wherein Stephen
Blackpool pronounces that 'life is a muddle'. In this modernist
moment we are condemned to muddle through. This does not mean
we should not, in Stephen Gill's words, 'theorize the interregnum'
(1995); to the contrary, and as Gill suggests, we should and we must.
An unsatisfying conclusion, to be sure. But from a 'green' perspective,
the only one possible.

Notes

1. For a comprehensive overview of the 'state of theory in IR', see Smith, Booth and Zalewski (1996).
2. Clearly, this is a bit of hyperbole. In the main, I am referring to that branch of IR theorizing which falls within the mainstream of the discipline. For a fuller treatment, see Smith, Booth and Zalewski (1996).
3. The use of the upper-case 'R' is in deference to Alan James's (1989) discussion of Morgenthau's search for theory. Morgenthau, James tells us, sought not merely to be a case for a realistic approach – that is analysis based on fact – but to elevate this small-'r' realism to the level of a paradigm, that is to cre-ate what James calls large-'r' Realism, or an accepted way of thinking about the world.
4. As in Morgenthau's nine-fold typology: geography; natural resources; raw materials; industrial capacity; military preparedness; population; national character; national morale; diplomacy. For Morgenthau, state-power is dependant fundamentally on the natural resources contained within its

territorially delimited space. These resources may be enhanced, depleted, or transformed over time. In the late-twentieth century industrial capacity is still the fundamental marker of state power (for example the G-7 against, say, the G-77), and industrial capacity rests on the ability to violently interrupt biotic pyramids in a sustained, if not sustainable, fashion (hence the classic image of the 'ghost towns' and 'boom towns' of *laissez-faire* America).

5. When using the acronym SADCC, I am referring to the original 10 members of the Southern African Development Coordination Conference (that is Angola, Botswana, Lesotho, Malawi, Mozambique, Namibia, Swaziland, Tanzania, Zambia and Zimbabwe) formed in 1980 with Namibia becoming a member 10 years later upon that state's independence from South Africa. When using SADC (created by treaty as the Southern African Development Community in 1992), unless otherwise stated, I am referring to the 12 continentally land-based members, that is the original 10-plus South Africa and Zaire (now known as the Democratic Republic of the Congo, or Congo-Kinshasa). For all intents and purposes, Mauritius and Seychelles are members in name only.

6. More than 600 people per flow unit (that is 1 million cubic metres of water) is said to lead to a condition of 'water stress'. More than 1,000 people per flow unit is said to mean there is 'absolute water scarcity'.

7. According to this measure, in 1995 there were said to be 4,257 people per flow unit in Botswana, 1,500 in Malawi, and about 1,200 in Namibia. These statistics are a crude measure meant to give a rough indication of conditions inhering in each SADC state. As Pallett points out, the statistics do not distinguish between total run-off or available run-off, nor do they account for groundwater resources or water available from lakes – hence the clearly misleading figures for Botswana, which derives almost all of its freshwater from groundwater sources, and for Malawi, whose major source of freshwater is Lake Malawi.

8. See, also, 'Scarce water "could cause friction" in southern Africa'. *Business Day*, 22 May 1997. It is interesting to note that the media chose to focus on the 'conflict' potential of water at a SADC-EU co-chaired meeting on the shared management of river basins. This meeting was attended by 11 of 12 SADC members, representatives of most members of the EU, the region's universities and think tanks, a number of other IGOs and several NGOs. The meeting was a model of cooperation and bargaining; in short, representative of the 'new multilateralism' discussed in Cox (1997).

9. See, 'Botswana/Namibia under WAR CLOUD', *Botswana Guardian*, 8 Oct. 1999.

10. Rather than rehearse the extensive history of environmentalism in international organization, I will simply acknowledge the intergovernmental historiography: from the 1972 Report of the UN Conference on the Human Environment, to the Brandt Report of 1980; from the World Commission on Environment and Development report *Our Common Future* (1987) to the Rio Summit and *Agenda 21* five years later, to, most recently, the Carlsson and Ramphal Commission on Global Governance (1995). For concise overviews of neo-institutionalism and environment, see Haas *et al.* (1993); Hurrell and Kingsbury (1992); and Imber (1994)

11. For an extended discussion of the evolution of environmental policy making in Southern Africa, see Johnson and Chenje (1994). For an overview of the Southern African environment, see Moyo *et al.* (1993).
12. For a detailed discussion of the Earth Summit and its implications for South Africa, see Wynberg (1993).
13. See, e.g., Fiona Macleod, 'Africa must pay for its wildlie', *Mail and Guardian*, 26 Sept.–2 Oct. 1997; Richard McNeill, 'Cites conference was more about money and politics than conservation', *Sunday Independent*, 29 June 1997; and Eddie Koch, 'Now to prevent the slaughter of the elephants', *Mail and Guardian*, 27 June–3 July 1997.
14. The author would like to acknowledge the assistance of Jesper Jonsson in the organization of this section. For a comprehensive treatment of CBMNR in the Botswana case, see Jonsson (1999).
15. The lineage of structuralist analysis is long and tortuous. For a steller overview and discussion of state and class see Pettman (1979). On the role of trade see Amin (1974; 1976). For an incisive analysis of the various theories of underdevelopment – e.g. dependency, world systems – see Hoogvelt (1982). On world systems theory see Wallerstein (1979); and for his treatment of Africa in world systems theory, see Wallerstein (1986). For a structuralist analysis of Southern Africa's position in the global economy and strategies for getting out from underdevelopment, see Amin *et al.* (1987). And, on various strategies for getting out from underdevelopment, see Mittelman (1988).
16. It is this kind of analysis and these sorts of insights that are sorely needed in neo-classical (development) economic thinking. Compare, for example, the chapters by Tsie and Holden above.
17. For a detailed discussion, see Cox (1987) and Mittelman (1988). How this analysis applies to the South African case is treated in Swatuk (1998).
18. In 1973, Arne Naess characterized the difference between 'deep ecology' and 'shallow ecology'. Shallow ecology, he felt, focused on short-term, anthropocentric reforms and is preoccupied with such issues as pollution and resource depletion. The ultimate goal of shallow ecology being the 'health and affluence of people in the developed countries'. Deep ecology, in contrast, proposes a major realignment of our philosophical worldview, culture and lifestyles (in Zimmerman *et al.*, 1993: p. 162). While many strands of GPT criticize modernity for its contribution to the environmental devastation of the planet, Dobson points out that 'ecologism is not anti-Enlightenment'. In Yearley's words, 'At risk of seeming sophistical, one might say that Greens put forward an enlightenment critique of the Enlightenment rather than a romantic one' (1992: p. 137).

References

Adams, Jonathan S., and Thomas O. McShane (1992), *The Myth of Wild Africa: conservation without illusion* (Berkeley: University of California Press).

Amin, Samir (1974), *Accumulation on a World Scale* (Cambridge: Cambridge University Press).

Amin, Samir (1976), *Unequal Development* (New York: Monthly Review Press).

Amin, Samir, Derrick Chitala and Ibbo Mandaza (eds) (1987), *SADCC: prospects for disengagement and development in Southern Africa* (London: Zed Press).
Berry, Thomas (1993), 'The Viable Human', in Michael E. Zimmerman *et al.*, eds, *Environmental Philosophy. From Animal Rights to Radical Ecology*, (Englewood Cliffs, NJ: Prentice-Hall).
Bookchin, Murray (1980), *Towards an Ecological Society* (Montreal: Black Rose Books).
Bookchin, Murray (1982), *The Ecology of Freedom: the emergence and dissolution of hierarchy* (Montreal: Black Rose Books).
Botswana Guardian (Gaborone), various.
Burchill, Scott and Andrew Linklater with Richard Devetak, Matthew Paterson and Jacqui True, 1996, *Theories of International Relations* (New York: St. Martin's Press).
Business Day (Johannesburg), various.
Chege, Michael (1995), 'Sub-Saharan Africa: underdevelopment's last stand,' in Barbara Stallings (ed.), *Global Change, Regional Response. The New International Context of Development* (Cambridge: Cambridge University Press).
Clapp, Jennifer (1995), 'Global Economic Factors in Africa's Environmental Crisis', unpublished manuscript, York University, Toronto, Canada.
Commission on Global Governance (the Carlsson and Ramphal Commission) (1995), *Our Global Neighbourhood* (Oxford: Oxford University Press).
Cox, Robert W. (1987), *Production, Power and World Order. Social Forces in the Making of History* (Columbia: Columbia University Press).
Cox, Robert W. (ed.) (1997), *The New Realism. Perspectives on Multilateralism and World Order* (London: Macmillan).
Crosby, Alfred W. (1986), *Ecological Imperialism. The Biological Expansion of Europe 900-1900* (Cambridge: Cambridge University Press).
Dobson, A. (1990), *Green Political Thought* (London: Unwin Hyman).
Gill, Stephen (1995), 'Theorizing the Interregnum: The Double Movement and Global Politics in the 1990s', in Björn Hettne (ed.), *International Political Economy: Understanding Global Disorder* (London: Zed & Halifax: Fernwood).
Globe & Mail (Toronto), various.
Goldblatt, David (1996), *Social Theory and the Environment* (Cambridge: Polity Press).
Graf, William D. (1996) 'Democratization "for" the Third World: critique of a hegemonic project', special issue of *Canadian Journal of Development Studies* entitled *Governance, Democracy and Human Rights* (eds Nasir Islam and David R. Morrison), 37–56.
Hass, Peter M., Robert O. Keohane and Marc A. Levy (1993), *Institutions for the Earth: Sources of International Environmental Protection* (Lanham, MD: UNIPUB).
Hall, Stuart, David Held and Tony McGrew (1992), *Modernity and Its Futures* (Oxford: Polity Press).
Harris, Nigel (1986), *The End of the Third World: Newly Industrialising Countries and the Decline of an Ideology* (Harmondsworth: Penguin).
Hasler, Richard (1996), *Agriculture, Foraging and Wildlife Resource Use in Africa. Cultural and Political Dynamics in the Zambezi Valley* (London: Kegan Paul).

Hettne, Björn (1997), 'The Double Movement: global market versus regionalism', in Robert W. Cox (ed.), *The New Realism: Perspectives on Multilateralism and World Order* (London: Macmillan).

Hoogvelt, Ankie M. M. (1982), *The Third World in Global Development* (London: Macmillan).

Hurrell, Andrew (1995), 'International Political Theory and the Global Environment', in Ken Booth and Steve Smith (eds), *International Relations Theory Today* (Cambridge: Polity Press).

Hurrell, Andrew, and Benedict Kingsbury (1992), *The International Politics of the Environment* (Oxford: Clarendon Press).

Imber, Mark (1994), *Environment, Security and UN Reform* (London: Macmillan).

James, Alan (1989), 'The realism of Realism: the state and the study of international relations', *Review of International Studies* 15/3 (July), 215–30.

Johnson, Phyllis, and Munyaradze Chenje (eds) (1994), *State of the Environment in Southern Africa* (Harare: SARDC, IUCN, SADC).

Kaplan, Robert (1994), 'The Coming Anarchy', *Atlantic Monthly* (February) 44–76.

Jones, B. T. B. (1995), *Wildlife Management, Utilization and Tourism in Communal Areas: Benefits to Communities and Improved Resource Management* (Windhoek, Namibia: Directorate of Environmental Affairs, Ministry of Environment and Tourism).

Jonsson, Jesper (1999), *Community Based Natural Resource Management in Botswana: Socioeconomic Impact*, unpublished MA thesis, Institute of Geography, University of Copenhagen (Oct.).

Keegan, John (1994), *A History of Warfare* (Toronto: Vintage Books).

Leopold, Aldo (1949), *A Sand County Almanac: And Sketches Here and There* (Oxford: Oxford University Press).

Lovelock, James E. (1979), *Gaia: A New Look At Life On Earth* (Oxford: Oxford University Press).

McKibbon, Bill (1998), 'A Special Moment in History', *The Atlantic Monthly* (May).

Mail & Guardian (Johannesburg), various.

Mittelman, James H. (1988), *Out from Underdevelopment* (London: Macmillan).

Moyo, Sam, Phil O'Keefe and Michael Sill (1993), *The Southern African Environment: Profiles of the SADC Countries* (London: Earthscan).

Mukute, M. (1994), 'Wildlife and Protected Areas', in P. Johnson and M. Chenje (eds), *State of the Environment in Southern Africa* (Harare: Zimbabwe Publishing House for SARDC, IUCN and SADC).

Pallett, John (ed.), (1997), *Sharing Water in Southern Africa* (Windhoek: Desert Research Foundation of Namibia).

Paterson, Matthew (1995), 'Green Politics', in Scott Burchill, Andrew Linklater *et al.*, *Theories of International Relations* (New York: St Martins Press).

Pettman, Ralph (1979), *State and Class: a sociology of international affairs* (London: Croom Helm).

Ramphele, Mamphela, with Chris McDowell (eds) (1991), *Restoring the Land: Environment and Change in Post-Apartheid South Africa* (London: Panos).

Rosenberg, Justin (1994), *The Empire of Civil Society: A Critique of the Realist Theory of International Relations* (London: Verso).

SADC (1998), *SADC Regional Human Development Report 1998* (Harare: SAPES Trust).

SADCC (1991), *Sustaining Our Common Future. Special Report to the UNCED Secretariat* (Maseru, Lesotho, October).

Smith, Steve, Ken Booth and Marysia Zalewski (eds) (1996), *International Theory: Positivism and Beyond* (Cambridge: Cambridge University Press).

Solomon, Hussein (ed.) (1996), *Sink or Swim? Water, Resource Security and State Co-operation* (Midrand: IDP Monograph Series, No. 6, October).

Sunday Independent (Johannesburg), various.

Swatuk, Larry A. (1991), *Between Choice in a Hard Place: contending theories of international relations* (Halifax: Centre for Foreign Policy Studies).

Swatuk, Larry A. (1996a), 'The End of History or Beginning of the End? Prospects for Botswana in the 21st Century', in Rukshana A. Siddiqui (ed.), *Challenges to Democracy and Development in Subsaharan Africa in the 1990s* (Praeger: New York).

Swatuk, Larry A. (1996b), *Power and Water: The Coming Order in Southern Africa* (Bellville: University of the Western Cape).

Swatuk, Larry A. (1996c), 'Learning the Hard Way: Environmental Policy Making in Southern Africa', in Gordon J. F. Macdonald *et al.* (eds), *Environmental Policy Making in Latin America in International Perspective* (Boulder, CO: Westview Press).

Swatuk, Larry A. (1996d), 'Environmental Issues and Prospects for Southern African Regional Cooperation', in Jakkie Cilliers and Hussein Solomon (eds), *People, Poverty and Peace: Human Security in Southern Africa*, IDP Monograph Series No. 4 (Midrand: Institute for Defence Policy, May 1996).

Swatuk, Larry A. (1998), 'Remaking the State: Assessing South Africa's Developmental Agenda', in Kidane Mengisteab and Cyril Kofie Daddieh (eds), *State Building and Democratisation in Africa: Faith, Hope and Realities* (Westport: Greenwood Press).

Swatuk, Larry A. and Peter Vale (1999), 'Why Democracy is Not Enough: Southern Africa and Human Security in the Twenty-first Century', *Alternatives* 24, 361–89.

Swatuk, Larry A. and Abillah H. Omari, (1997), 'Regional Security: Southern Africa's Mobile "Front Line"', *Southern African Perspectives, no. 61* (Bellville, South Africa: Centre for Southern African Studies).

Taylor, Paul W. (1993), 'The Ethics of Respect for Nature', in Michael E. Zimmerman *et al.*, eds, *Environmental Philosophy: From Animal Rights to Radical Ecology* (Englewood Cliffs, NJ: Prentice-Hall)

Thomas, J. S. (1991), 'The Legacy of Dualism and Decision-Making: the prospects for local institutional development in "CAMPFIRE"' (Harare: Centre for Applied Social Sciences, University of Zimbabwe).

Toronto Star (Toronto), various.

UNDP (1997), *Human Development Report 1997* (New York: Oxford University Press).

VanDeveer, Stacy, and Geoffrey D. Dabelko (1999), 'Redefining Security Around the Baltic: Environmental Issues in Regional Context', *Global Governance* 5/2 (April–June), 221–49.

Wallerstein, Immanuel (1979), *The Capitalist World Economy* (Cambridge: Cambridge University Press).

Wallerstein, Immanuel (1986), *Africa and the Modern World* (Trenton, NJ: Africa World Press).

World Bank (1997), *World Development Report 1997: the state in a changing world* (New York: Oxford University Press).

World Commission on Environment and Development (The Bruntland Commission) (1987), *Our Common Future* (Oxford: Oxford University Press).

Wynberg, Rachel (1993), *Exploring the Earth Summit: implications for South Africa* (Johannesburg: Penrose Press).

Yearley, Steven (1992), 'Environmental Challenges', in Stuart Hall, David Held and Tony McGrew (eds), *Modernity and its Futures* (Oxford: Polity Press).

Zimmerman, Michael E., J. Baird Callicott, George Sessions, Karen J. Warren and John Clark (eds) (1993), *Environmental Philosophy. From Animal Rights to Radical Ecology* (Englewood Cliffs, NJ: Prentice-Hall).

Index